Origami Symphony No. 3

Duet of Magestic Dragons & Dinosaurs

Books by John Montroll
www.johnmontroll.com
Instagram: @montrollorigami

Origami Symphonies

Origami Symphony No. 1: The Elephant's Trumpet Call
First movement: Allegro: Theme and Variation on the Classic Crane
Second Movement: Andante: Crawling Simple Bugs
Third Movement: Minuet of Platonic Solids with a Trio of Sunken Solids
Fourth Movement: March of the Large African Animals

Origami Symphony No. 2: Trio of Sharks & Playful Prehistoric Mammals
First Movement: Allegro Agitato: Sharks in the Sea
Second Movement: Andante: Dulce, Peaceful Creatures
Third Movement: Minuet of Dimpled Polyhedra with a Trio of Archimedean Solids
Fourth Movement: March of the Prehistoric Mammals

Origami Symphony No. 3: Duet of Majestic Dragons & Dinosaurs
First Movement: Allegro: Quacking Chorus of Dinosaurs
Second Movement: Andante: Colorful Australian Birds
Third Movement: Minuet of Diamonds with a Trio of Dimpled Diamonds
Fourth Movement: Presto: Flight of the Dragons

General Origami

Origami Fold-by-Fold
DC Super Heroes Origami
Origami Worldwide
Teach Yourself Origami: Second Revised Edition
Christmas Origami: Second Edition
Storytime Origami
Origami Inside-Out: Third Edition

Animal Origami

Dogs in Origami
Perfect Pets Origami
Dragons and Other Fantastic Creatures in Origami
Bugs in Origami
Horses in Origami
Origami Birds
Origami Gone Wild
Dinosaur Origami
Origami Dinosaurs for Beginners
Prehistoric Origami: Dinosaurs and other Creatures: Third Edition
Mythological Creatures and the Chinese Zodiac Origami
Origami Under the Sea
Sea Creatures in Origami
Origami Sea Life: Third Edition
Bringing Origami to Life: Second Edition
Bugs and Birds in Origami
Origami Sculptures: Fourth Edition
African Animals in Origami: Third Edition
North American Animals in Origami: Third Edition

Geometric Origami

Origami Stars
Galaxy of Origami Stars: Second Edition
Origami and Math: Simple to Complex
Origami & Geometry
3D Origami Platonic Solids & More: Second Edition
3D Origami Diamonds
3D Origami Antidiamonds
3D Origami Pyramids
A Plethora of Polyhedra in Origami: Third Edition
Classic Polyhedra Origami
A Constellation of Origami Polyhedra
Origami Polyhedra Design

Dollar Bill Origami

Dollar Origami Treasures: Second Edition
Dollar Bill Animals in Origami: Second Revised Edition
Dollar Bill Origami
Easy Dollar Bill Origami

Simple Origami

Fun and Simple Origami: 101 Easy-to-Fold Projects: Second Edition
Super Simple Origami
Easy Dollar Bill Origami
Easy Origami Animals
Easy Origami Polar Animals
Easy Origami Ocean Animals
Easy Origami Woodland Animals
Easy Origami Jungle Animals
Meditative Origami

Origami Symphony No. 3

Duet of Majestic Dragons & Dinosaurs

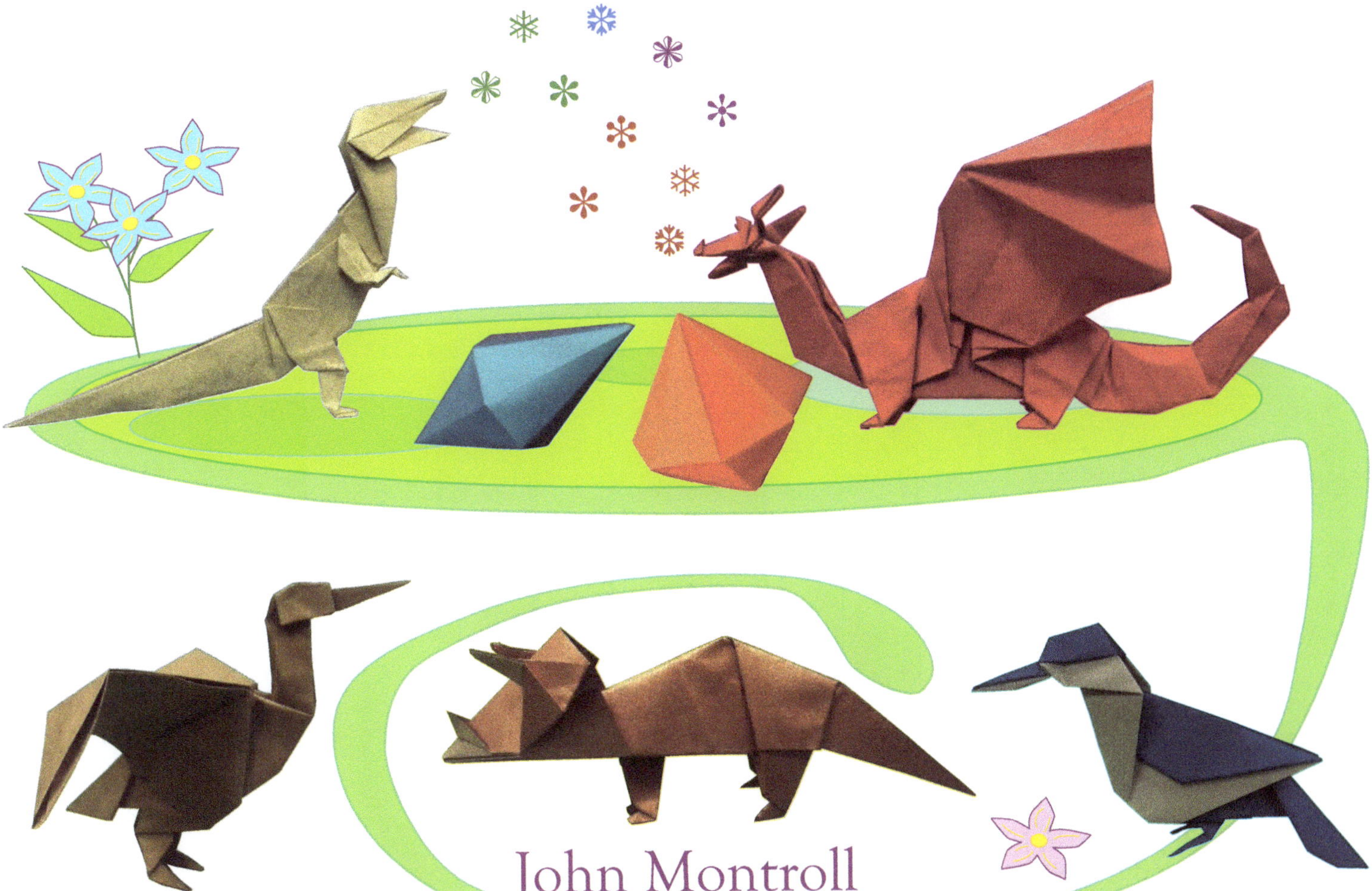

John Montroll

Antroll Publishing Company

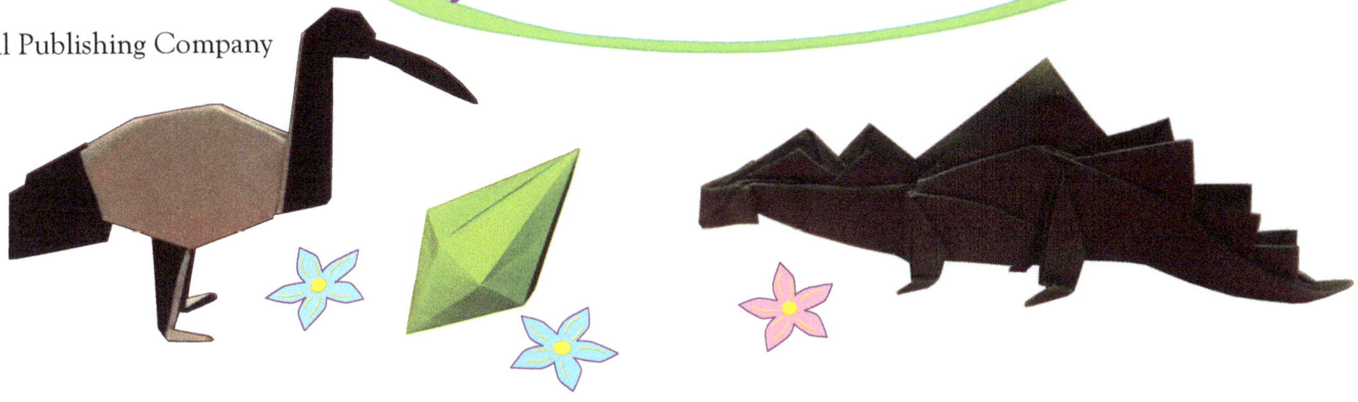

To Toby and Frank

Origami Symphony No. 3: *Duet of Majestic Dragons & Dinosaurs*

ISBN-10: 1-877656-50-X
ISBN-13: 978-1-877656-50-7

Antroll Publishing Company

Introduction

Welcome to the world premier of the Third Origami Symphony! Just as in a musical symphony, an origami symphony is an elaborate composition in usually four movements of various themes and styles that flow together. As a musical symphony brought music to new heights, I wish to do the same for origami.

The four movements of this symphony encompass favorite themes in origami. Dinosaurs, Dragons, colorful Australian birds, and a display of dazzling diamonds unite the four movements. The symphony opens in Prehistoric times, as a quacking chorus of dinosaurs fills the first movement. In the chorus is an Apatosaurus, Tyrannosaurus, Triceratops, Stegosaurus, and more. Time passes and the dinosaurs evolve into birds. For the second movement, we meet a dozen colorful Australian birds. In symphonic form, every other bird has a color-change pattern. The colorful birds include a Spangled Drongo, Red-necked Avocet, Collared Kingfisher, White-Bellied Sea-Eagle, and more. The third movement is a minuet of Diamonds with a trio of Dimpled Diamonds. The three-dimensional diamonds vary in number of faces, and the trio presents mind-boggling dimpled designs. The diamonds are protected by the Dragons of the fourth movement. Not only do the dragons have special powers, but you will gain their powers by folding them.

Each of the 37 models of this symphony are folded from a single uncut square. All can be folded from standard origami paper. The models are specifically designed to be as simple as possible for the given detail. Most of the dinosaurs can be folded in about 20 steps. This includes the Triceratops, with legs, horns, and head detail, all accomplished in 22 steps. All the birds have wings and legs, and several include color-change patterns, yet, with all the detail, can each be folded in under 30 steps. The diamonds are polyhedra which hold together through tabs and locks, and each is also under 30 steps. Even the more complex dragons are under 50 steps. The simplicity in folding complex shapes brings origami to a higher level.

The diagrams are drawn in the internationally approved Randlett-Yoshizawa style. You can use any kind of square paper for these models, but the best results will be achieved with standard origami paper, which is colored on one side and white on the other (in the diagrams in this book, the shading represents the colored side). Large sheets, such as nine inches squared, are easier to use than small ones.

Origami supplies can be found in arts and craft shops, or at Dover Publications online: www.doverpublications.com. You can also visit OrigamiUSA at www.origamiusa.org for origami supplies and other related information including an extensive list of local, national, and international origami groups.

Please follow me on Instagram @montrollorigami to see posts of my origami.

I thank Jay Sella and Christian Gonzalez for the photography. I thank my editor, Charley Montroll. I also thank the many folders who continued to encourage me to develop the presentation of origami through an origami symphony.

I hope you enjoy Origami Symphony No. 3.

John Montroll
www.johnmontroll.com

Contents

Symbols	9
Realms of Existence	9
Origami Symphony No. 3	10
First Movement	11
Second Movement	44
Third Movement	78
Fourth Movement	106

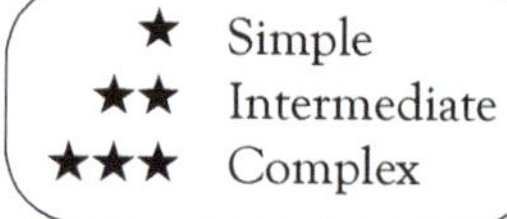

First Movement
Allegro: Quacking Chorus of Dinosaurs

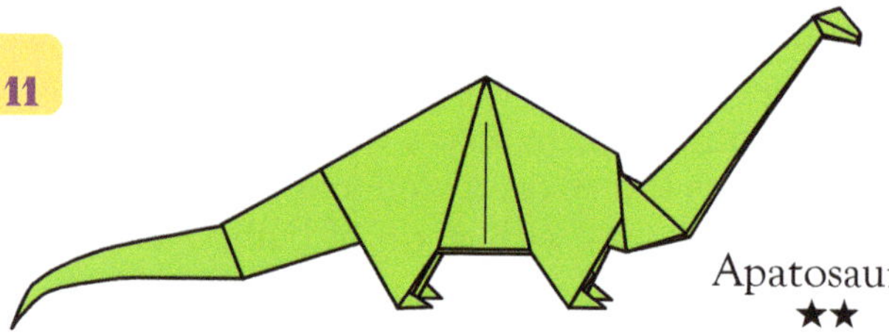

11 Apatosaurus ★★

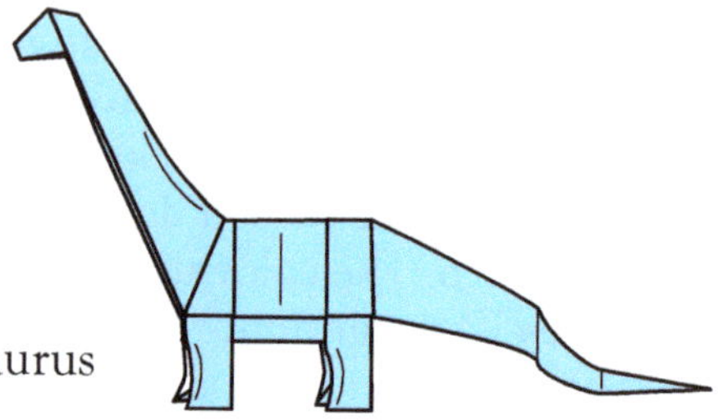

14 Brachiosaurus ★★

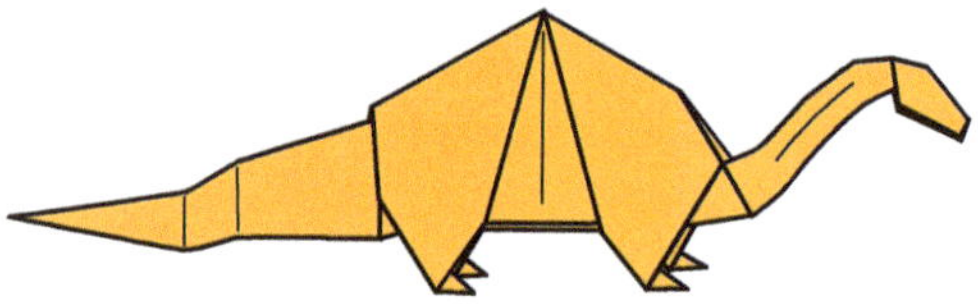

17 Plateosaurus ★★

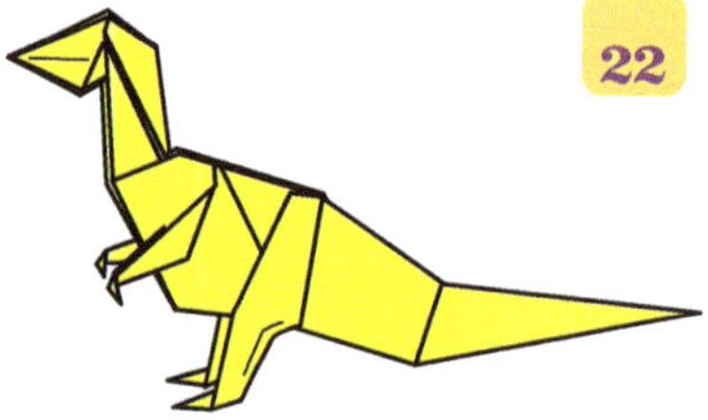

20 Hypsilophodon ★★

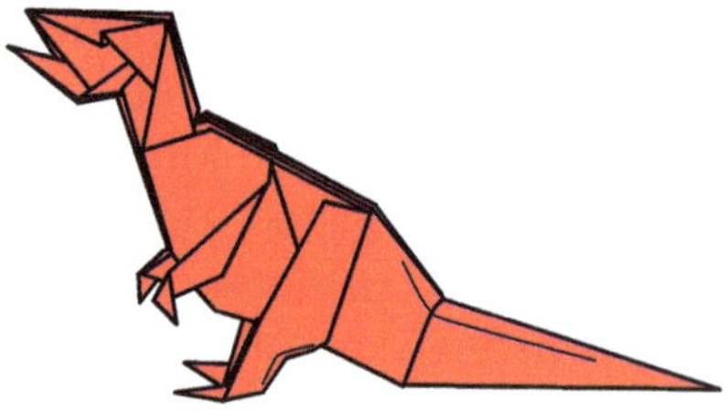

22 Tyrannosaurus ★★

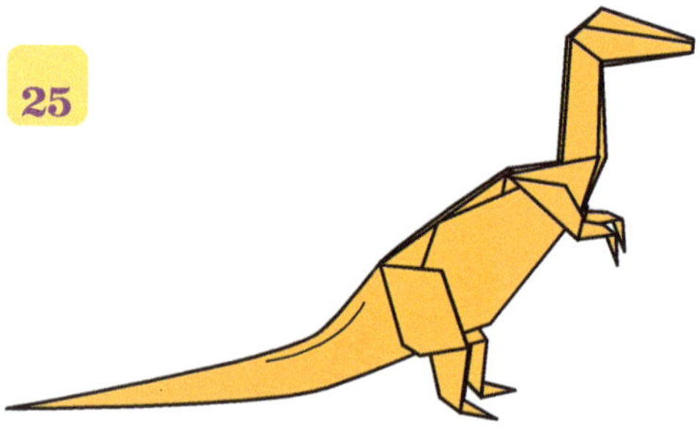

25 Megapnosaurus ★★

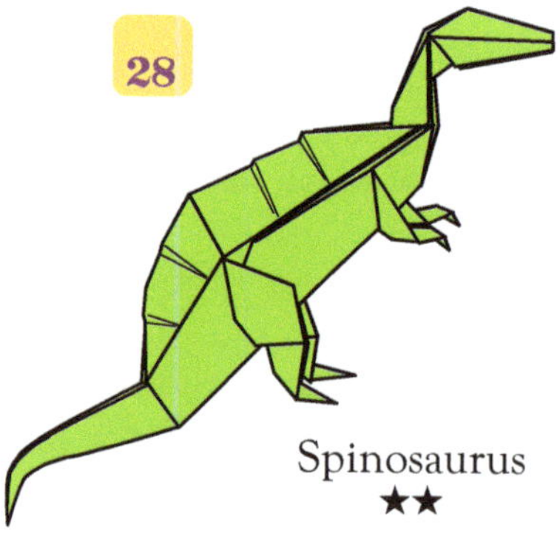

28 Spinosaurus ★★

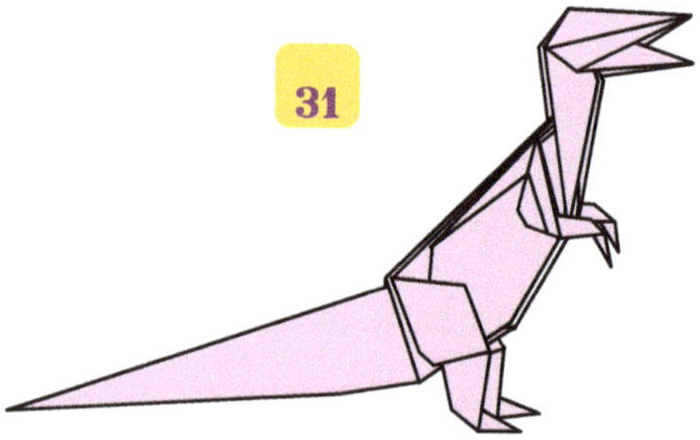

31 Allosaurus ★★

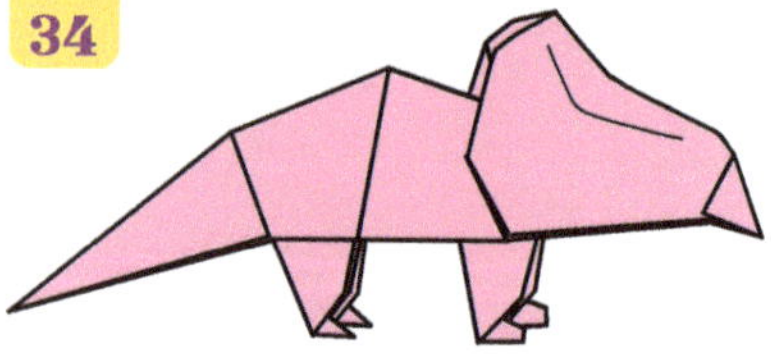

34 Protoceratops ★★

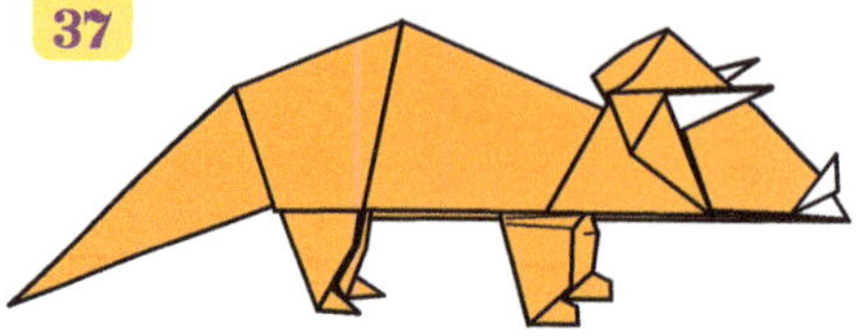

37 Triceratops ★★

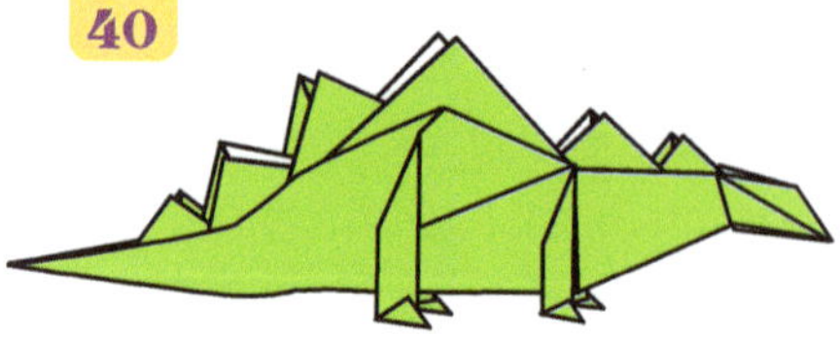

40 Stegosaurus ★★★

Second Movement
Andante: Colorful Australian Birds

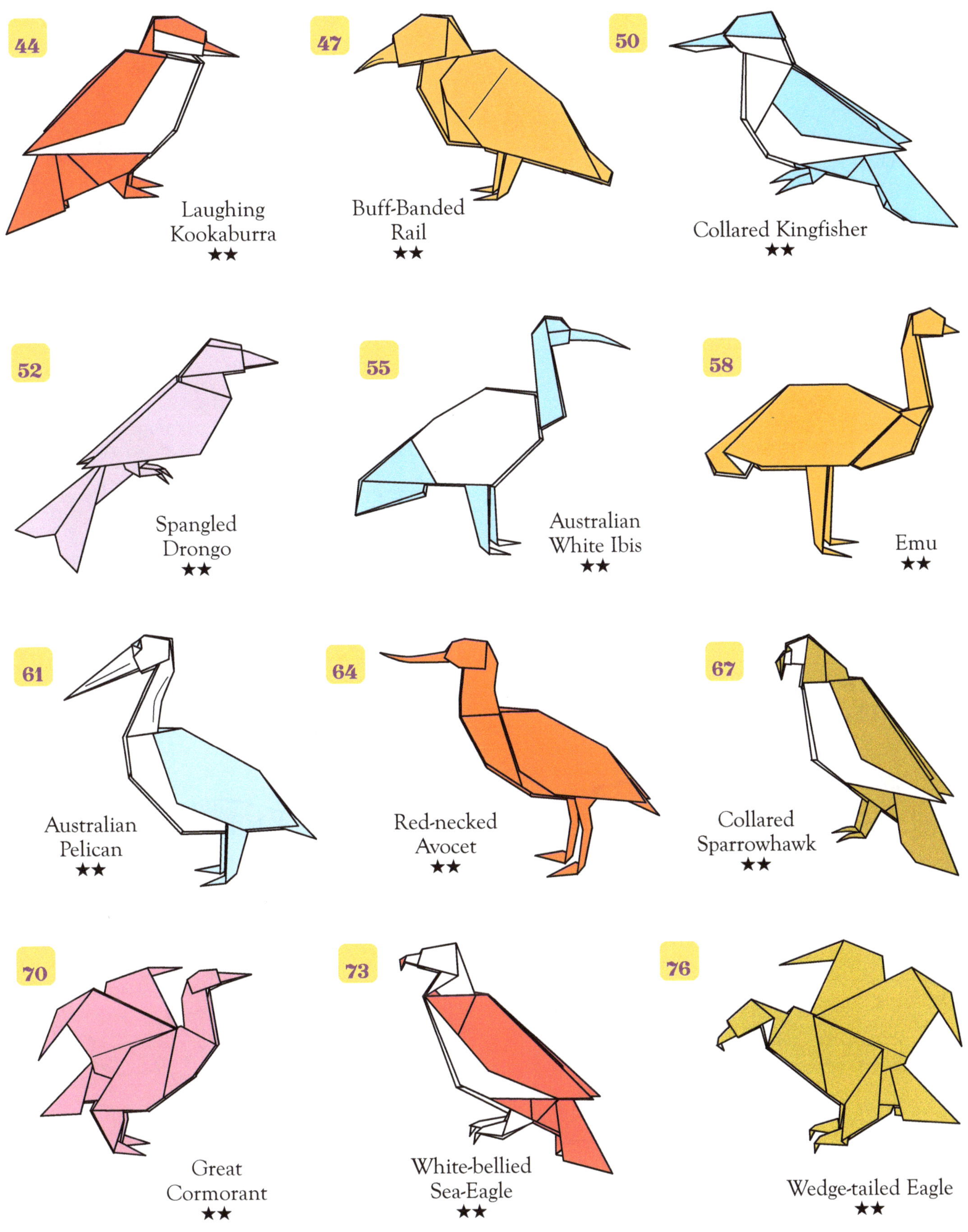

Third Movement
Minuet of Diamonds with a Trio of Dimpled Diamonds

78 Triangular Diamond ★★

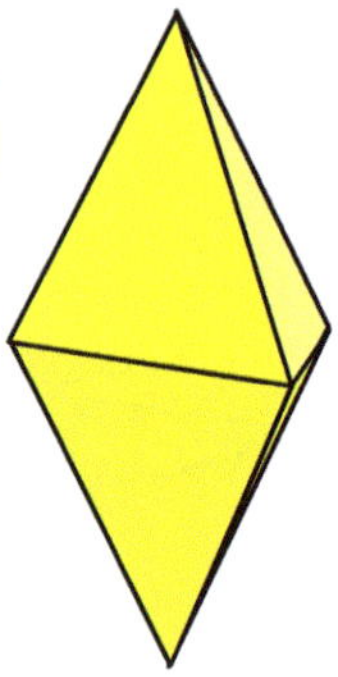

81 Square Diamond ★★

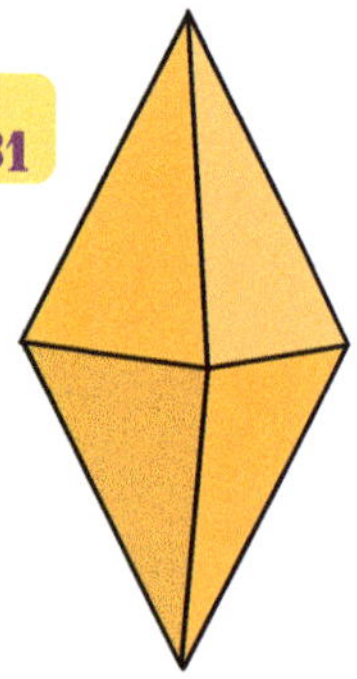

84 Pentagonal Diamond ★★

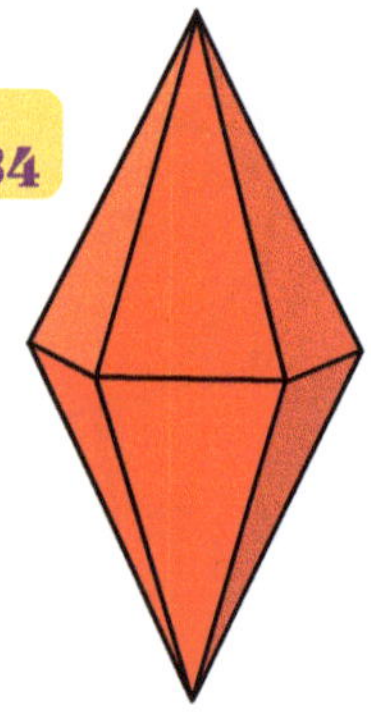

87 Hexagonal Diamond ★★

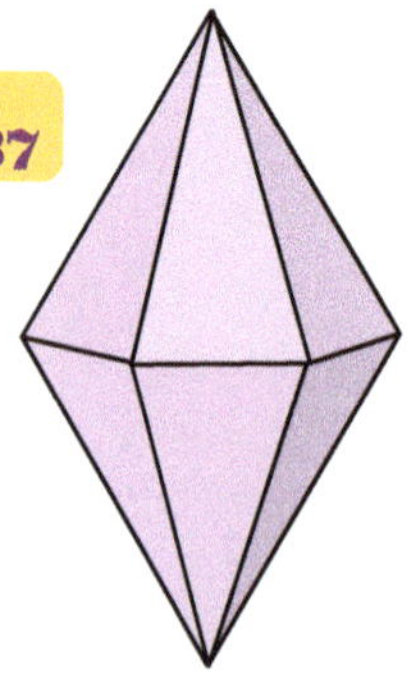

90 Heptagonal Diamond ★★

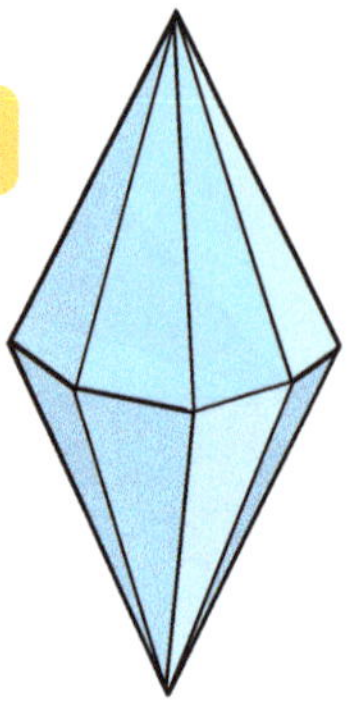

93 Octagonal Diamond ★★

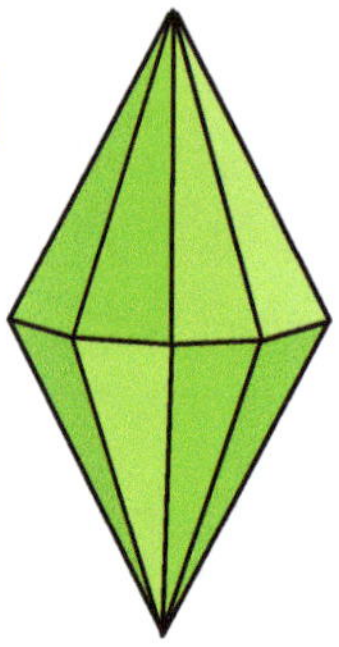

96 Dimpled Square Diamond ★★

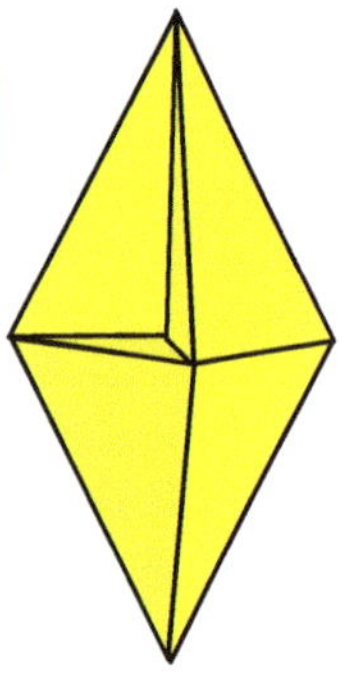

99 Dimpled Hexagonal Diamond ★★★

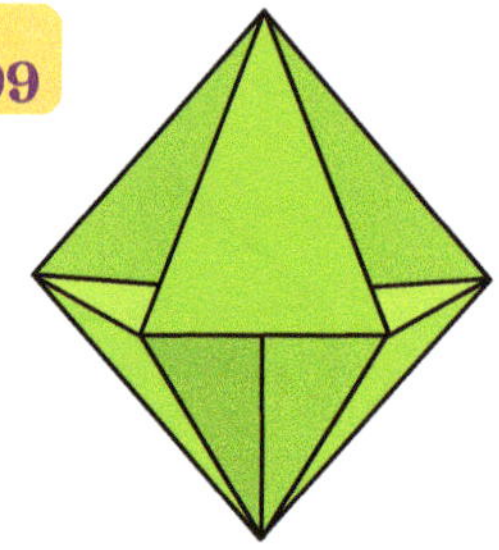

102 Dimpled Octagonal Diamond ★★★

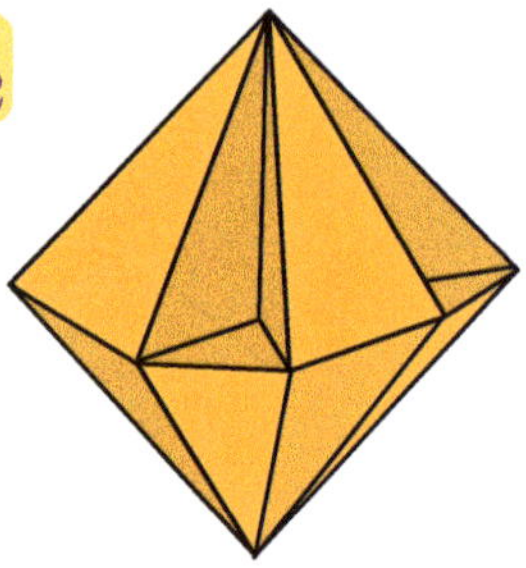

Fourth Movement
Presto: Flight of the Dragons

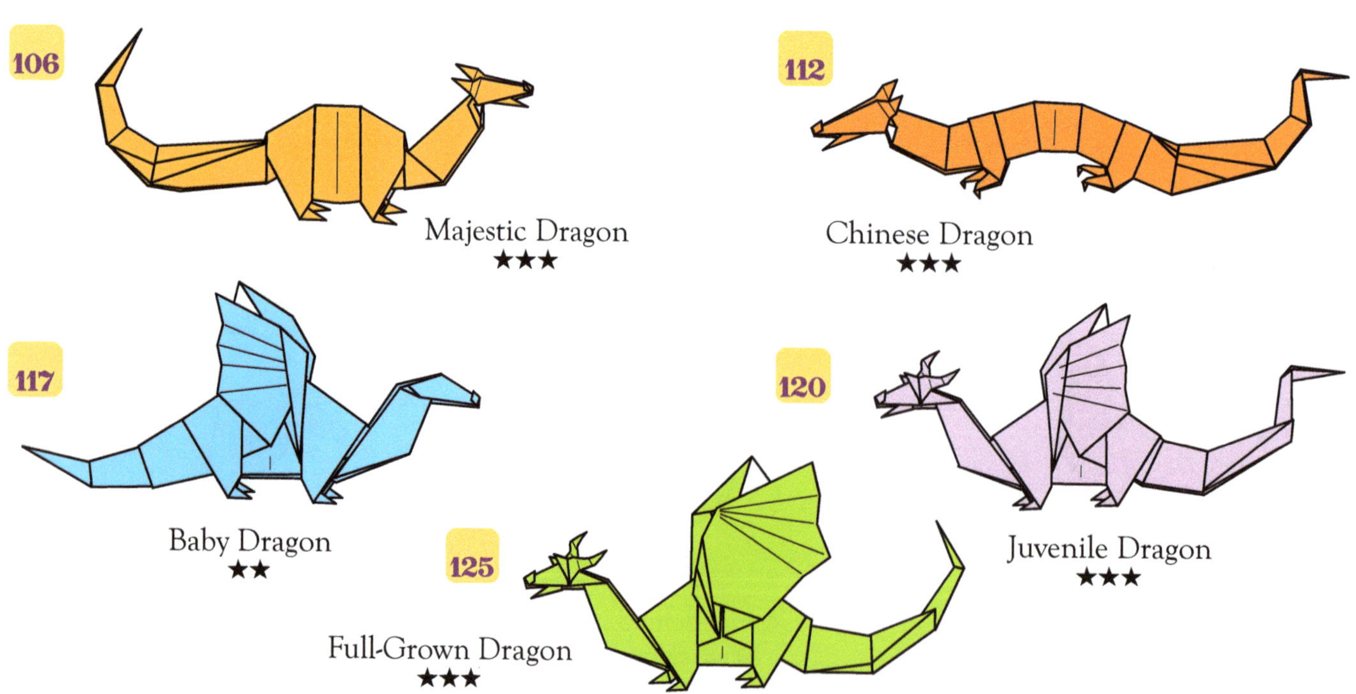

106 Majestic Dragon ★★★

112 Chinese Dragon ★★★

117 Baby Dragon ★★

120 Juvenile Dragon ★★★

125 Full-Grown Dragon ★★★

Symbols

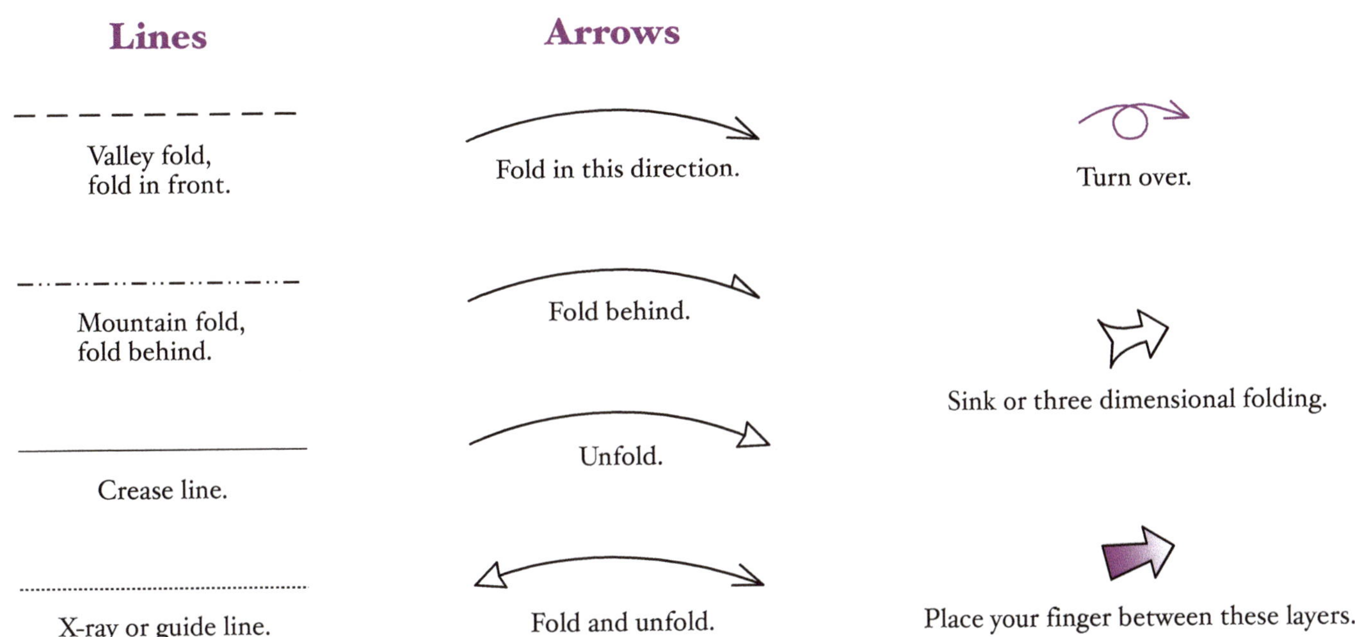

Realms of Existence

The four movements take on different themes of Dinosaurs, Australian Birds, Diamonds, and Dragons. Dinosaurs existed in the past and Australian Birds exist in the present and at a specific corner of the world. The existence of Diamonds is timeless and they are found in stardust and on other worlds. Dragons exist in our imagination.

Theories have suggested that early mammals, during the time of dinosaurs, knew to fear large, scaled creatures with claws and wings. Their memories became instinct, carried through evolution, and finally humans can communicate this thought, which created the dragon.

Birds exist in a different realm than us. Knowing they are free to fly and not bound by fences changes everything. They can sense the magnetic field, probably through vision. Birds experience more colors than us, which are invisible in our realm. They process vision far faster, and see clearly flying through a forest whereas we could not. Their songs and chirps, when slowed down, are more musical. Most likely, they also process sound faster than us, so chirps are more musical. I suspect their passage of time is different than for us. If a bird turned into a human, they would feel so heavy, lumber around in slow motion, and wonder what happened to their detailed, colorful world and freedom.

We origami folk are in our realm of existence. We see value in simply folding paper to create models that sometimes defy the imagination including a wide range of animals and objects. The mystery of design, dexterity of folding, and delight of the artistic outcome is very rewarding. Engaged in folding, we are at peace.

It is fun to symbolize these realms of existence through an origami symphony.

Origami Symphony No. 3

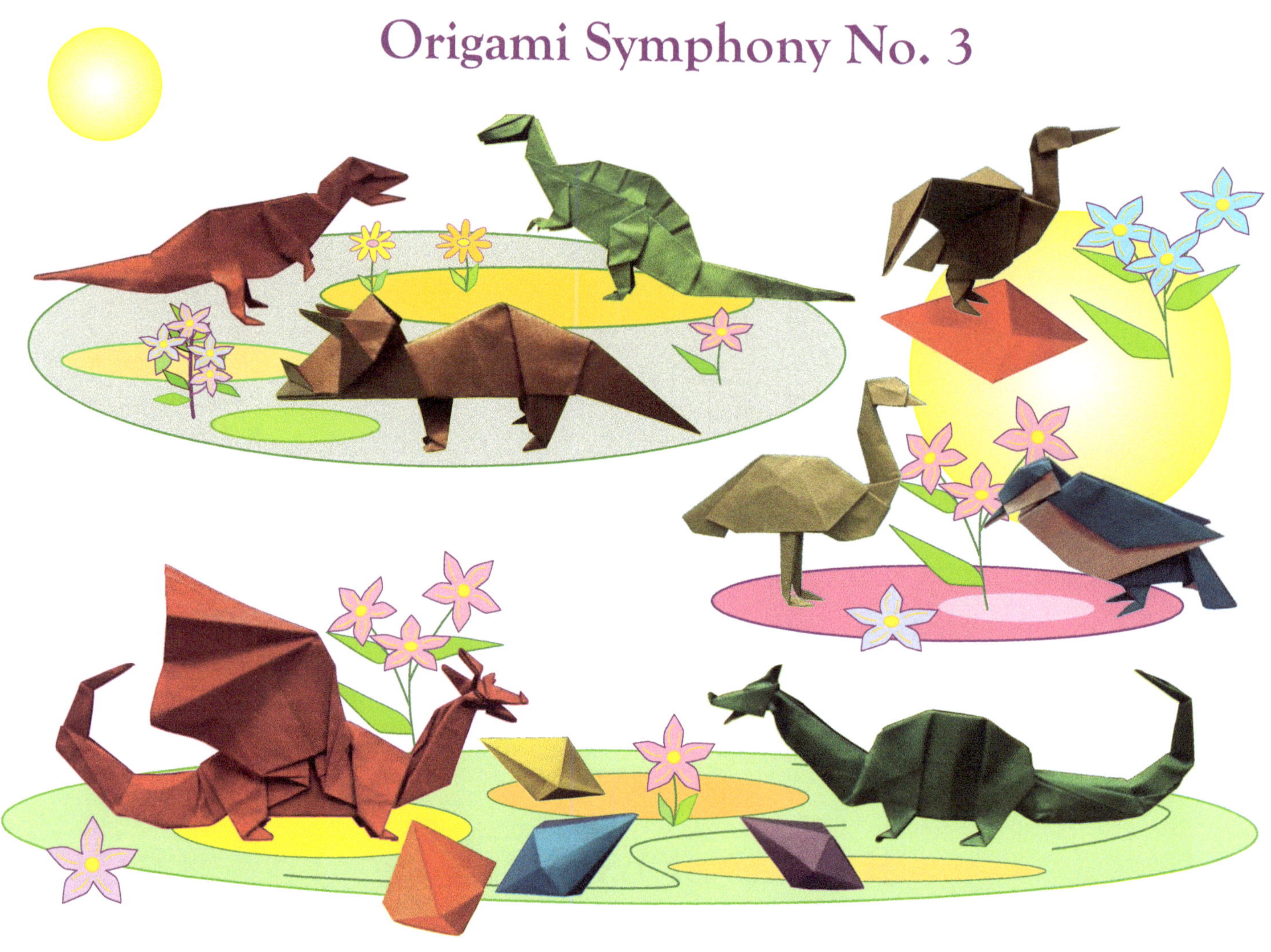

Majestic creatures come to life in this origami symphony. Dinosaurs, colorful Australian Birds, and Dragons delight us on every page. Diamonds and Dimpled Diamonds bring treasured possessions to the Dragons.

The first movement of Origami Symphony No. 3 opens in the prehistoric period. A parade of walking Dinosaurs sing prehistoric songs by quacking. In the parade is an Apatosaurus, Brachiosaurus, Spinosaurus, and several more. With detail of body structure, these Dinosaur designs are intended to be as simple as possible. Most of the models are accomplished in about 20 steps. The regal Stegosaurus walks on stage to close the movement of Quacking Dinosaurs.

Time passes by as we proceed to the Second movement. Dinosaurs have evolved into birds, and we travel to Australia to enjoy these colorful birds. We meet twelve birds, and in symphonic form, every other one is either solid in color or has a two-color pattern. Birds include a Kingfisher, Spangled Drongo, Australian White Ibis, Emu, and a Great Cormorant. Two Eagles fly by and close the second movement.

The third movement is a Minuet of Diamonds with a trio of Dimpled Diamonds. These diamonds can be dinosaur or bird eggs, or geometric objects for the birds to perch upon. However, the Dragons (coming soon) will be protecting the Diamonds. Beginning with a Triangular Diamond, each new diamond will have more faces, up to an Octagonal Diamond. The trio of Dimpled Diamonds dazzles us with mind-boggling complexity.

Five Dragons entertain us for the fourth movement. A Majestic Dragon, Chinese Dragon, and Family of three Dragons keep watch over their Diamonds. Dragons are especially fun to fold, and as you fold them, you will gain super powers.

Throughout this symphony, prehistoric Dinosaurs, colorful Australian Birds, dazzling Diamonds, and majestic Dragons weave a story. Folding these and making scenes bring origami to life.

First Movement

Allegro: Quacking Chorus of Dinosaurs

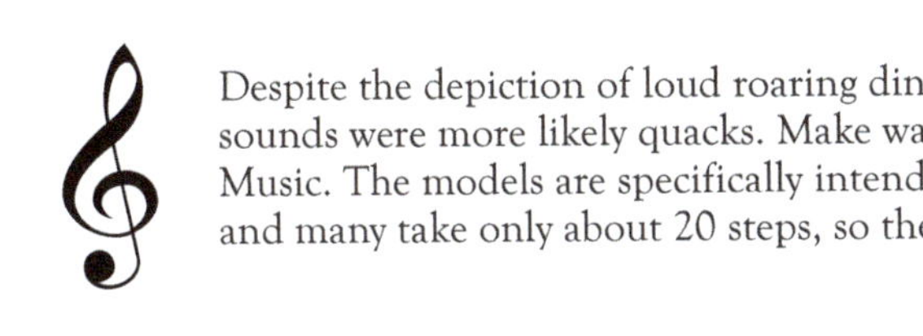

Despite the depiction of loud roaring dinosaurs, they, like birds, possessed no vocal chords. Any sounds were more likely quacks. Make way for a parade of Quacking Dinosaurs set to Prehistoric Music. The models are specifically intended to be much easier than most other origami depictions, and many take only about 20 steps, so these intermediate level models appear complex.

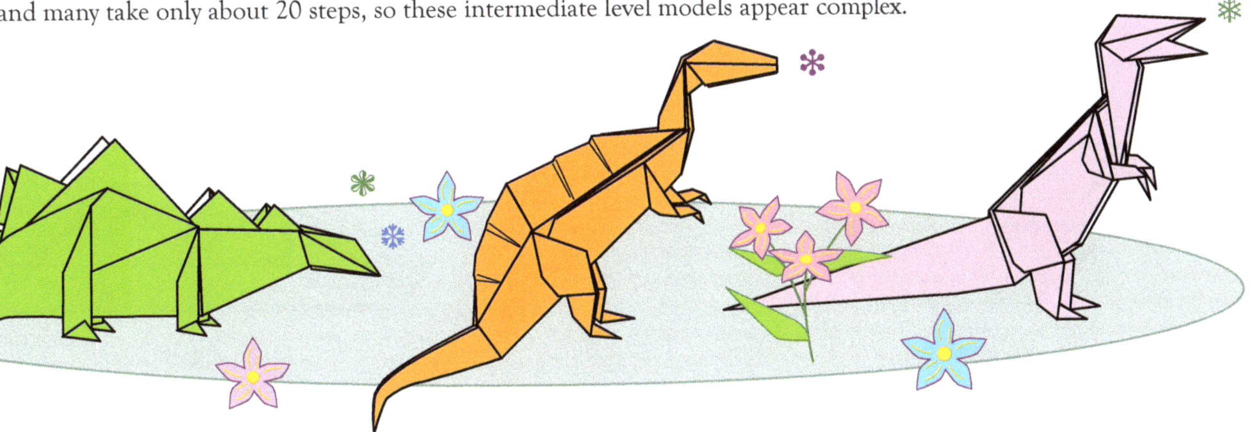

Apatosaurus

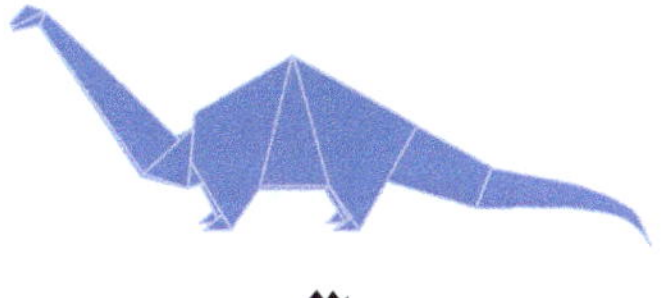

These large dinosaurs lived during the late Jurassic Period in North America, and at one time were known by the name Brontosaurus, though many paleontologists now believe that these two types of dinosaurs are distinct types unto themselves. They were extremely large, reaching lengths of around 70 feet.

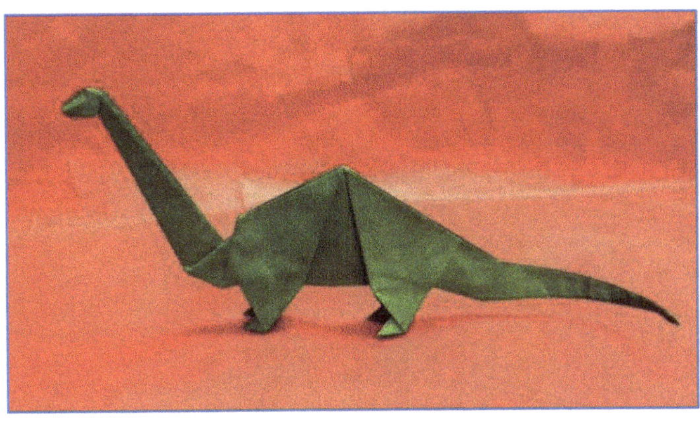

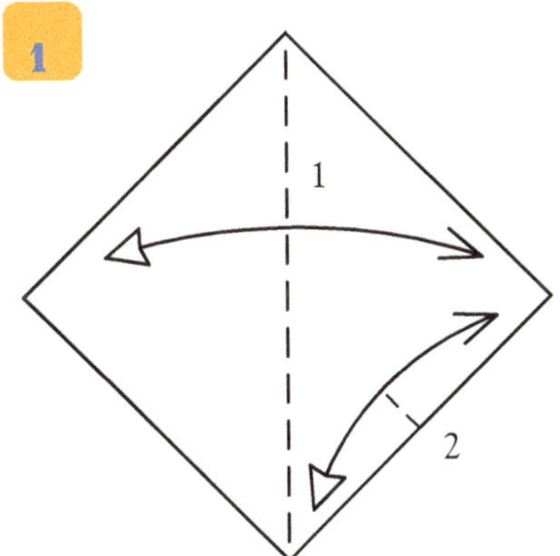

1. Fold and unfold.
2. Fold and unfold on the edge.

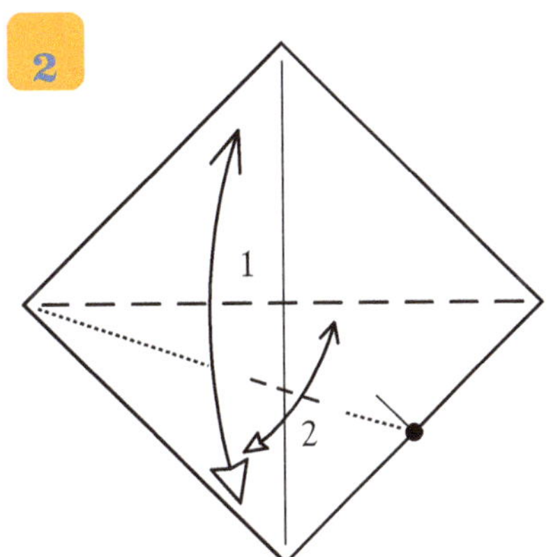

1. Fold and unfold.
2. Fold and unfold on the diagonal.

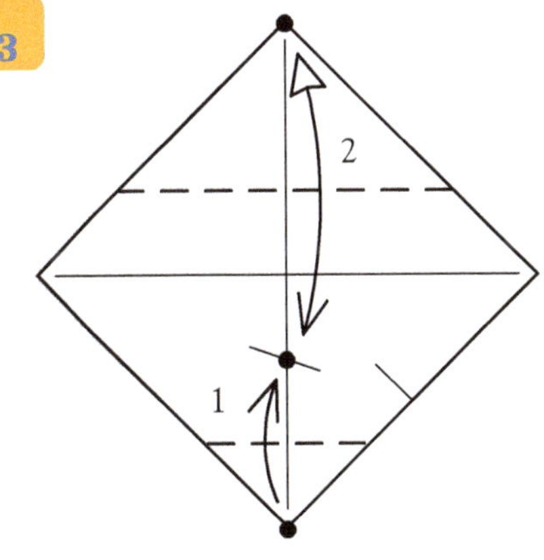

1. Fold up.
2. Fold and unfold.

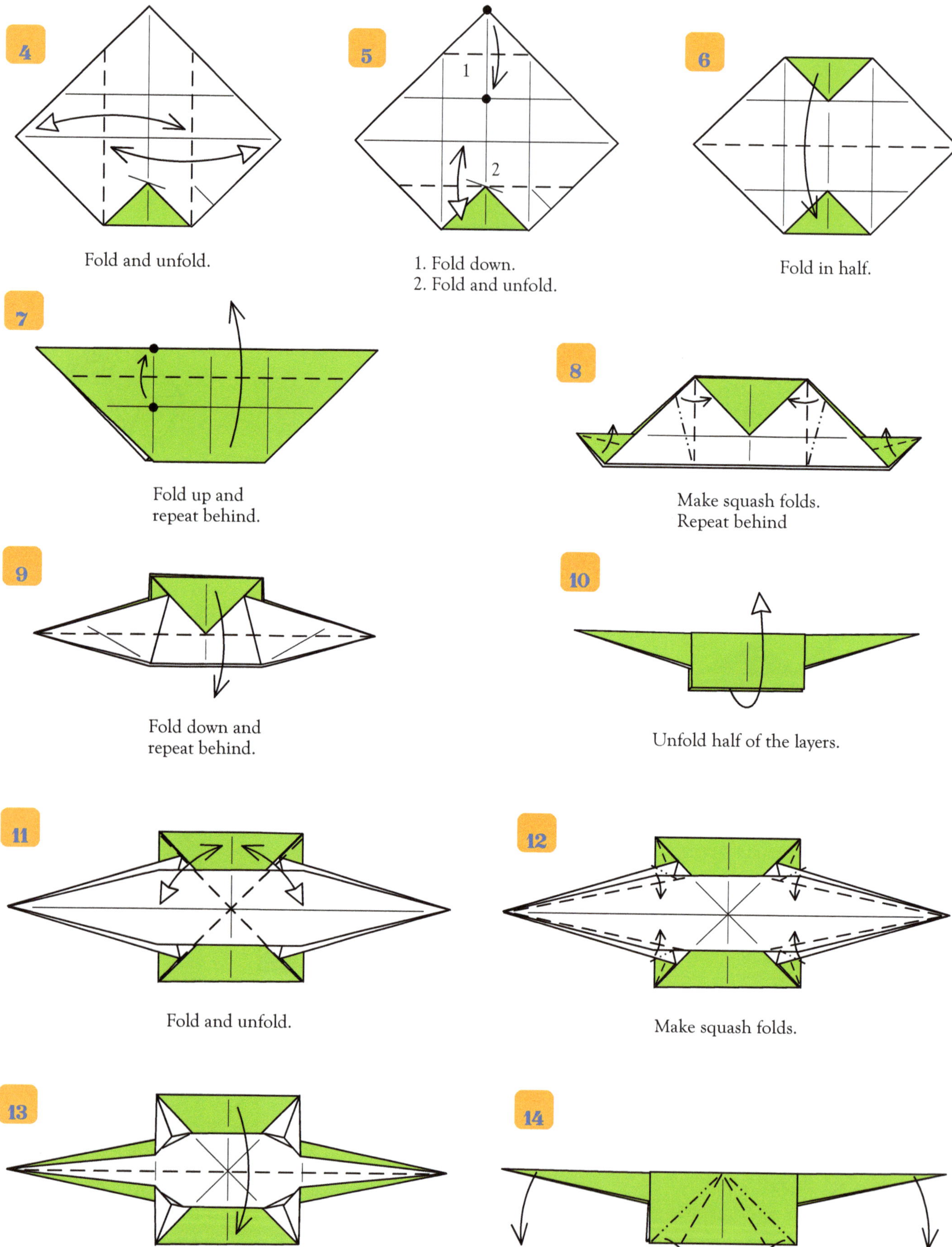
4
Fold and unfold.
5
1
2
1. Fold down.
2. Fold and unfold.
6
Fold in half.
7
Fold up and
repeat behind.
8
Make squash folds.
Repeat behind
9
Fold down and
repeat behind.
10
Unfold half of the layers.
11
Fold and unfold.
12
Make squash folds.
13
Fold in half.
14
Make crimp folds.

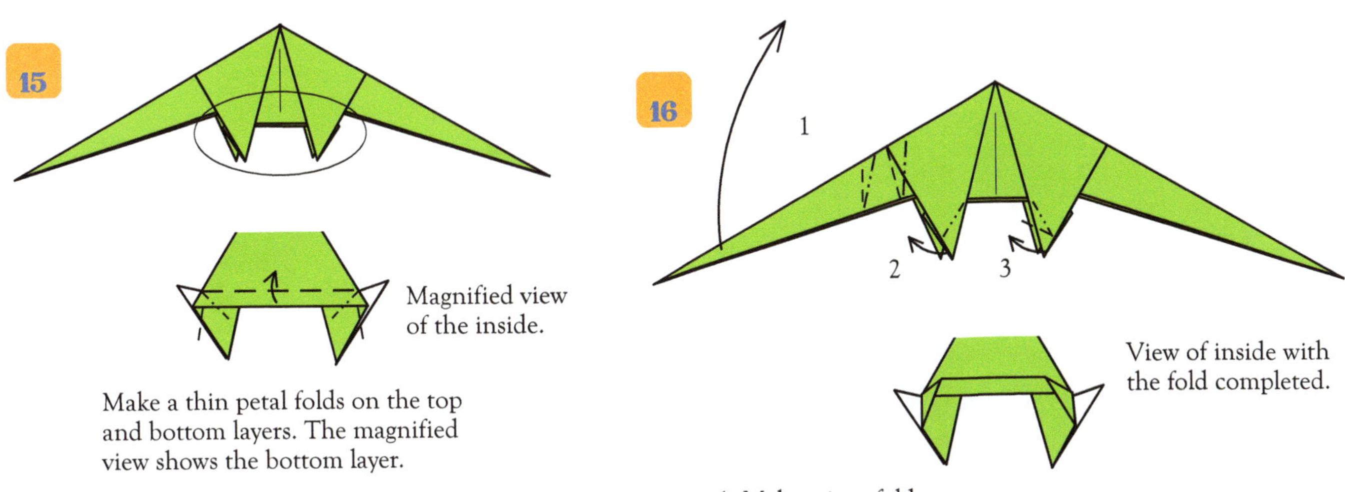

Make a thin petal folds on the top and bottom layers. The magnified view shows the bottom layer.

1. Make crimp folds.
2. Reverse-fold, repeat behind.
3. Crimp-fold, repeat behind.

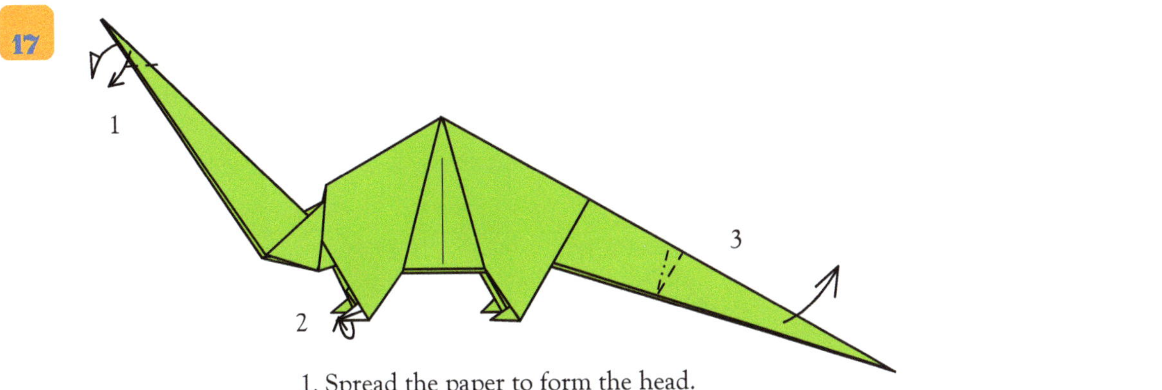

1. Spread the paper to form the head.
2. Fold the small, top white layer up, repeat behind.
3. Crimp-fold.

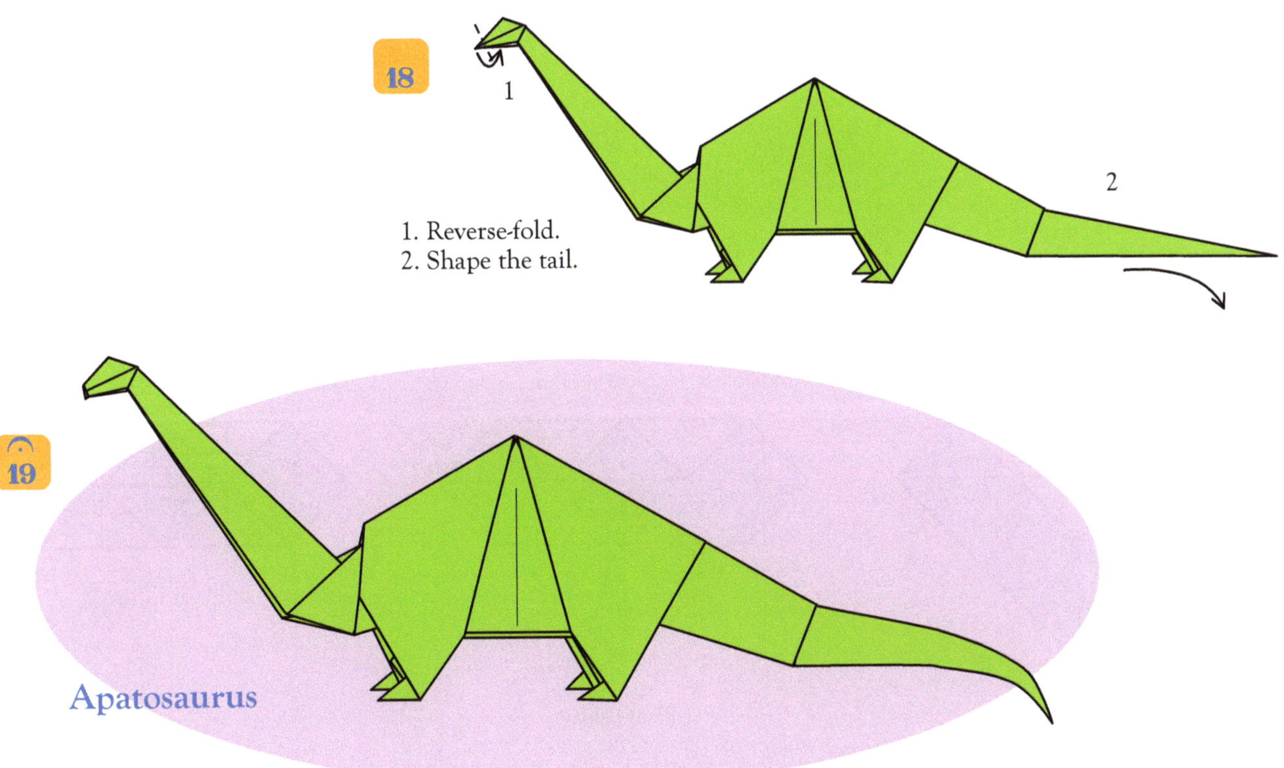

1. Reverse-fold.
2. Shape the tail.

Brachiosaurus

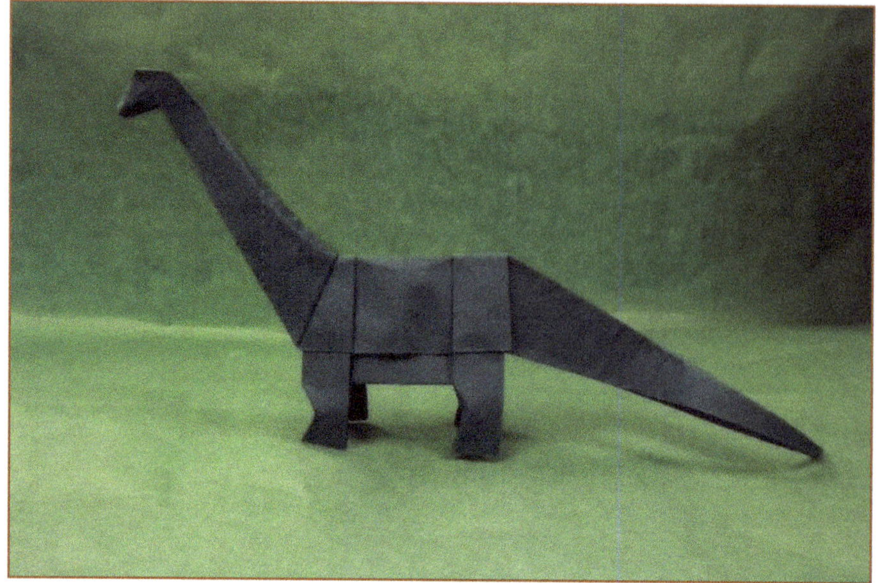

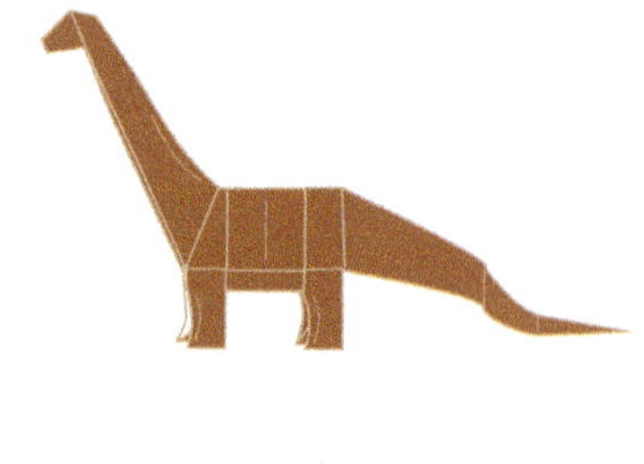

Reaching 85 to almost 100 feet in length, this massive dinosaur is believed to have had a lifespan of approximately 100 years. A herbivore, the Brachiosaurus belonged to the sauropod genus. It lived during the Jurassic Period.

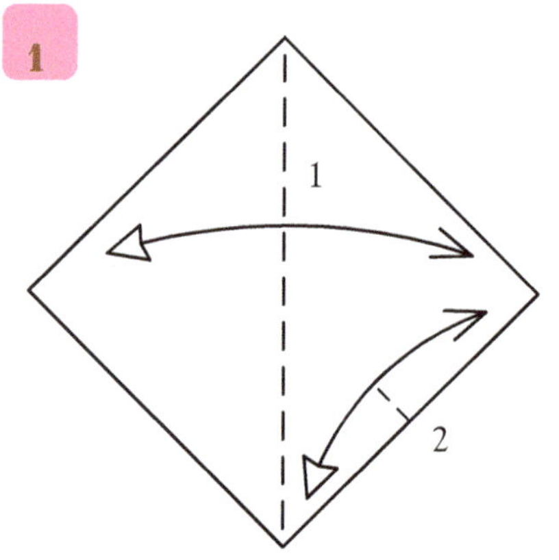

1. Fold and unfold.
2. Fold and unfold on the edge.

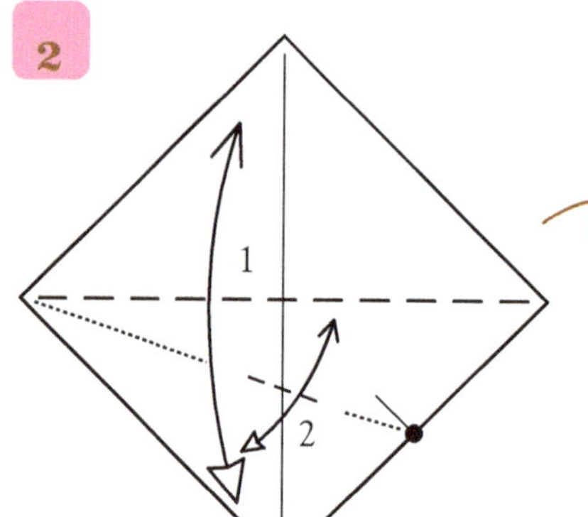

1. Fold and unfold.
2. Fold and unfold on the diagonal.

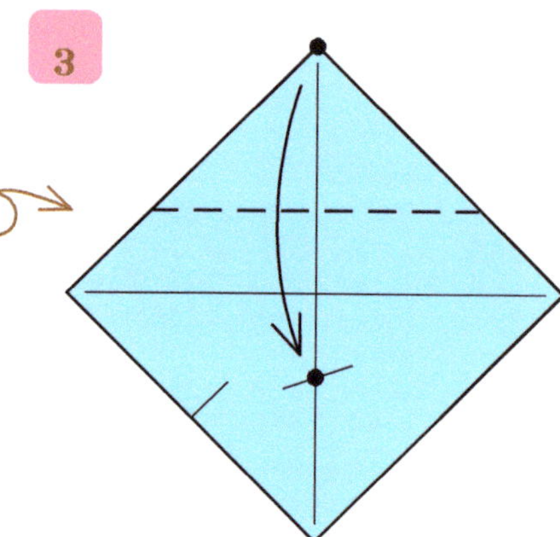

The dots will meet.

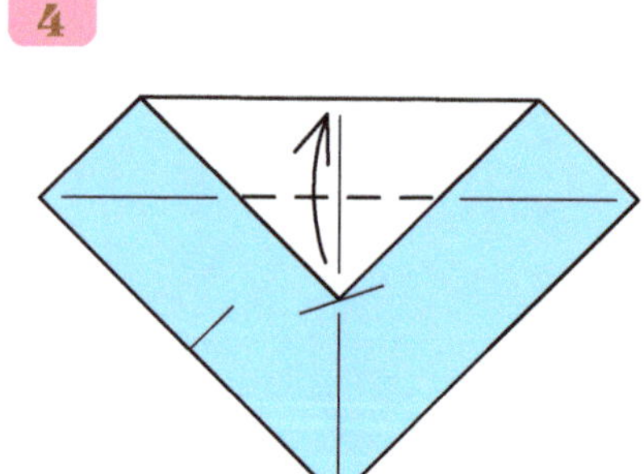

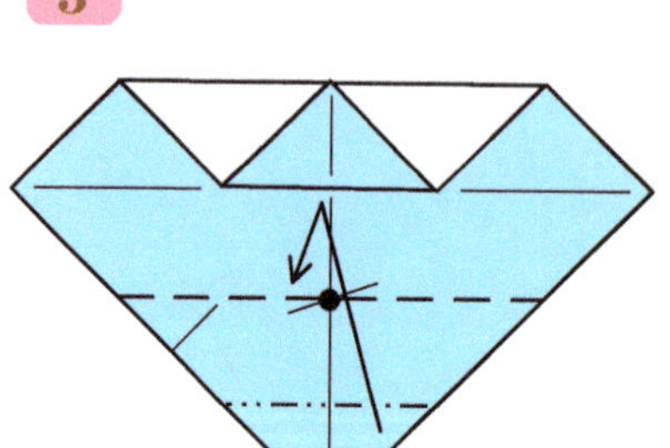

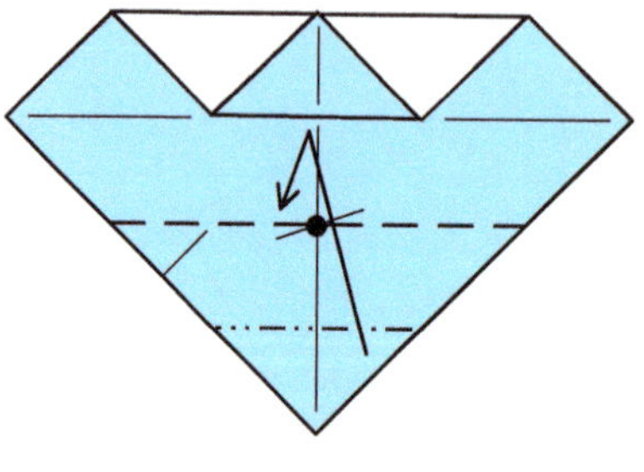

Pleat-fold.

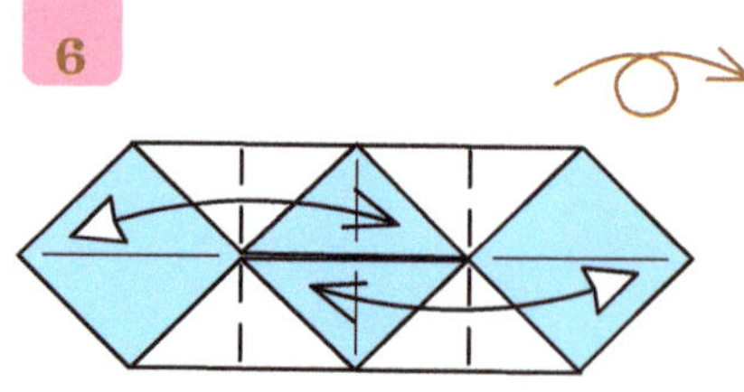

Fold and unfold.

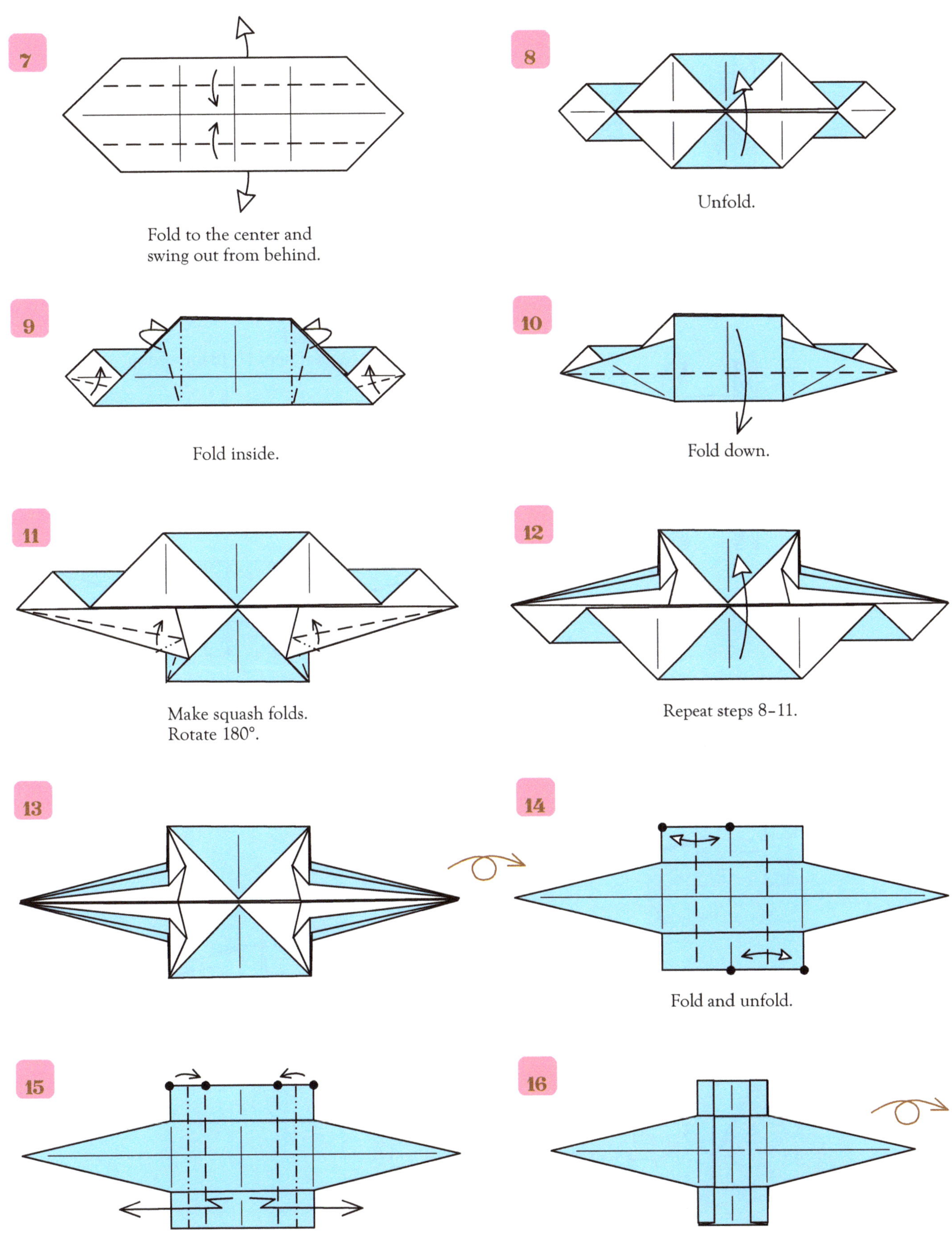

Fold to the center and swing out from behind.

Unfold.

Fold inside.

Fold down.

Make squash folds. Rotate 180°.

Repeat steps 8–11.

Fold and unfold.

Make pleat folds so the dots meet. Valley-fold along the creases.

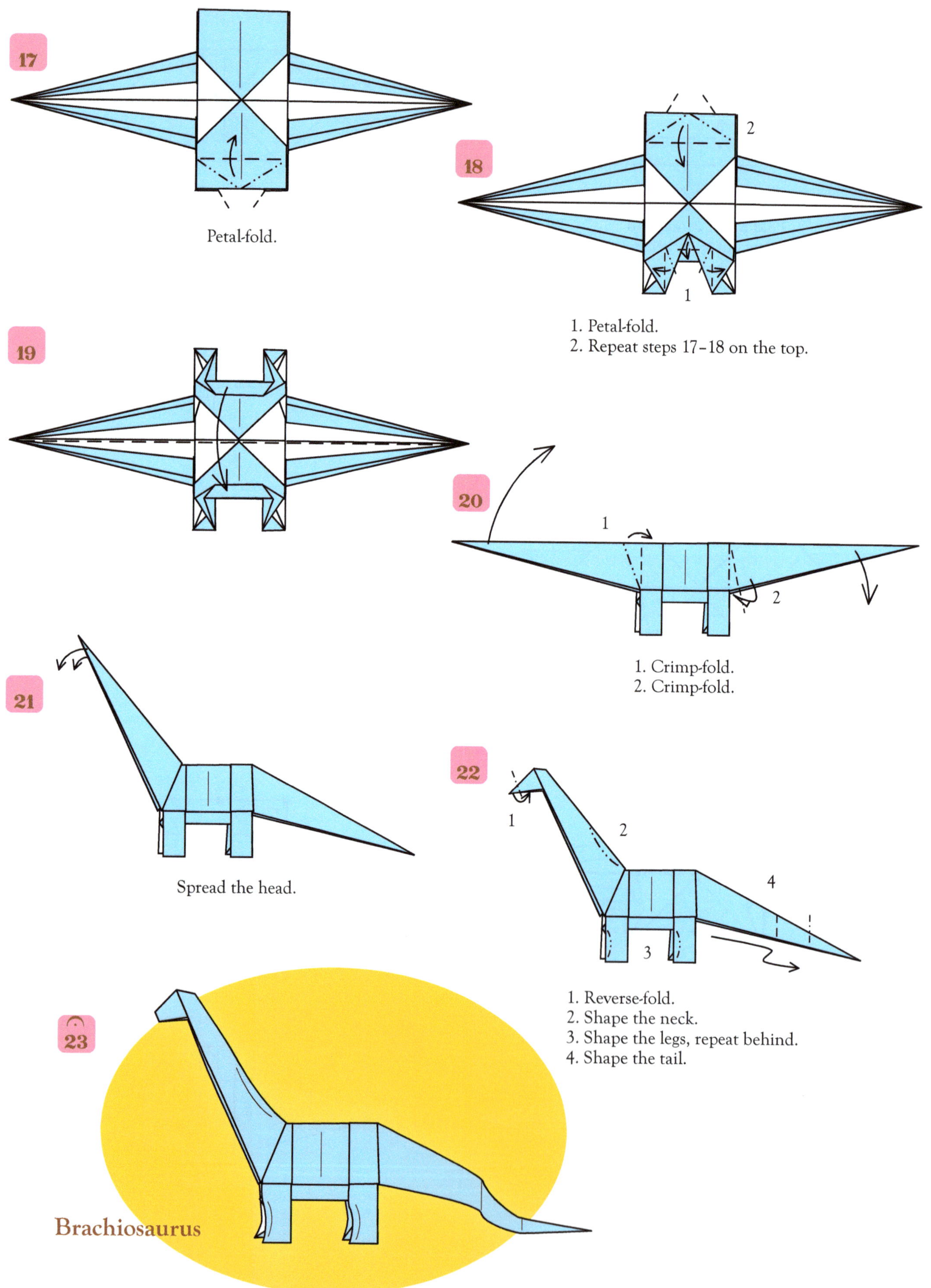
17
Petal-fold.
18
2
1
1. Petal-fold.
2. Repeat steps 17–18 on the top.
19
20
1
2
1. Crimp-fold.
2. Crimp-fold.
21
Spread the head.
22
1
2
4
3
1. Reverse-fold.
2. Shape the neck.
3. Shape the legs, repeat behind.
4. Shape the tail.
23
Brachiosaurus

Plateosaurus

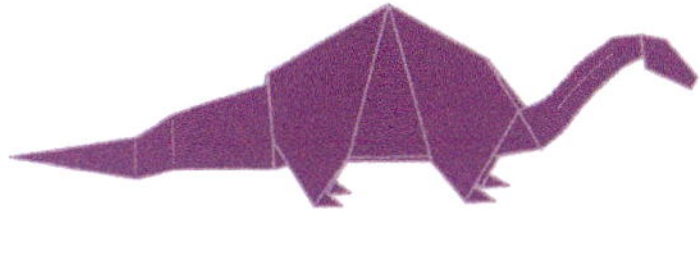

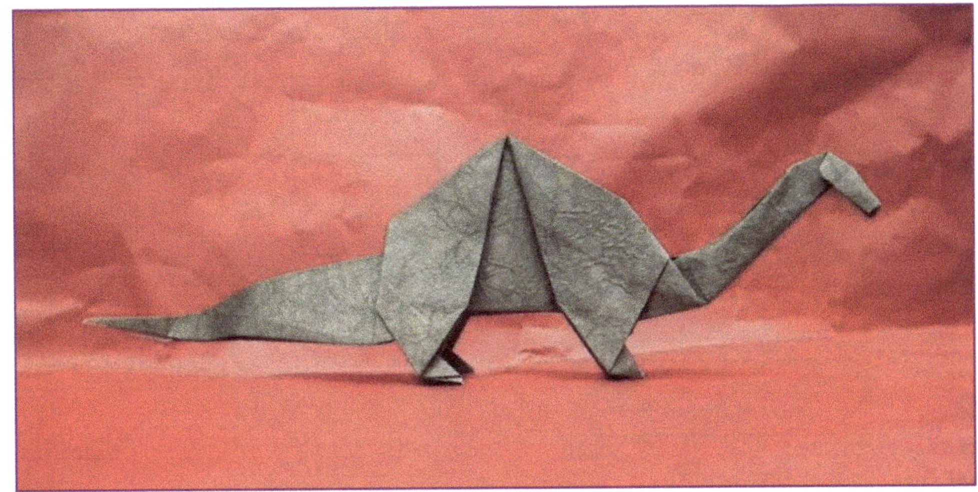

Found in abundance in Europe and Greenland, its name means "Broad Lizard" in Latin. The Plateosaurus lived during the Late Triassic Period and at 27 feet long, it was one of the earliest known large herbivores.

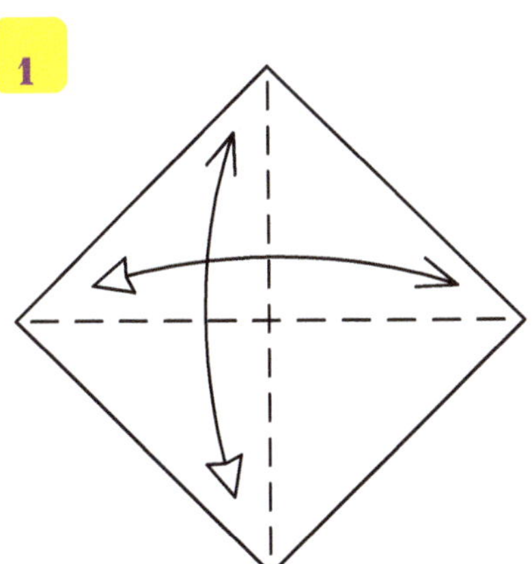

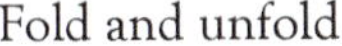

Fold and unfold.

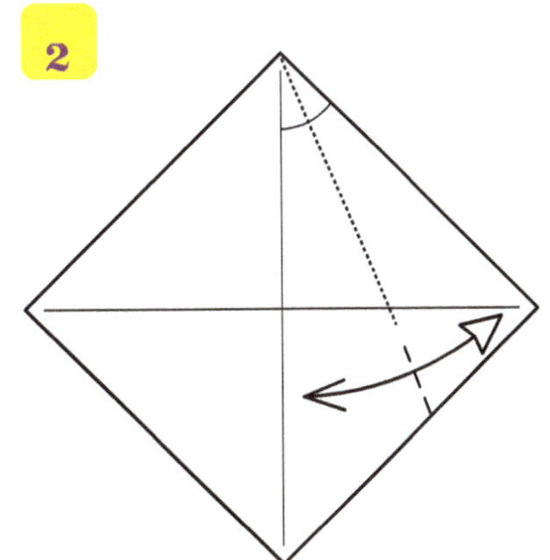

Fold and unfold on the edge.

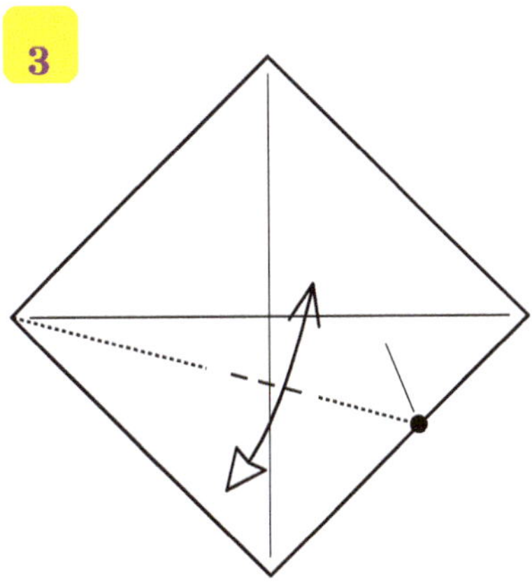

Fold and unfold on the diagonal.

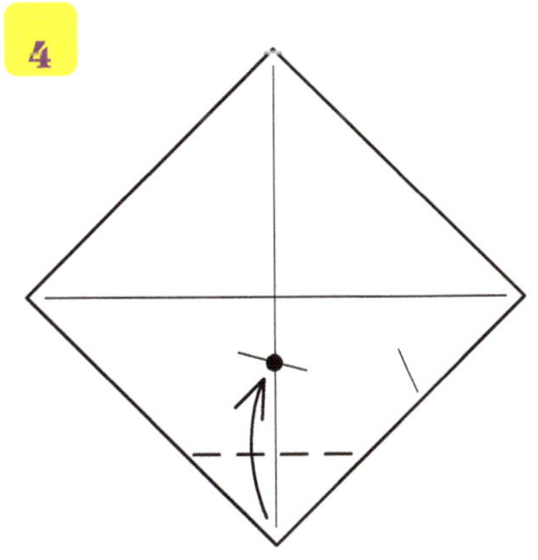

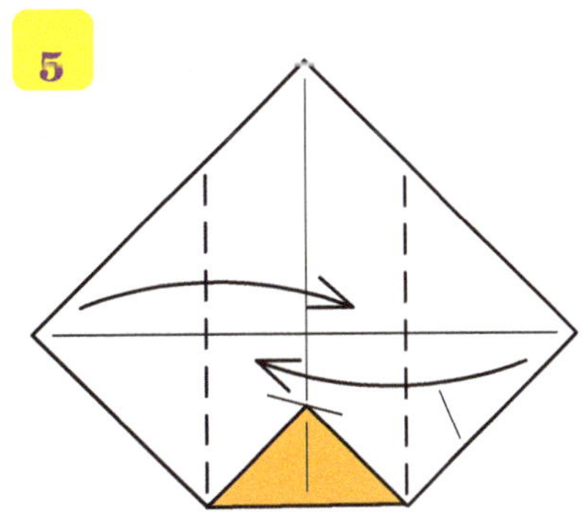

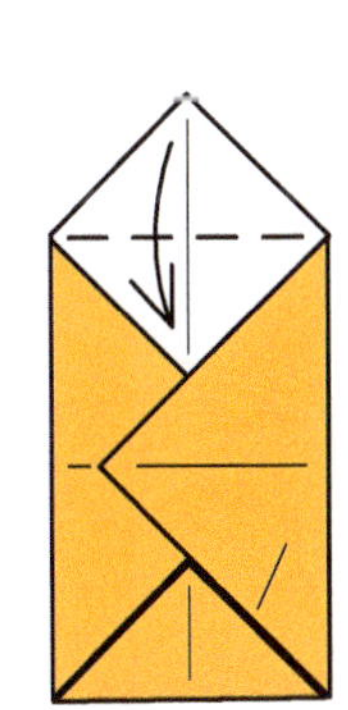

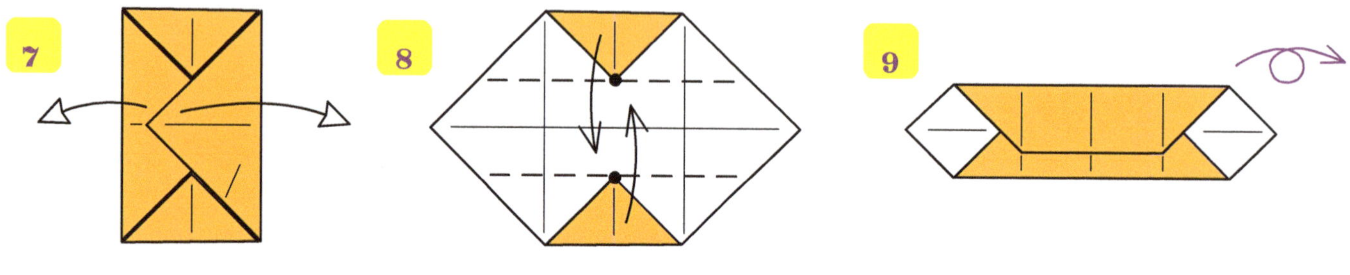

Unfold.

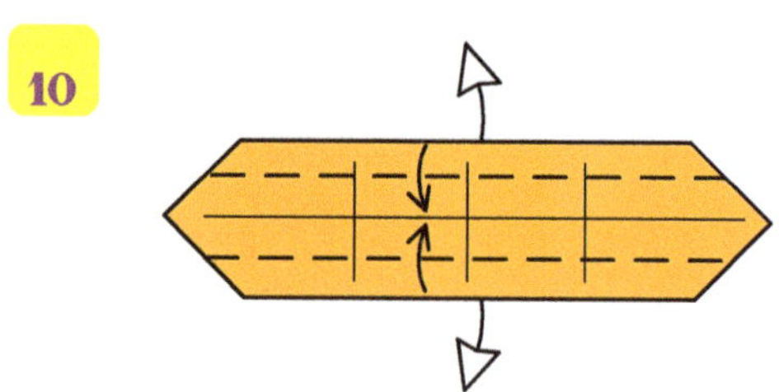

Fold to the center and swing out from behind.

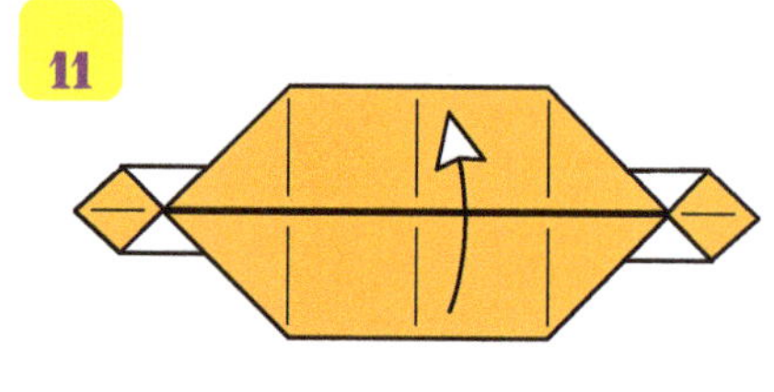

Unfold.

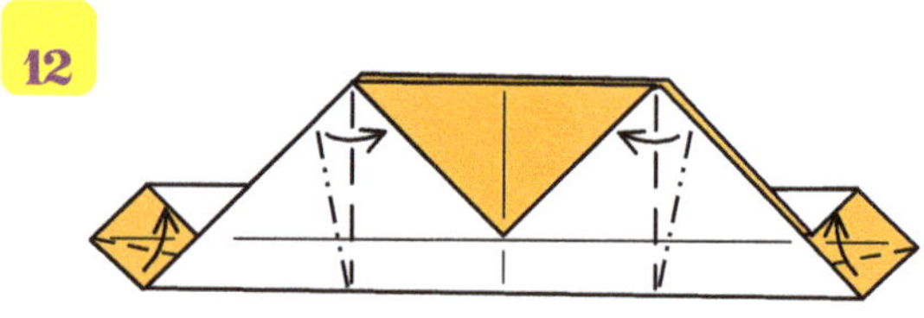

Make squash folds.

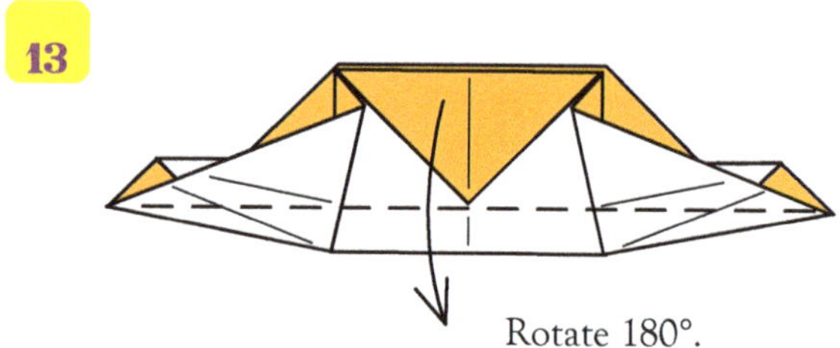

Rotate 180°.

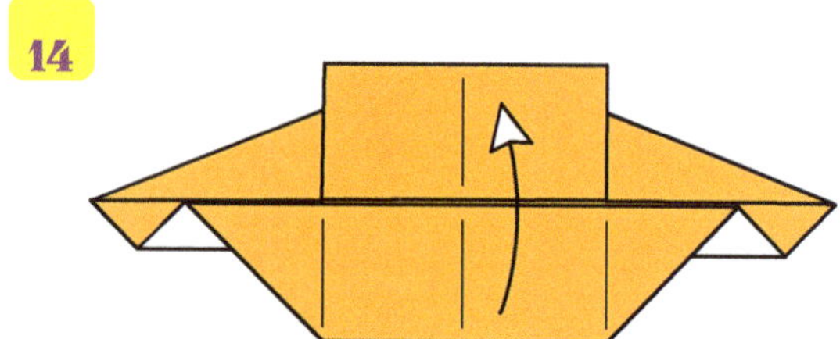

Repeat steps 11–13.

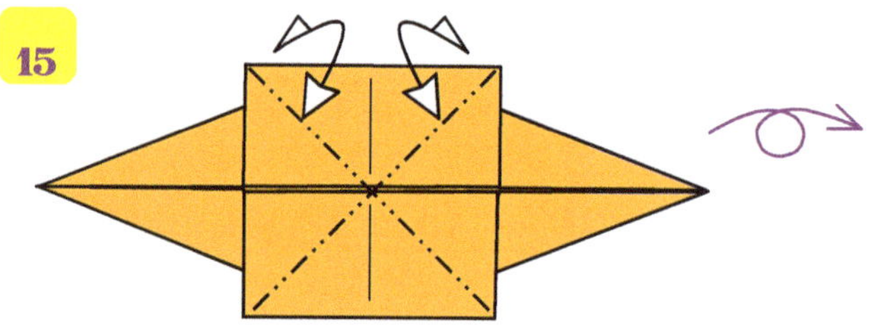

Fold and unfold.

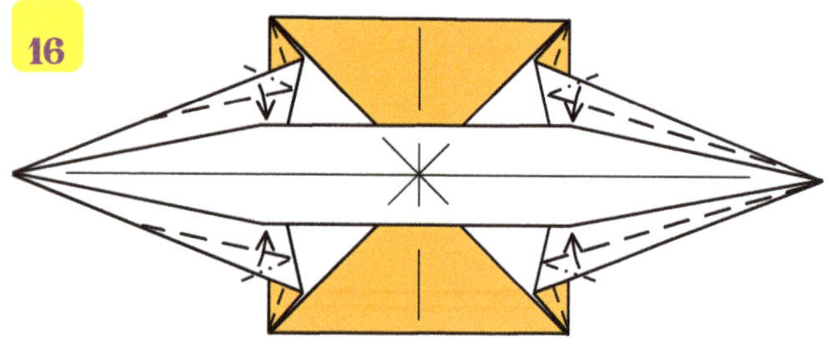

Make squash folds. Do not fold to the tip on the left.

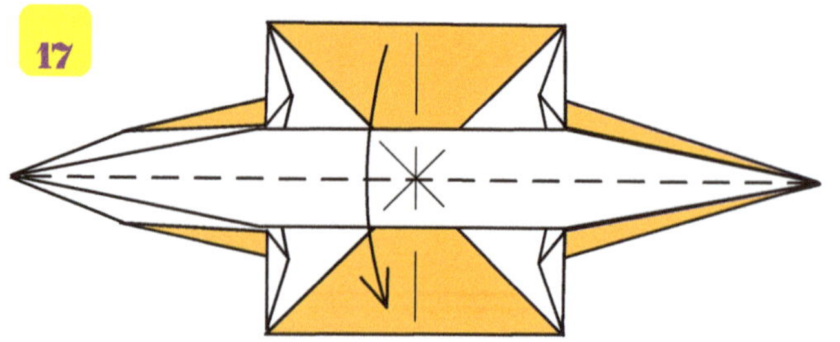

18

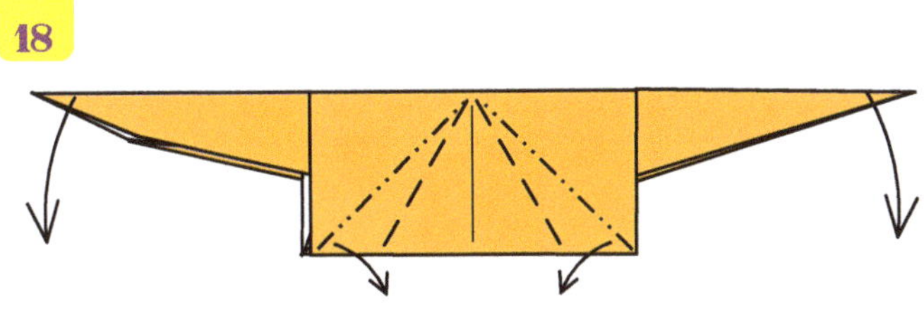

Make crimp folds.

19

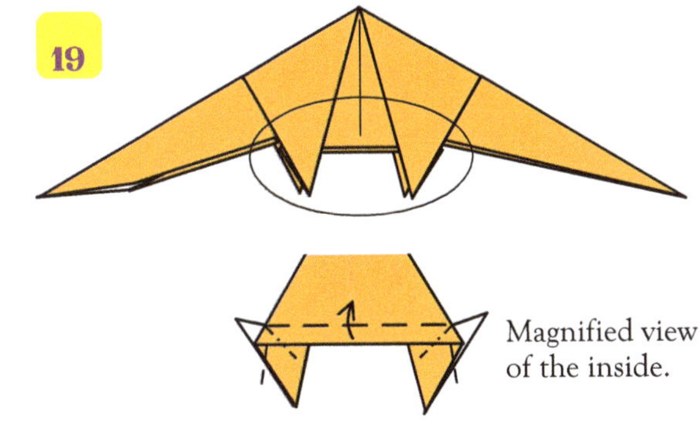

Magnified view of the inside.

Make a thin petal folds on the top and bottom layers. The magnified view shows the bottom layer.

20

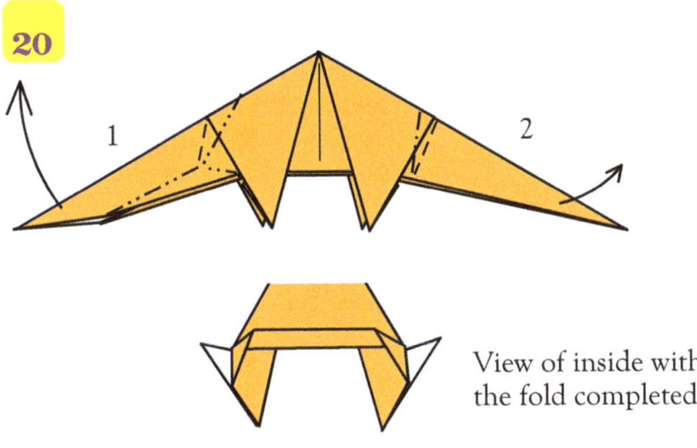

View of inside with the fold completed.

1. Double-rabbit-ear.
2. Crimp-fold.

21

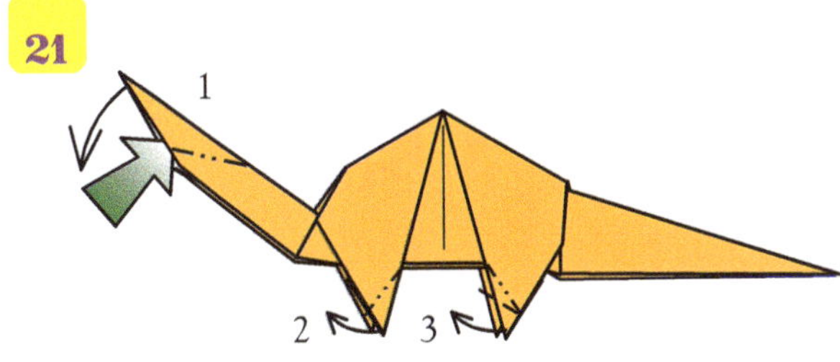

1. Reverse-fold.
2. Reverse-fold,repeat behind.
3. Crimp-fold, repeat behind.

22

23

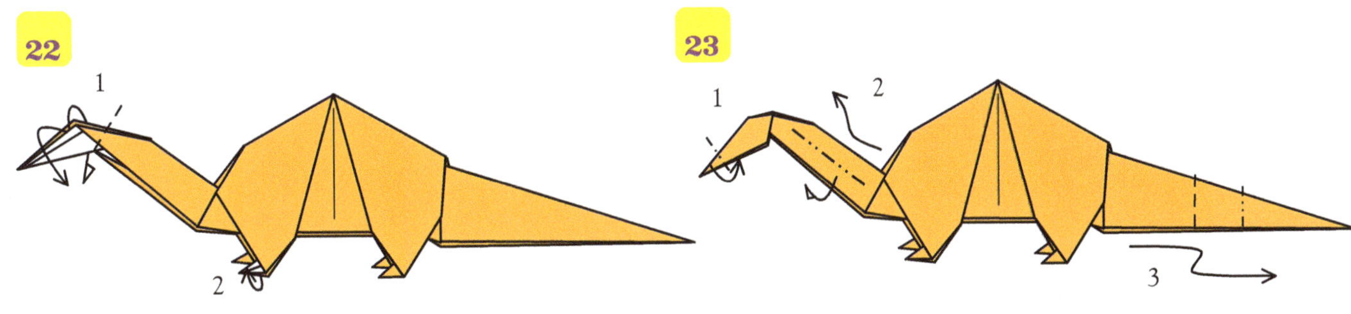

1. Outside-reverse-fold.
2. Fold the small, top white layer up, repeat behind.

1. Reverse-fold.
2. Shape the neck.
3. Shape the tail.

24

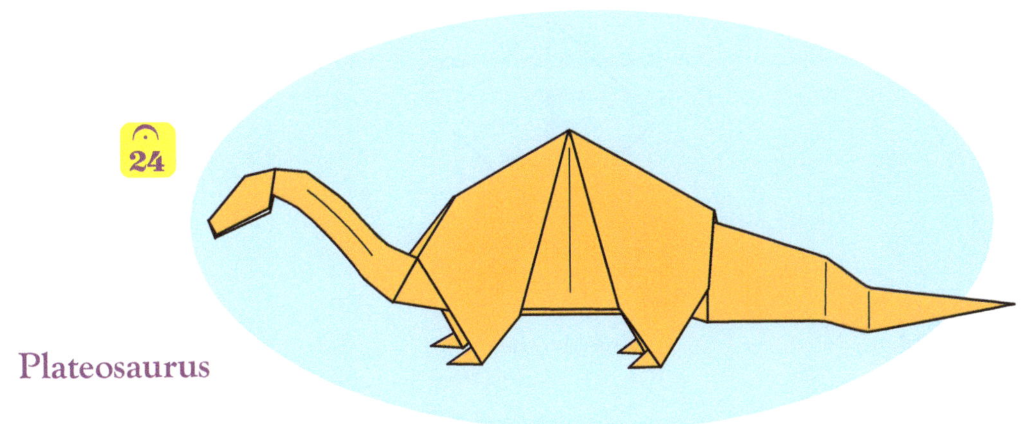

Plateosaurus

Hypsilophodon

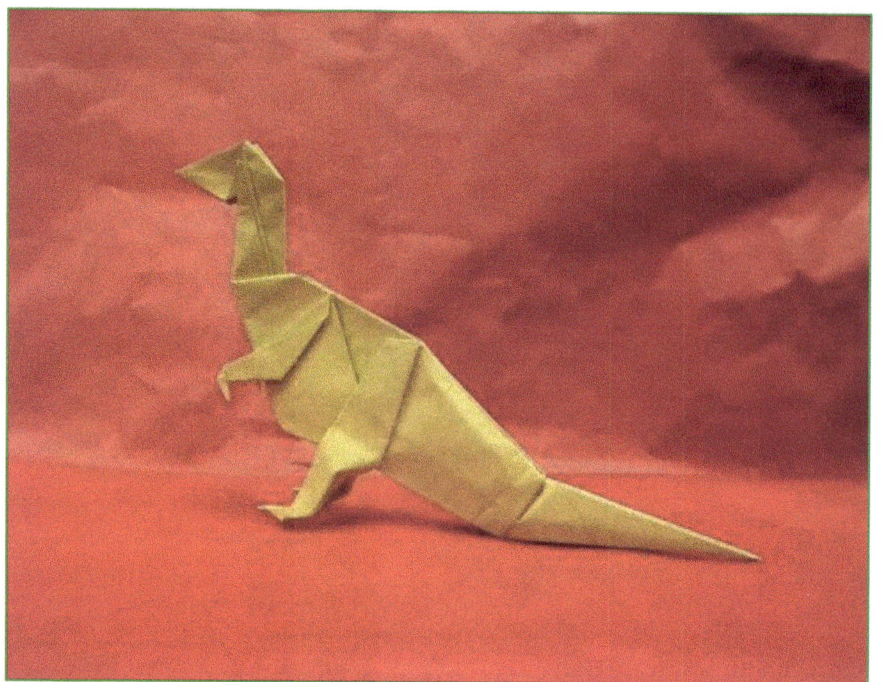

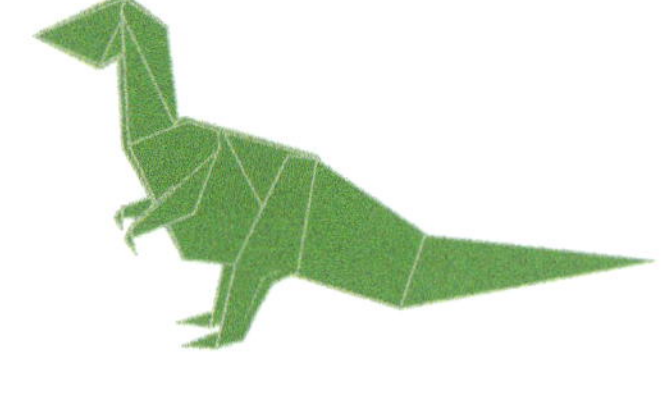

A relatively small dinosaur, the Hypsilophodon lived in what is now England during the Early Cretaceous Period and was bird-like in its appearance and eating habits. With a length of seven feet, it had long legs and was well adapted for running.

1

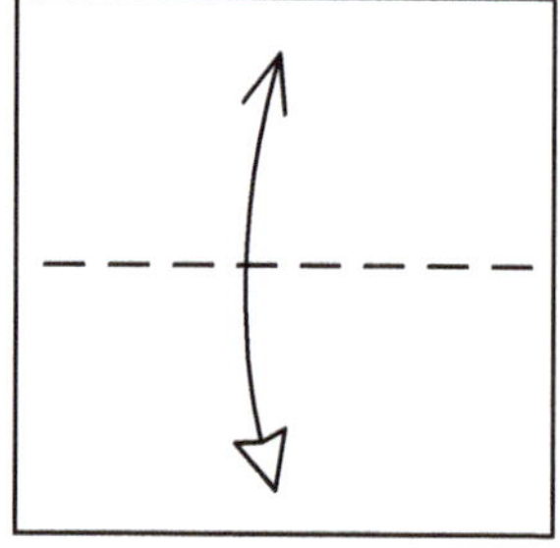

Fold and unfold.

2

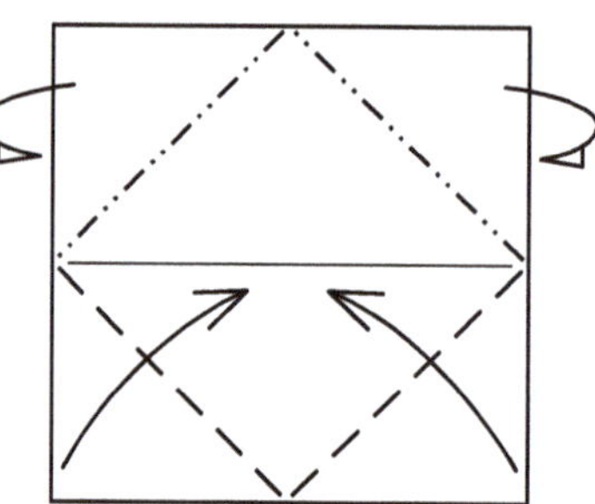

Fold to the center.

3

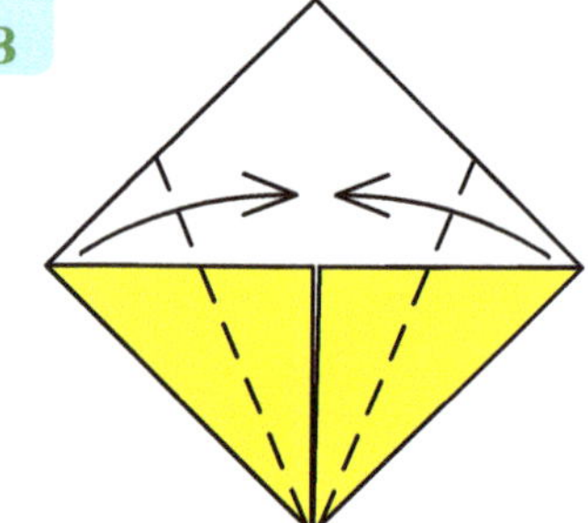

Fold to the center.

4

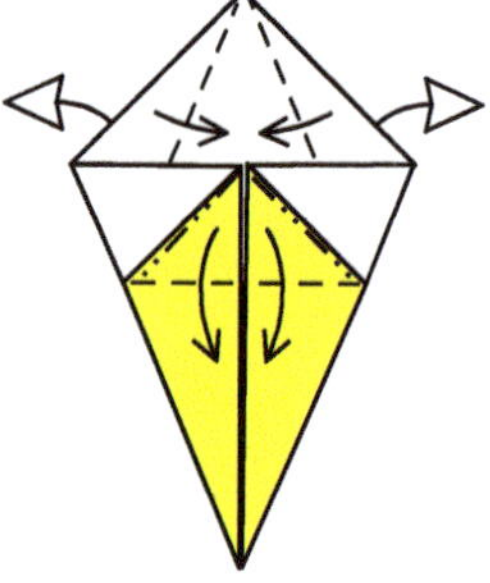

Make squash folds and swing out from behind.

5

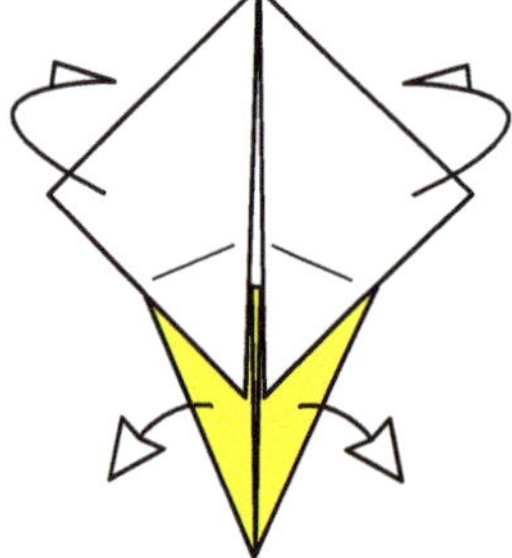

Unfold to step 3.

6

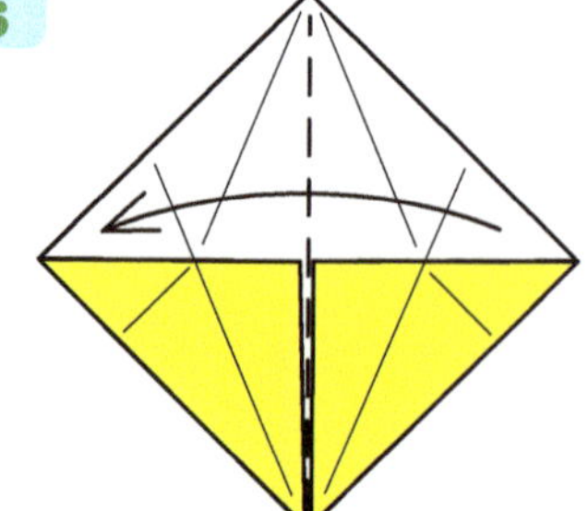

Fold in half.

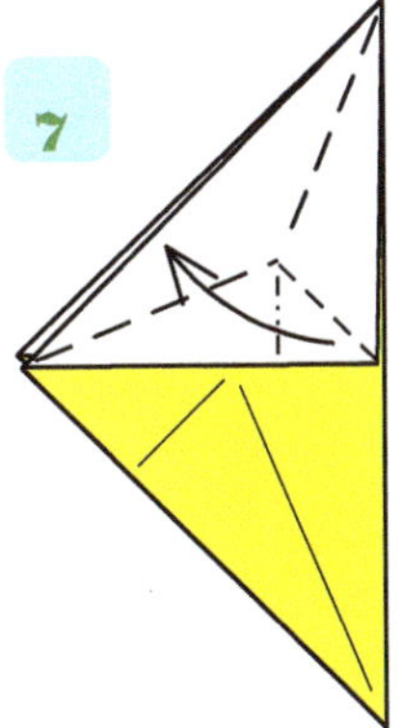

Rabbit-ear,
repeat behind.

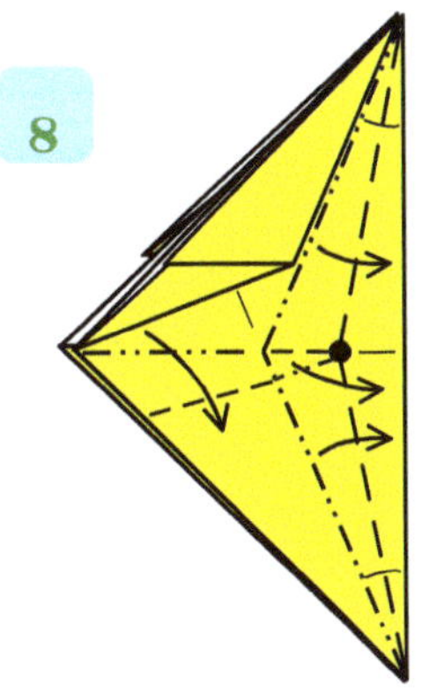

Push in at the dot to bisect
the angles. This is similar to
a rabbit ear. Repeat behind.

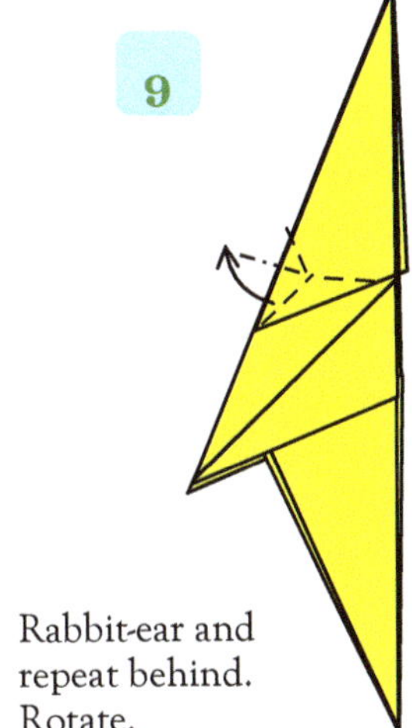

Rabbit-ear and
repeat behind.
Rotate.

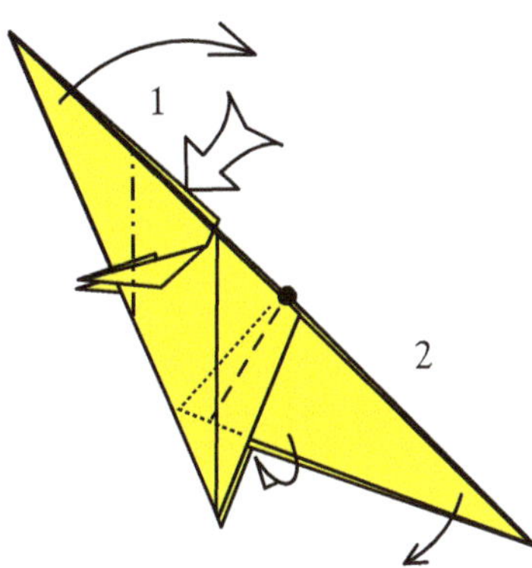

1. Push into the center flap.
   This is similar to a reverse fold.
2. Pivot at the dot. This is
   similar to a crimp fold.

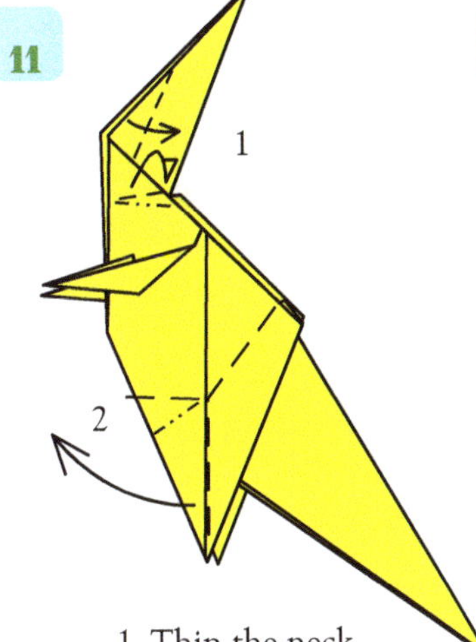

1. Thin the neck.
2. Rabbit-ear.
Repeat behind.

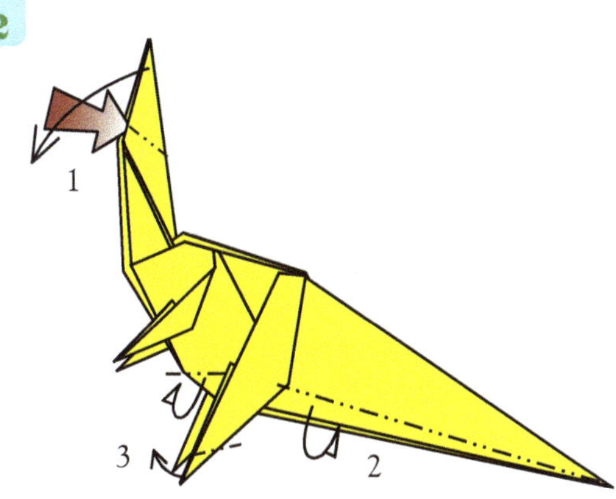

1. Reverse-fold.
2. Fold inside, repeat behind.
3. Reverse-fold, repeat behind.

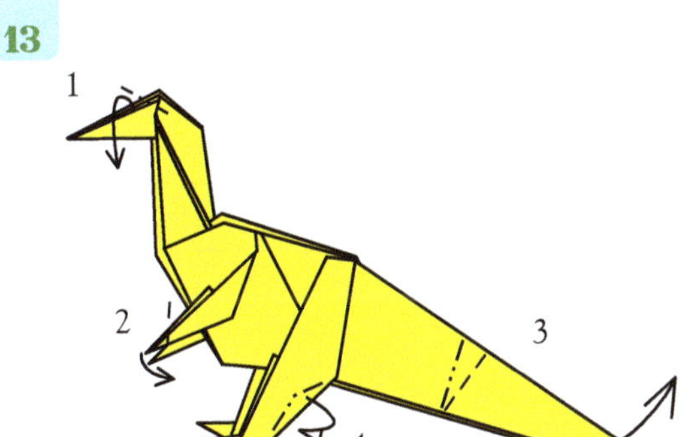

1. Pull out the top layer.
2. Outside-reverse-fold.
3. Crimp-fold.
4. Shape the legs.
Repeat behind.

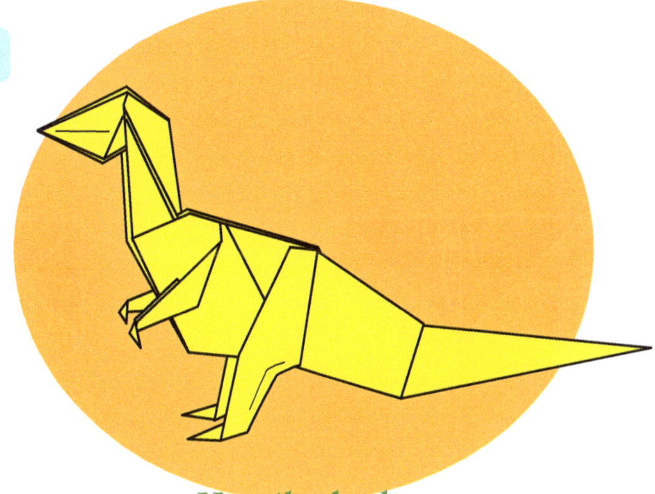

Hypsilophodon

Tyrannosaurus

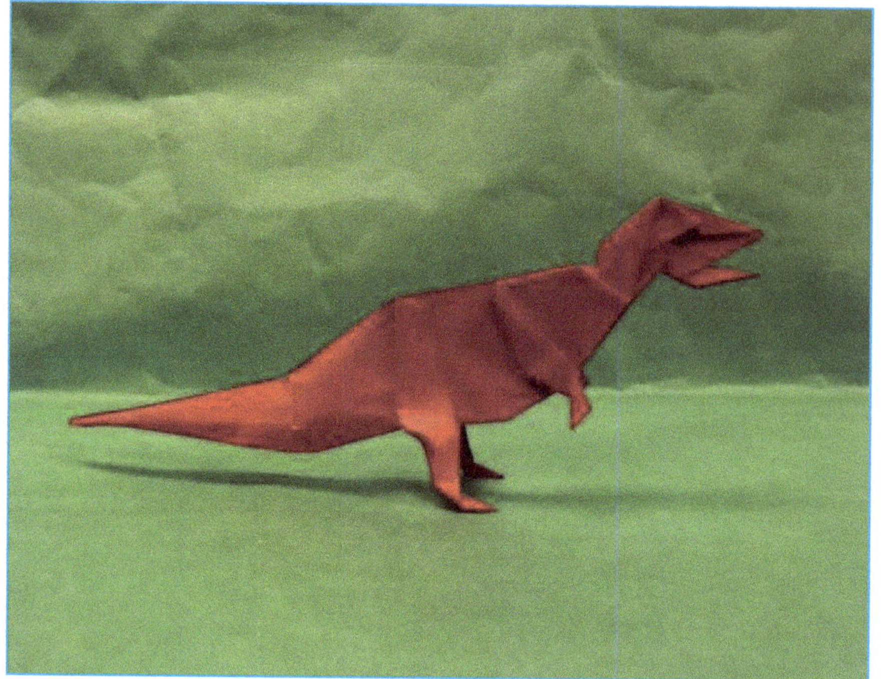

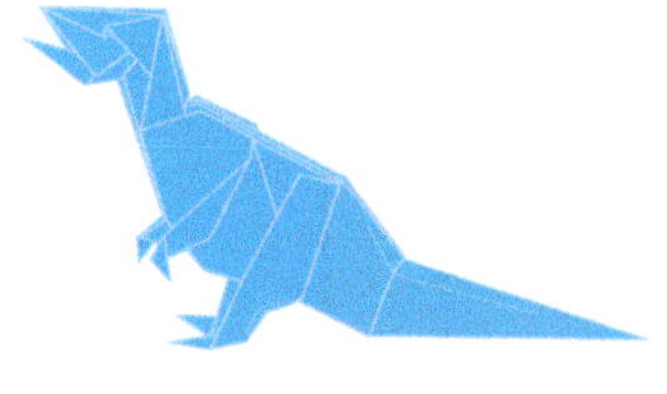

The Tyrannosaurus is one of the largest carnivorous dinosaurs. With its large skull and huge teeth, it would enjoy a meal of hundreds of pounds. It lived during the Cretaceous period, in the island continent of Laramidia, now western North America. At 40 feet long, it had a life span of 30 years.

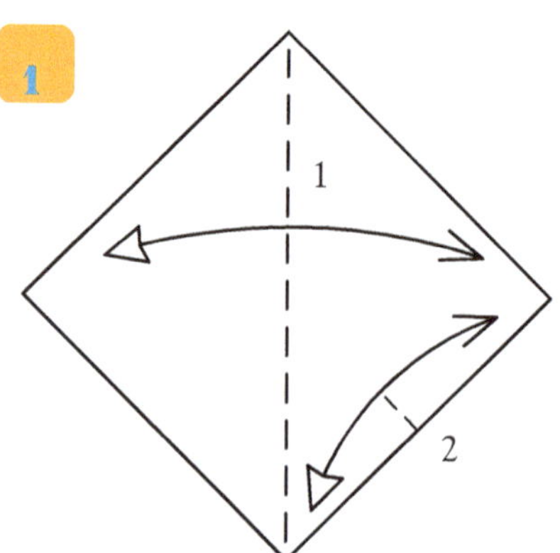

1. Fold and unfold.
2. Fold and unfold on the edge.

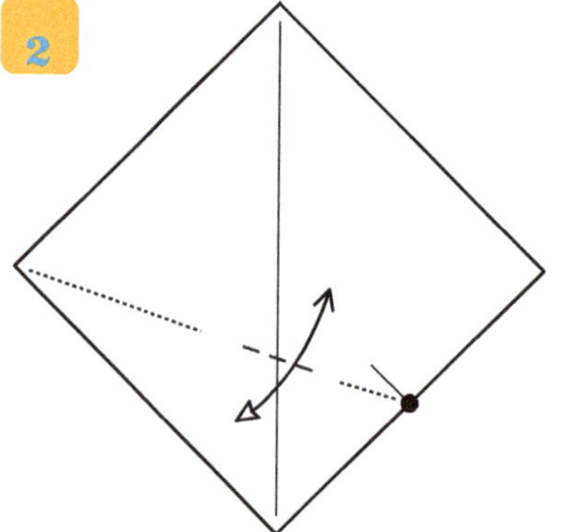

Fold and unfold on the diagonal.

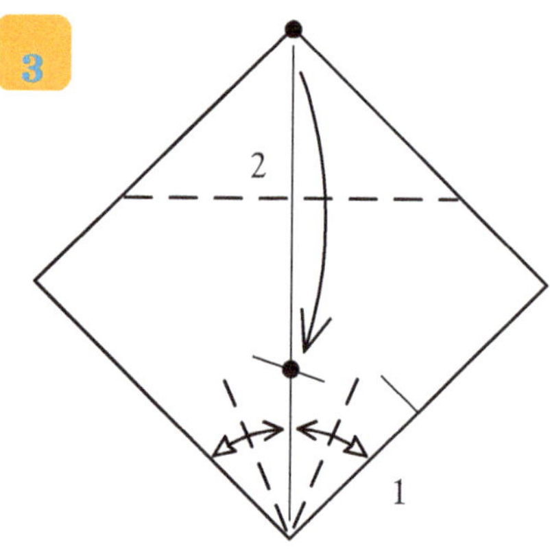

1. Fold and unfold.
2. The dots will meet.

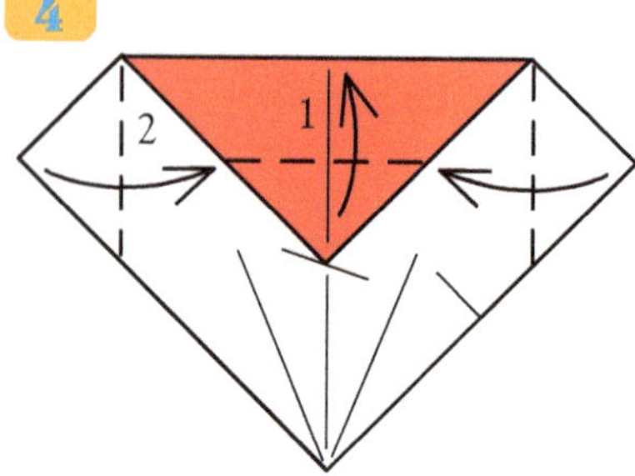

1. Fold up.
2. Fold on the left and right.

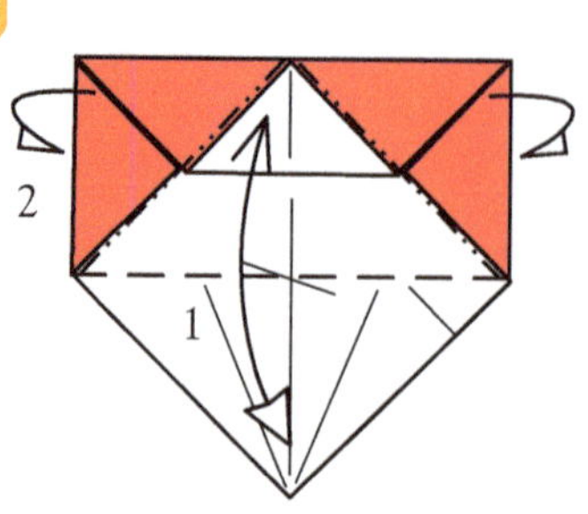

1. Fold and unfold.
2. Fold behind on the left and right.

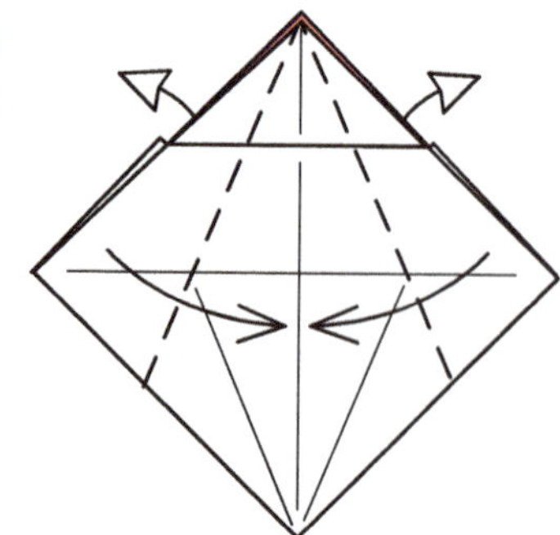

Fold to the center and swing out from behind.

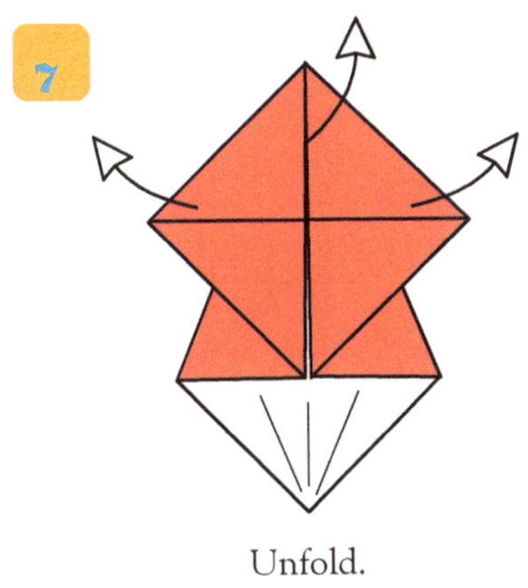

Unfold.

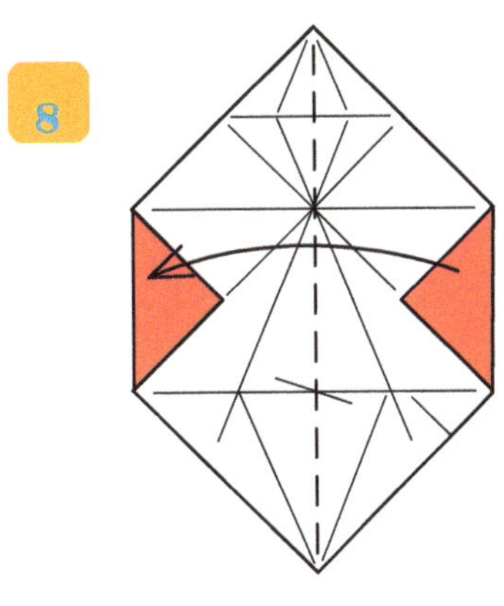

Fold in half.

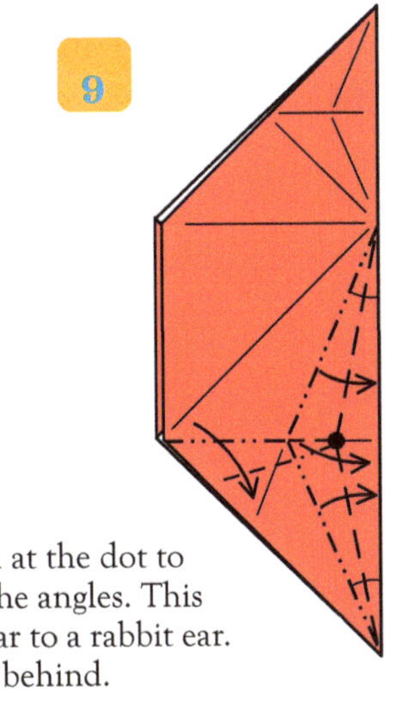

Push in at the dot to bisect the angles. This is similar to a rabbit ear. Repeat behind.

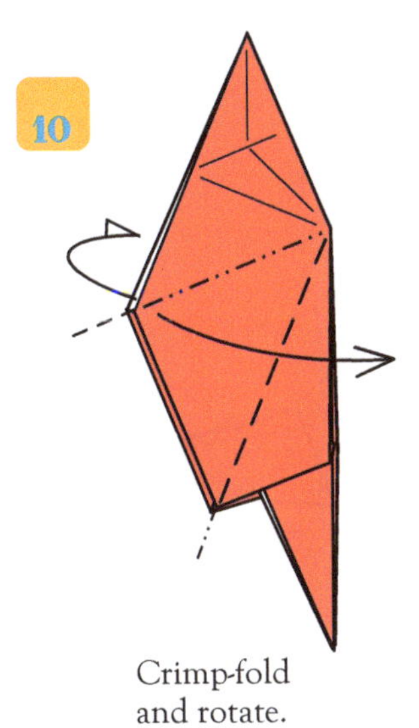

Crimp-fold and rotate.

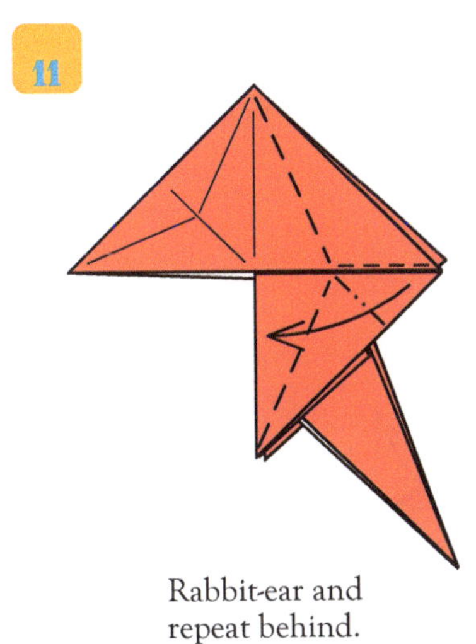

Rabbit-ear and repeat behind.

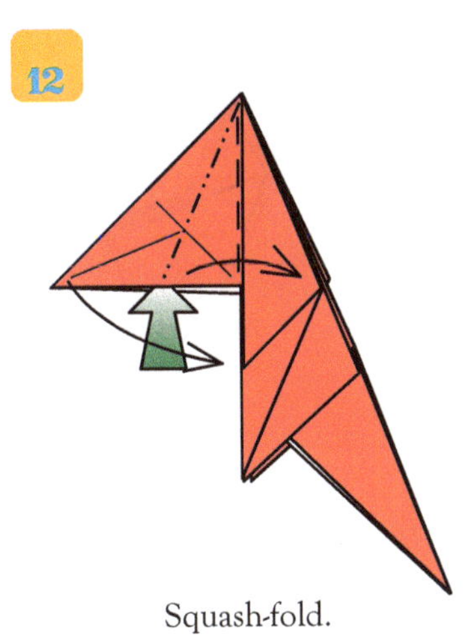

Squash-fold.

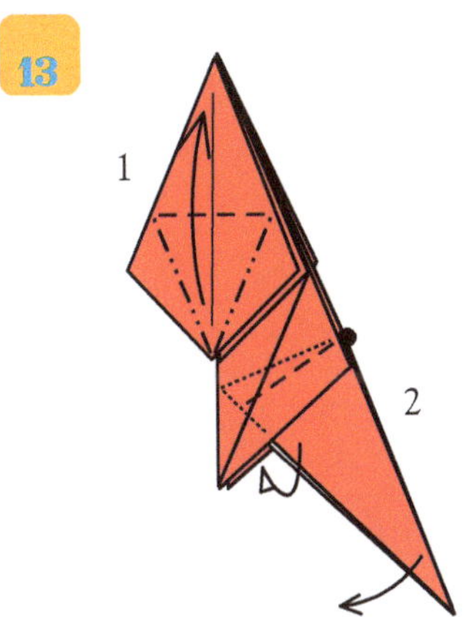
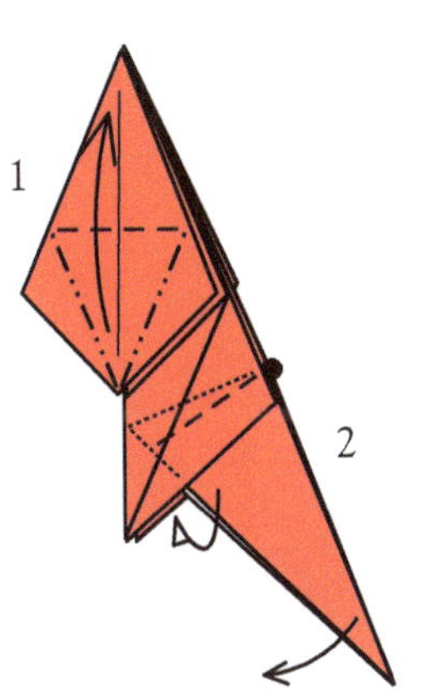

1. Petal-fold.
2. Pivot at the dot. This is similar to a crimp fold.

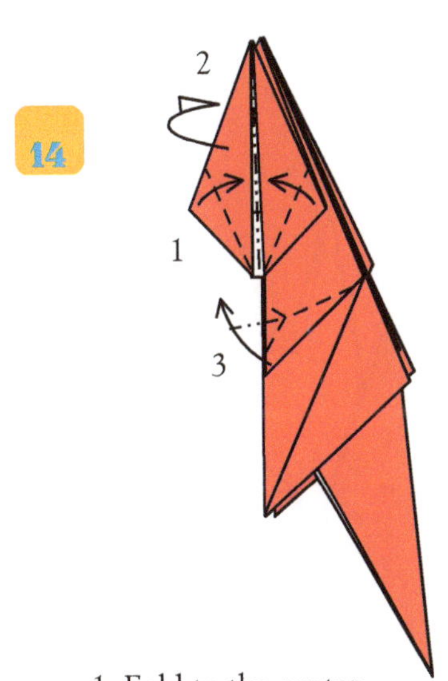

1. Fold to the center.
2. Fold behind.
3. Rabbit-ear, but not to a point. Repeat behind.

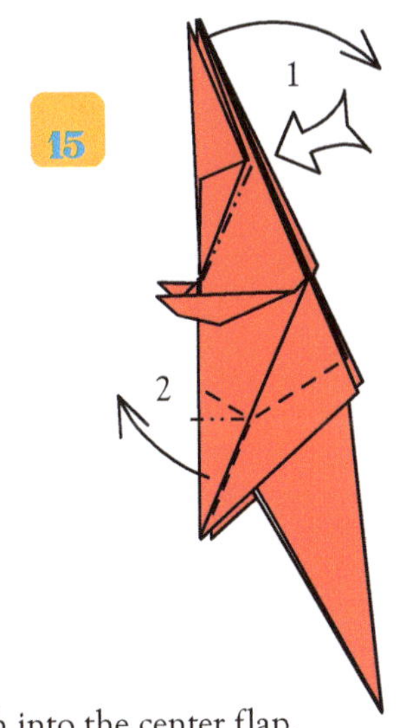

1. Push into the center flap. This is similar to a reverse fold.
2. Rabbit-ear, repeat behind.
Rotate.

16

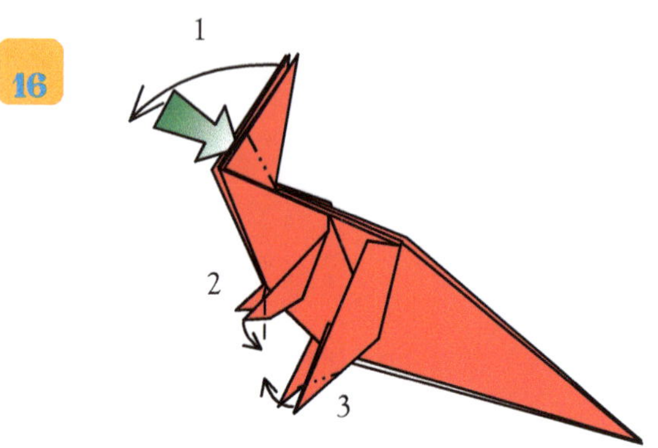

1. Reverse-fold.
2. Fold the tip, repeat behind.
3. Reverse-fold, repeat behind.

17

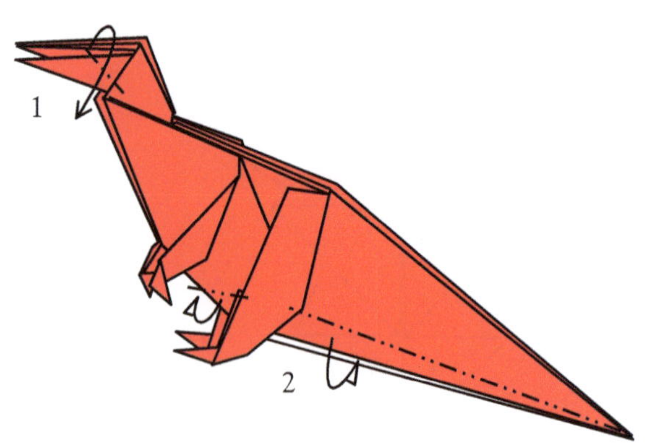

1. Fold down the mouth and one layer of the head.
2. Fold inside.

Repeat behind.

18

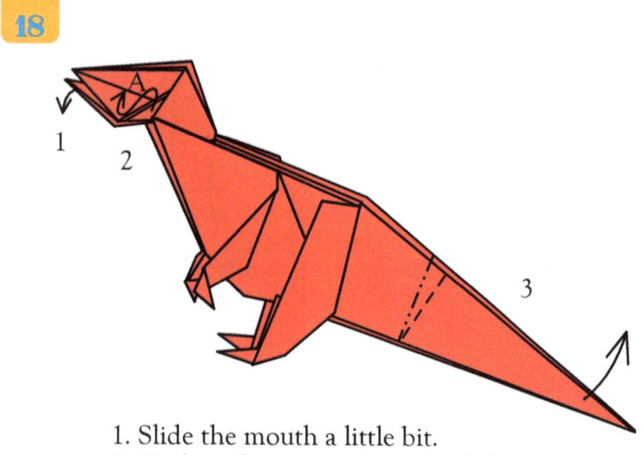

1. Slide the mouth a little bit.
2. Tuck under region A, repeat behind.
3. Crimp-fold.

19

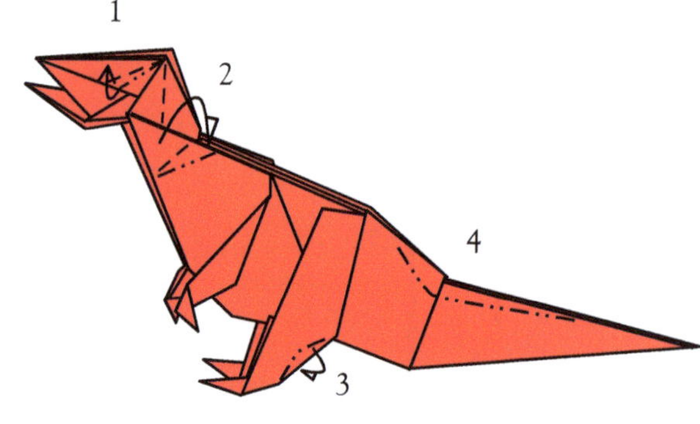

1. Pleat-fold to shape the eye.
2. Fold the neck.
3. Shape the legs.
4. Shape the tail.

Repeat behind.

20

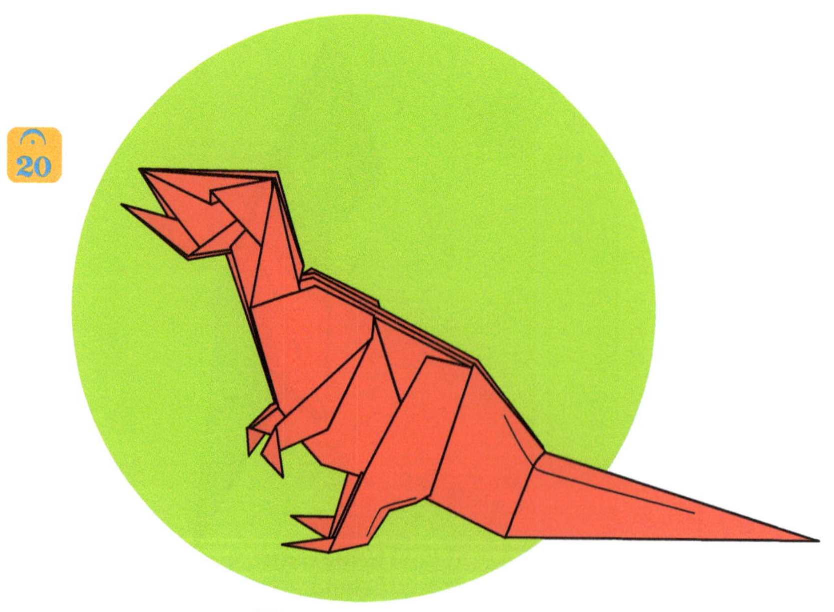

Tyrannosaurus

Megapnosaurus

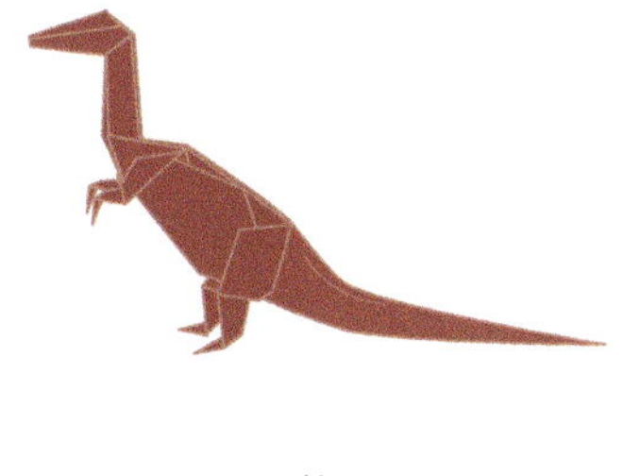

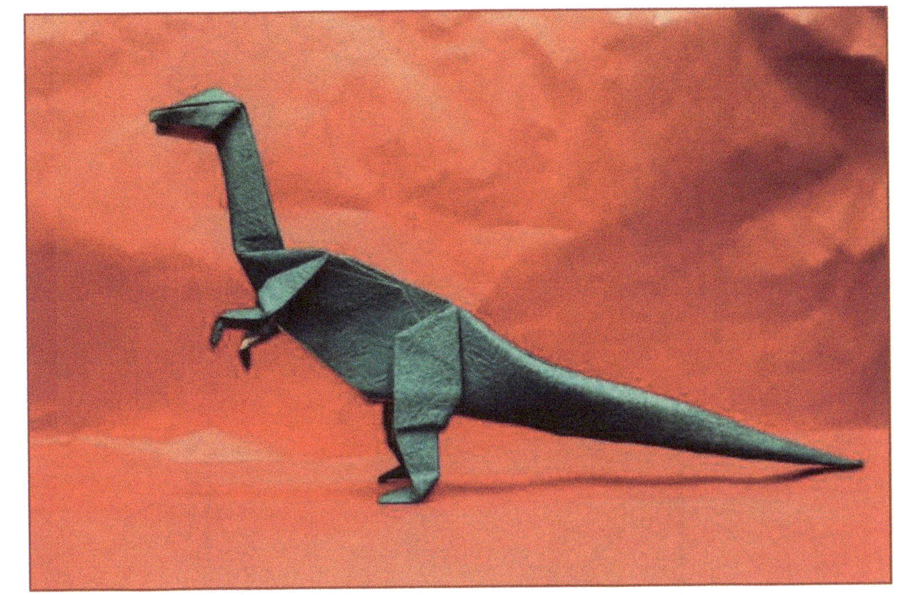

The Megapnosaurus was a carnivore during the early Jurassic period. It was about six feet long and lived in South Africa with an average life span of seven years. This long-necked creature is also known as Syntarsus.

1

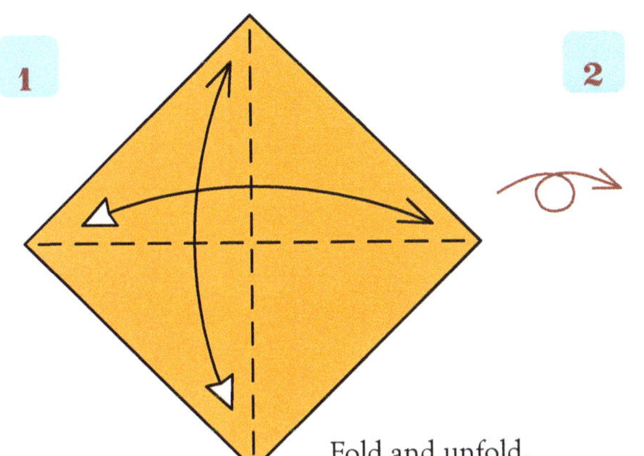

Fold and unfold.
Rotate 45°.

2

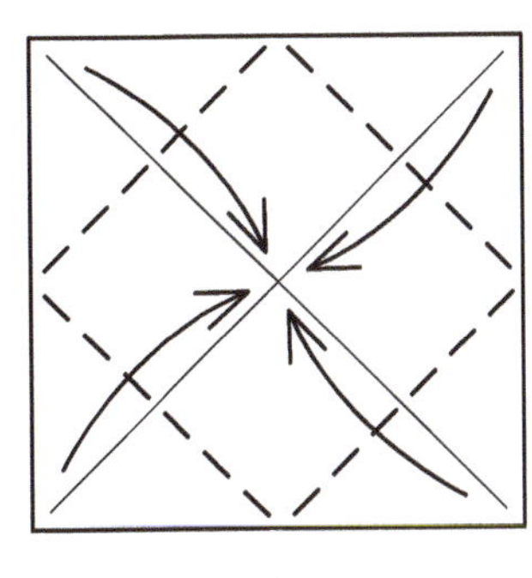

Fold to the center.

3

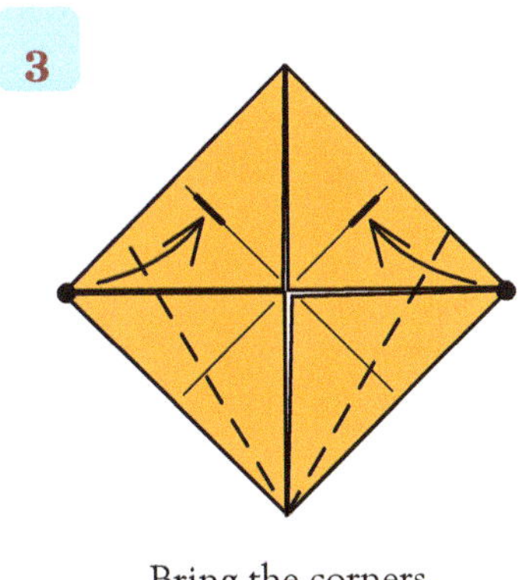

Bring the corners to the lines.

4

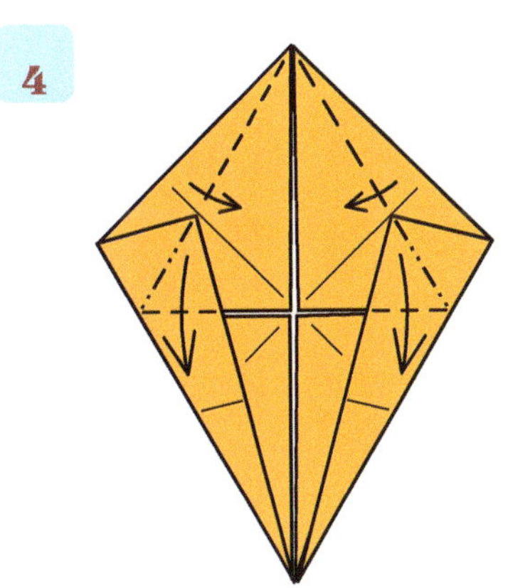

Make squash folds.

5

6

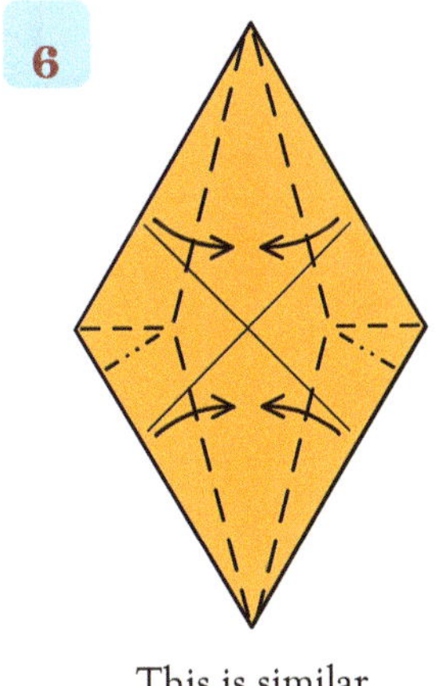

This is similar to rabbit ears.

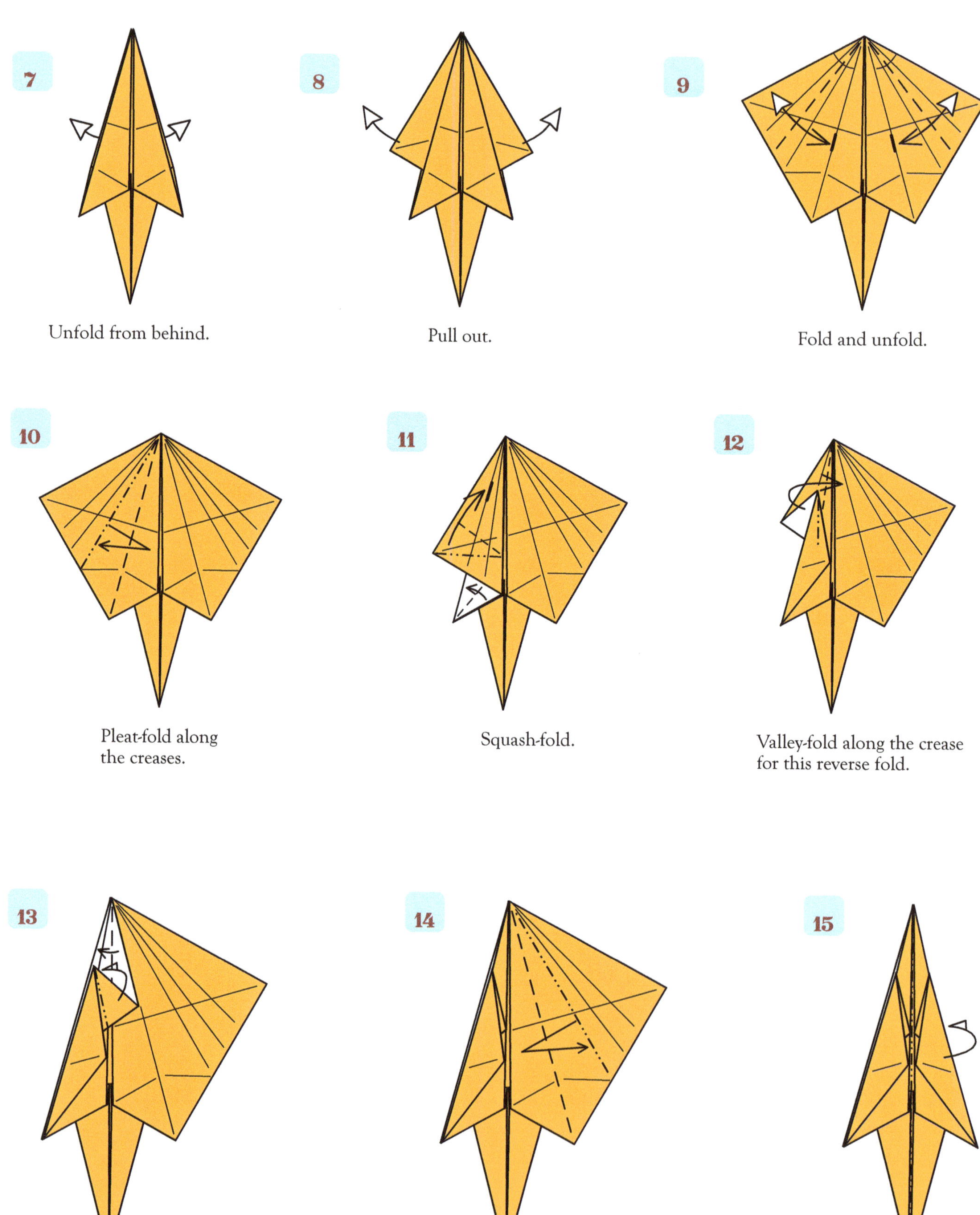
7
Unfold from behind.
8
Pull out.
9
Fold and unfold.
10
Pleat-fold along
the creases.
11
Squash-fold.
12
Valley-fold along the crease
for this reverse fold.
13
Reverse-fold.
14
Repeat steps 10–13
on the right.
15
Fold in half
and rotate.

16

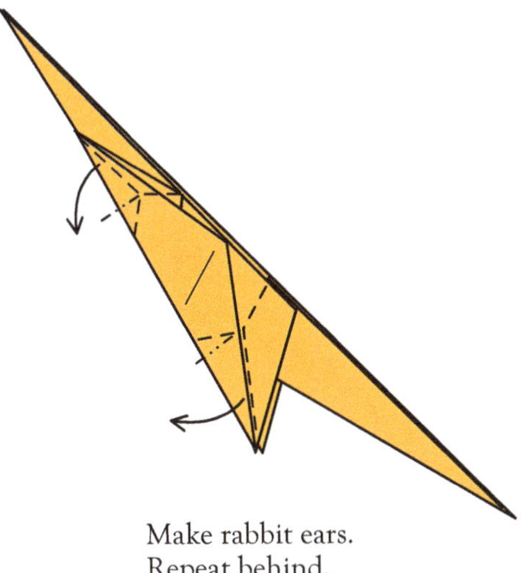

Make rabbit ears.
Repeat behind.

17

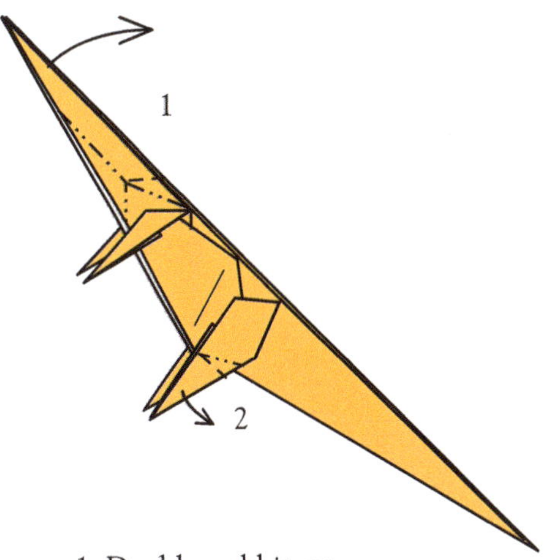

1. Double-reabbit-ear.
2. Crimp-fold, repeat behind.

18

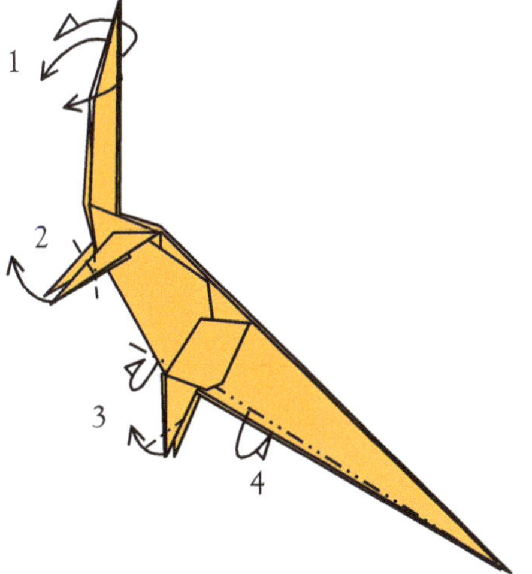

1. Spread and shape the head.
2. Crimp-fold, repeat behind.
3. Reverse-fold, repeat behind.
4. Thin the tail, repeat behind.

19

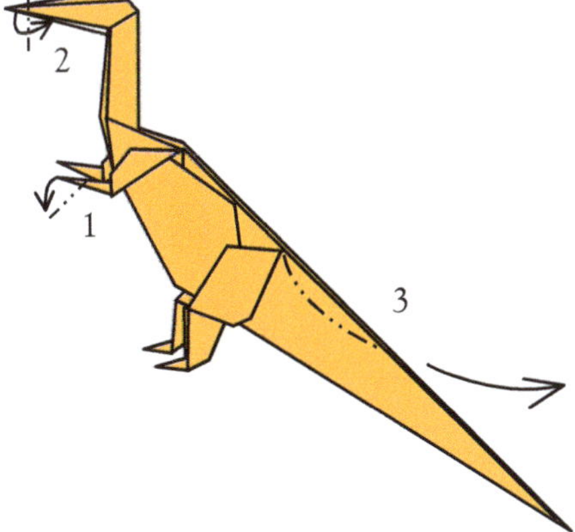

1. Reverse-fold, repeat behind.
2. Reverse-fold.
3. Shape the tail.

20

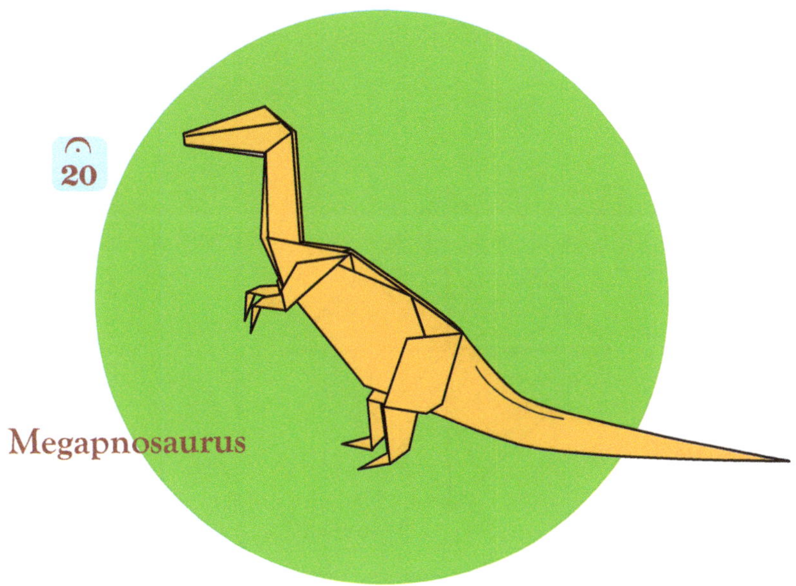

Megapnosaurus

Spinosaurus

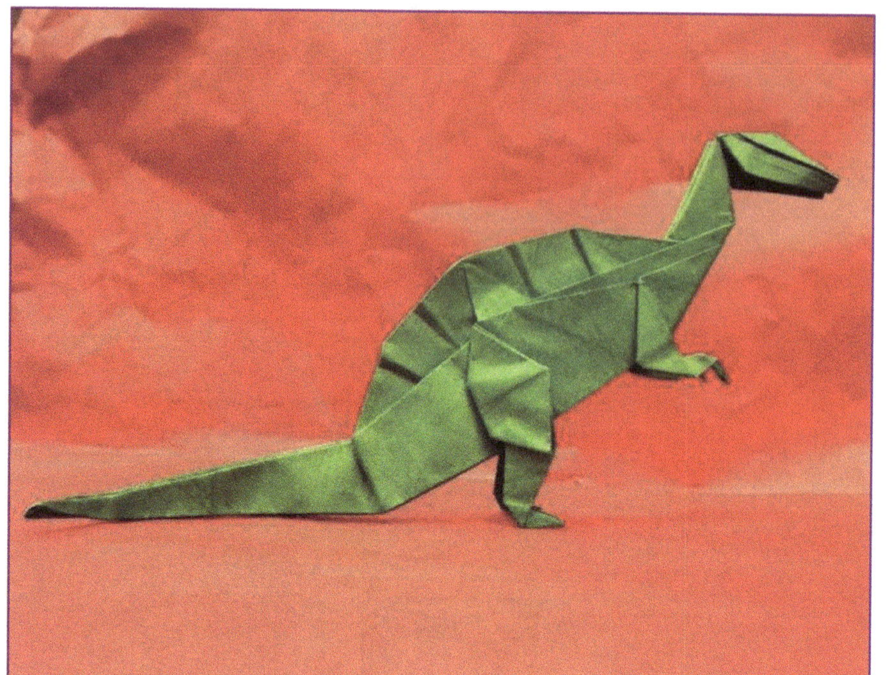

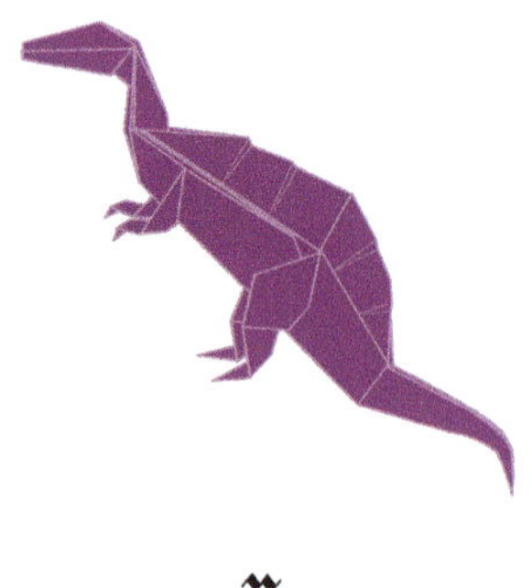

The Spinosaurus lived in Egypt and Morocco during the Cretaceous Period. It lived by the shores and dined on fish. Its large distinctive sail was used to regulate body temperature and for display. At over 50 feet in length, this large dinosaur had a skull which is similar to that of a crocodile. The head suggests it lived both in the water and on land.

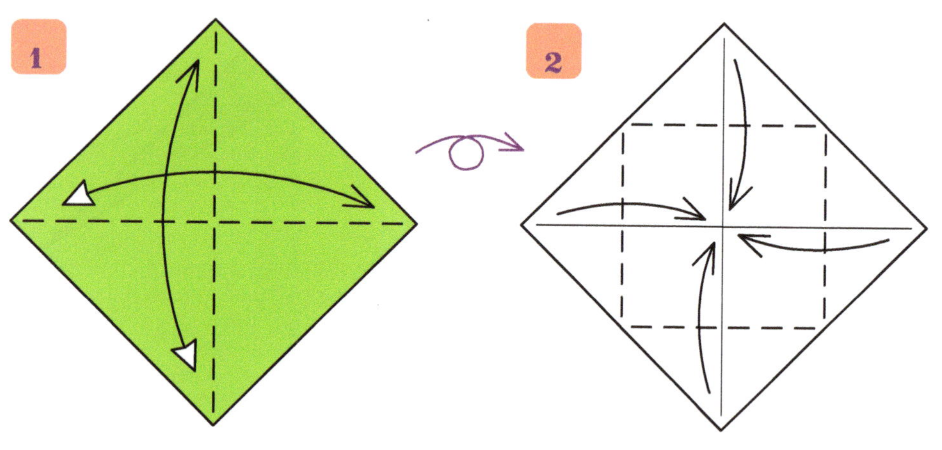

Fold and unfold.

Fold to the center.

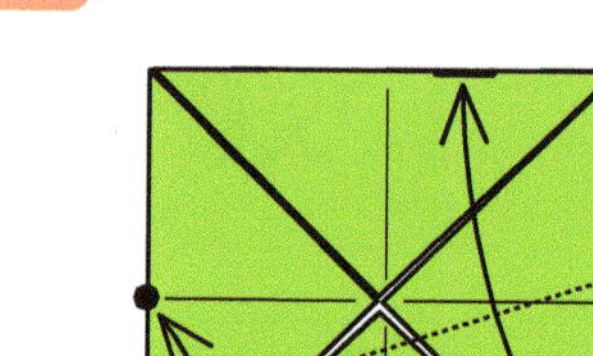

Bring the lower right corner to the top edge and the bottom edge to the left center. Crease on the left.

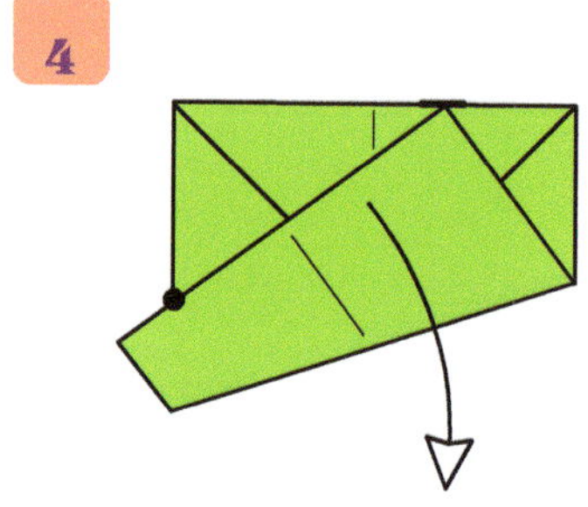

Unfold and rotate 45°.

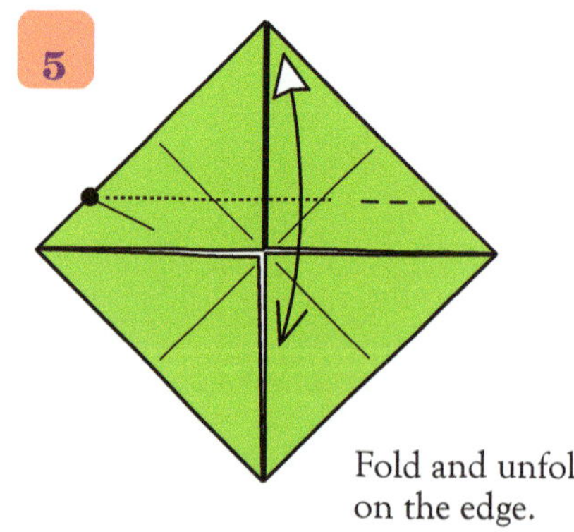

Fold and unfold on the edge.

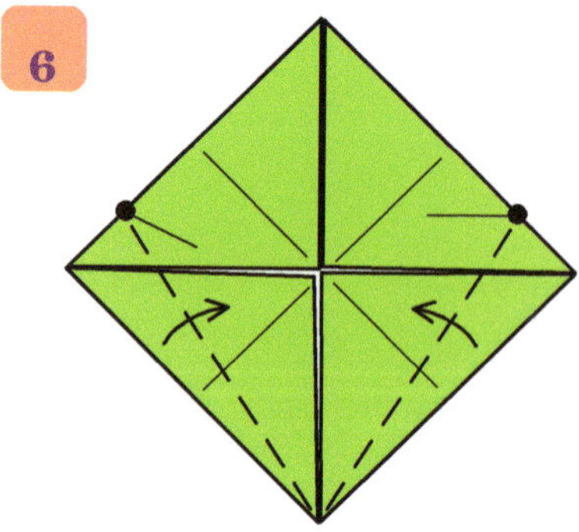

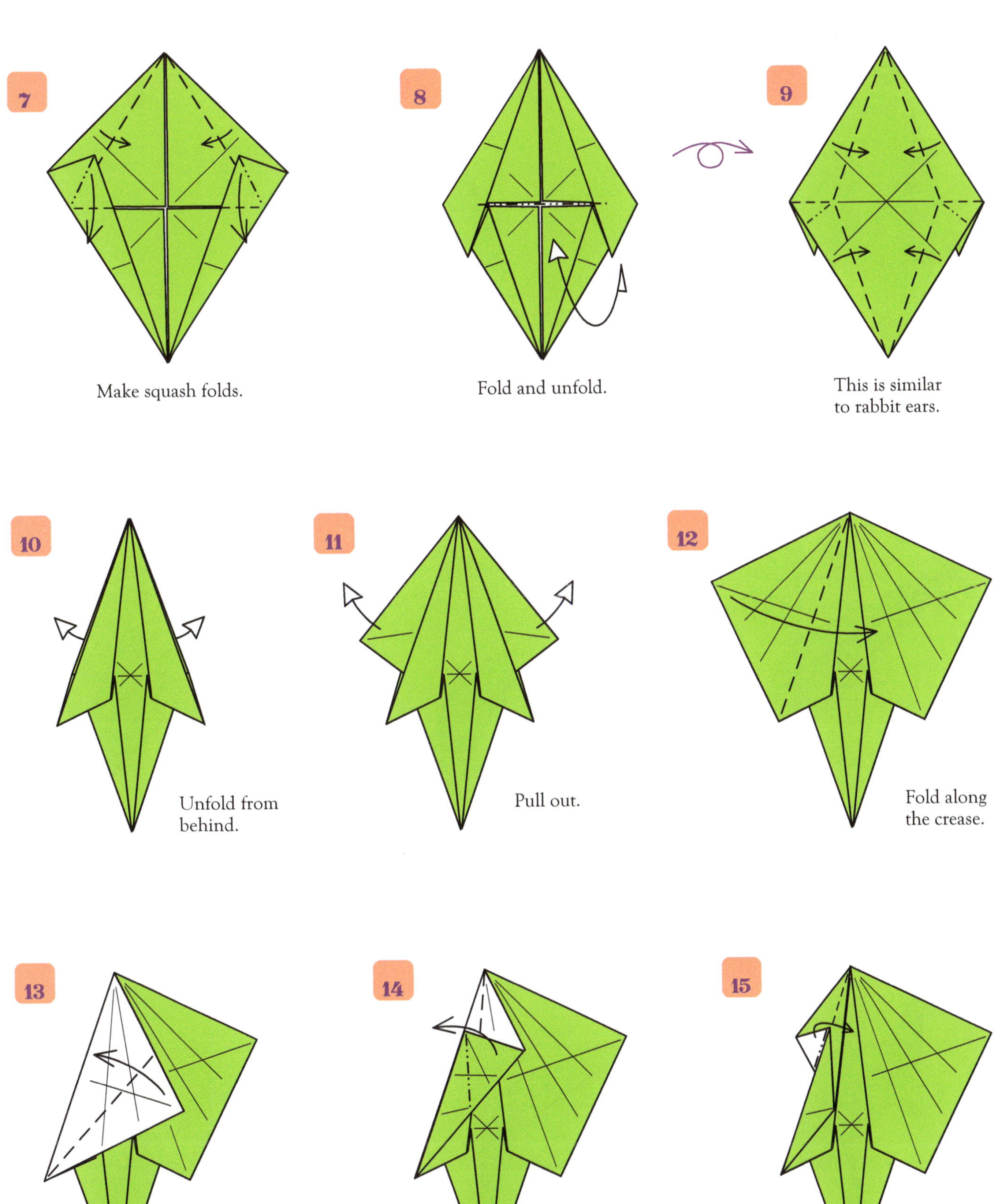

Make squash folds.

Fold and unfold.

This is similar to rabbit ears.

Unfold from behind.

Pull out.

Fold along the crease.

Valley-fold along the crease for this reverse fold.

Reverse-fold.

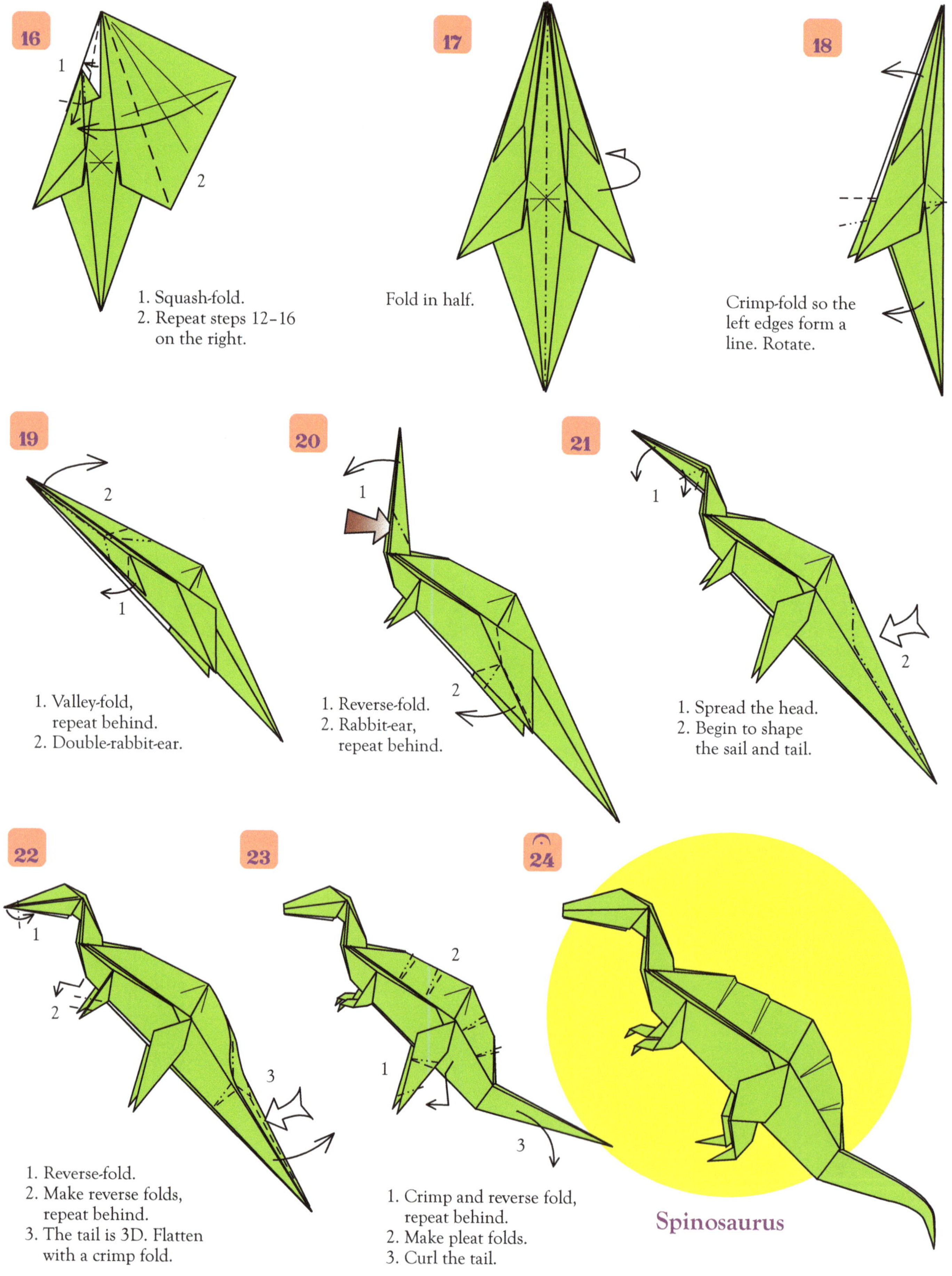
16
1
2
1. Squash-fold.
2. Repeat steps 12–16 on the right.
17
Fold in half.
18
Crimp-fold so the left edges form a line. Rotate.
19
2
1
1. Valley-fold, repeat behind.
2. Double-rabbit-ear.
20
1
2
1. Reverse-fold.
2. Rabbit-ear, repeat behind.
21
1
2
1. Spread the head.
2. Begin to shape the sail and tail.
22
1
2
3
1. Reverse-fold.
2. Make reverse folds, repeat behind.
3. The tail is 3D. Flatten with a crimp fold.
23
2
1
3
1. Crimp and reverse fold, repeat behind.
2. Make pleat folds.
3. Curl the tail.
24
Spinosaurus

Allosaurus

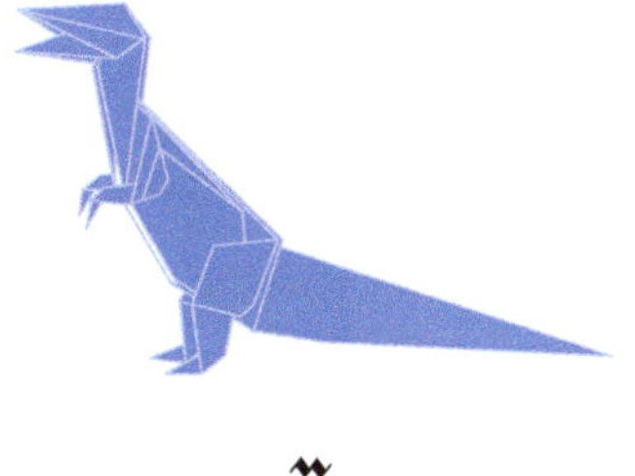

The Allosaurus was a large carnivorous dinosaur that walked on two legs. Its name means "different lizard", because the neck bones curved differently than other known dinosaurs. They roamed in Utah, Portugal, and Tanzania. The Allosaurus lived during the late Jurassic Period and were 30 to 40 feet long.

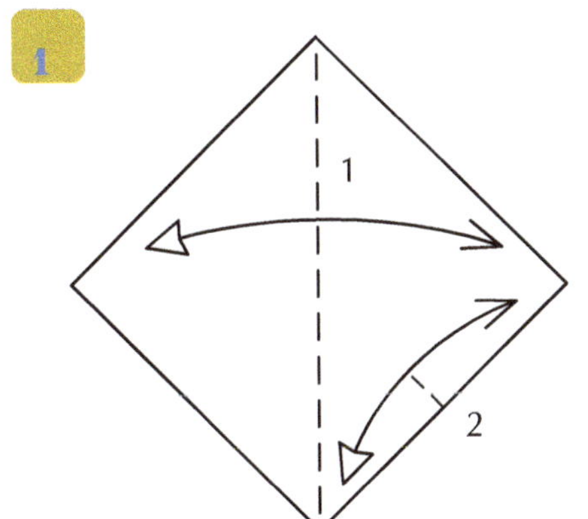

1. Fold and unfold.
2. Fold and unfold on the edge.

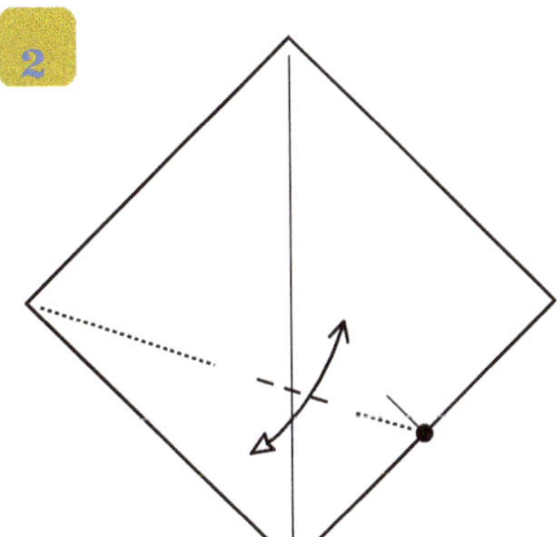

Fold and unfold on the diagonal.

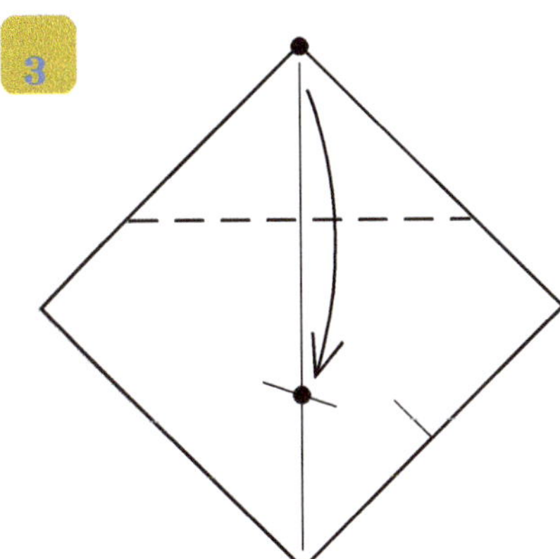

The dots will meet.

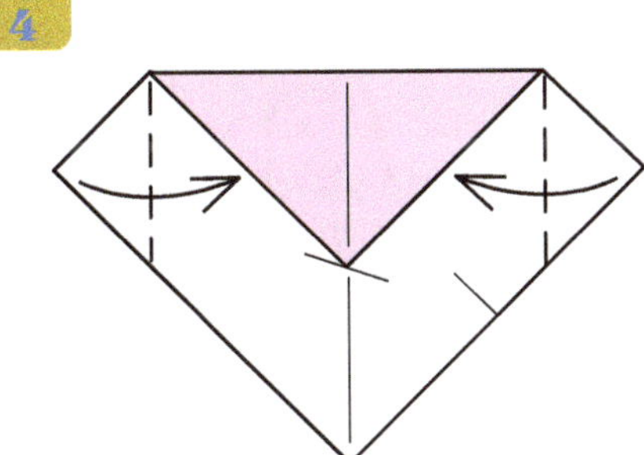

Fold on the left and right.

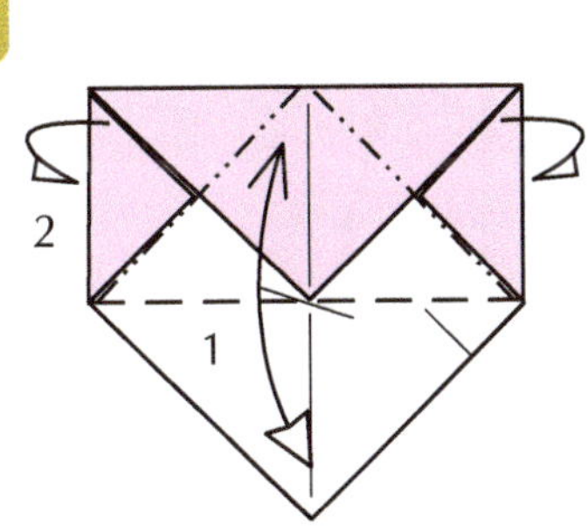

1. Fold and unfold.
2. Fold behind on the left and right.

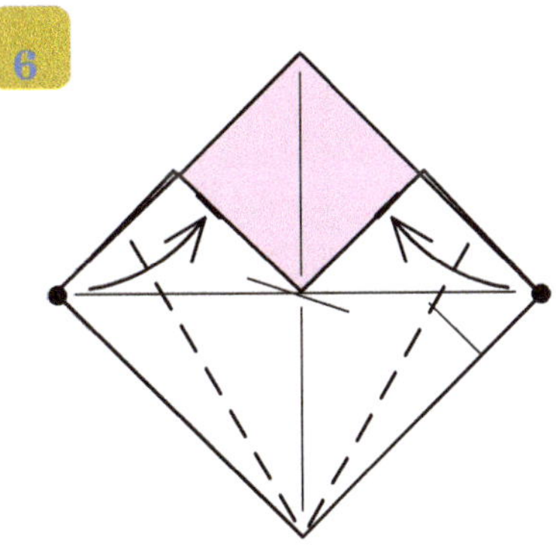

Bring the corners to the lines.

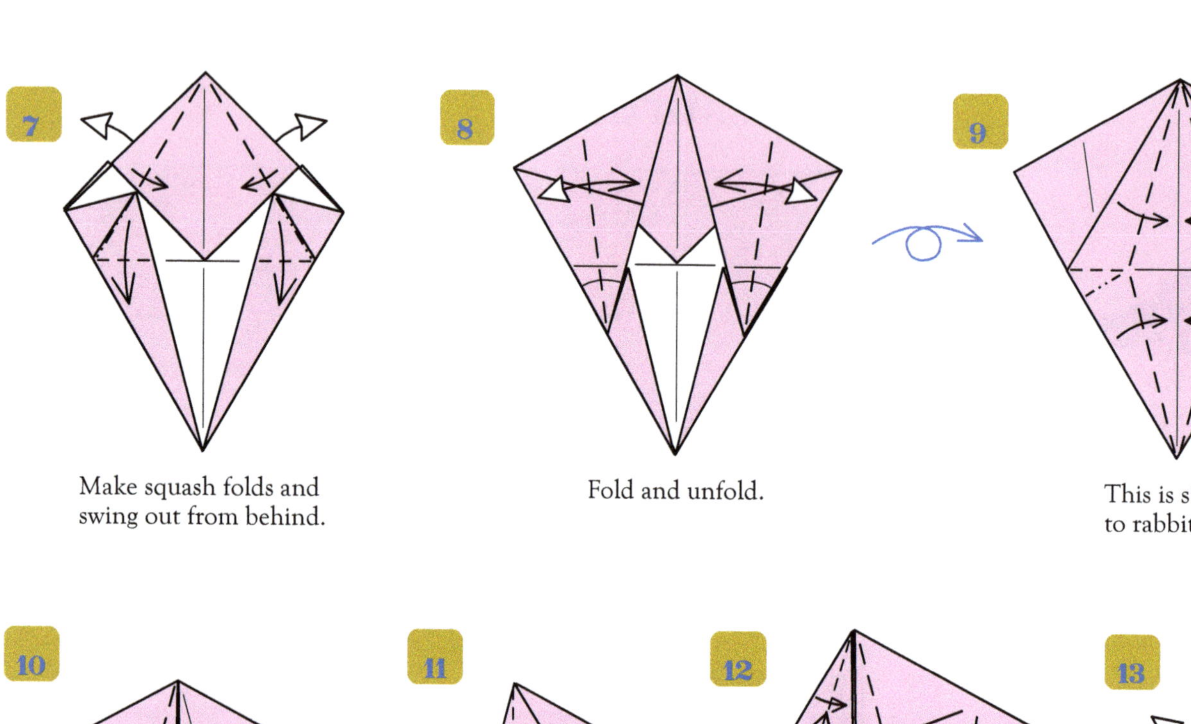

Make squash folds and swing out from behind.

Fold and unfold.

This is similar to rabbit ears.

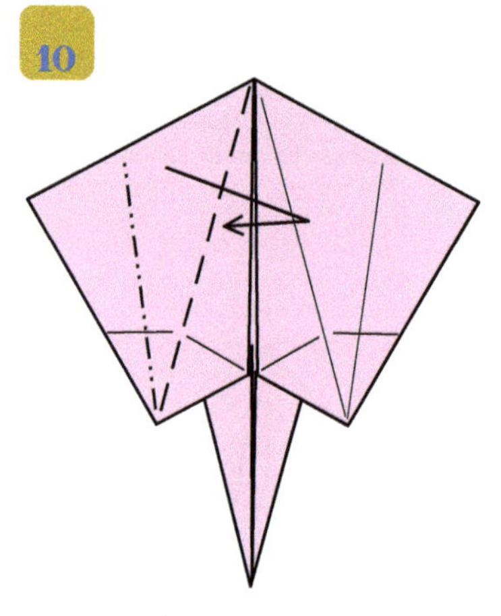

Pleat-fold along the creases.

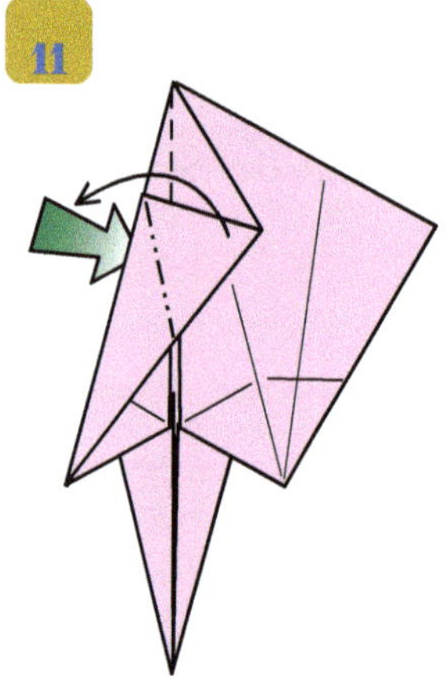

Reverse-fold.

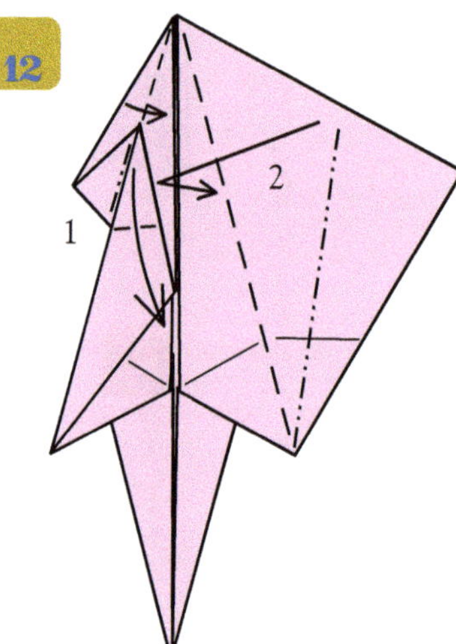

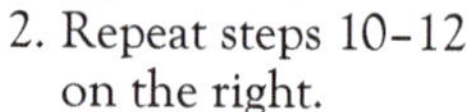

1. Squash-fold.
2. Repeat steps 10–12 on the right.

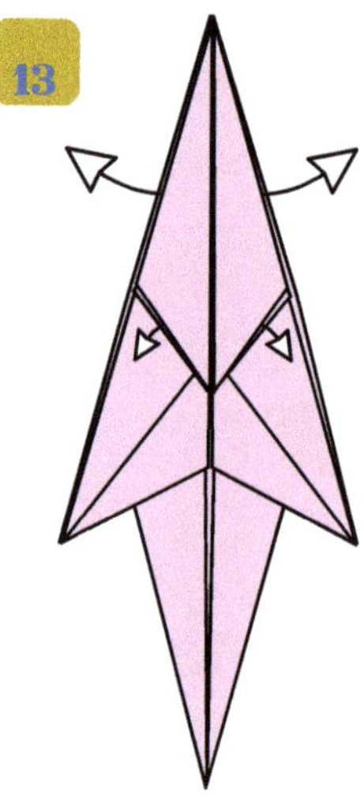

Unlock the paper.

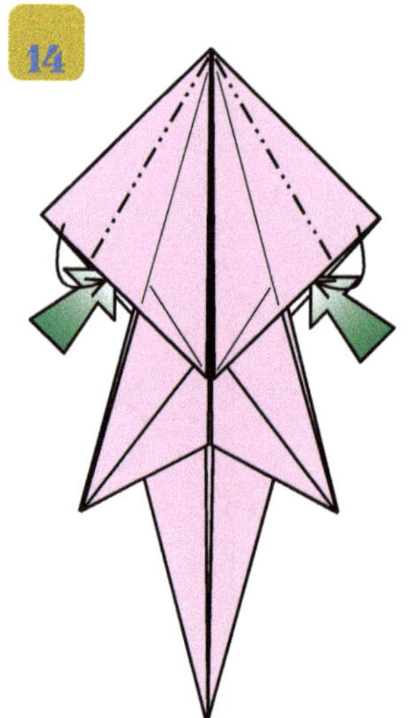

Make reverse folds along the creases.

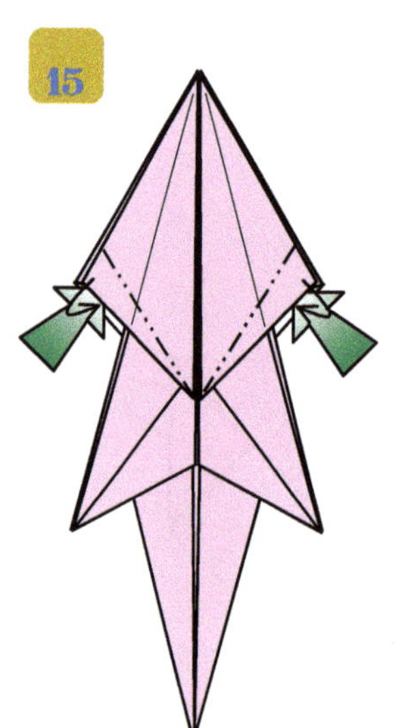

Make reverse folds along the creases.

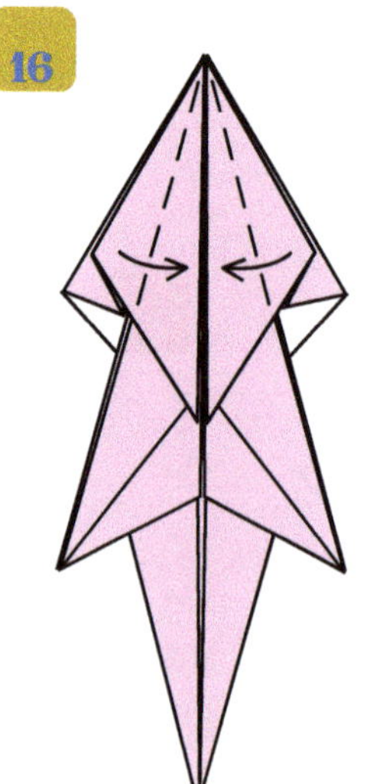

Fold to the center.

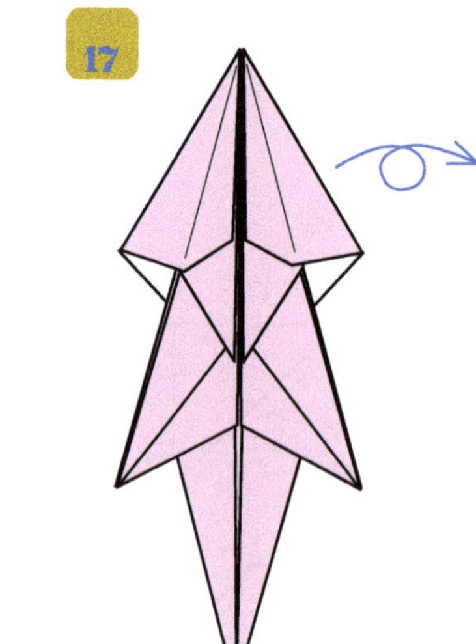

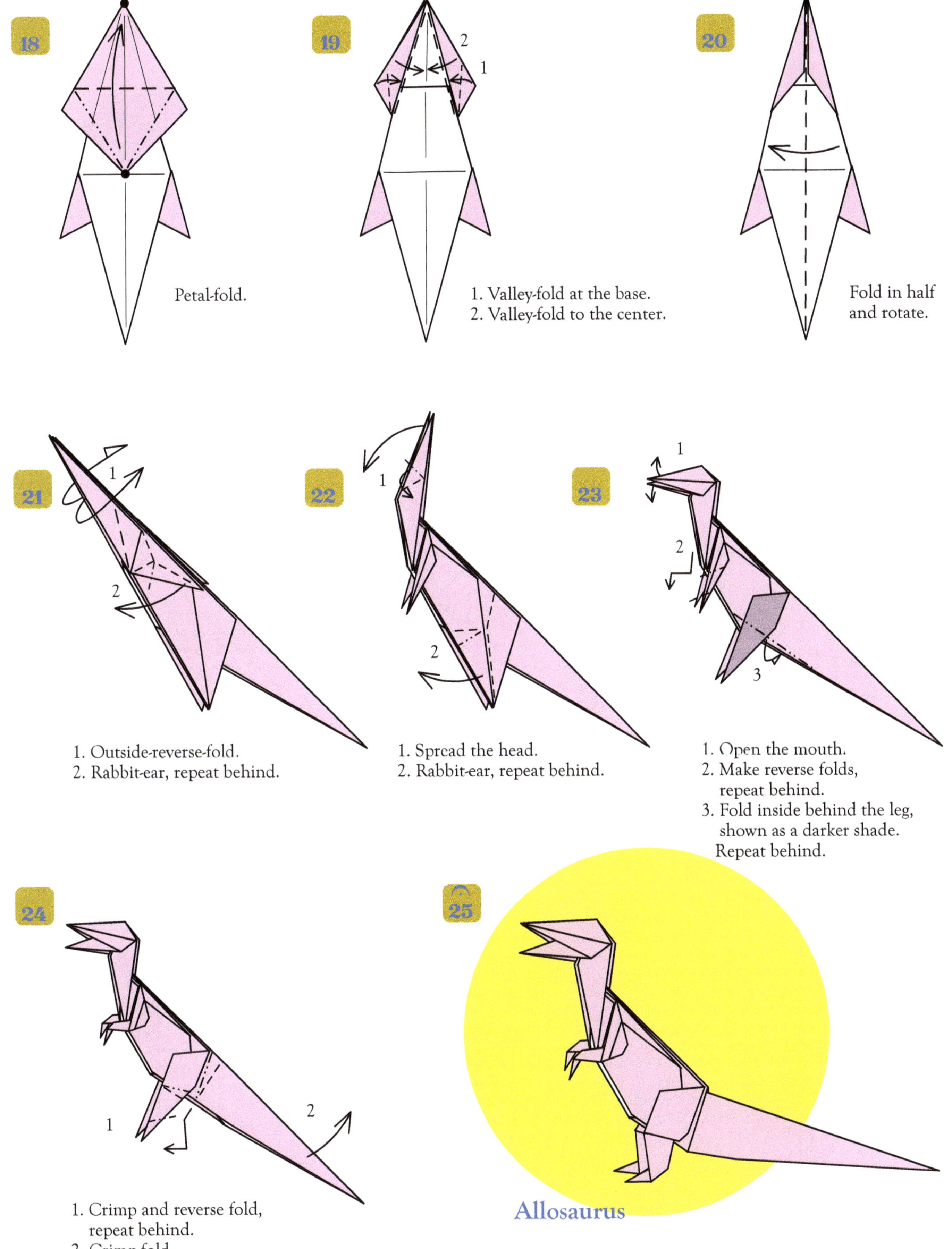
18
Petal-fold.
19
2
1
1. Valley-fold at the base.
2. Valley-fold to the center.
20
Fold in half
and rotate.
21
1
2
1. Outside-reverse-fold.
2. Rabbit-ear, repeat behind.
22
1
2
1. Spread the head.
2. Rabbit-ear, repeat behind.
23
1
2
3
1. Open the mouth.
2. Make reverse folds,
repeat behind.
3. Fold inside behind the leg,
shown as a darker shade.
Repeat behind.
24
1
2
1. Crimp and reverse fold,
repeat behind.
2. Crimp-fold.
25
Allosaurus

Protoceratops

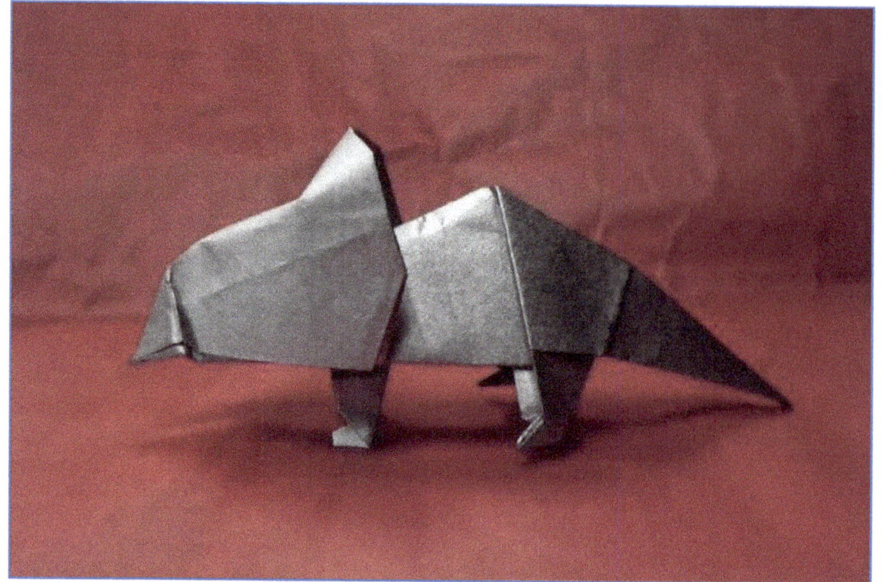

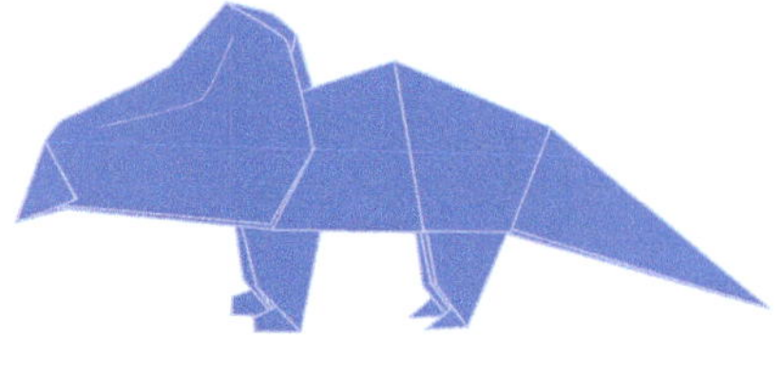

The Protoceratops was a smaller dinosaur at 6 feet in length. They were abundant and lived in herds during the late Cretaceous Period in China and Mongolia. Protoceratops ate plants with its parrot-like beak. The frills on their heads were larger for the males and most likely used to show dominance.

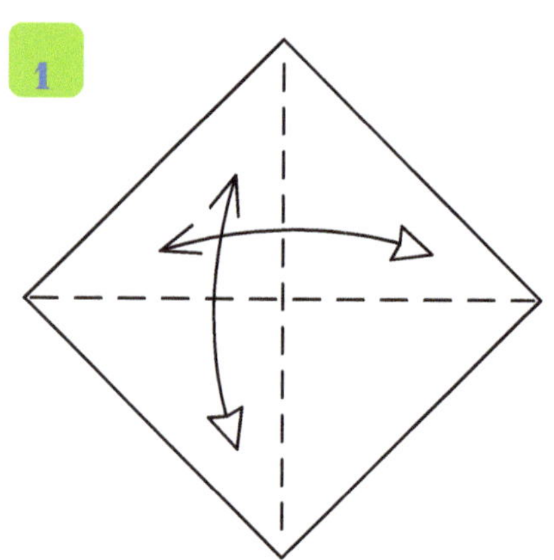

Fold and unfold.

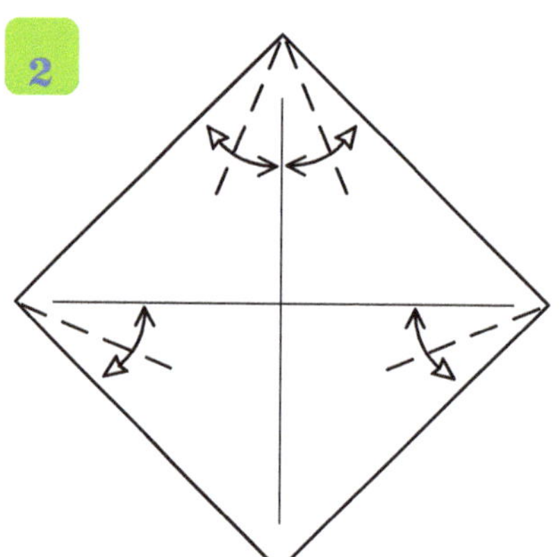

Fold and unfold.

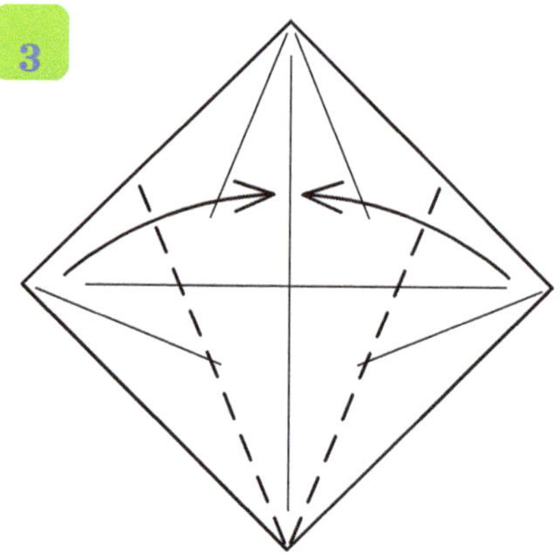

Fold to the center.

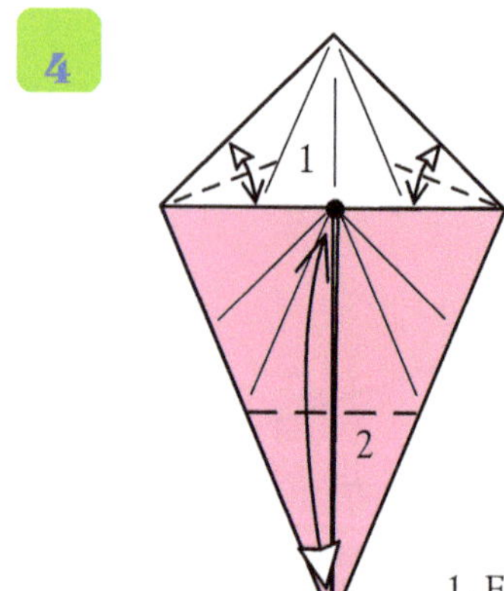

1. Fold and unfold on the left and right.
2. Fold and unfold.

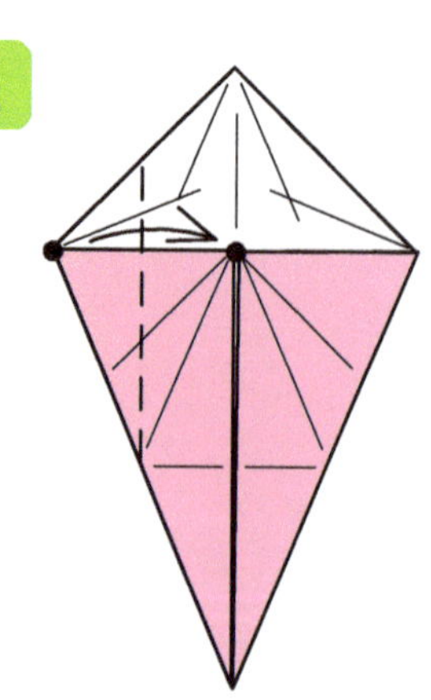

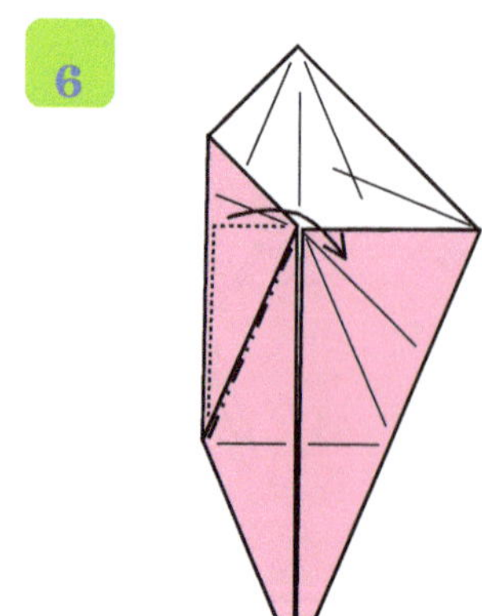

Fold the hidden flap.

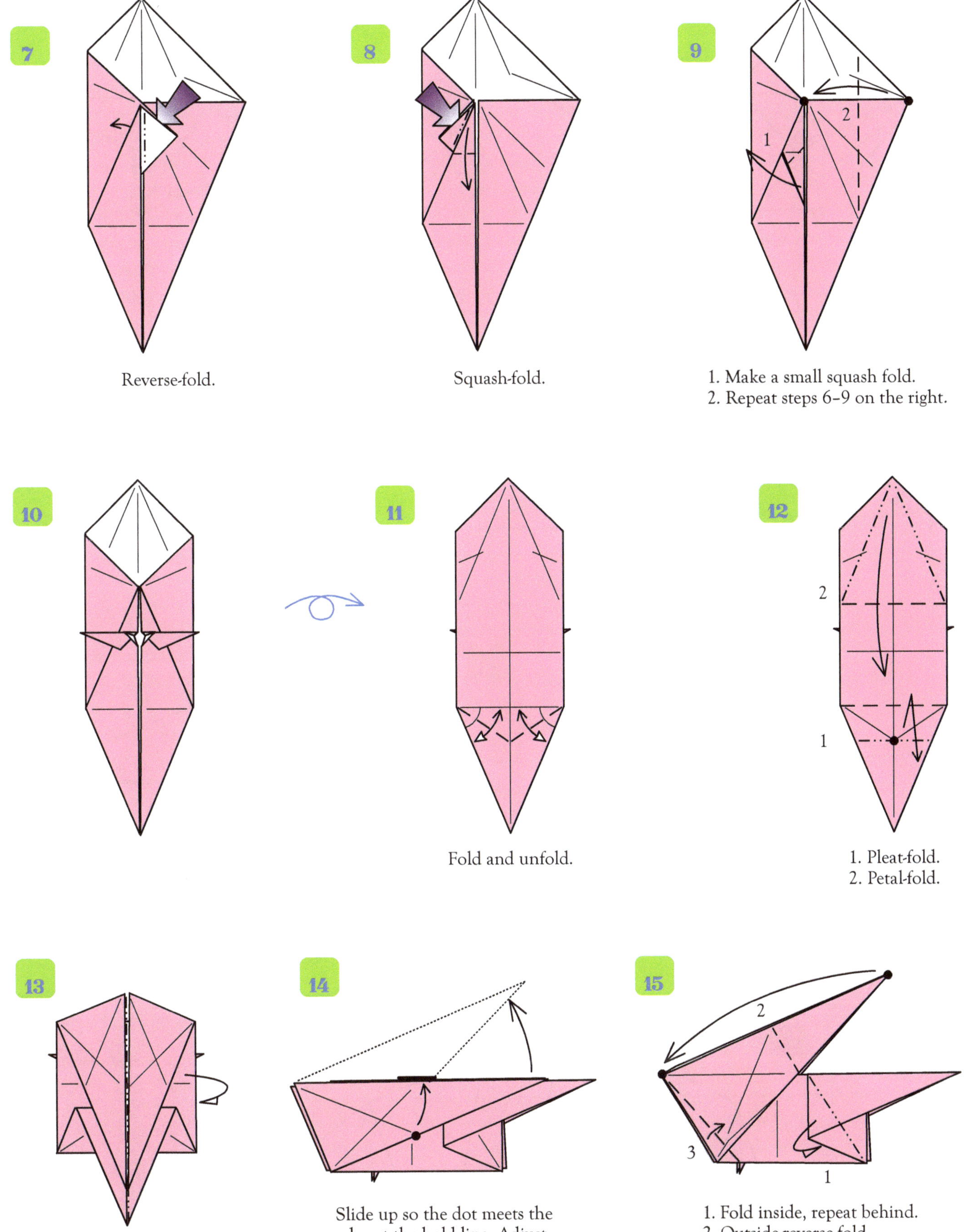

7. Reverse-fold.

8. Squash-fold.

9. 1. Make a small squash fold.
2. Repeat steps 6–9 on the right.

11. Fold and unfold.

12. 1. Pleat-fold.
2. Petal-fold.

13. Fold in half and rotate 90°.

14. Slide up so the dot meets the edge at the bold line. Adjust the folds at the bottom.

15. 1. Fold inside, repeat behind.
2. Outside-reverse-fold.
3. Fold along the crease, repeat behind.

16

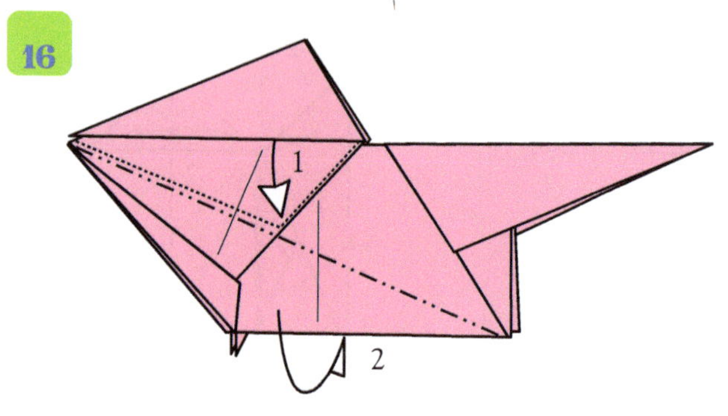

1. Pull out.
2. Tuck inside.
Repeat behind.

17

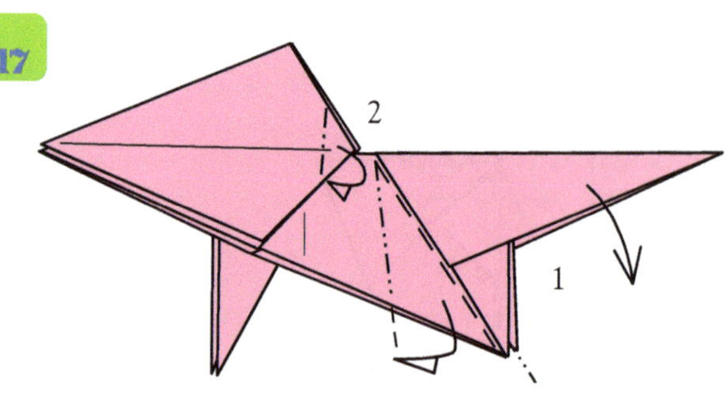

1. Crimp-fold.
2. Fold behind, repeat behind.

18

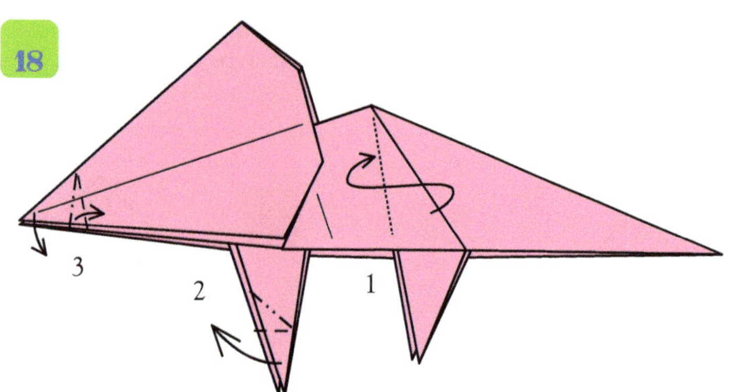

1. Tuck inside, repeat behind.
2. Crinp-fold, repeat behind.
3. Crinp-fold.

19

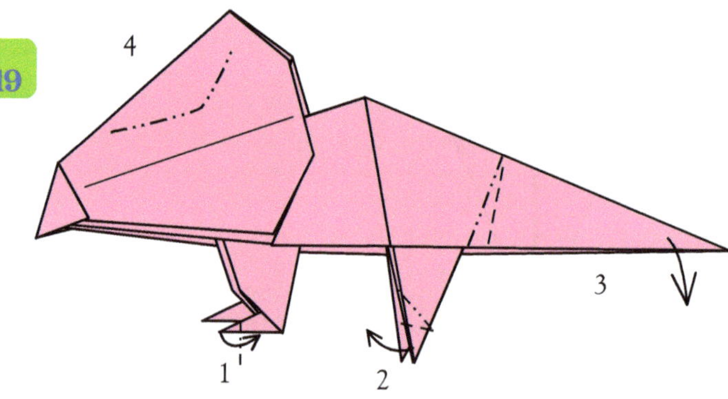

1. Reverse-fold, repeat behind.
2. Crimp-fold, repeat behind.
3. Crimp-fold
4. Spread and shape the crown.

20

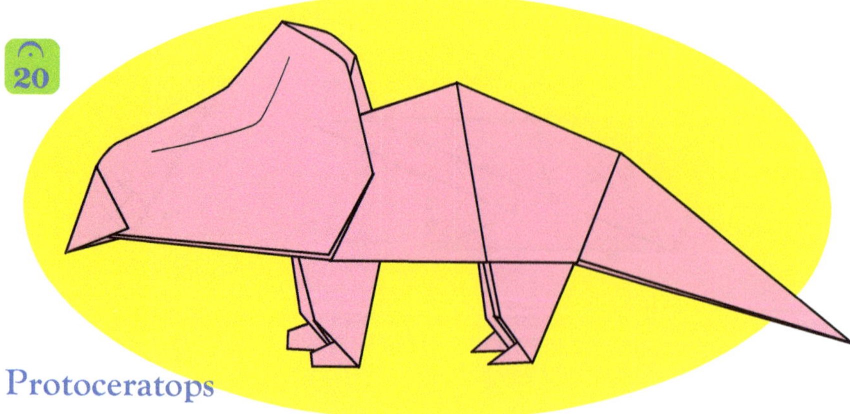

Protoceratops

Triceratops

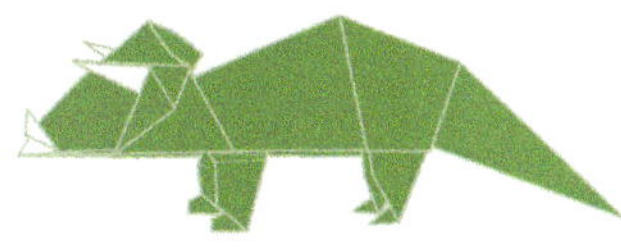

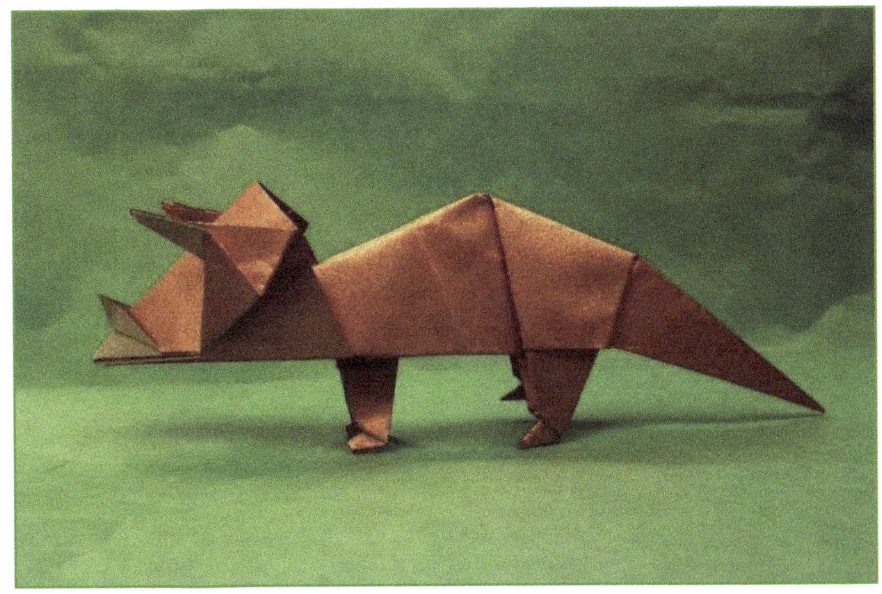

Triceratops is named from the Greek words for "three-horn-face". It lived in North America toward the end of the Cretaceous Period. The bony frill and horns on its head were used for defense and possibly also for show and to help regulate body temperature. This herbivore grew to 30 feet in length.

1

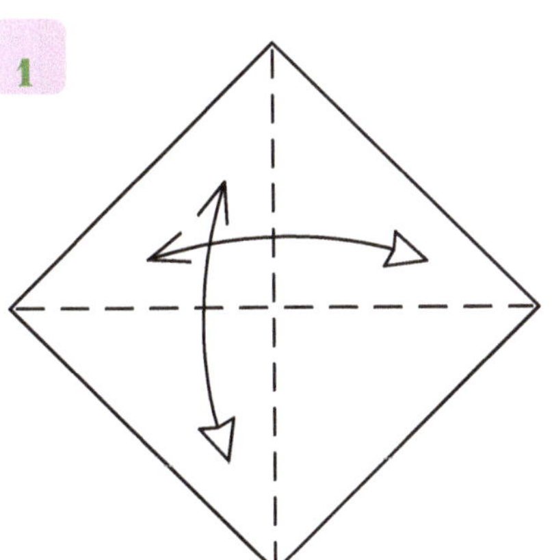

Fold and unfold.

2

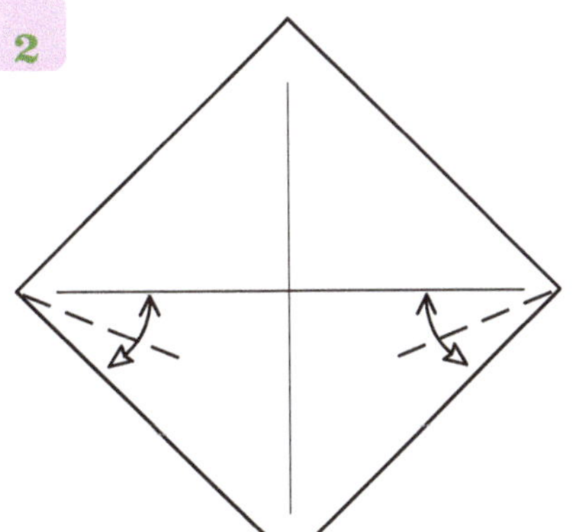

Fold and unfold.

3

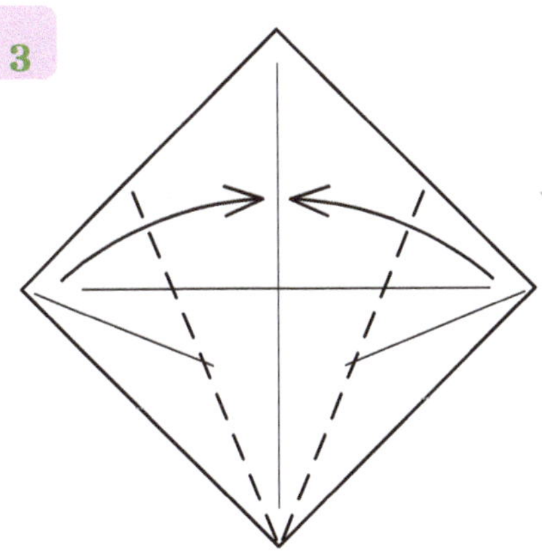

Fold to the center.

4

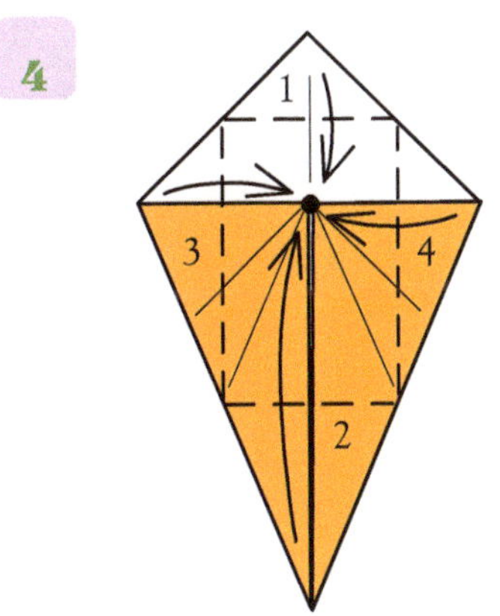

Fold to the dot.

5

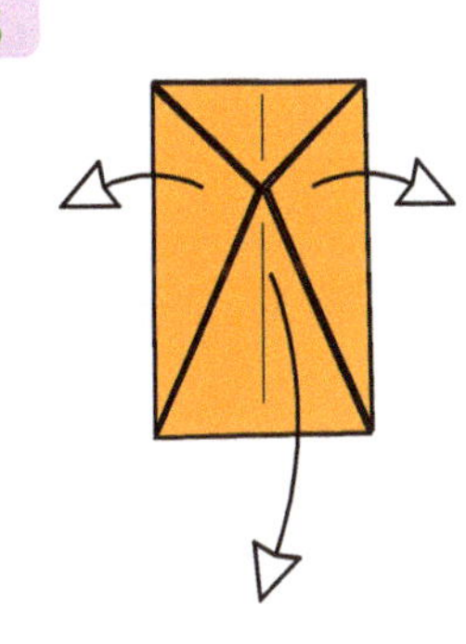

Unfold.

6

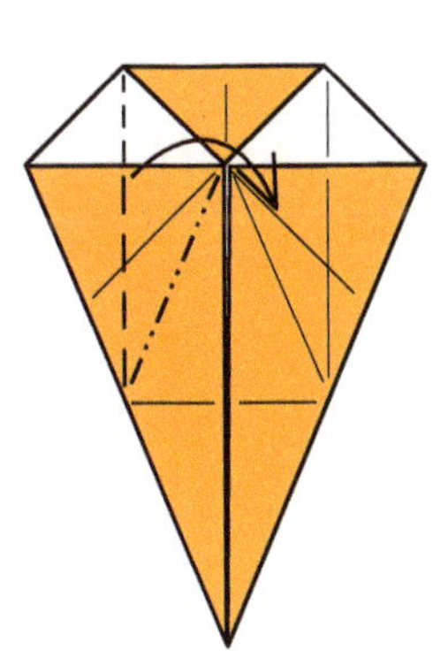

Fold along the creases. This is similar to a reverse fold.

7

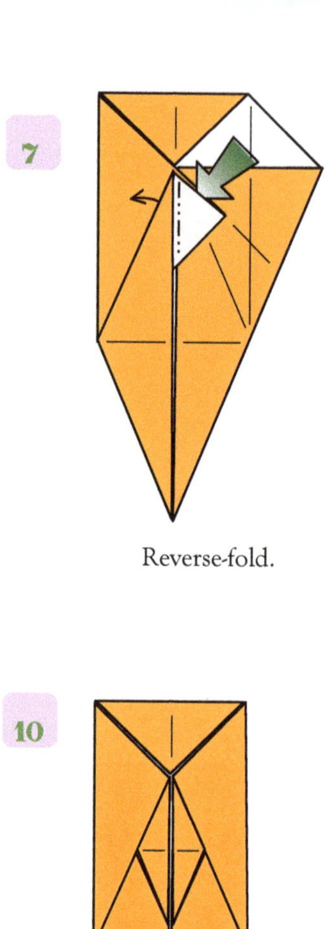

Reverse-fold.

8

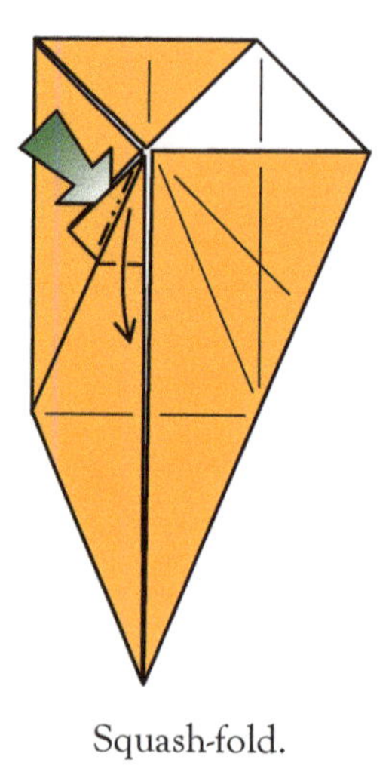

Squash-fold.

9

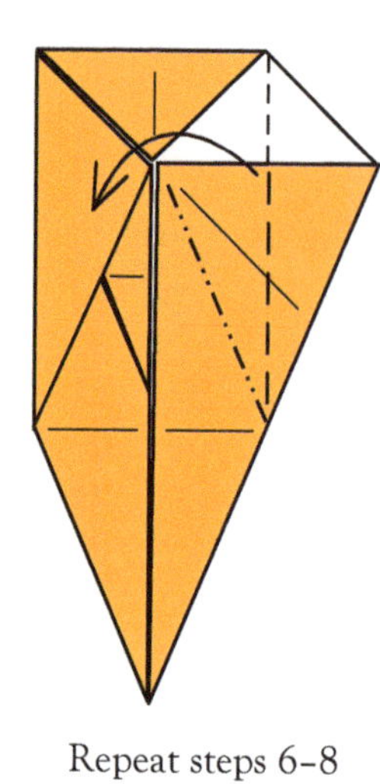

Repeat steps 6–8 on the right.

10

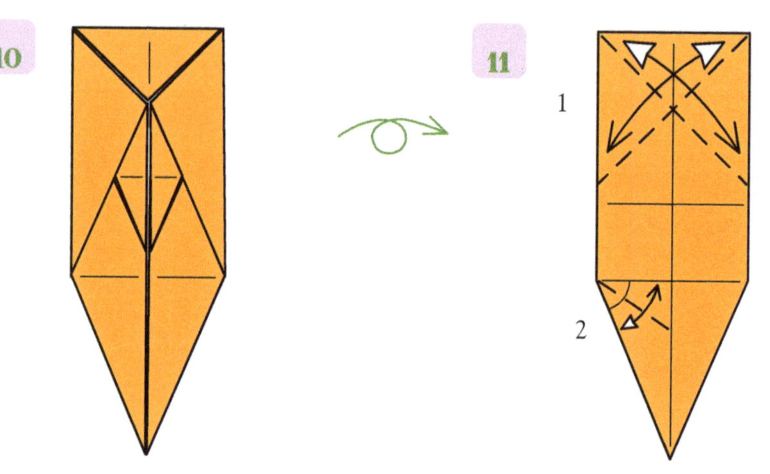

11

1. Fold and unfold.
2. Fold and unfold.

12

1. Rabbit-ear.
2. Fold and unfold.

13

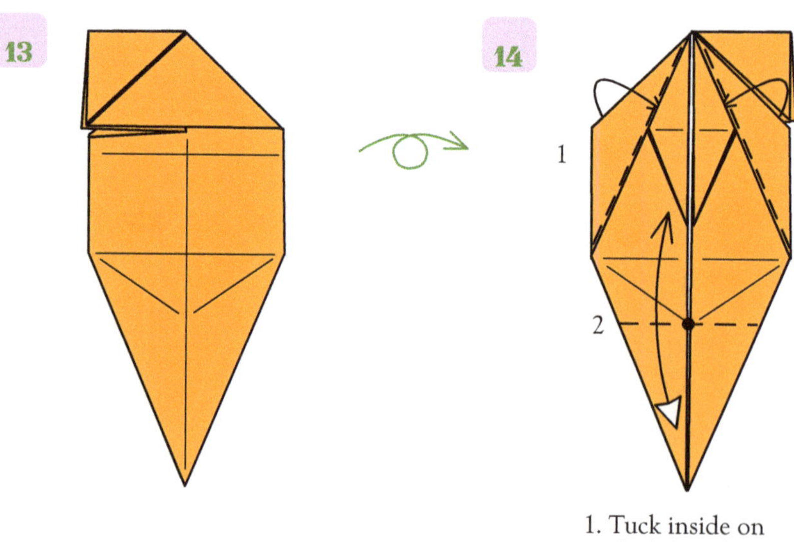

14

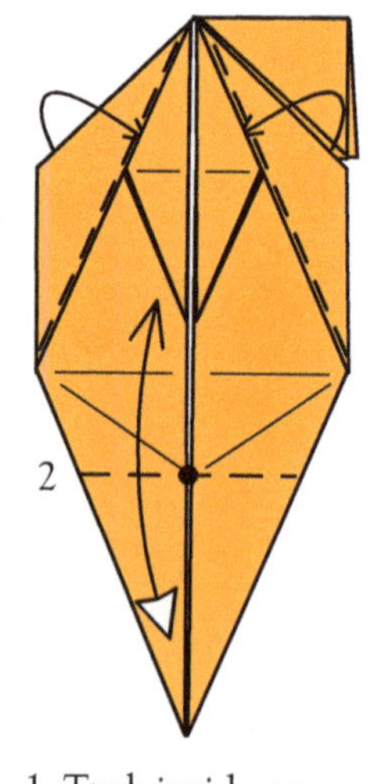

1. Tuck inside on the left and right.
2. Fold and unfold.

15

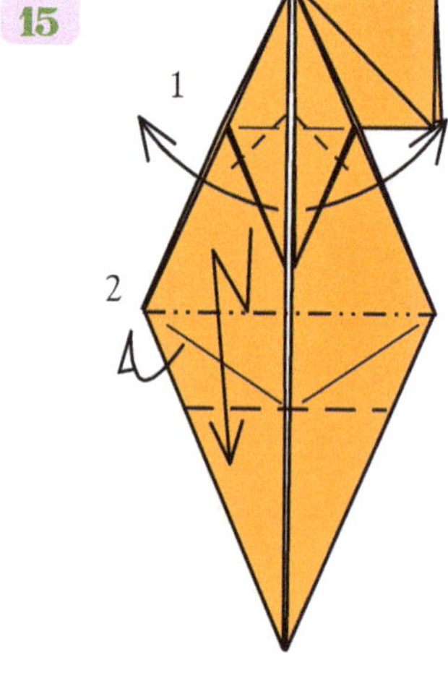

1. Make small squash folds.
2. Pleat-fold.

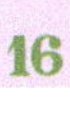

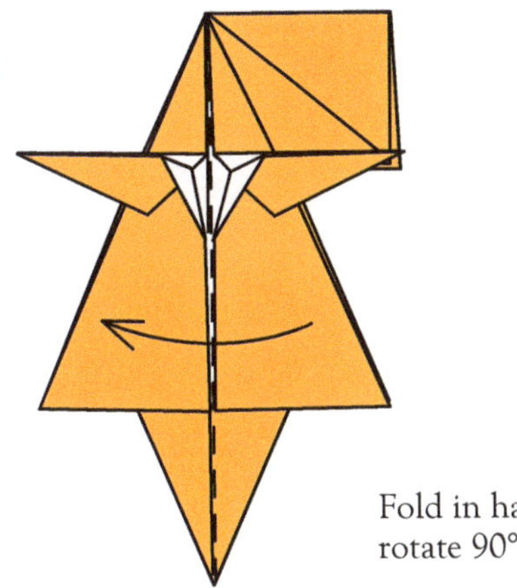

Fold in half and rotate 90°.

17

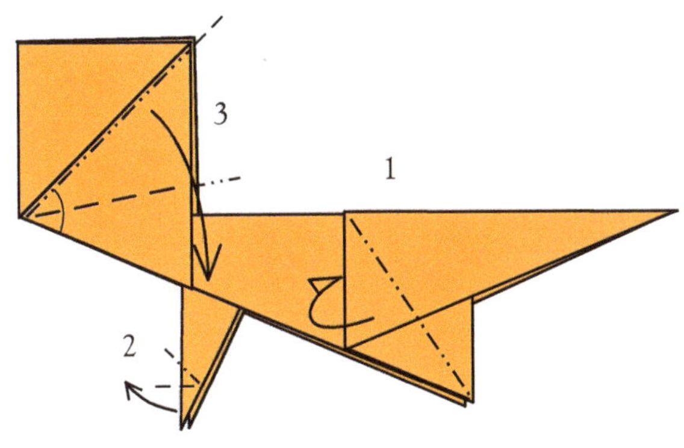

1. Fold inside, repeat behind.
2. Crimp-fold, repeat behind.
3. Crimp-fold.

18

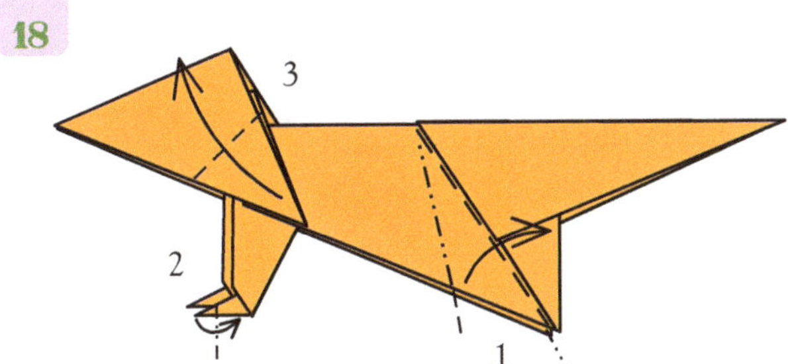

1. Crimp-fold.
2. Reverse-fold, repeat behind.
3. Fold up, repeat behind.

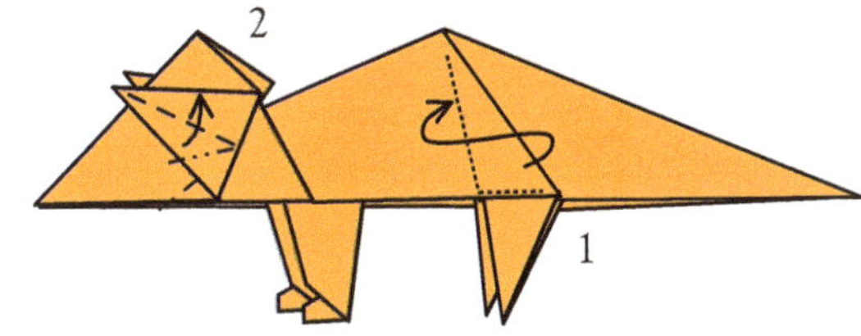

1. Tuck inside.
2. Squash-fold.
Repeat behind.

20

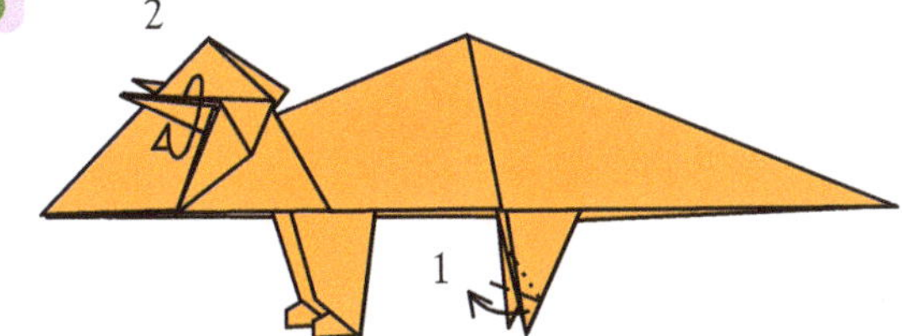

1. Crimp-fold.
2. Wrap one layer around.
Repeat behind.

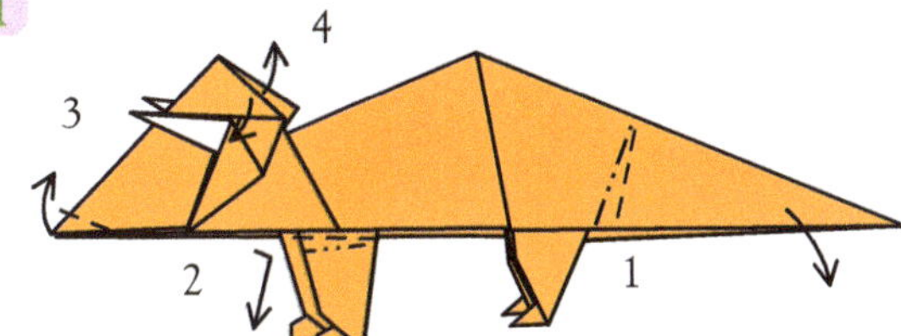

1. Crimp-fold.
2. Pleat-fold, repeat behind.
3. Outside-reverse-fold.
3. Spread the crown with soft folds.

22

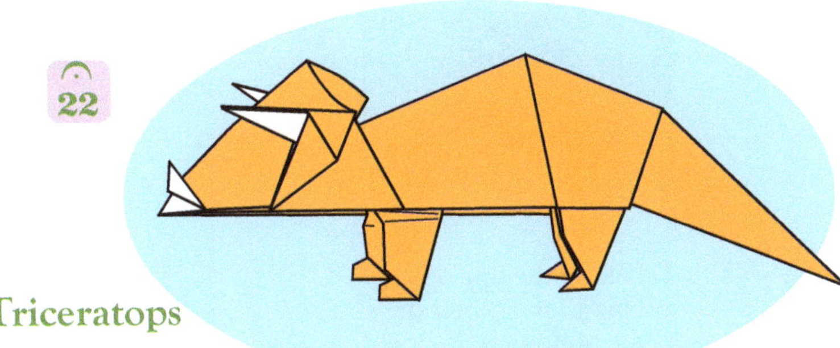

Triceratops

Stegosaurus

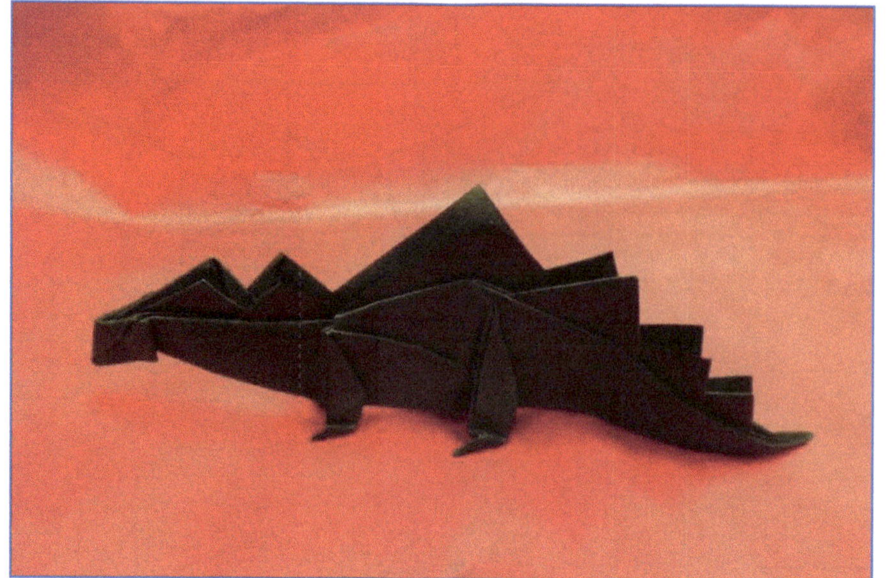

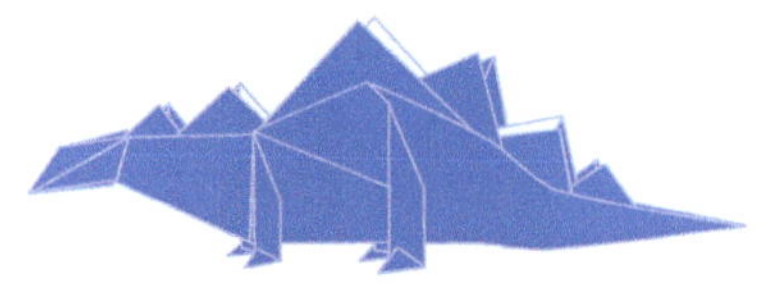

The Stegosaurus is named for the Greek words "stegos" for roof and "saurus" for lizard. The Stegosaurus lived in the Late Jurassic Period and grew to 20 or 30 feet in length. This herbivore is easily recognized by its plates. Theories suggest the plates helped it control its temperature by acting as radiators though they could also be used for show or defense.

1

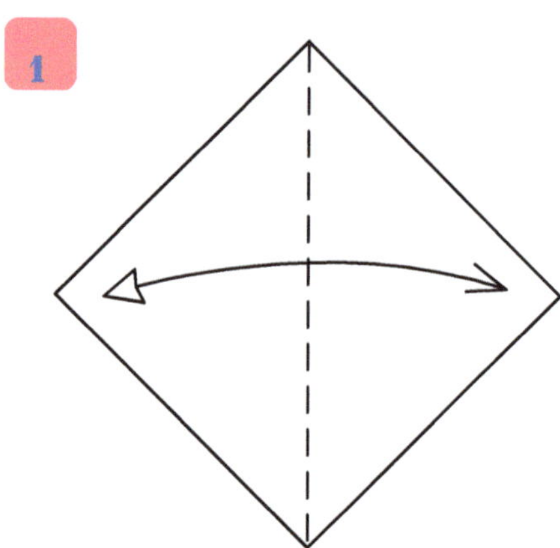

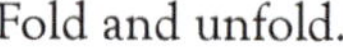

Fold and unfold.

2

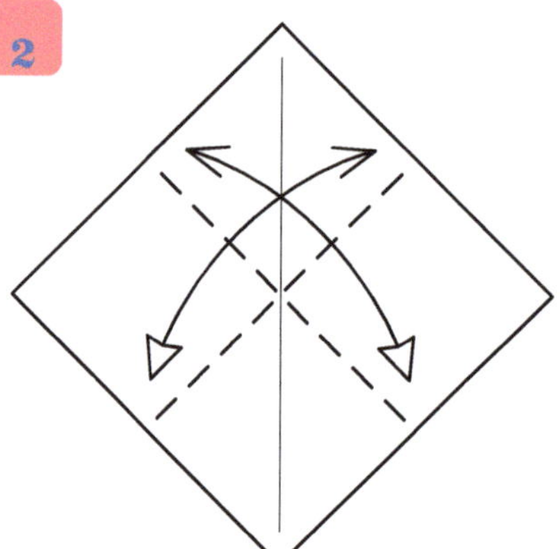

Fold and unfold.

3

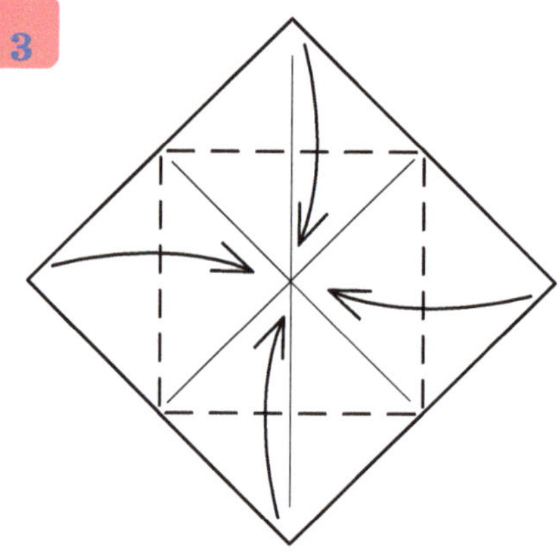

Fold to the center.

4

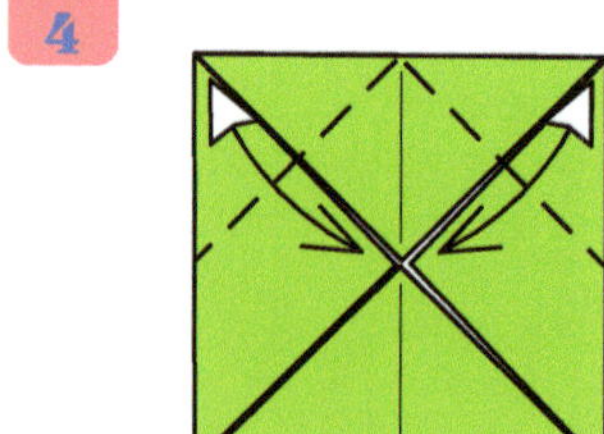

Fold and unfold on the top.

5

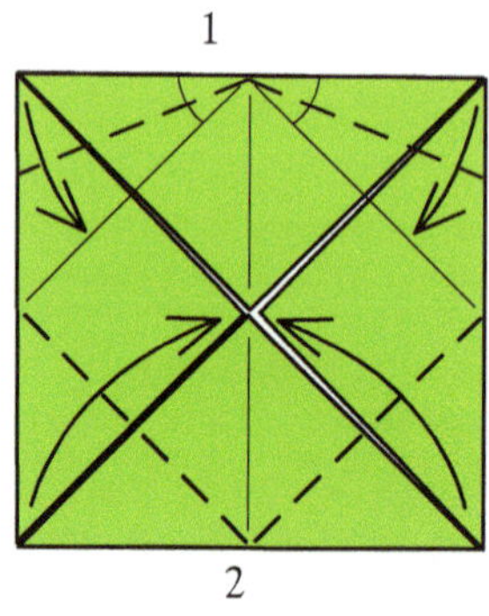

1. Fold to the line on top.
2. Fold to the center on the bottom.

6

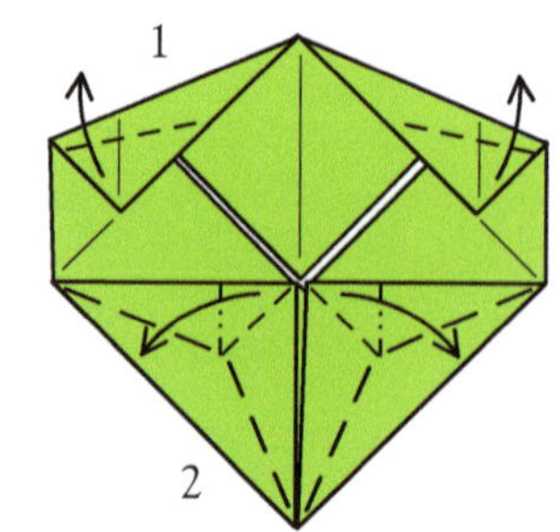

1. Fold up.
2. Make rabbit ears.

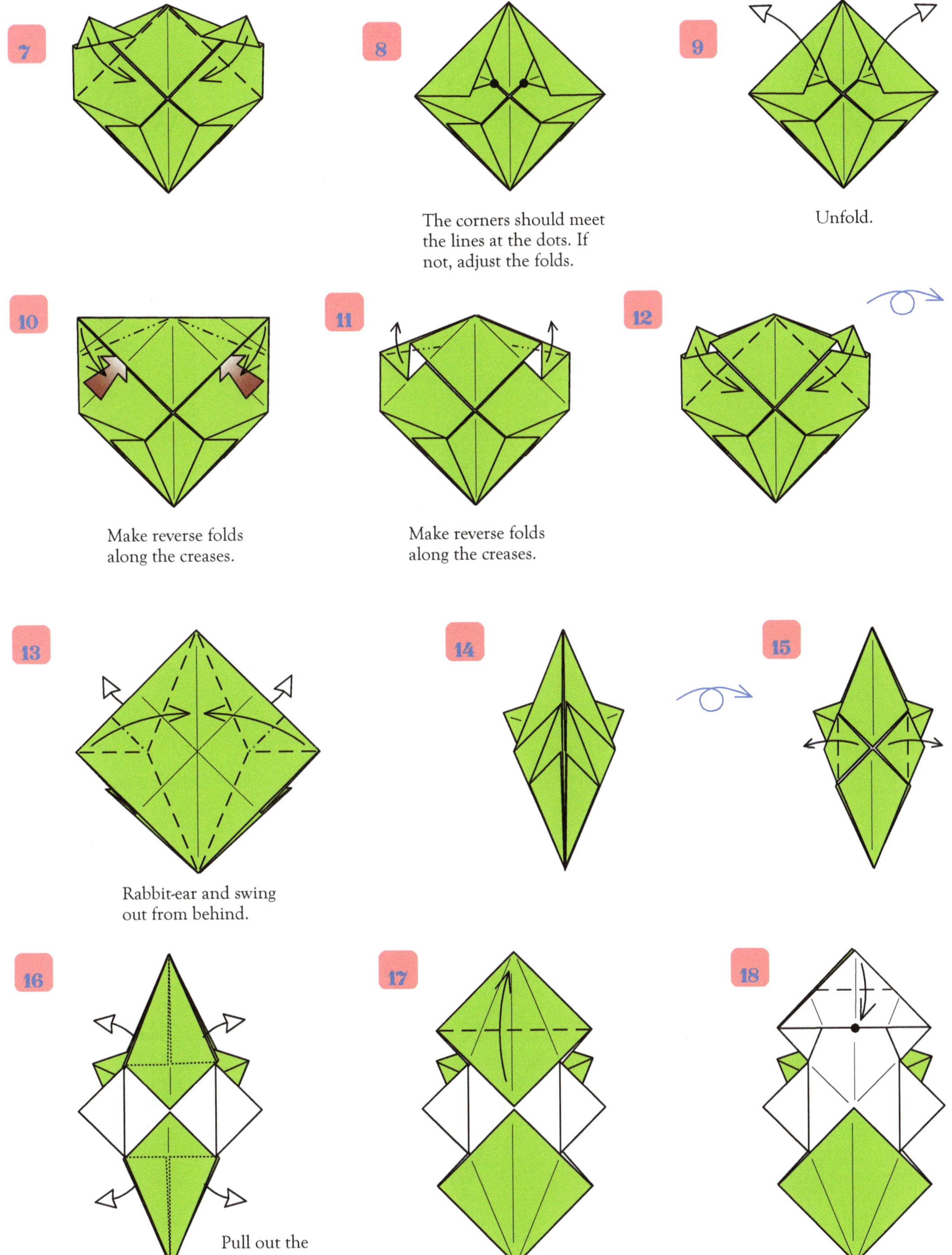
7
8
The corners should meet the lines at the dots. If not, adjust the folds.
9
Unfold.
10
Make reverse folds along the creases.
11
Make reverse folds along the creases.
12
13
Rabbit-ear and swing out from behind.
14
15
16
Pull out the locked layers.
17
18

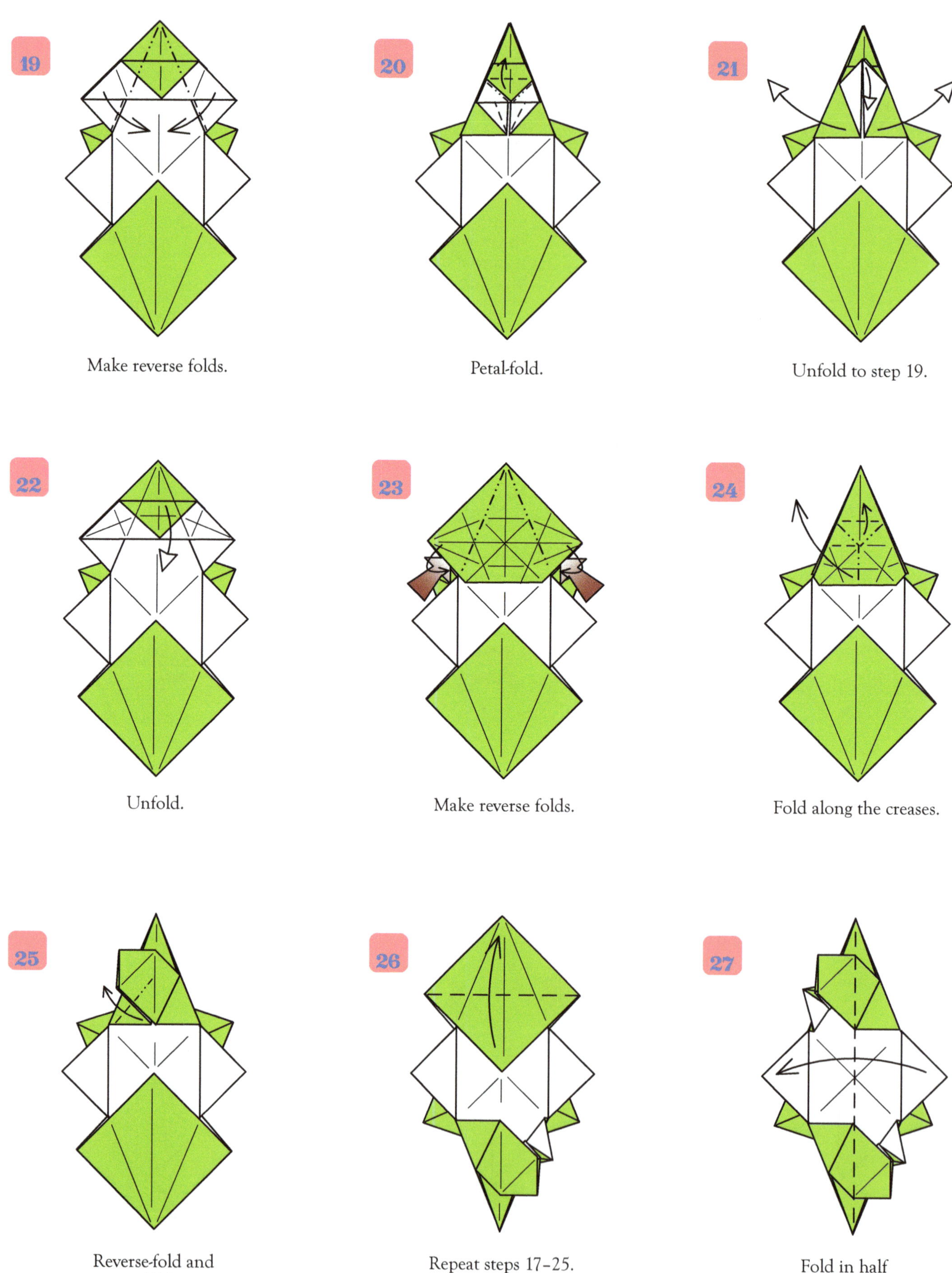
19
Make reverse folds.
20
Petal-fold.
21
Unfold to step 19.
22
Unfold.
23
Make reverse folds.
24
Fold along the creases.
25
Reverse-fold and
rotate 180°.
26
Repeat steps 17–25.
27
Fold in half
and rotate 90°.

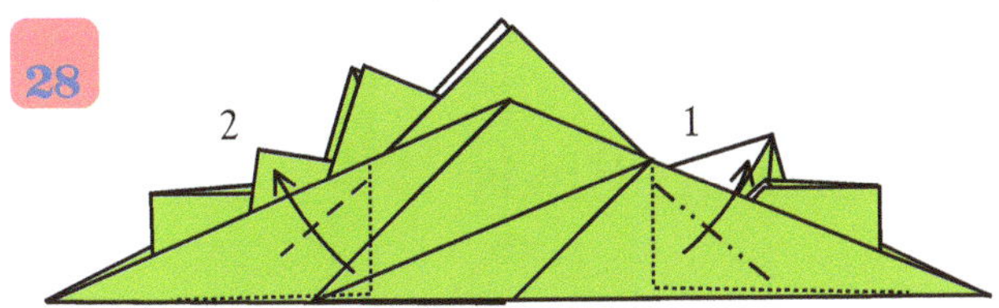

1. Reverse-fold inside, on the front side.
2. Reverse-fold inside, on the back side.
These are the same as step 25.

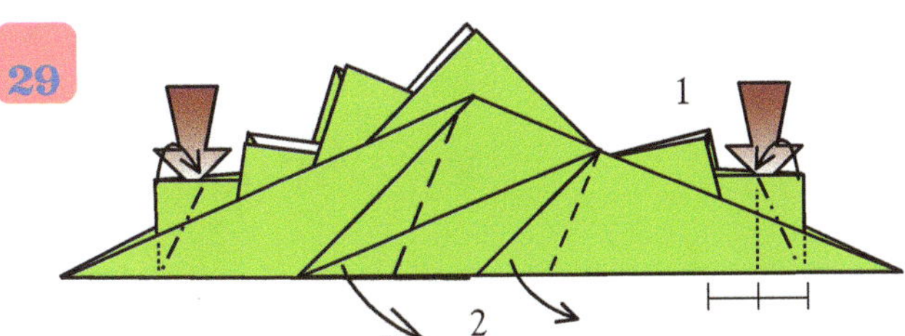

1. Make reverse folds on the left and right.
   Use the half-way mark at the top of the flap.
2. Make valley folds, repeat behind.

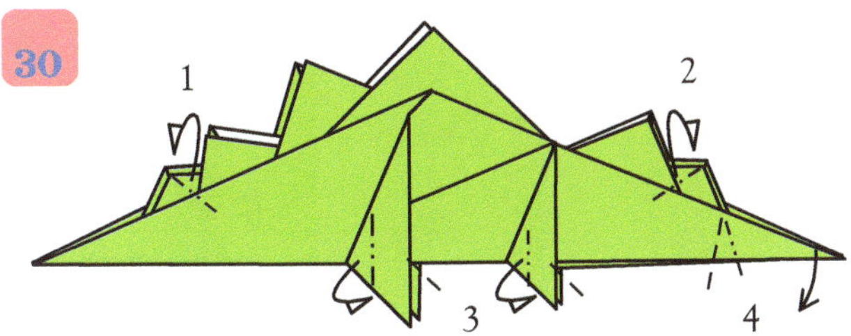

1, 2. Fold inside, repeat behind.
3. Make small reverse folds to
   shape the legs, repeat behind.
4. Spread the head.

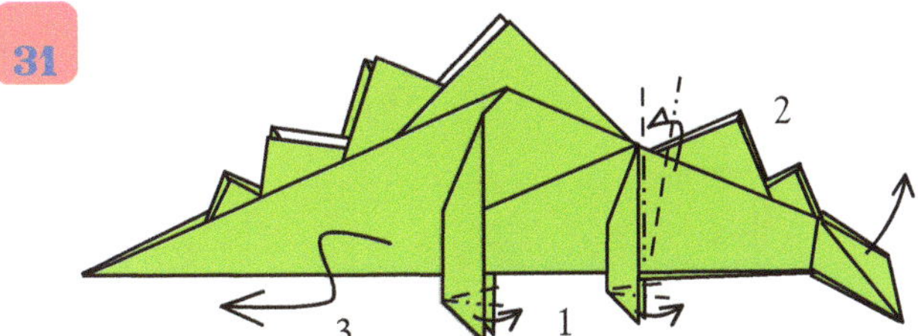

1. Shape the feet with soft folds,
   repeat behind.
2. Crimp-fold.
3. Curl the tail. This keeps the
   layers together.

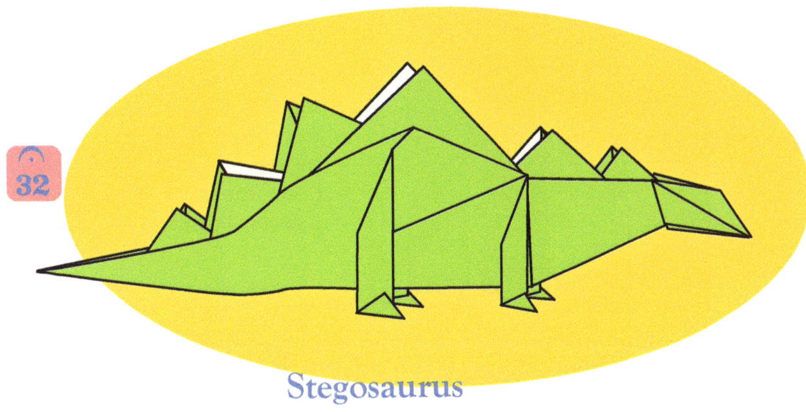

Second Movement

Andante: Colorful Australian Birds

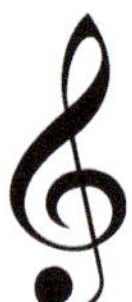

As the dinosaurs evolved into birds, we find ourselves in Australia, admiring the evolved birds. In symphonic form, every other origami bird is either solid in color or two-colored with a color-change pattern. Listen to their songs and admire their variety as you wander through Australia. Models are of intermediate level.

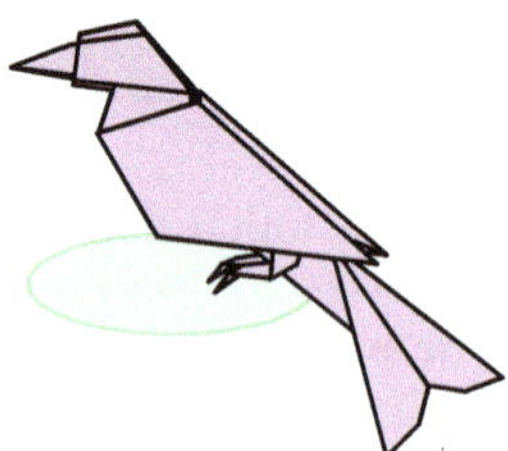

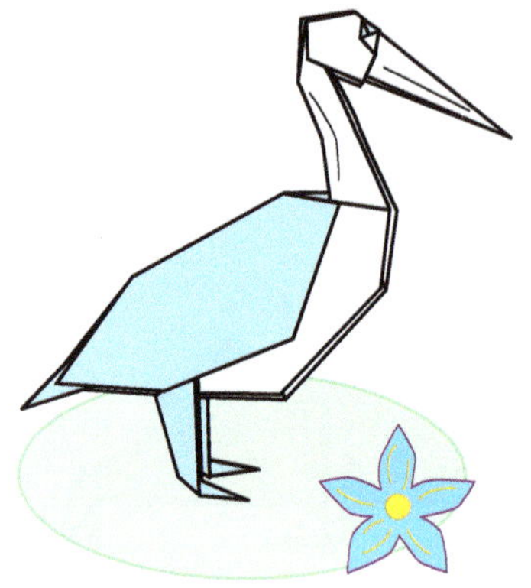

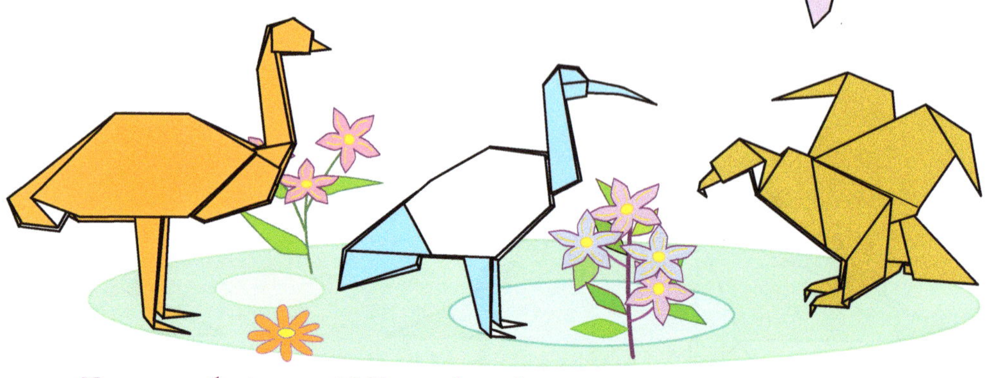

Laughing Kookaburra

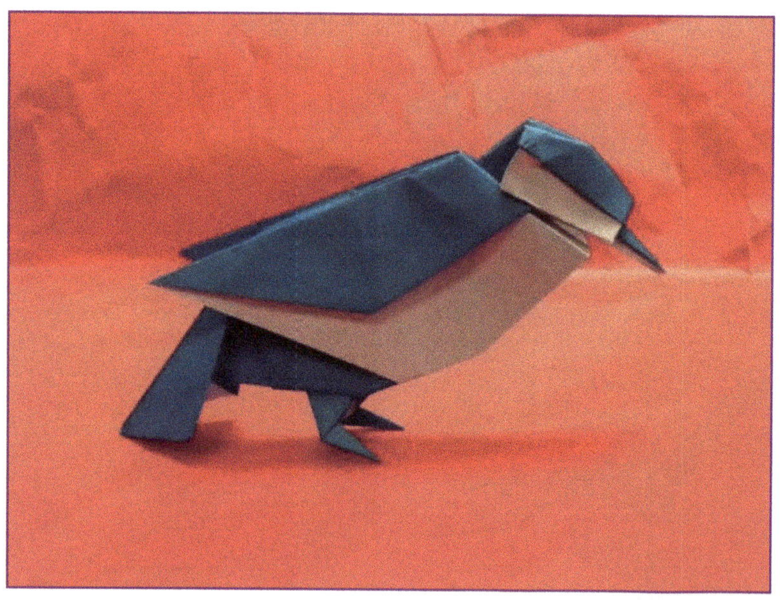

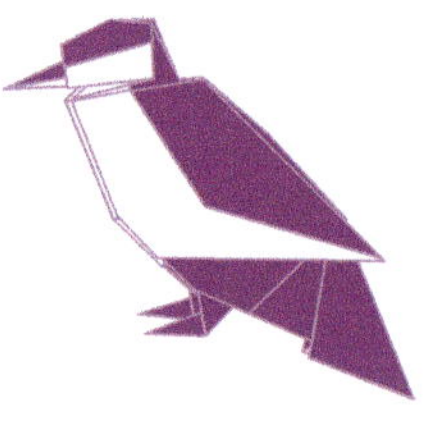

The Laughing Kookaburra is the largest member of the kingfisher family. Found in woodland territories, they live in family groups and make their distinctive laughing calls to protect their territory. One bird starts the laughter and the rest join in, creating a lively jungle sound. Perched in trees, they wait for prey below and swoop down for the catch. They feed on mice, lizards, insects, worms, and other small creatures.

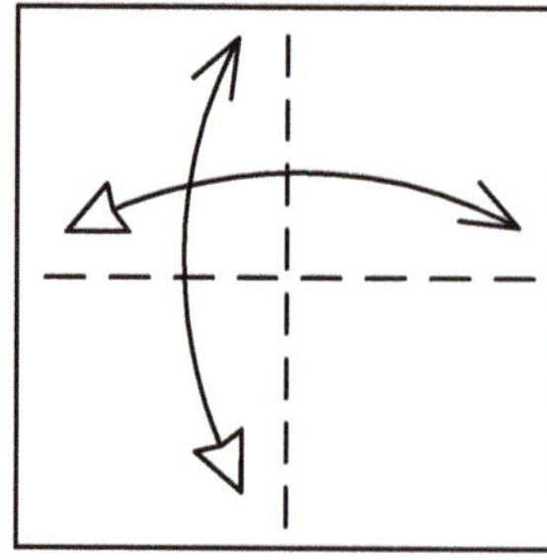

Fold and unfold.

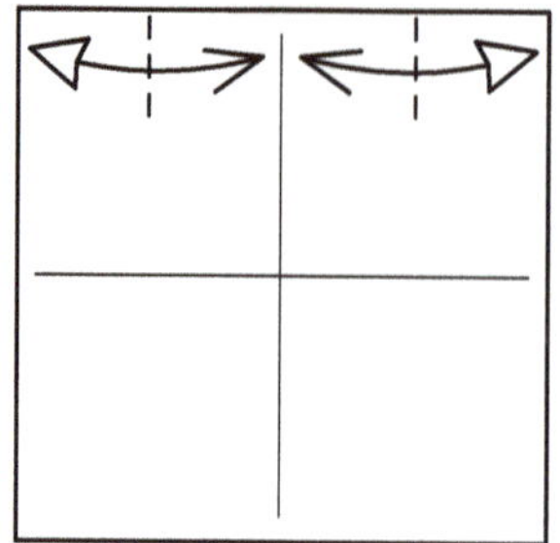

Fold and unfold.

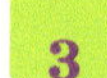

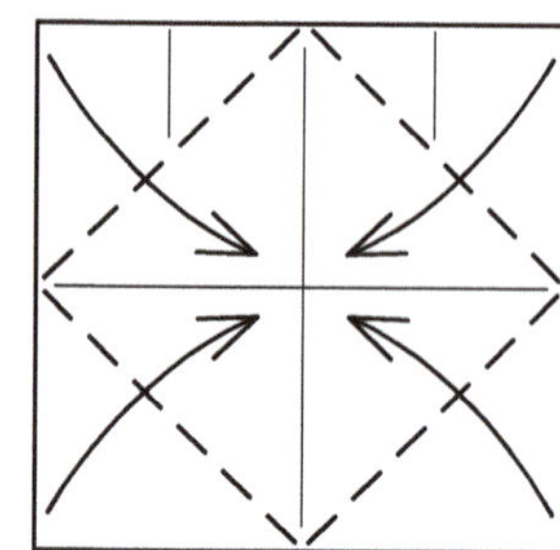

Fold to the center.

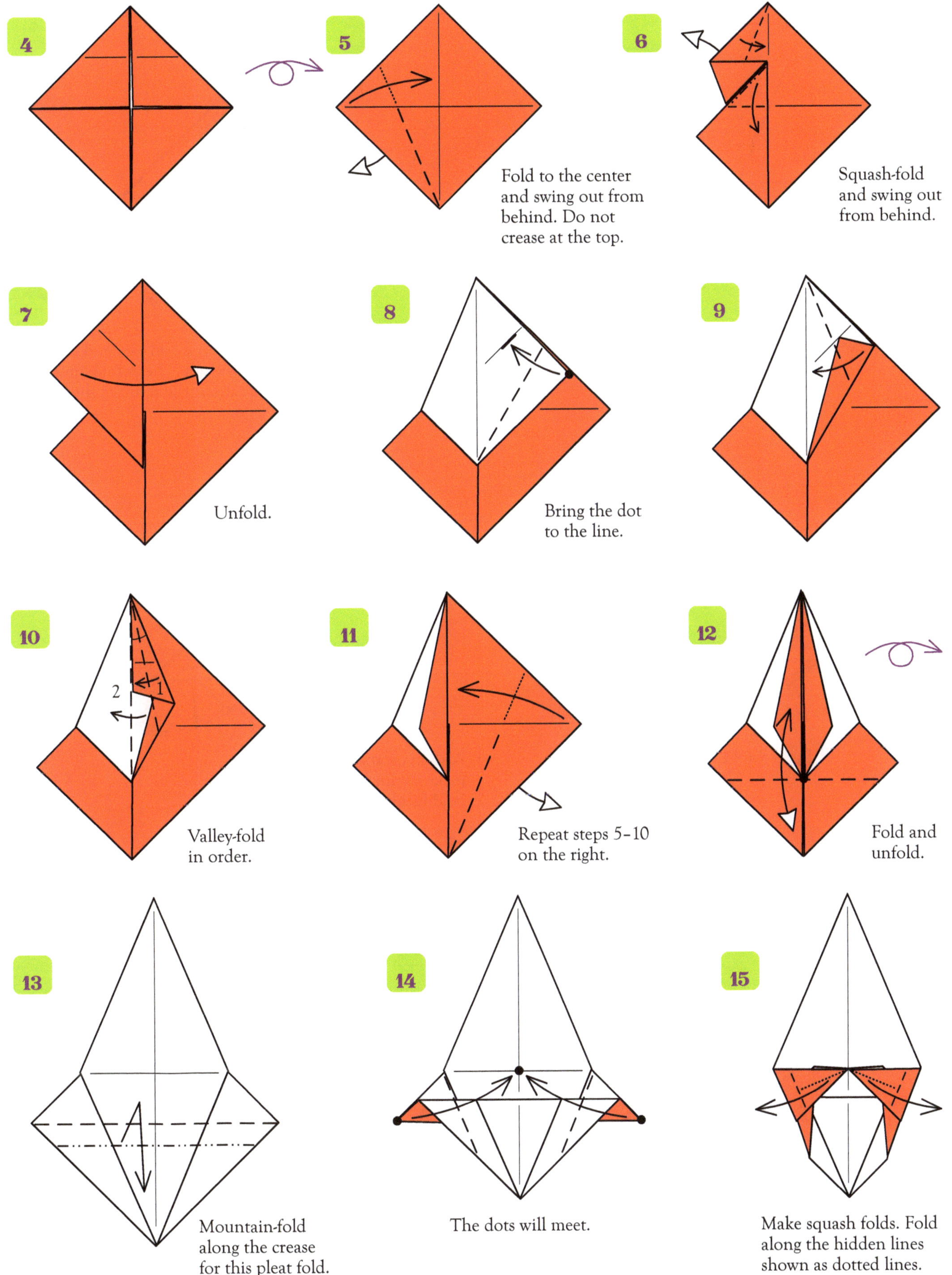
4
5
Fold to the center
and swing out from
behind. Do not
crease at the top.
6
Squash-fold
and swing out
from behind.
7
Unfold.
8
Bring the dot
to the line.
9
10
2
1
Valley-fold
in order.
11
Repeat steps 5–10
on the right.
12
Fold and
unfold.
13
Mountain-fold
along the crease
for this pleat fold.
14
The dots will meet.
15
Make squash folds. Fold
along the hidden lines
shown as dotted lines.

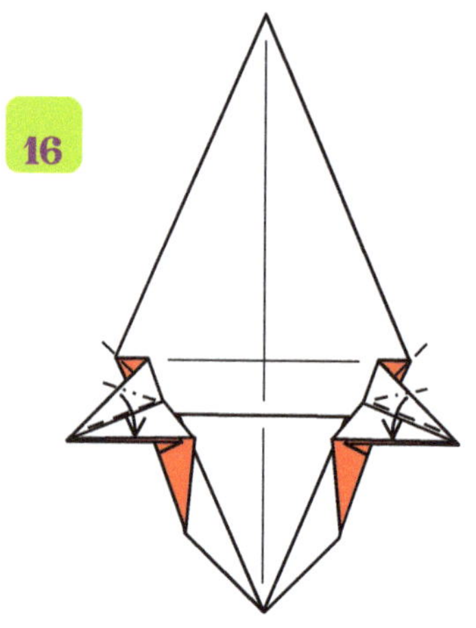

Make squash folds.

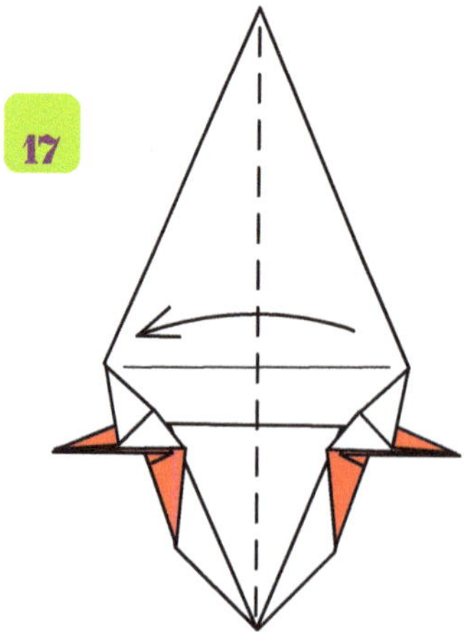

Fold in half
and rotate.

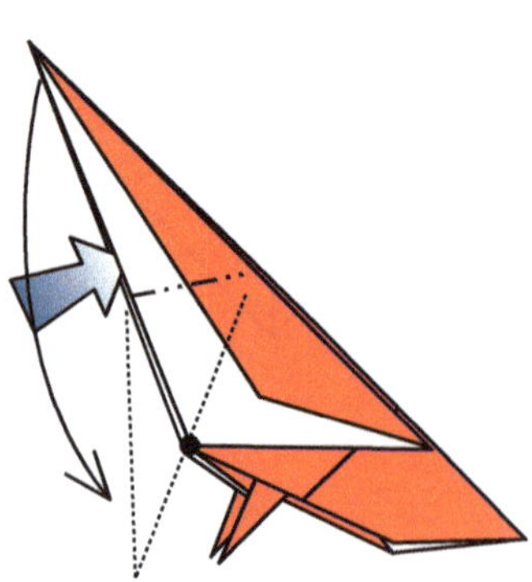

Reverse-fold so the edge meets the dot. The dotted lines shows the result of the fold.

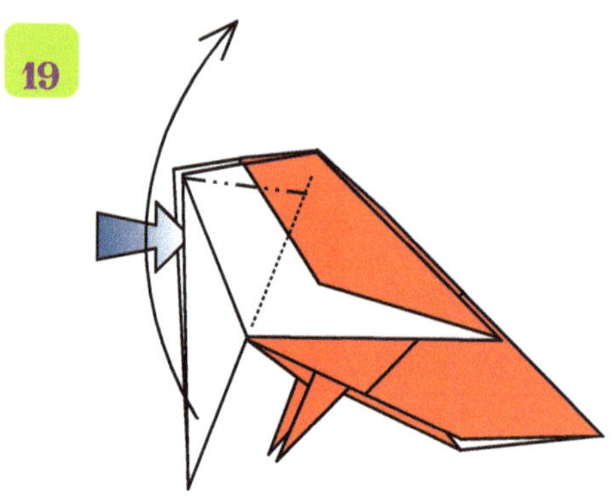

Reverse-fold.

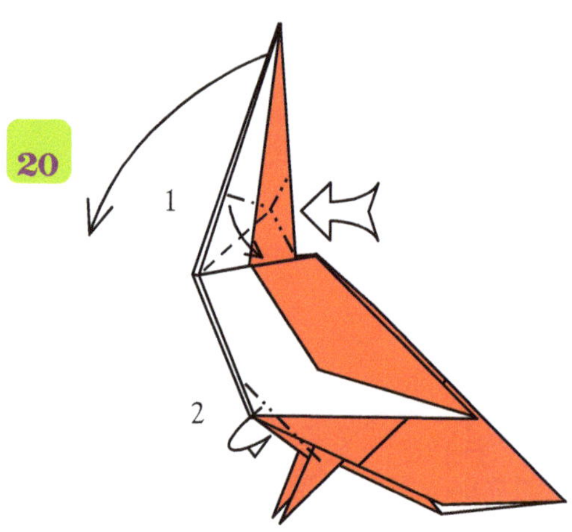

1. Push in on the right and make a crimp fold.
2. Fold inside, repeat behind.

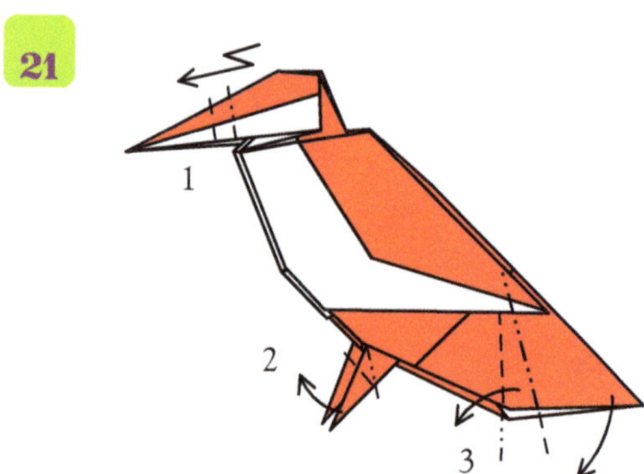

1. Crimp-fold the beak.
2. Crimp-fold the leg, repeat behind.
3. Crimp-fold the tail.

The bird perches.

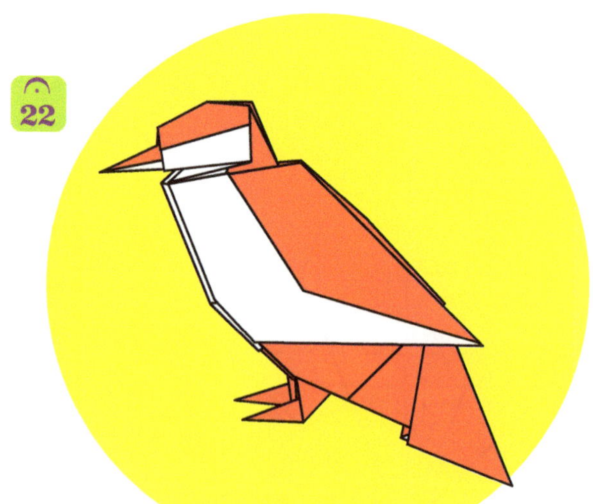

Laughing Kookaburra

Buff-Banded Rail

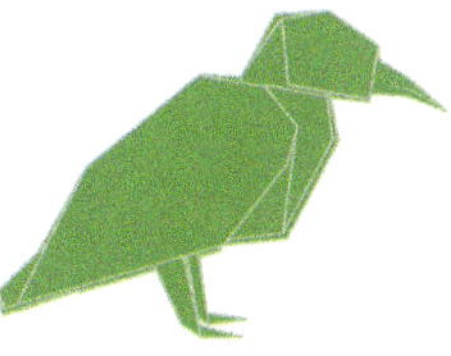

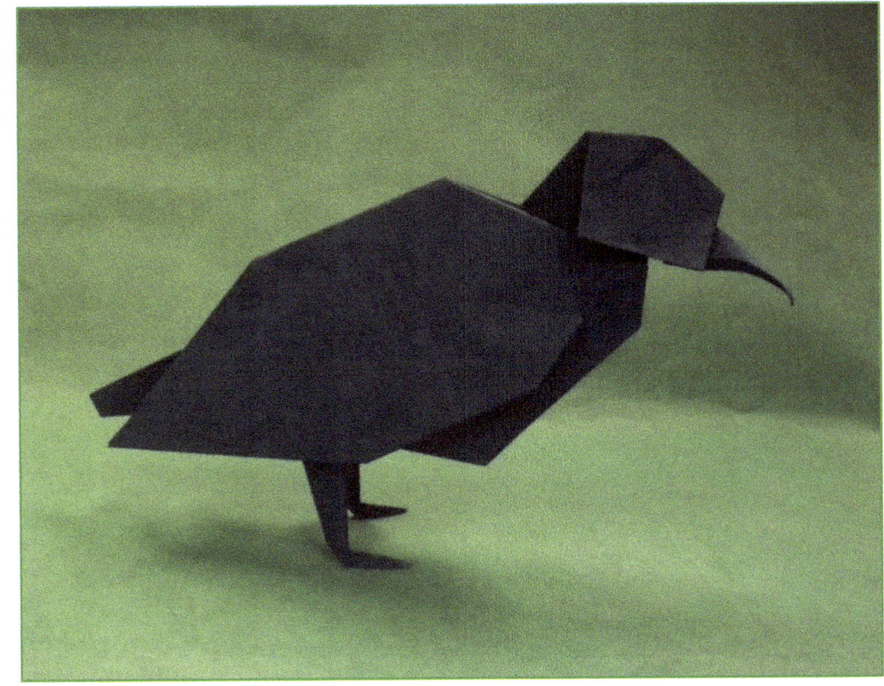

Known as a Misery chicken in Australia, the Buff-Banded Rail lives along the coast and in wetlands. It feeds on seeds, fruit, insects, crustaceans, and small vertebrates. About the size of a domestic chicken, this bird is usually shy. Living by water, it likes to hide among the reeds and vegetation.

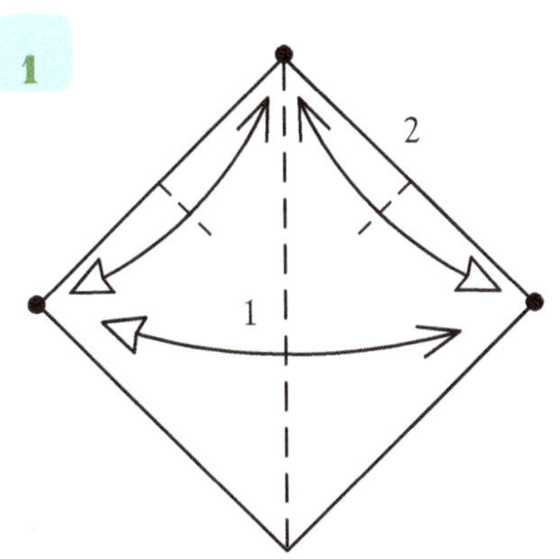

1. Fold and unfold.
2. Fold and unfold on the edge.

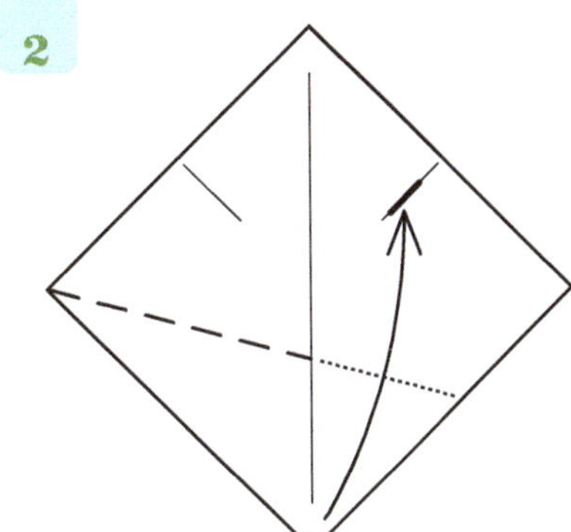

Bring the dot to the line.

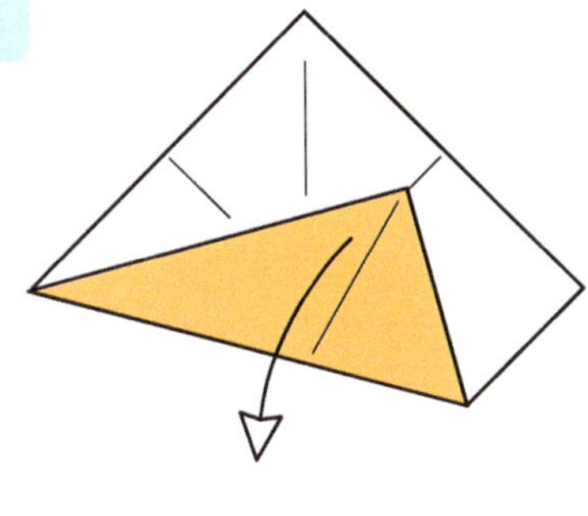

Unfold.

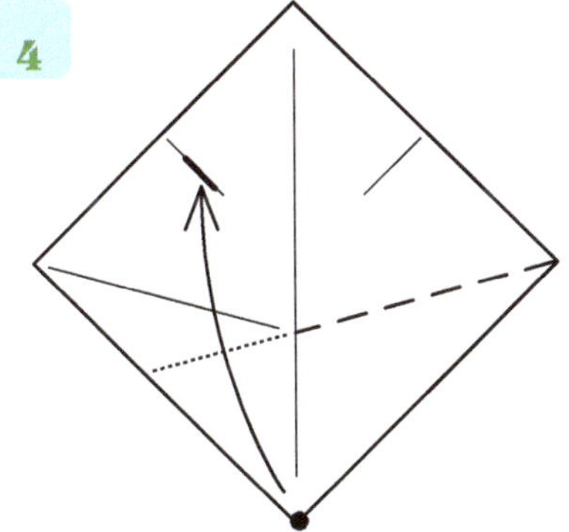

Repeat steps 2–3 on the right.

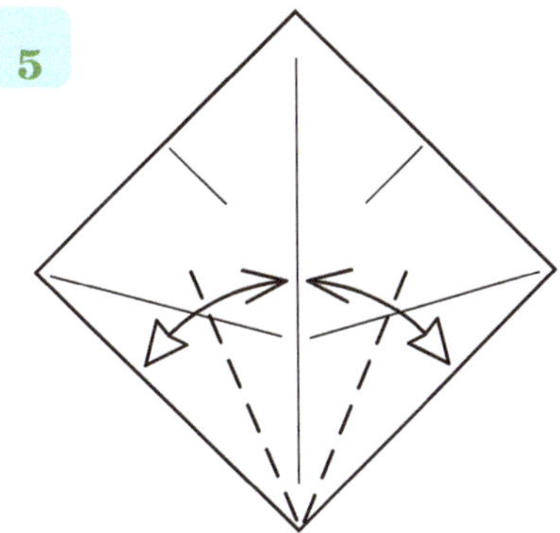

Fold to the center and unfold. Rotate 180°.

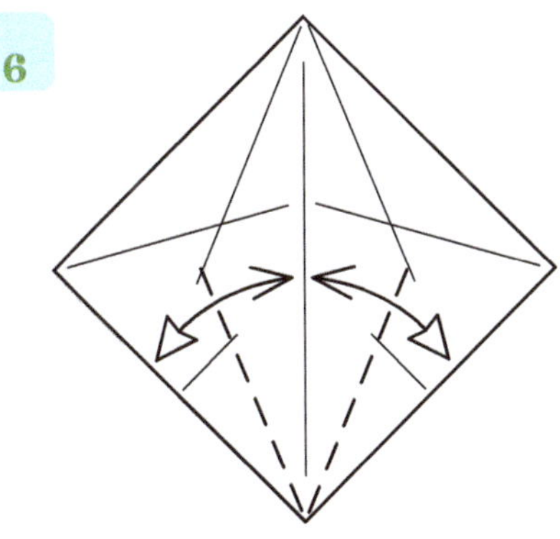

Fold to the center and unfold.

7

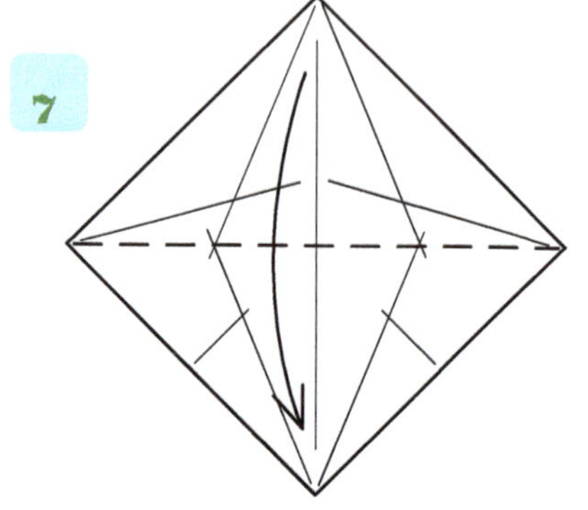

8

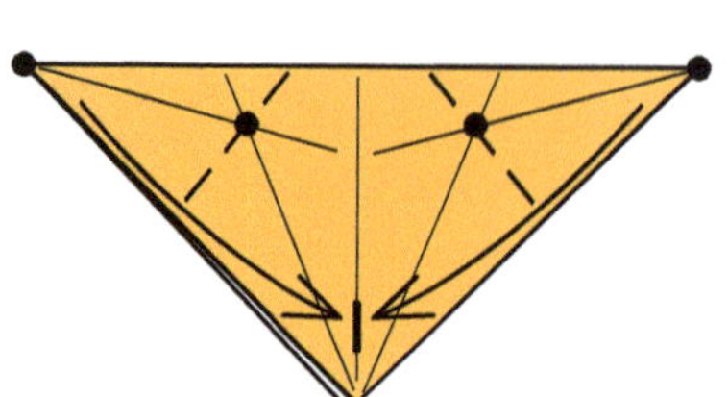

Fold through the inner dots and bring the outer dots to the center.

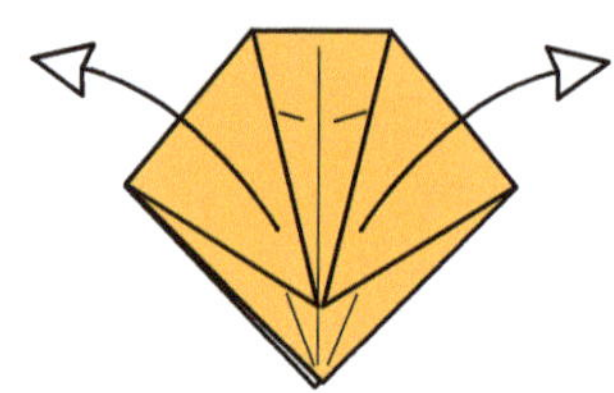

Unfold.

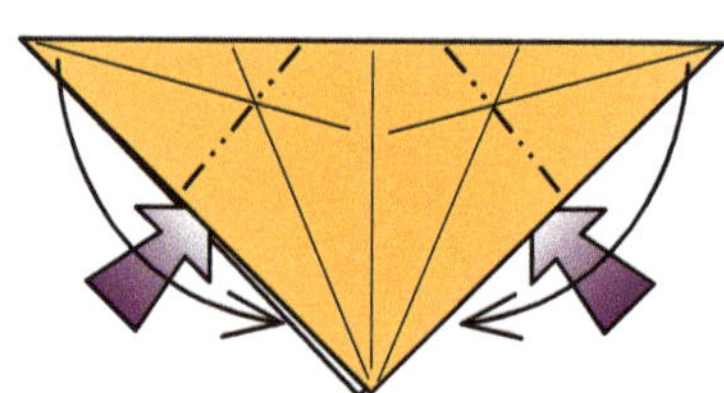

Make reverse folds.

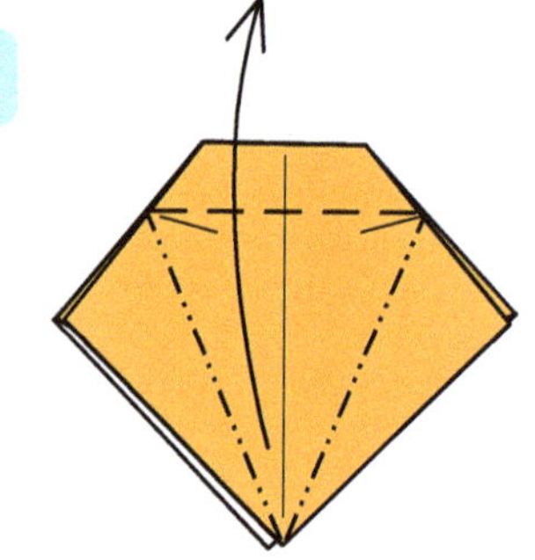

Petal-fold.

12

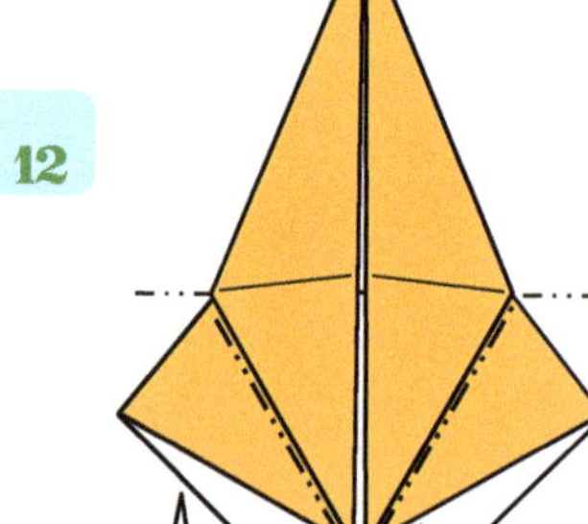

Petal-fold behind.

13

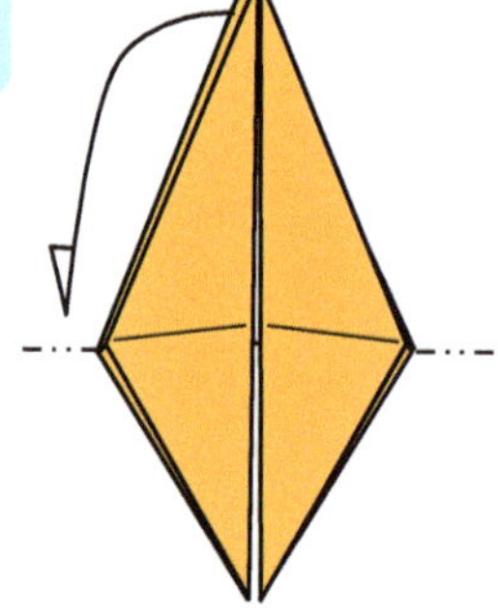

Fold the flap down from behind.

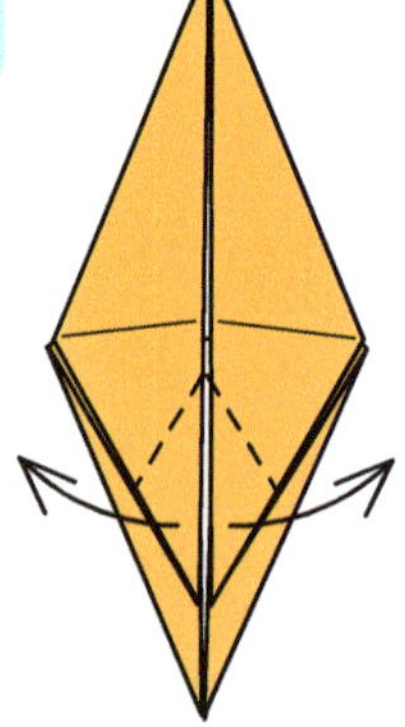

Make valley folds.

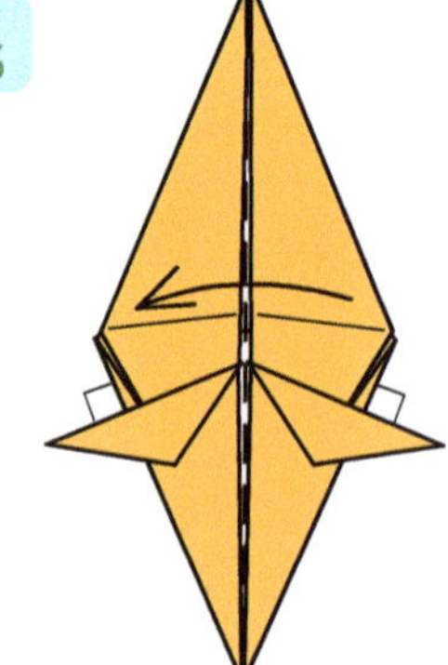

Note the right angles. Fold in half and rotate.

16

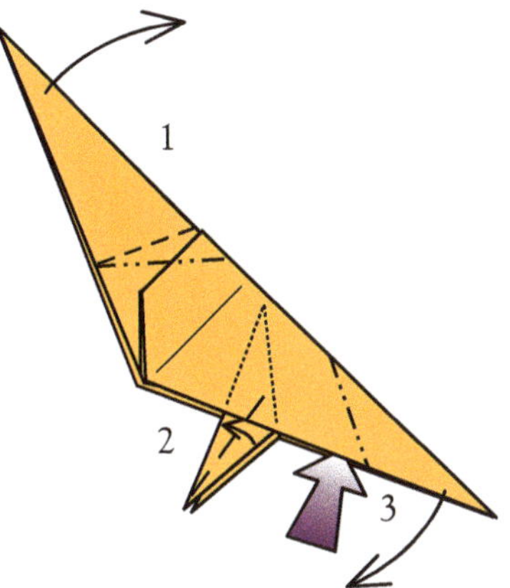

1. Crimp-fold.
2. Fold in half, repeat behind.
3. Reverse-fold.

17

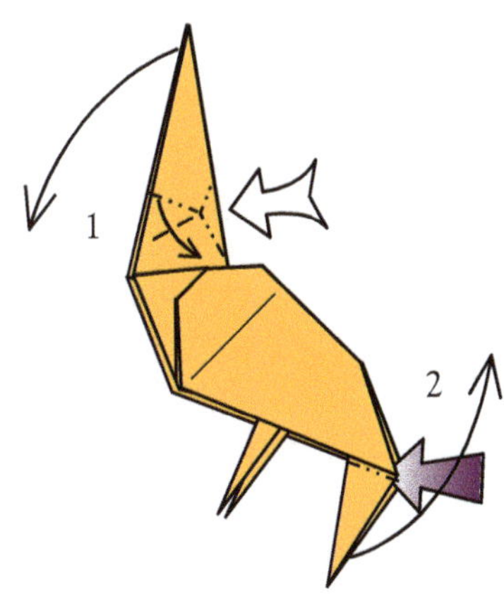

1. Push in on the right and make a crimp fold.
2. Reverse-fold.

18

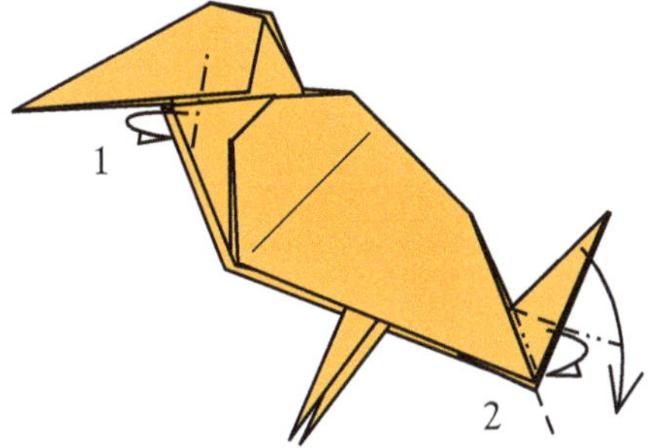

1. Fold inside, repeat behind.
2. Crimp-fold.

19

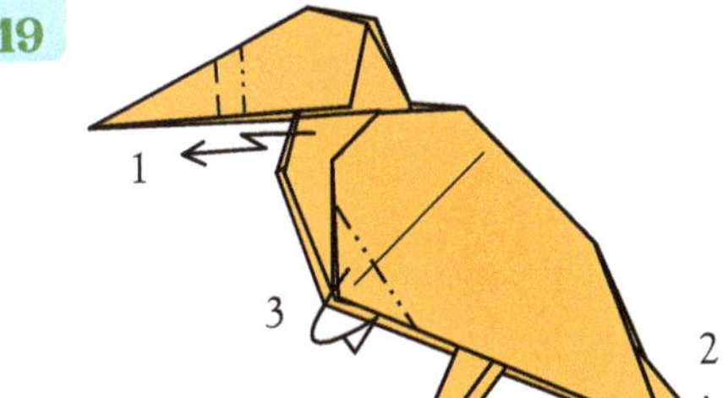

1. Crimp-fold.
2. Reverse-fold.
3. Fold inside, repeat behind.

20

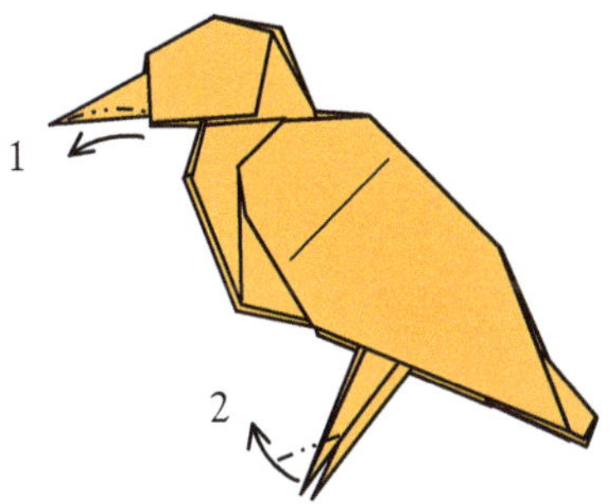

1. Curl the beak.
2. Reverse-fold, repeat behind.

The Rail can stand.

21

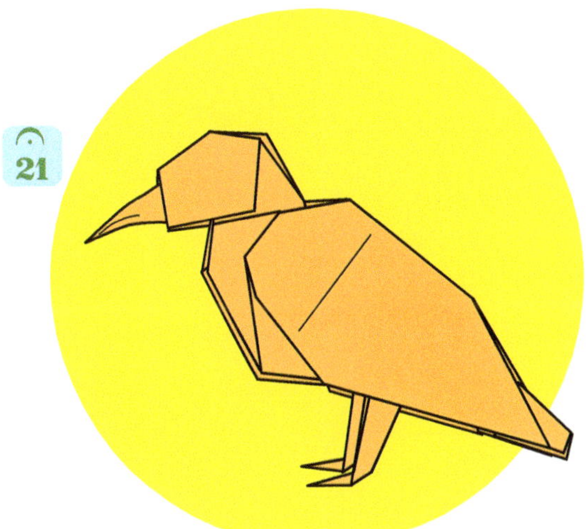

Buff-Banded Rail

Collared Kingfisher

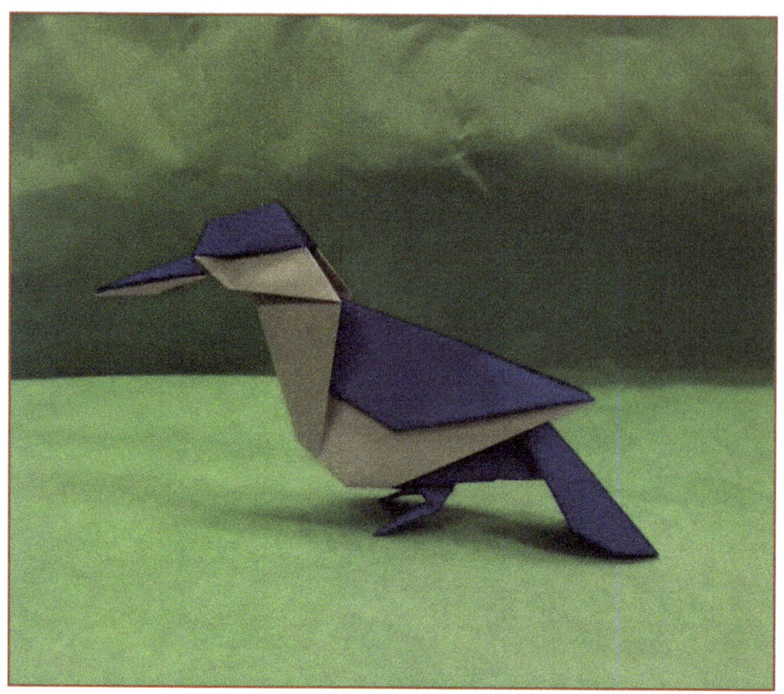

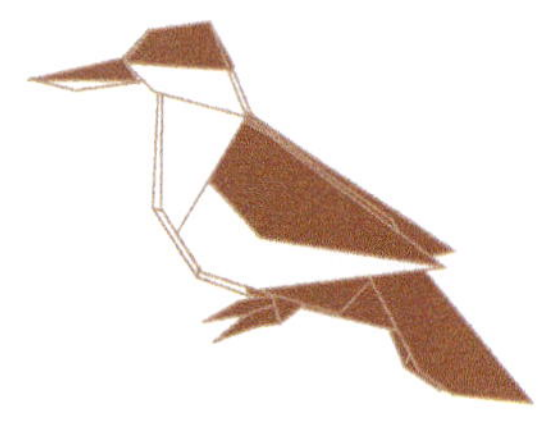

The Collared Kingfisher is named for the white collar around its neck. This medium-sized kingfisher lives by coastal regions. Perching in a tree, it waits for its meal of small fish, shrimp, crabs, and other small creatures. With its hard beak, it can spear a fish. It enjoys the water and will dive in for a bath.

Begin with step 14 of the Laughing Kookaburra (page 44).

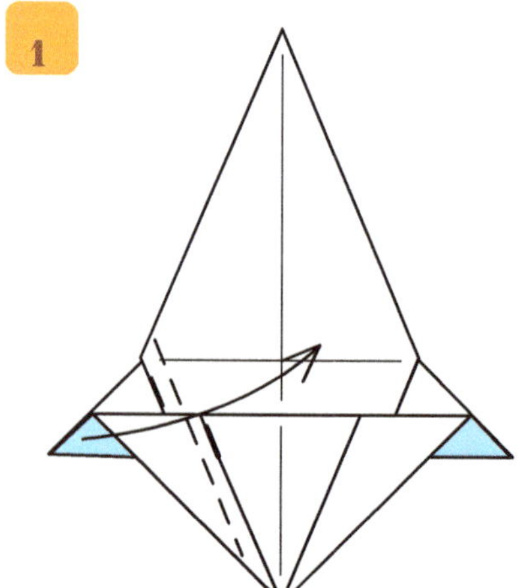

Fold between the bold lines.

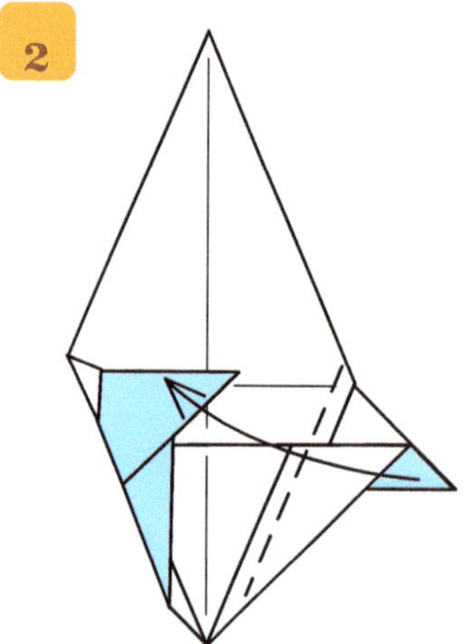

Repeat on the right.

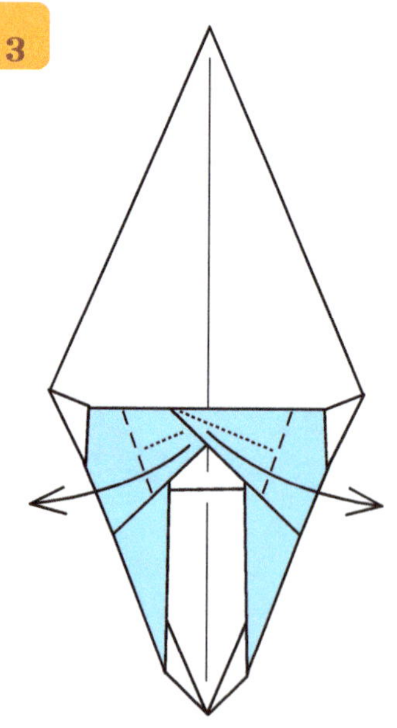

Make squash folds. Fold along the hidden lines shown as dotted lines.

4

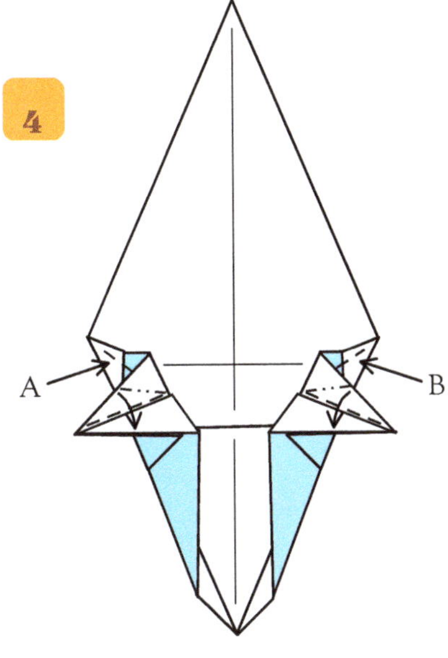

Make squash folds. Some of the folds are hidden under triangles A and B.

5

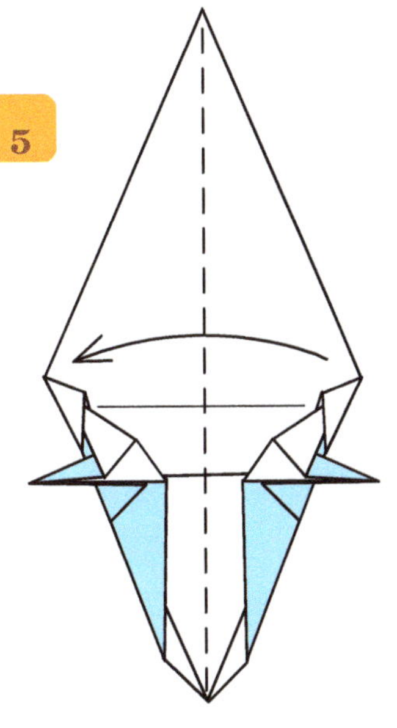

Fold in half and rotate.

6

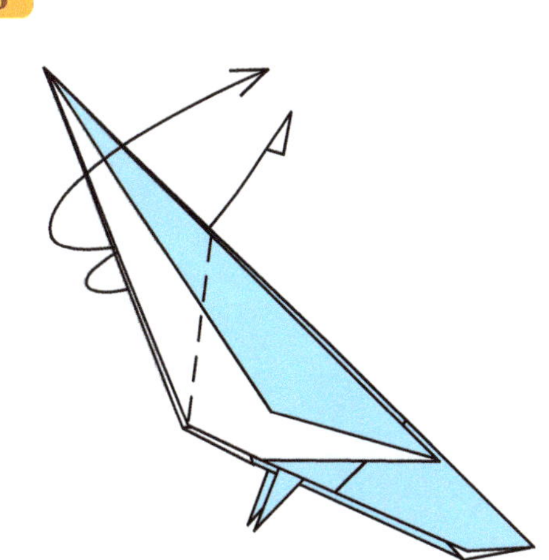

Outside-reverse-fold.

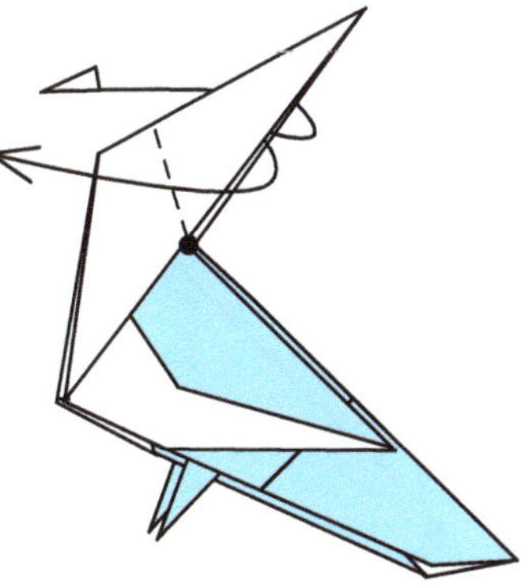

Outside-reverse-fold.

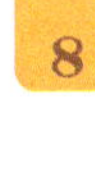

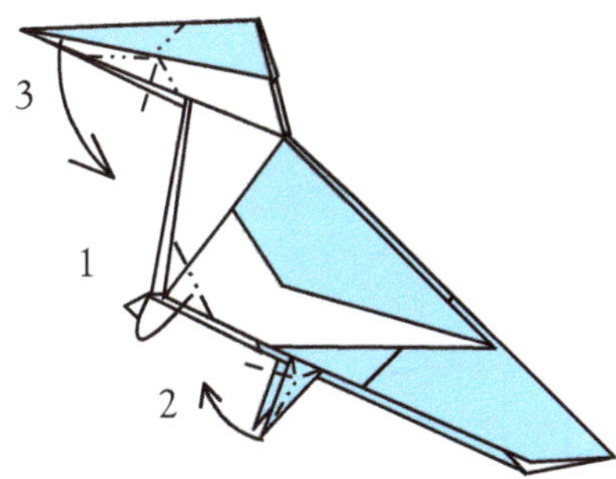

1. Fold inside, repeat behind.
2. Double-rabbit-ear, repeat behind.
3. Double-rabbit-ear but not to a point.

9

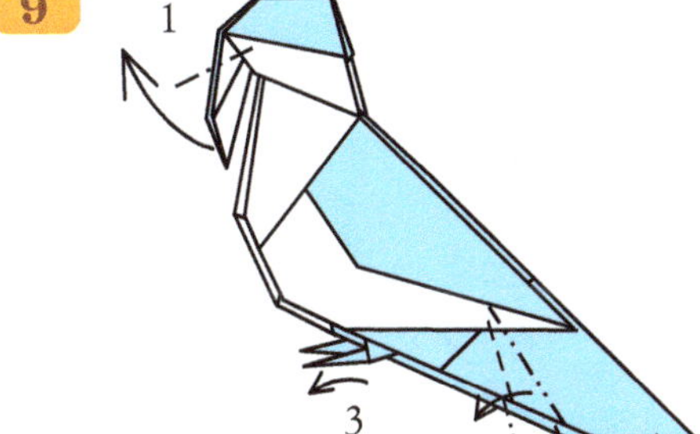

1. Reverse-fold.
2. Crimp-fold.
3. Curl the legs, repeat behind.

10

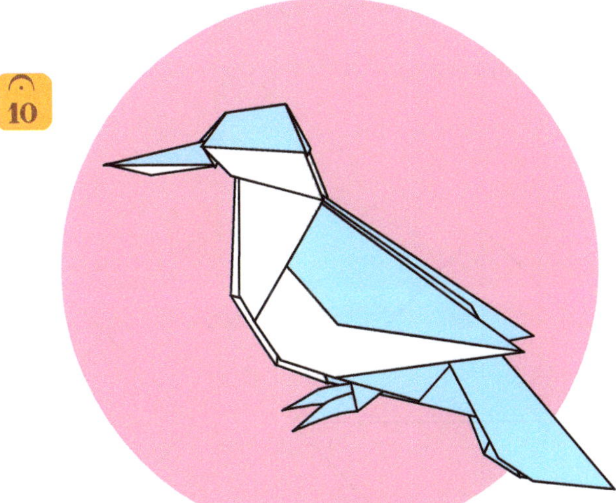

Collared Kingfisher

Spangled Drongo

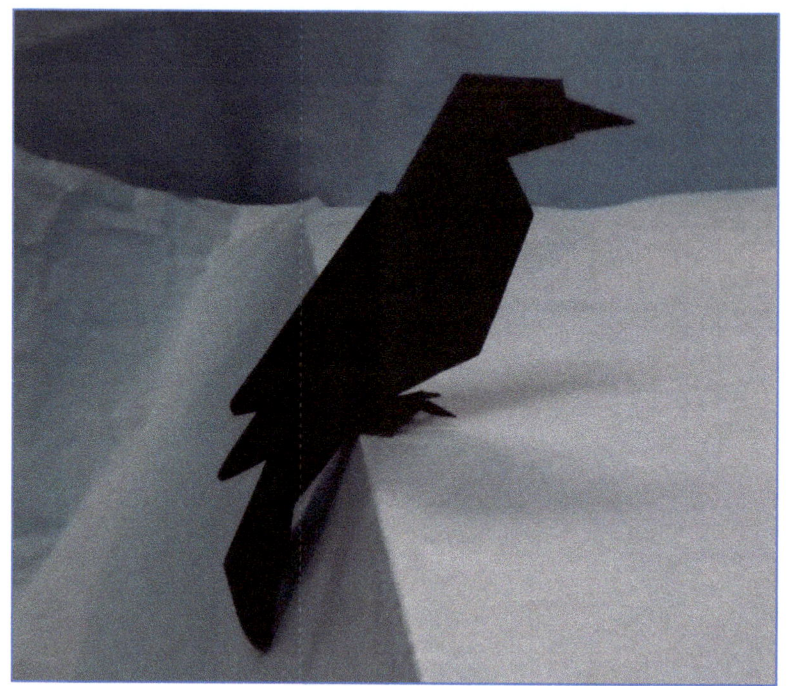

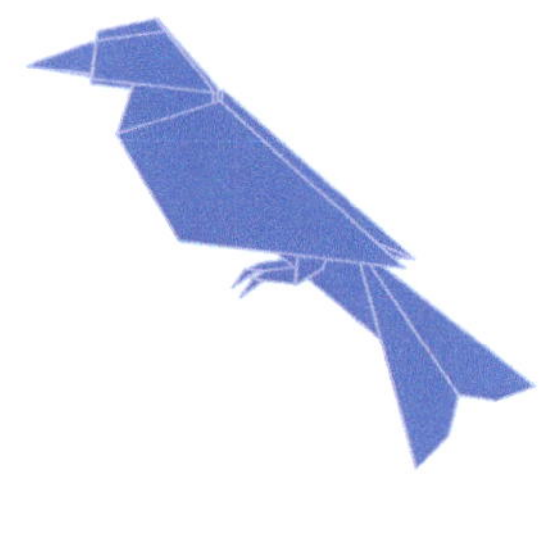

The Spangled Drongo has a forked tail. The feathers are black with iridescent blue and purple spots. It mimics nearby sounds and creates its own symphonic music. Found in wet forests, woodlands, and parks, it waits patiently perched on branches, to catch insects with its hooked bill.

1

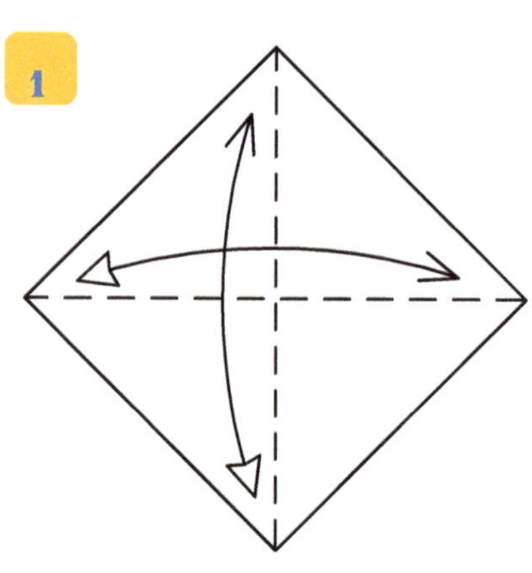

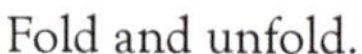

Fold and unfold.

2

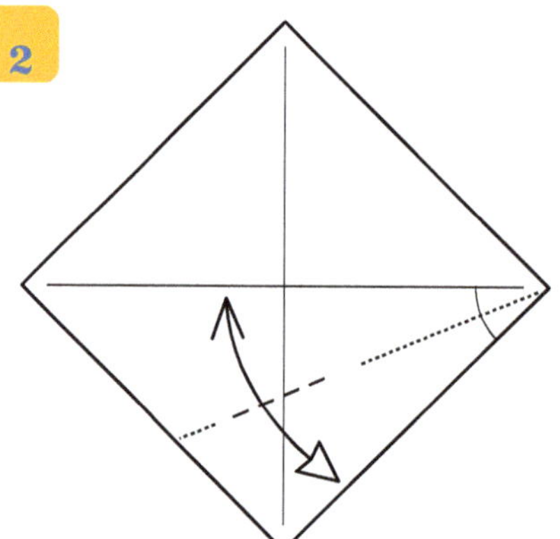

Fold and unfold on the diagonal.

3

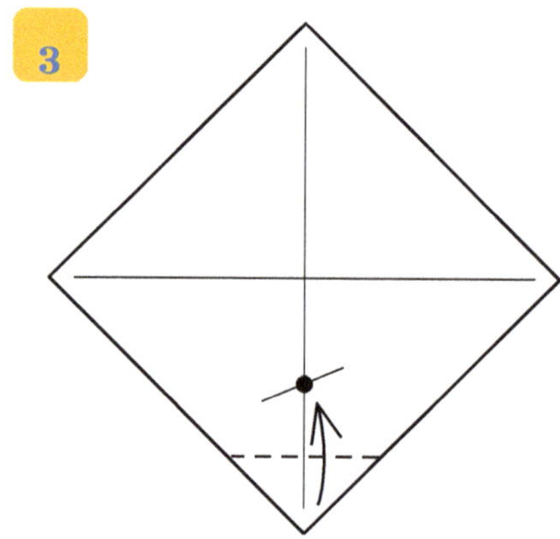

4

5

Fold and unfold.

6

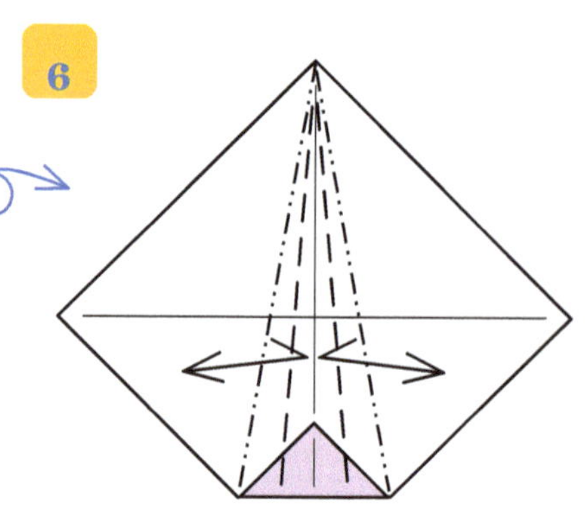

Pleat-fold to the center.

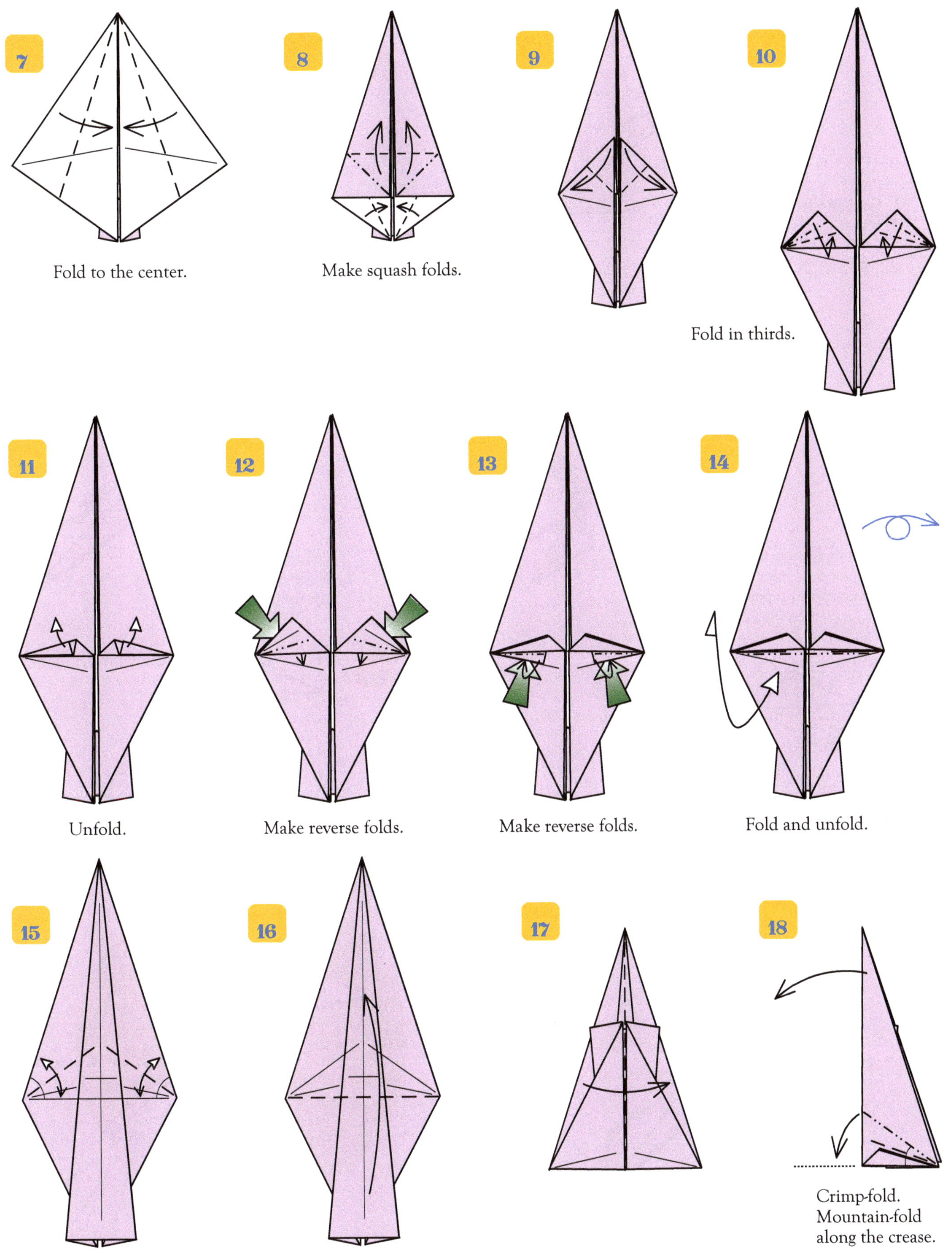
7
Fold to the center.
8
Make squash folds.
9
10
Fold in thirds.
11
Unfold.
12
Make reverse folds.
13
Make reverse folds.
14
Fold and unfold.
15
Fold and unfold.
16
17
18
Crimp-fold.
Mountain-fold
along the crease.

19

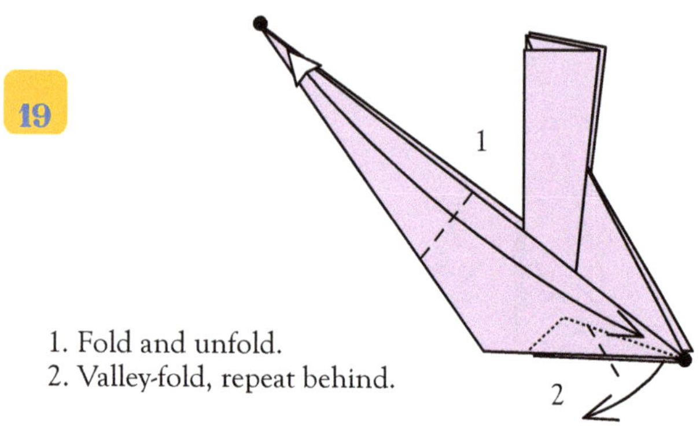

1. Fold and unfold.
2. Valley-fold, repeat behind.

20

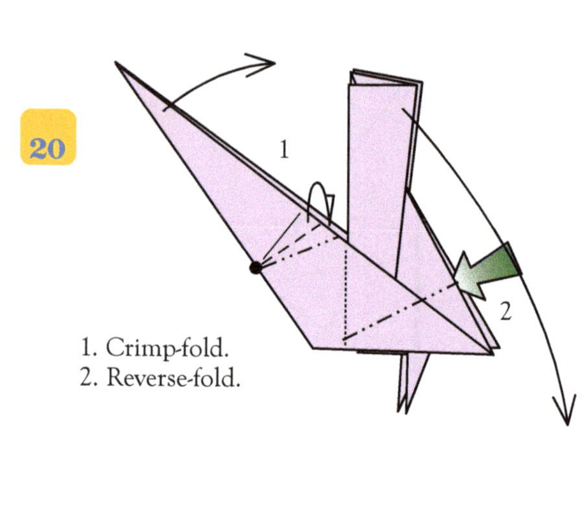

1. Crimp-fold.
2. Reverse-fold.

21

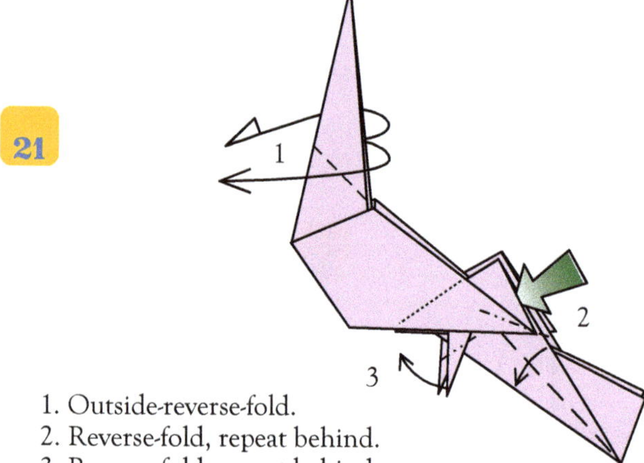

1. Outside-reverse-fold.
2. Reverse-fold, repeat behind.
3. Reverse-fold, repeat behind.

22

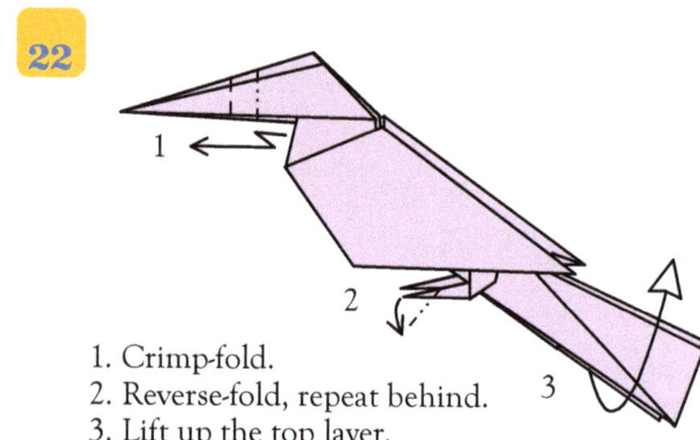

1. Crimp-fold.
2. Reverse-fold, repeat behind.
3. Lift up the top layer.

23

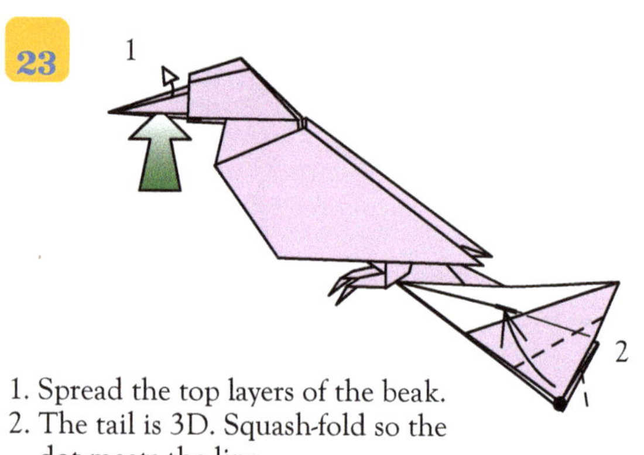

1. Spread the top layers of the beak.
2. The tail is 3D. Squash-fold so the dot meets the line.

24

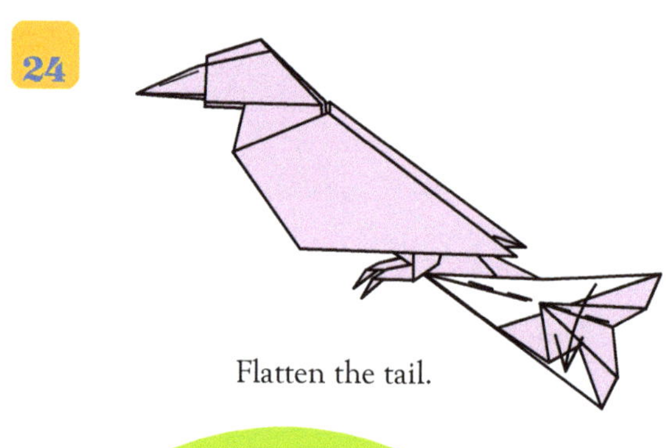

Flatten the tail.

25

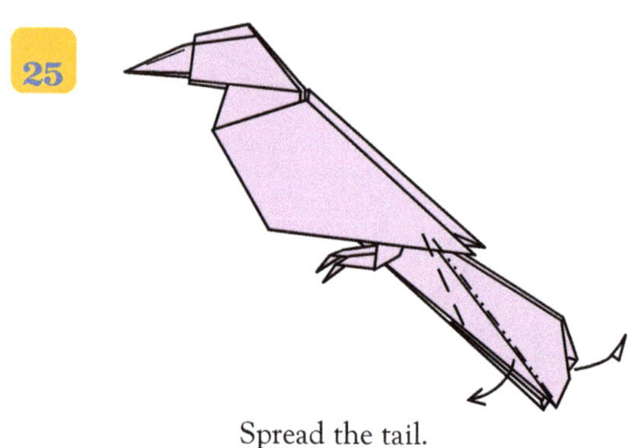

Spread the tail.

26

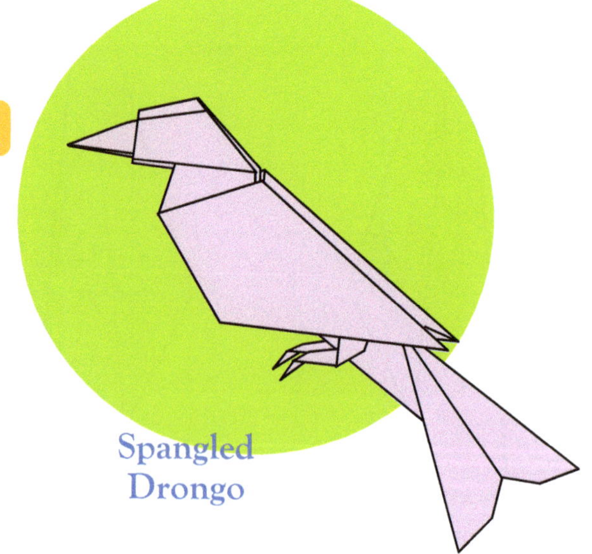

Spangled Drongo

Australian White Ibis

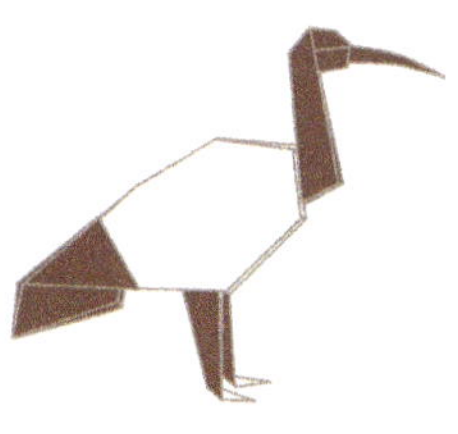

The Australian White Ibis lives in wetlands, coastal lagoons, along with gardens and parks. With their long bills, they search for insects, snakes, crustaceans, and other small animals. They especially enjoy rubbish from human trash and have settled into Australian coastal cities. To the locals, these black and white birds are revered and despised.

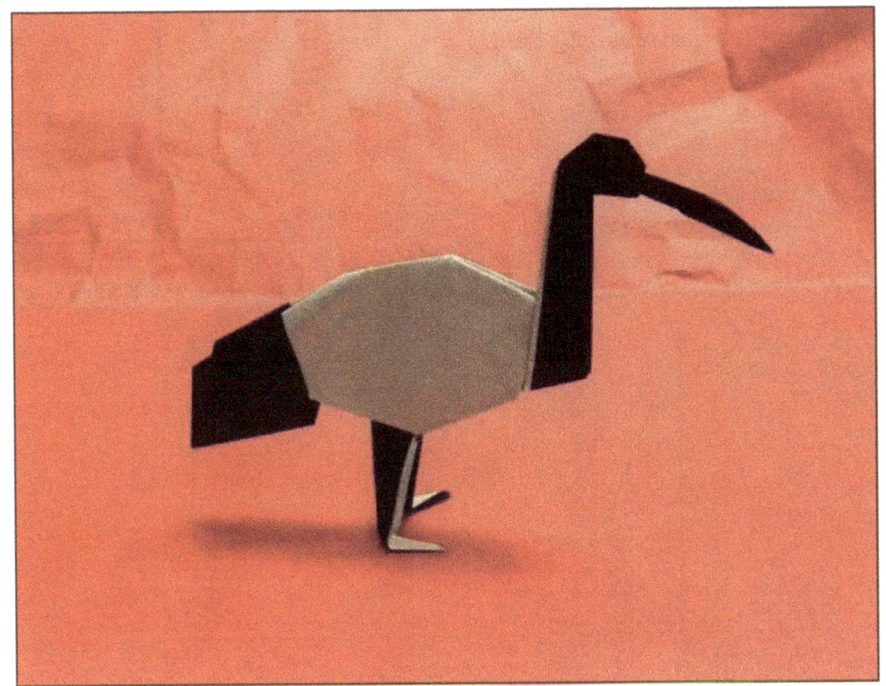

1

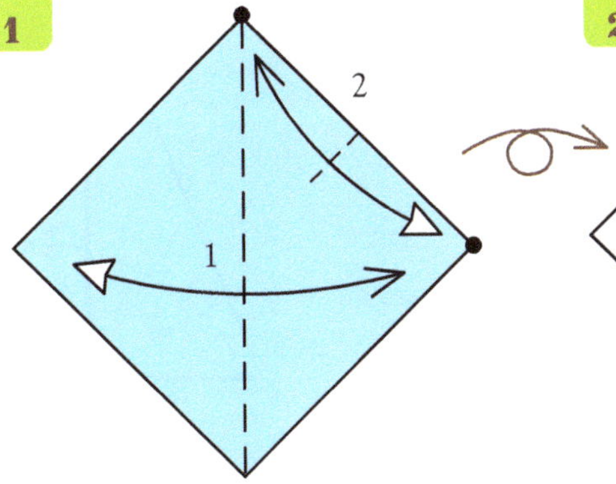

1. Fold and unfold.
2. Fold and unfold on the edge.

2

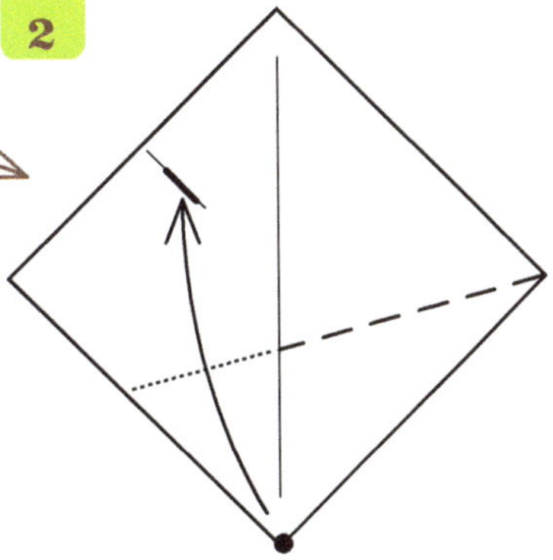

Bring the dot to the line.

3

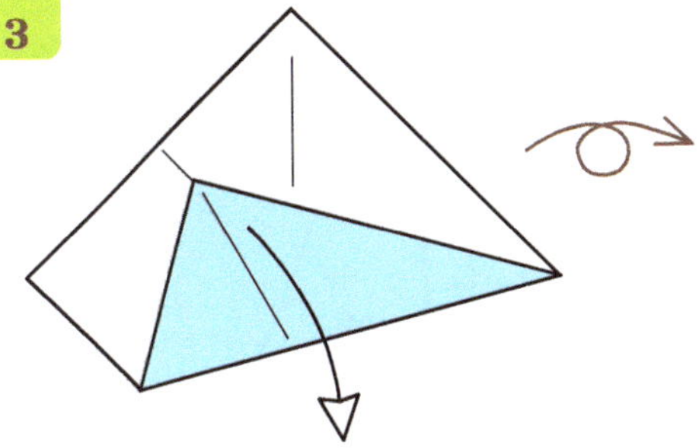

Unfold.

4

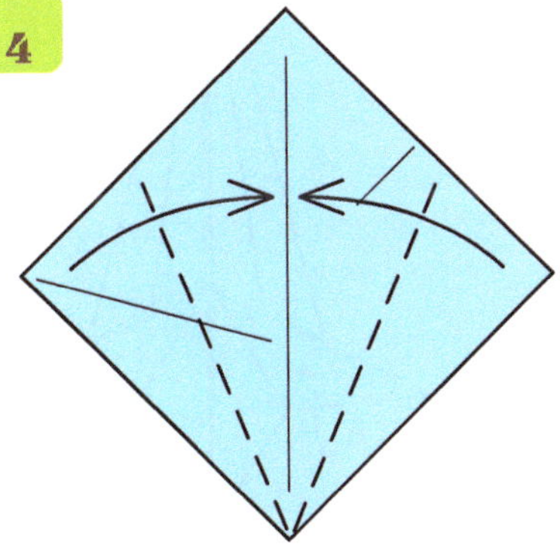

Fold to the center.

5

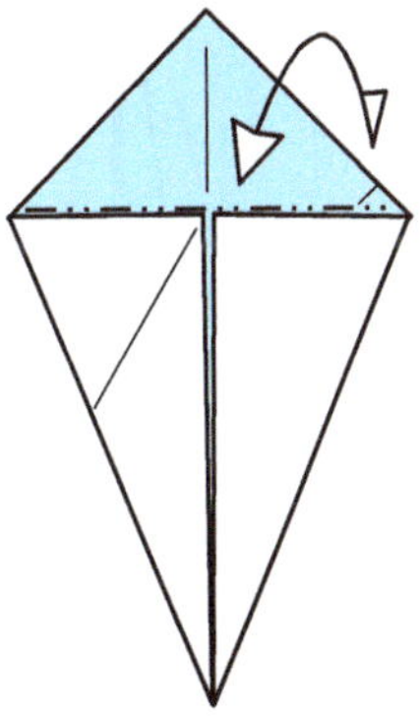

Fold and unfold. Rotate 180°.

6

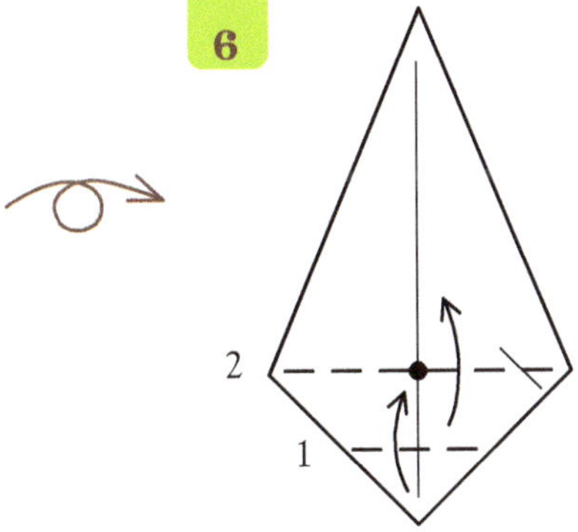

Fold in order.

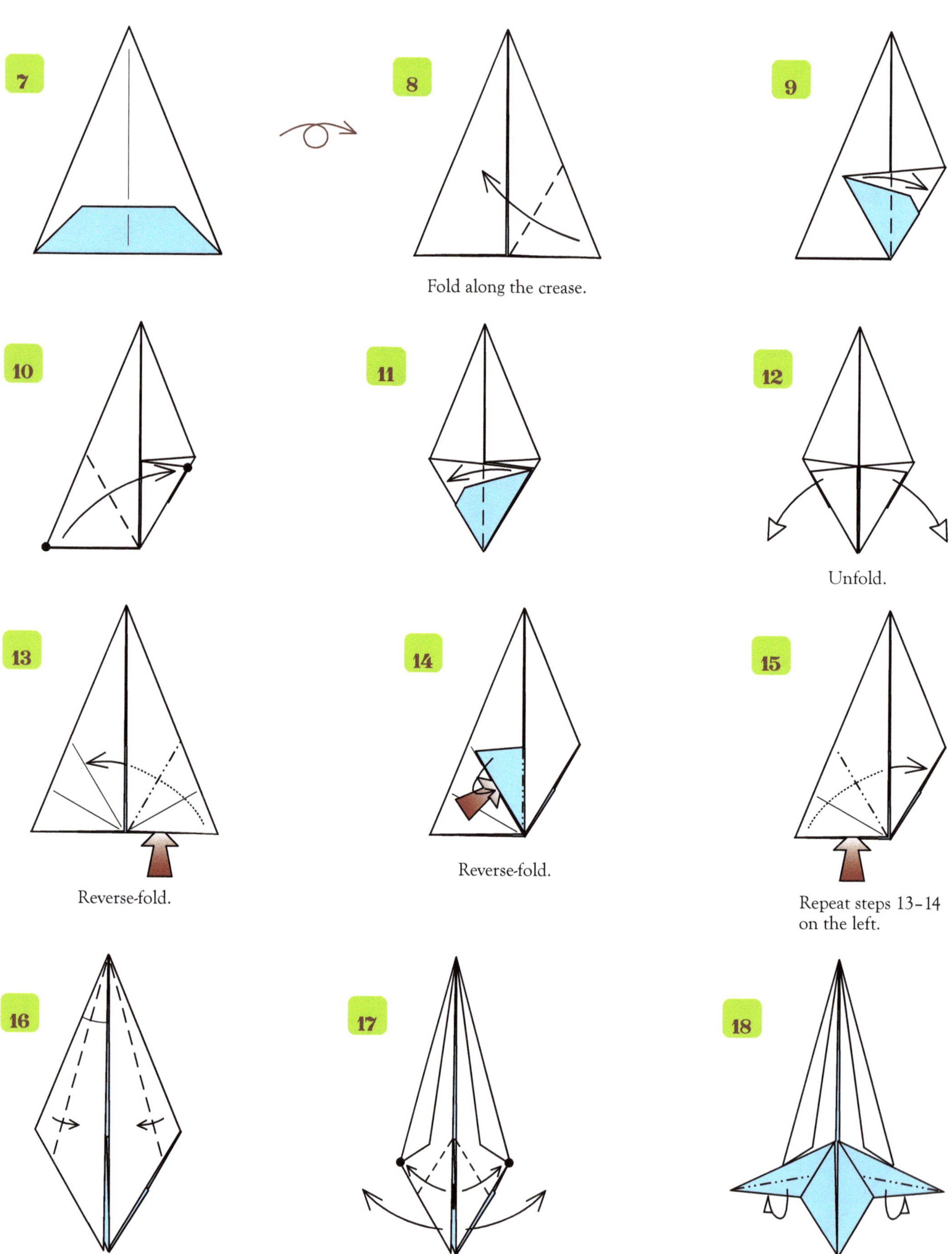

Fold along the crease.

Unfold.

Reverse-fold.

Reverse-fold.

Repeat steps 13–14 on the left.

Fold at an angle of one-third.

The edges will meet the dots.

Fold in half.

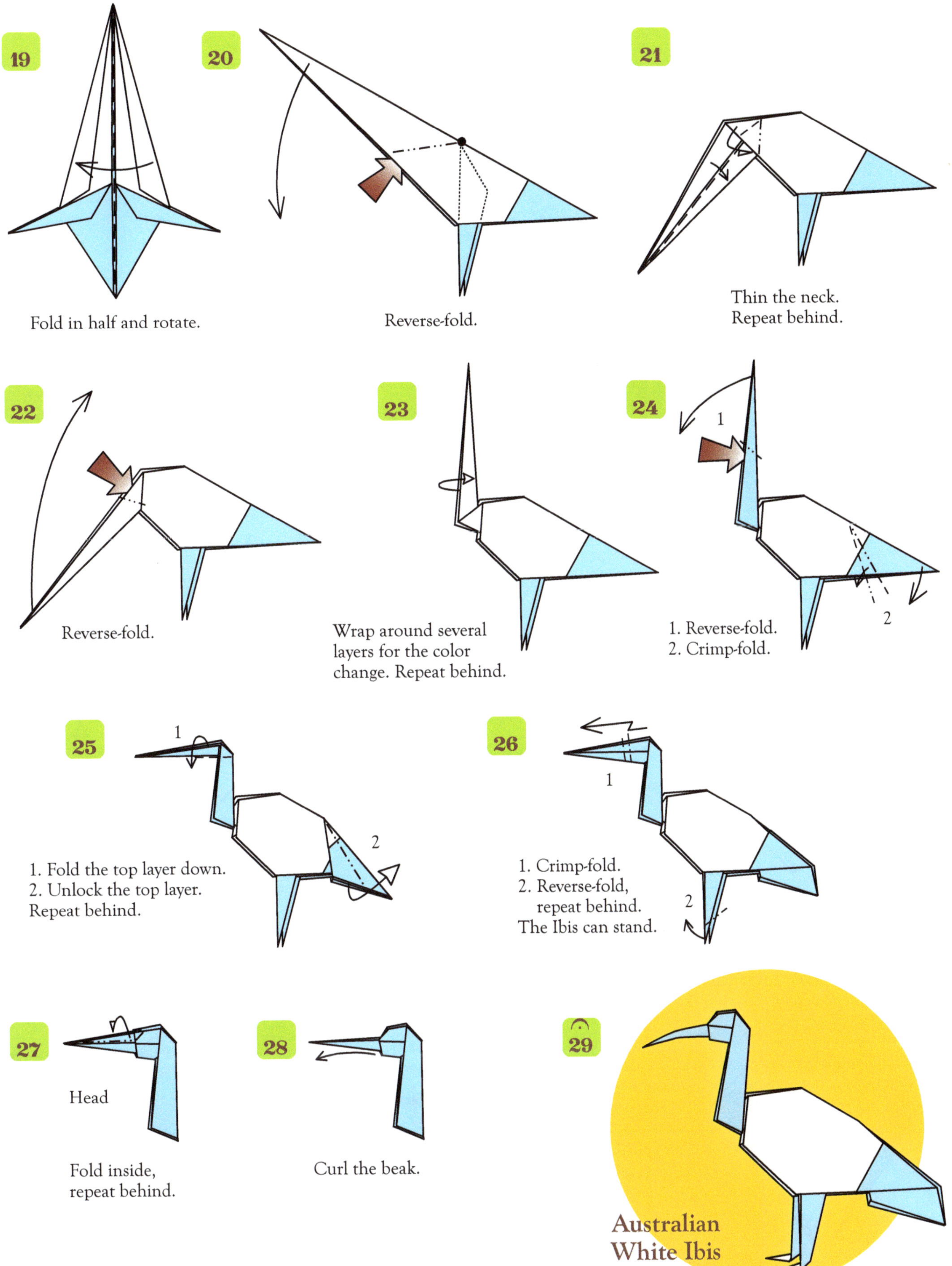
19
Fold in half and rotate.
20
Reverse-fold.
21
Thin the neck.
Repeat behind.
22
Reverse-fold.
23
Wrap around several
layers for the color
change. Repeat behind.
24
1
2
1. Reverse-fold.
2. Crimp-fold.
25
1
2
1. Fold the top layer down.
2. Unlock the top layer.
Repeat behind.
26
1
2
1. Crimp-fold.
2. Reverse-fold,
repeat behind.
The Ibis can stand.
27
Head
Fold inside,
repeat behind.
28
Curl the beak.
29
Australian
White Ibis

Emu

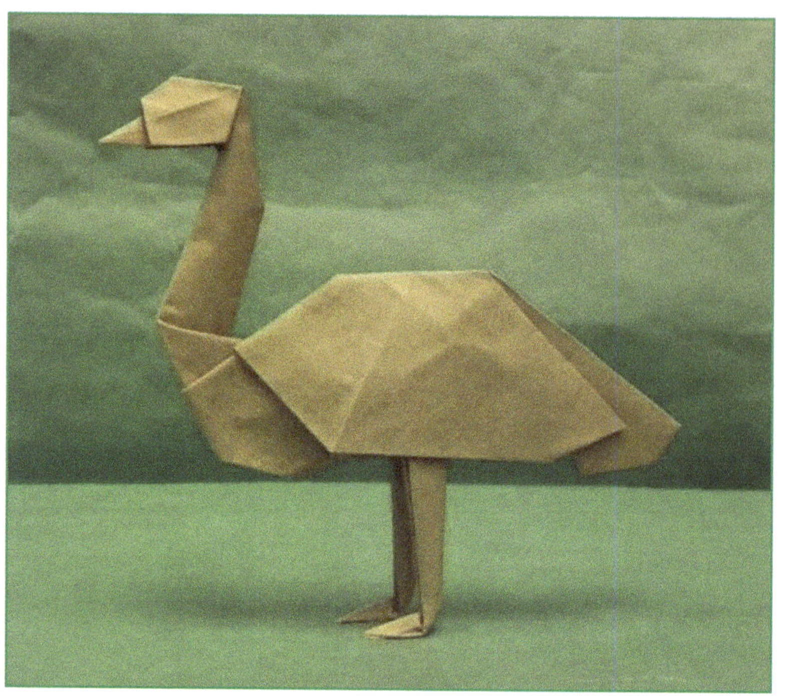

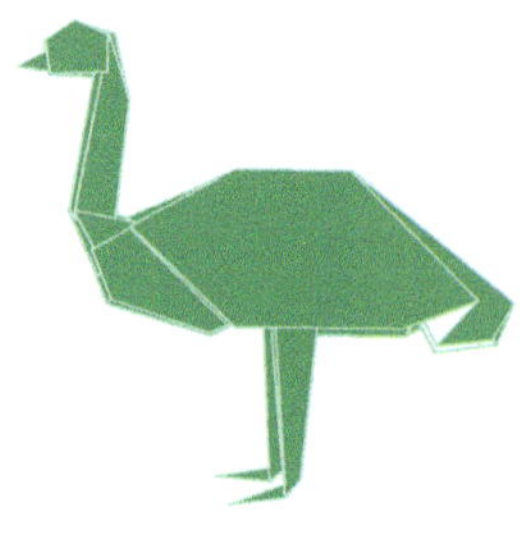

The Emu is the second tallest living bird. This flightless bird uses its wings for running at speeds up to 30 miles per hour. It feeds on plants and insects. It will also swallow small stones to aid in digestion. Emus travel in groups, in search of food.

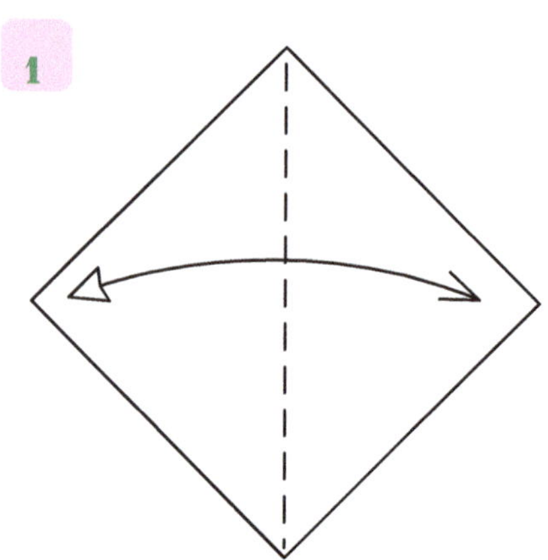

Fold and unfold.

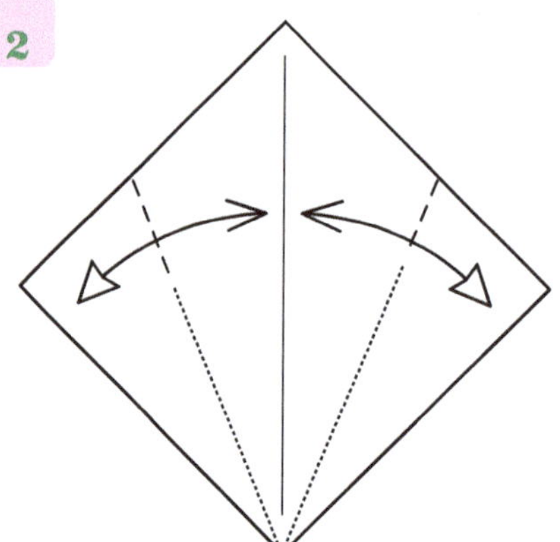

Fold to the center and unfold. Crease at the top.

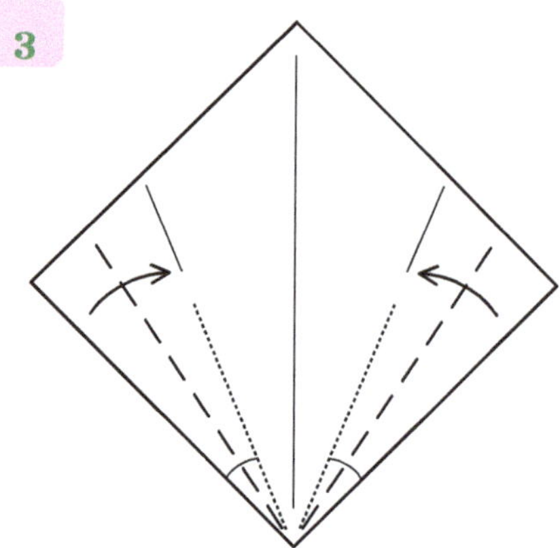

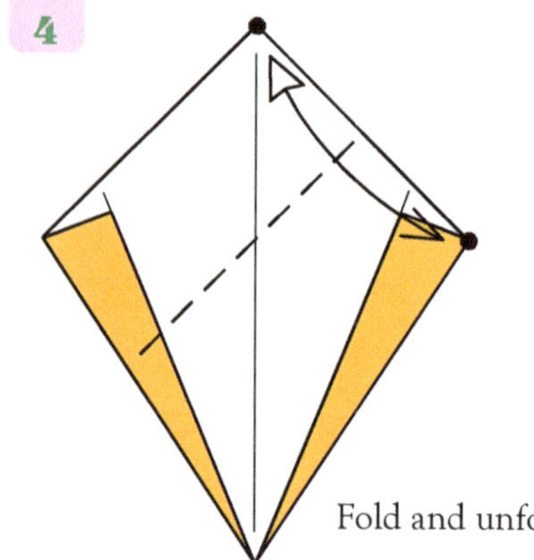

Fold and unfold.

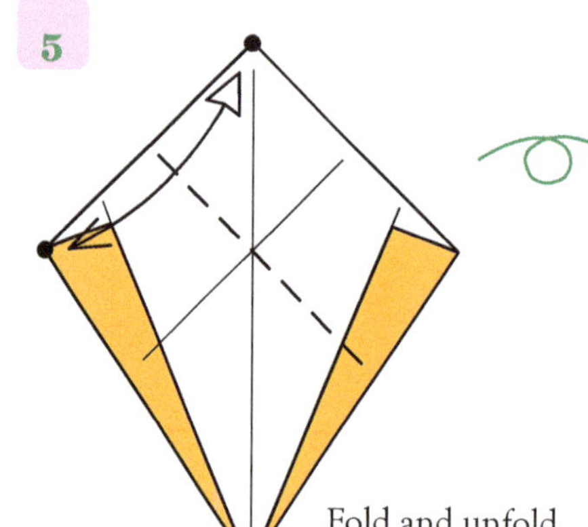

Fold and unfold.

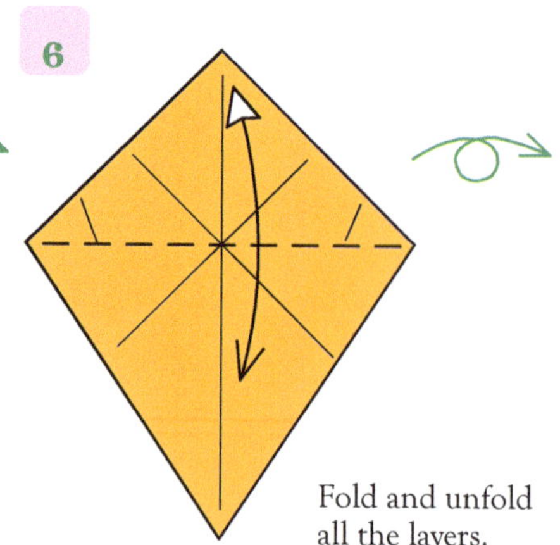

Fold and unfold all the layers.

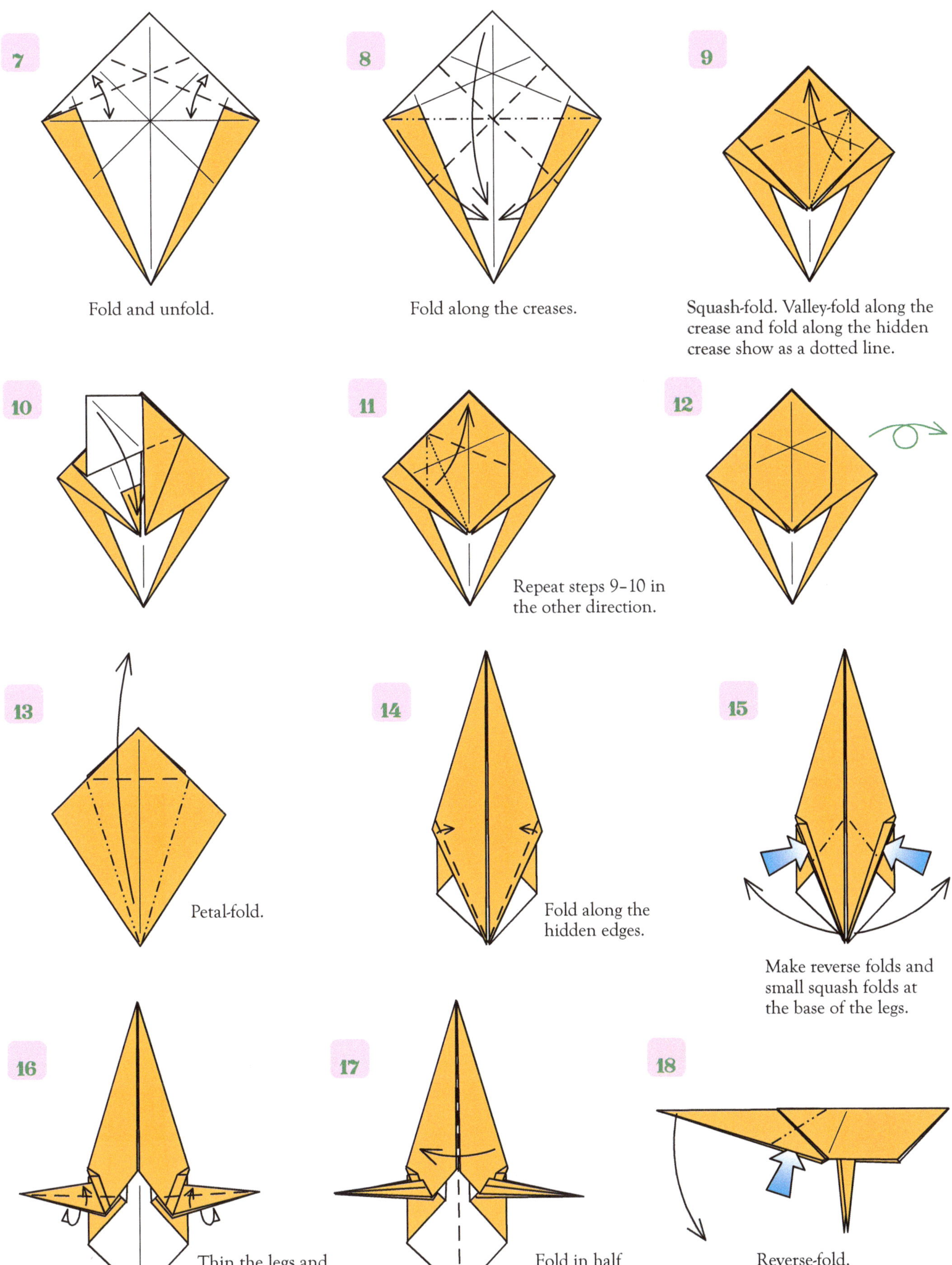
7
Fold and unfold.
8
Fold along the creases.
9
Squash-fold. Valley-fold along the crease and fold along the hidden crease show as a dotted line.
10
11
Repeat steps 9–10 in the other direction.
12
13
Petal-fold.
14
Fold along the hidden edges.
15
Make reverse folds and small squash folds at the base of the legs.
16
Thin the legs and repeat behind.
17
Fold in half and rotate.
18
Reverse-fold.

19

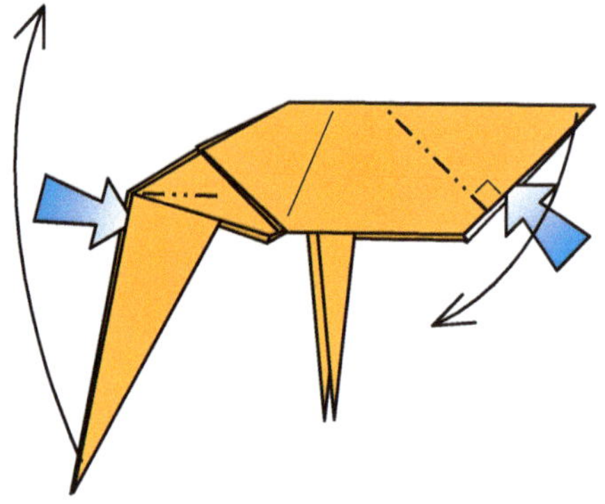

Make reverse folds.

20

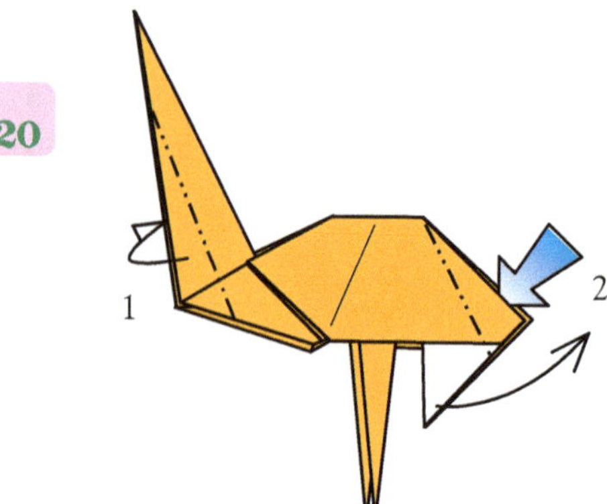

1. Fold inside, repeat behind.
2. Reverse-fold.

21

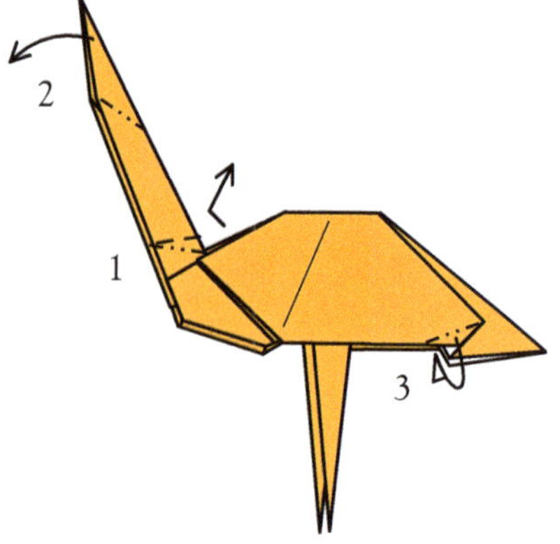

1. Crimp-fold.
2. Reverse-fold.
3. Fold inside, repeat behind.

22

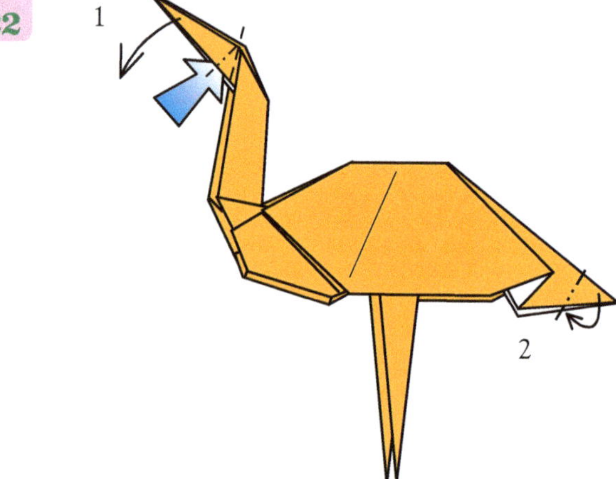

1. Crimp-fold and spread the head.
2. Reverse-fold.

23

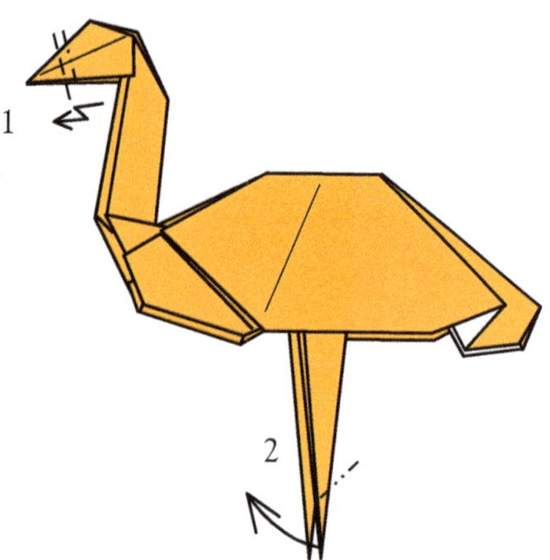

1. Crimp-fold.
2. Reverse-fold, repeat behind.
The Emu can stand.

24

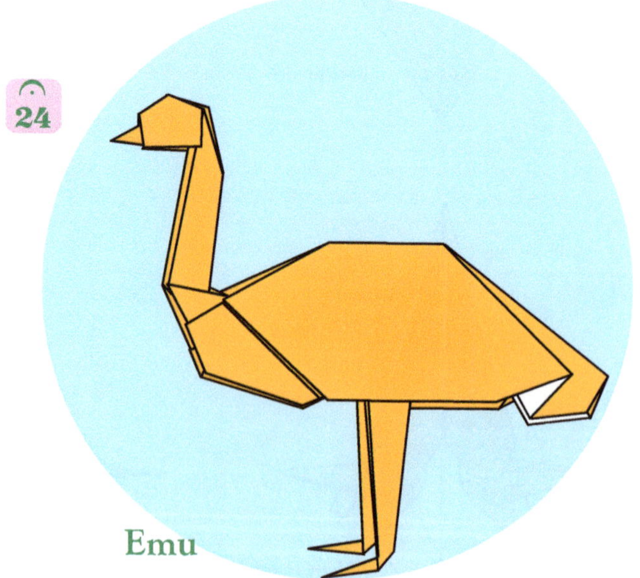

Emu

Australian Pelican

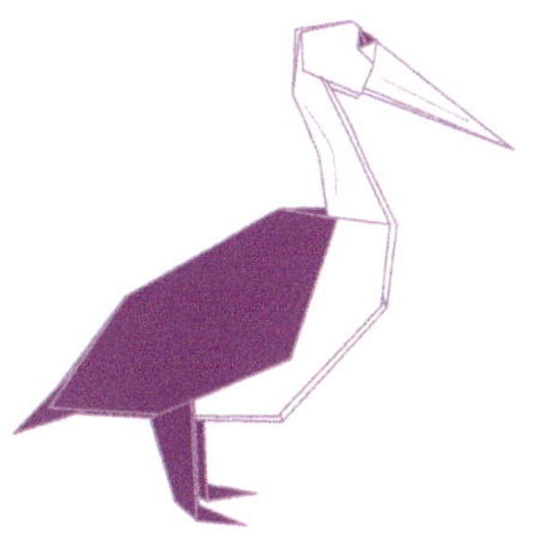

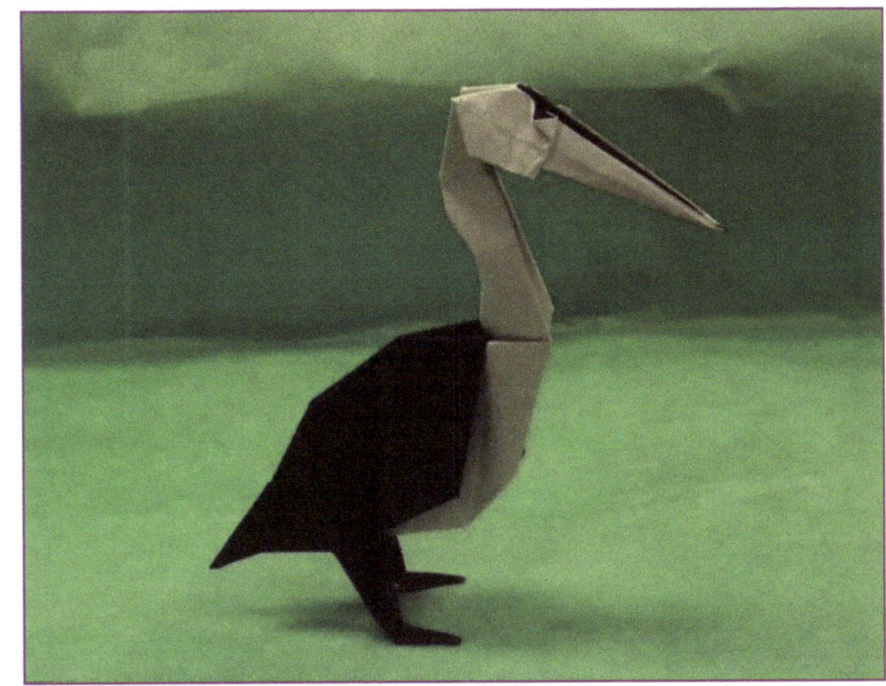

The Australian Pelican's pink bill is known to be the largest bill of any bird. This white bird has black wings. They feed on fish, insects, crustaceans, and occasionally other birds.

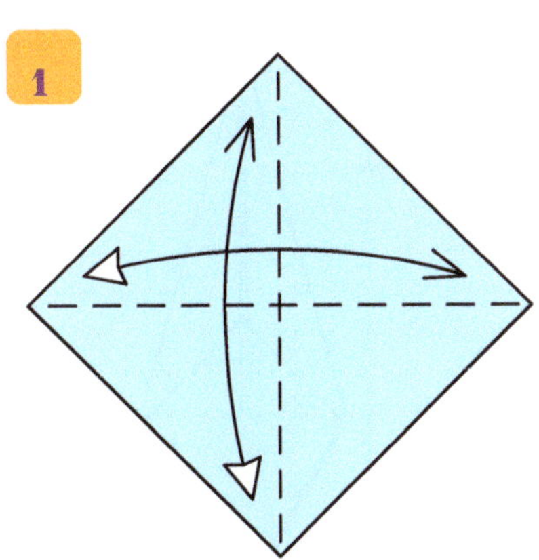

Fold and unfold.

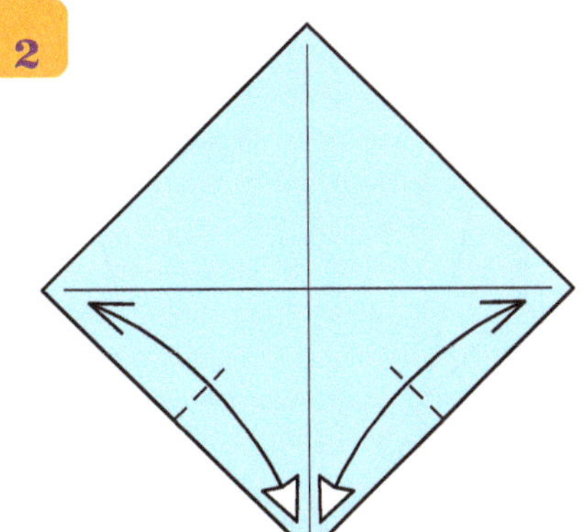

Fold and unfold on the edge.

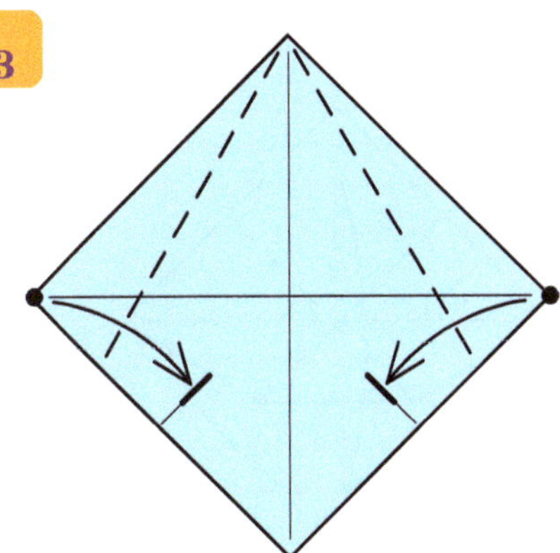

Bring the corners to the lines.

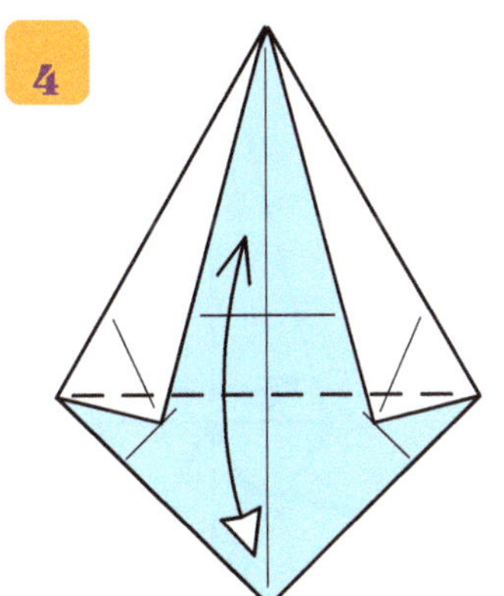

Fold and unfold.

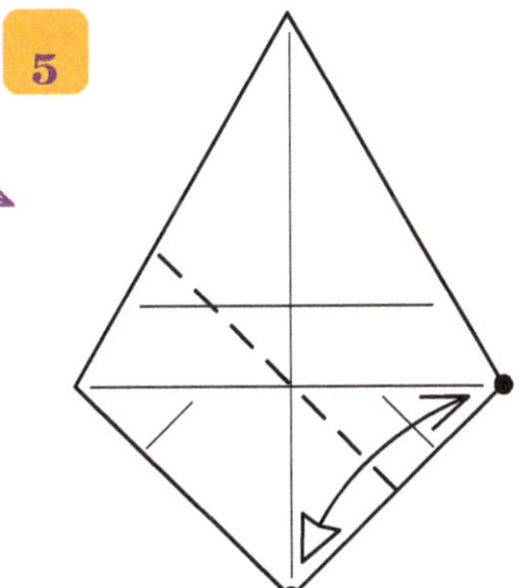

Fold and unfold.

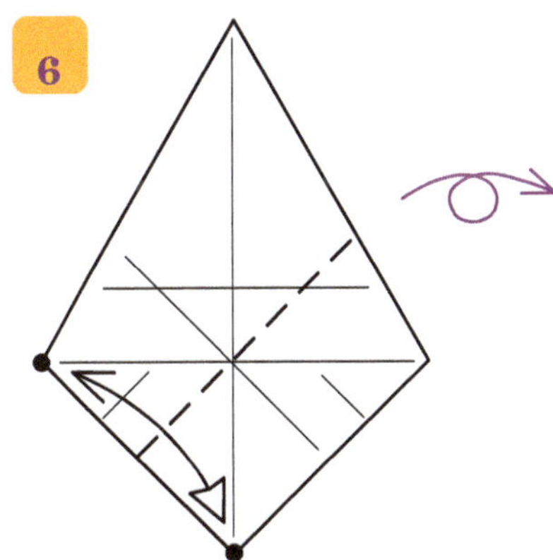

Fold and unfold.

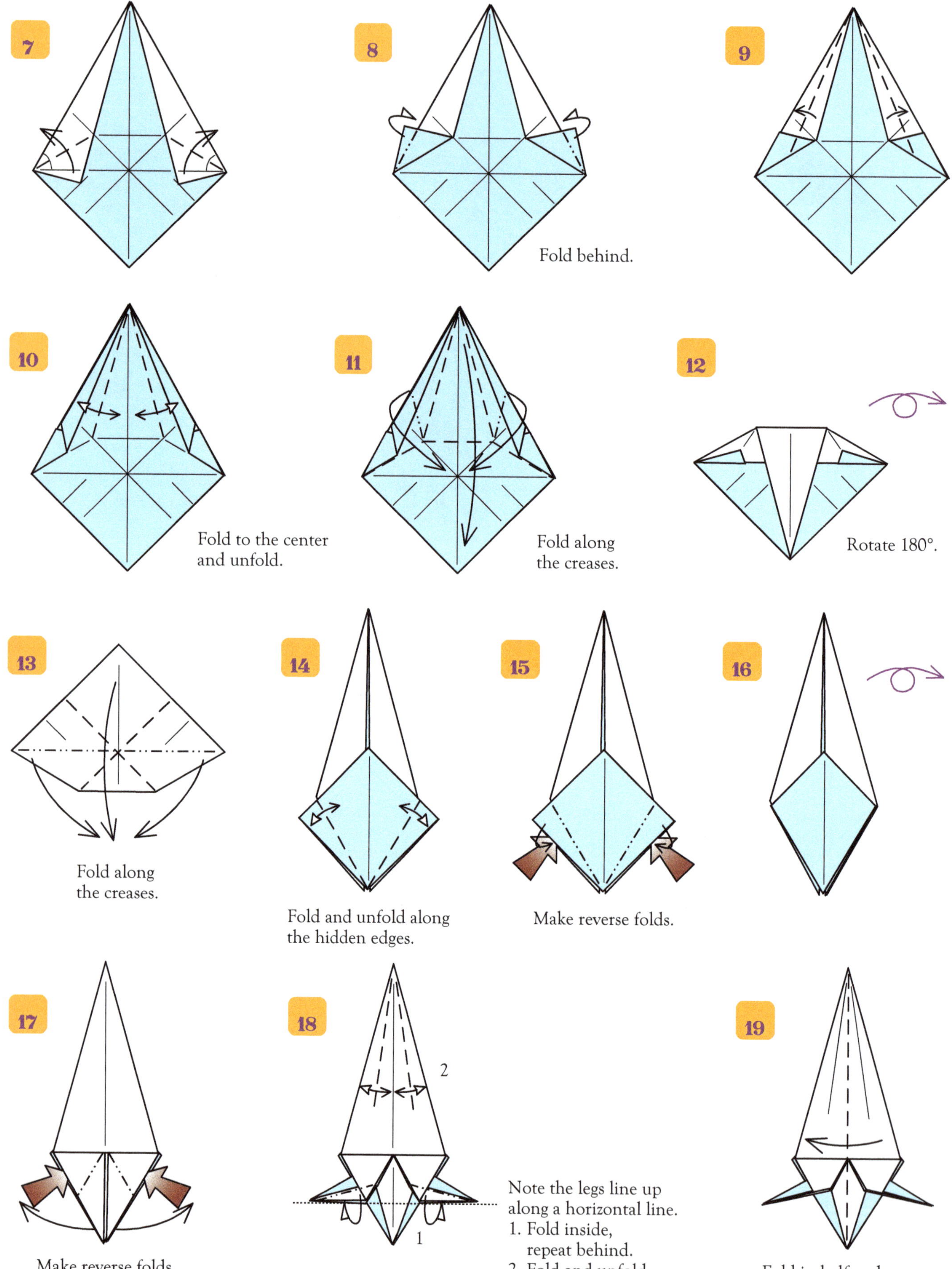
7
8
9
Fold behind.
10
Fold to the center
and unfold.
11
Fold along
the creases.
12
Rotate 180°.
13
Fold along
the creases.
14
Fold and unfold along
the hidden edges.
15
Make reverse folds.
16
17
Make reverse folds.
18
2
1
Note the legs line up
along a horizontal line.
1. Fold inside,
repeat behind.
2. Fold and unfold.
19
Fold in half and rotate.

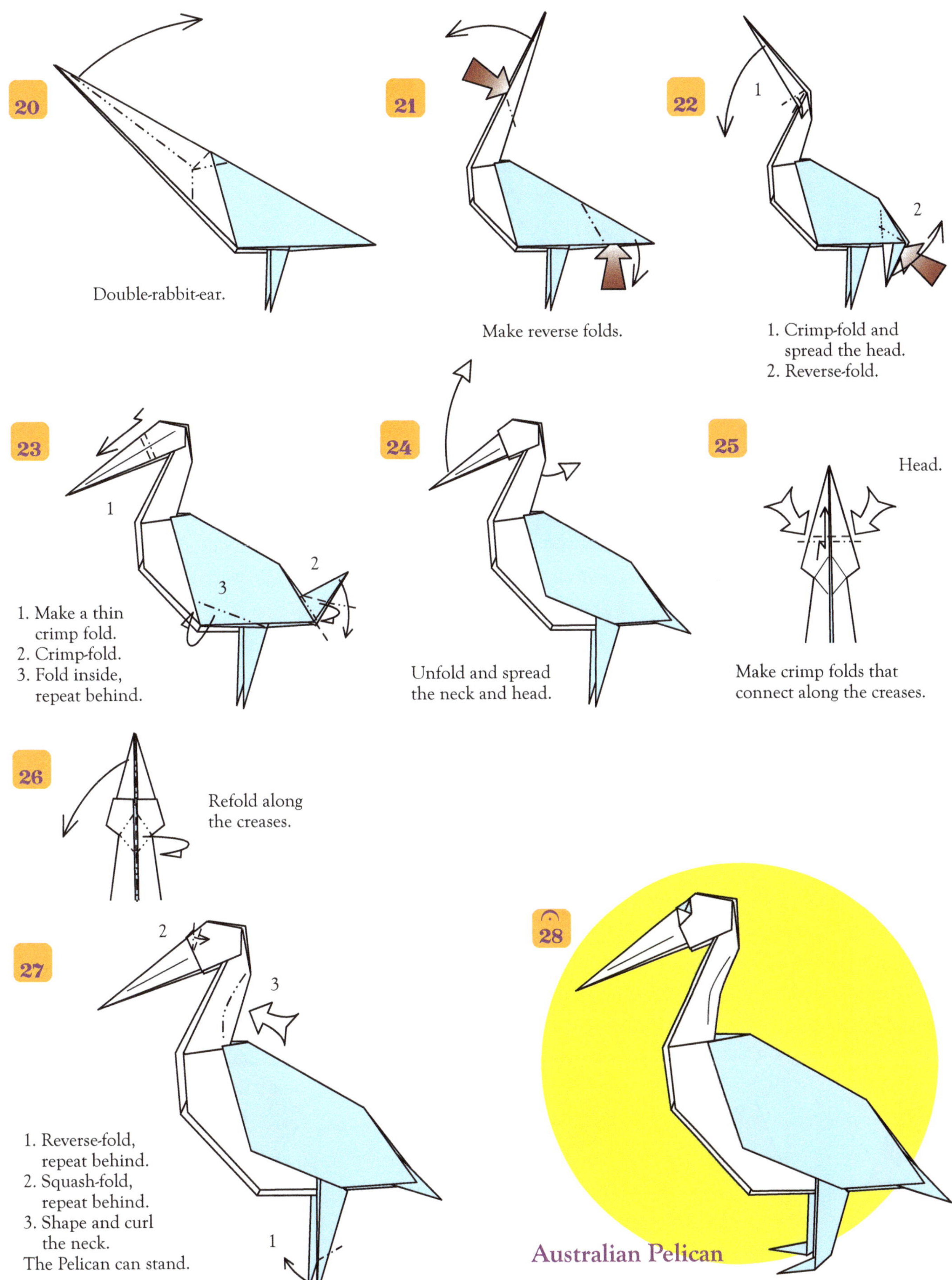
20
Double-rabbit-ear.
21
Make reverse folds.
22
1
2
1. Crimp-fold and
spread the head.
2. Reverse-fold.
23
1
2
3
1. Make a thin
crimp fold.
2. Crimp-fold.
3. Fold inside,
repeat behind.
24
Unfold and spread
the neck and head.
25
Head.
Make crimp folds that
connect along the creases.
26
Refold along
the creases.
27
2
3
1
1. Reverse-fold,
repeat behind.
2. Squash-fold,
repeat behind.
3. Shape and curl
the neck.
The Pelican can stand.
28
Australian Pelican

Red-necked Avocet

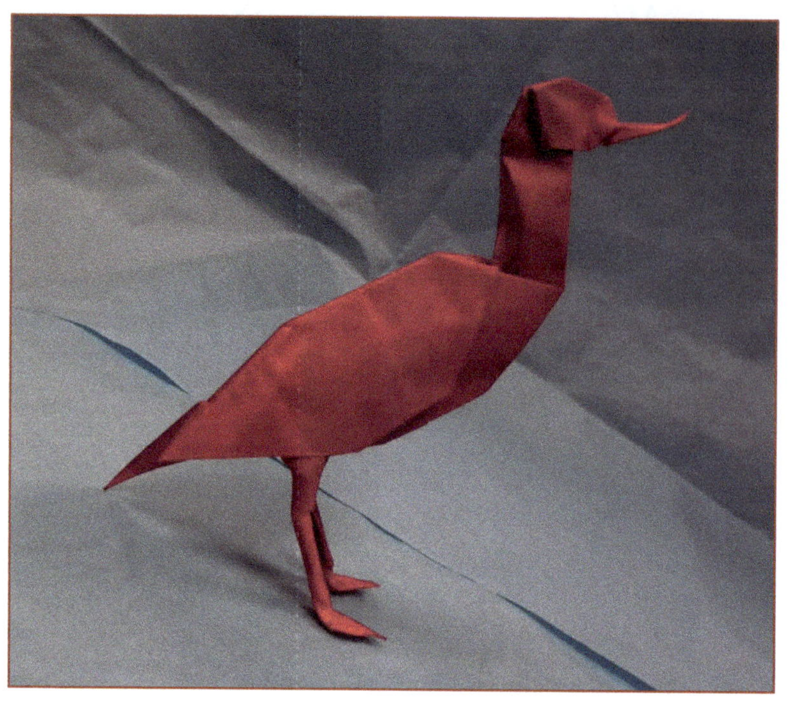

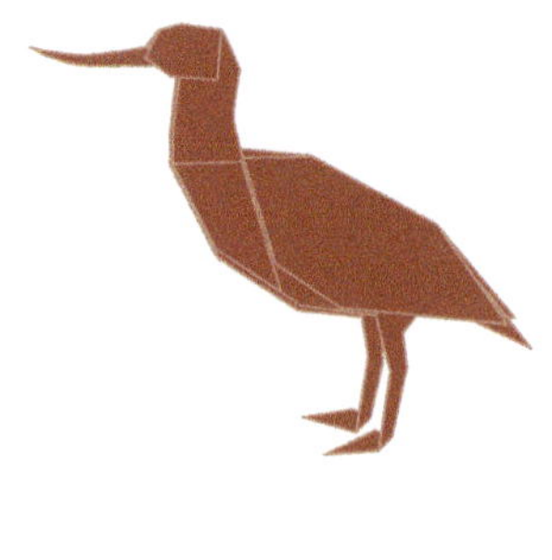

While swimming, the Red-necked Avocet uses its curved bill at the water's surface to scoop up aquatic bugs and crustaceans. It spends much of its time in shallow water but can swim in deeper water. These Avocets can gather at large nesting colonies.

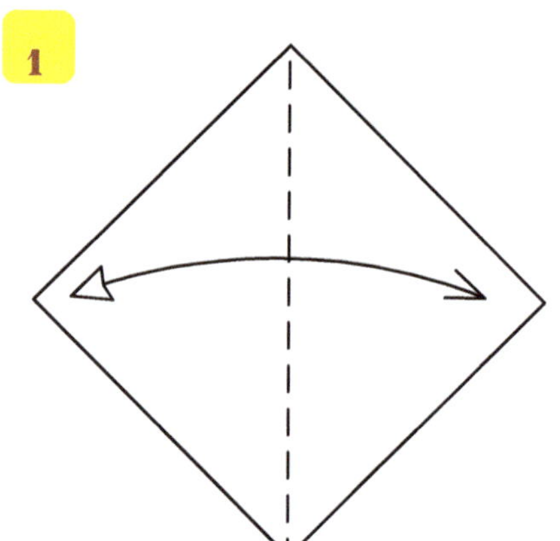

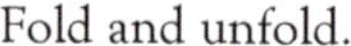

Fold and unfold.

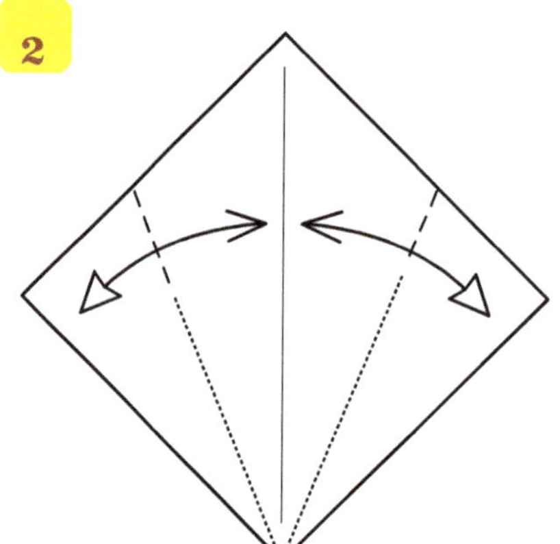

Fold to the center and unfold. Crease at the top.

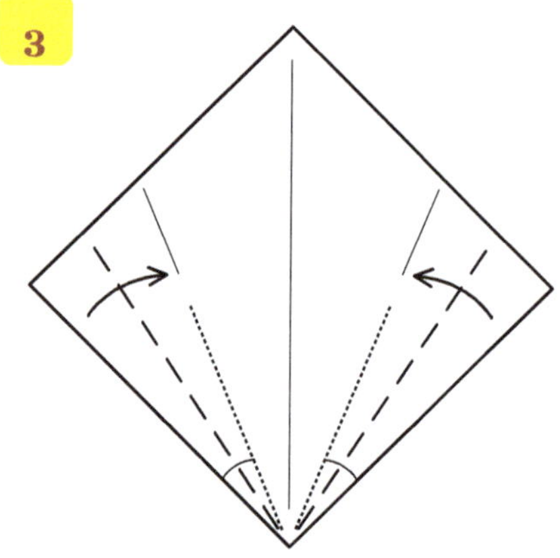

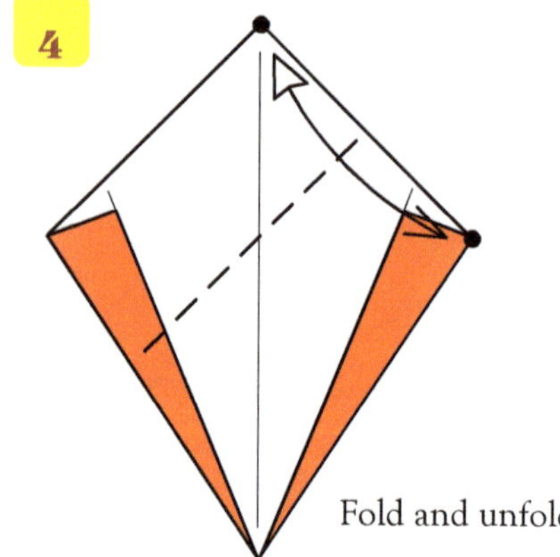

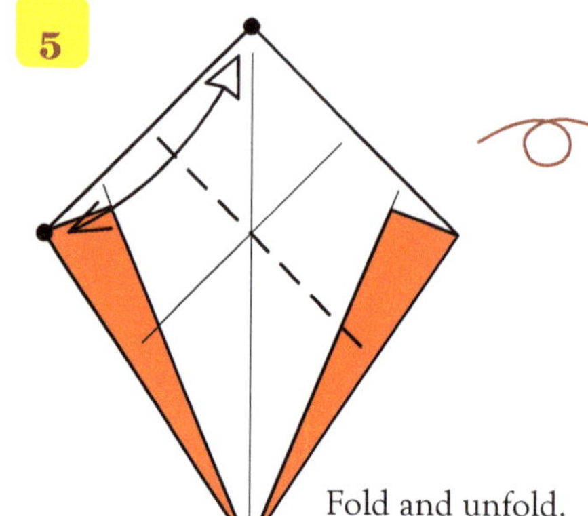

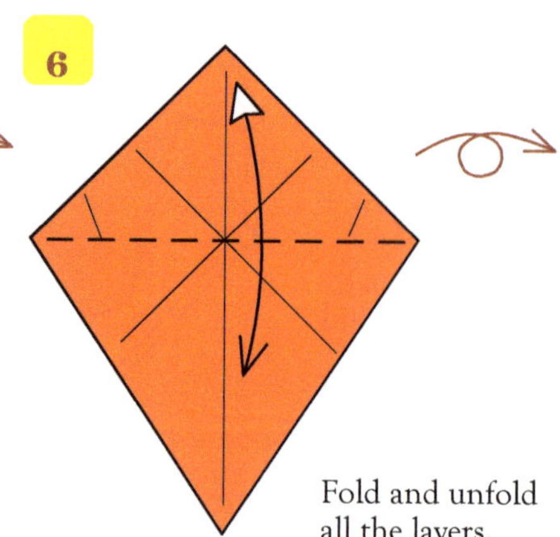

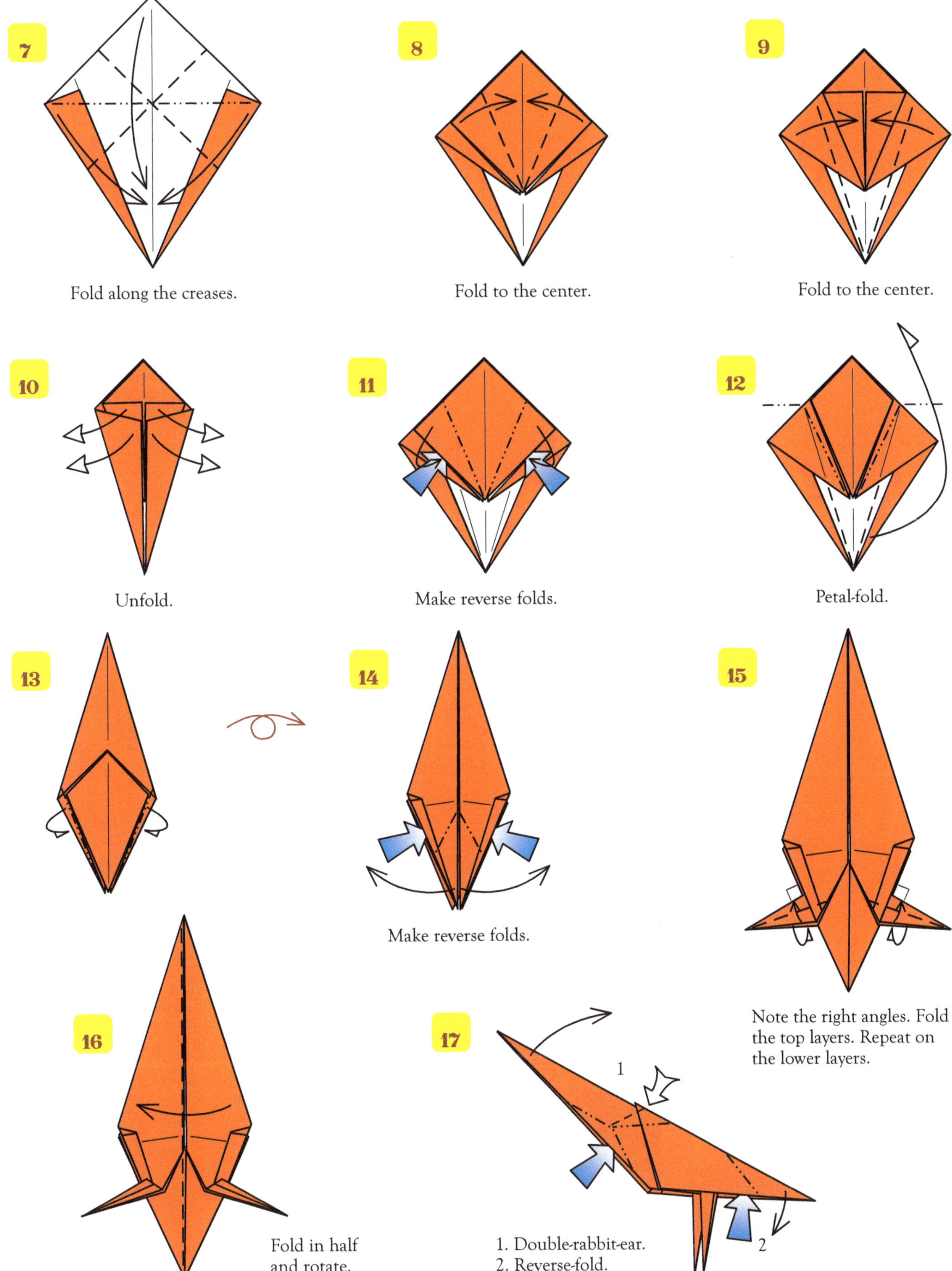
7
Fold along the creases.
8
Fold to the center.
9
Fold to the center.
10
Unfold.
11
Make reverse folds.
12
Petal-fold.
13
14
Make reverse folds.
15
Note the right angles. Fold the top layers. Repeat on the lower layers.
16
Fold in half and rotate.
17
1
2
1. Double-rabbit-ear.
2. Reverse-fold.

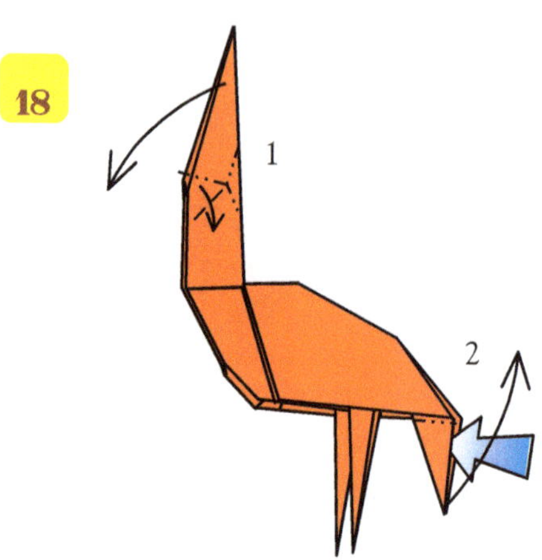

1. Push in on the right and make a crimp fold.
3. Reverse-fold.

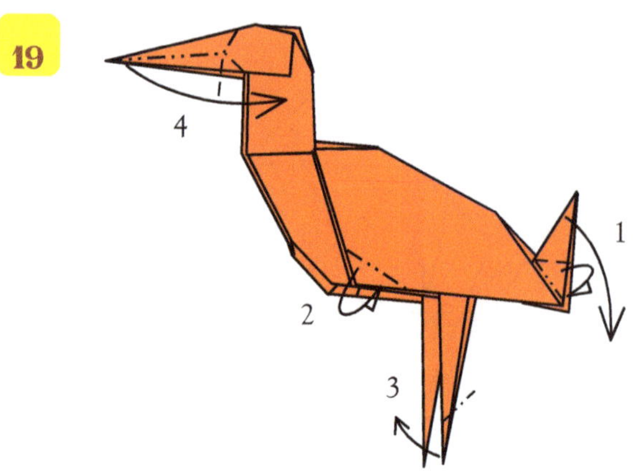

1. Crimp-fold.
2. Fold inside, repeat behind.
3. Reverse-fold and spread the foot, repeat behind.
4. Double-rabbit-ear.

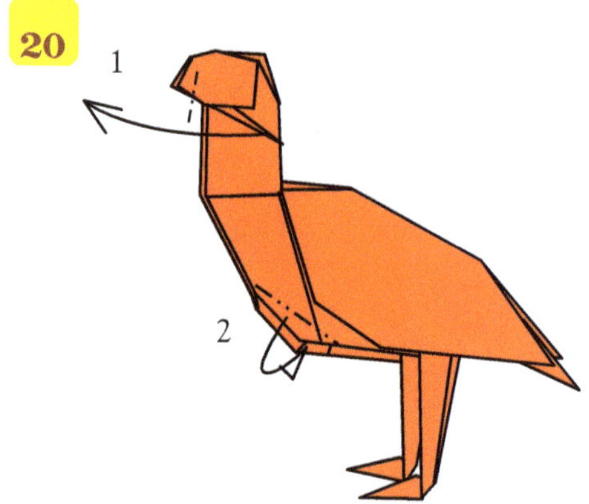

1. Reverse-fold. It is easier to form the beak from steps 19 and 20 in one step.
2. Fold inside, repeat behind.

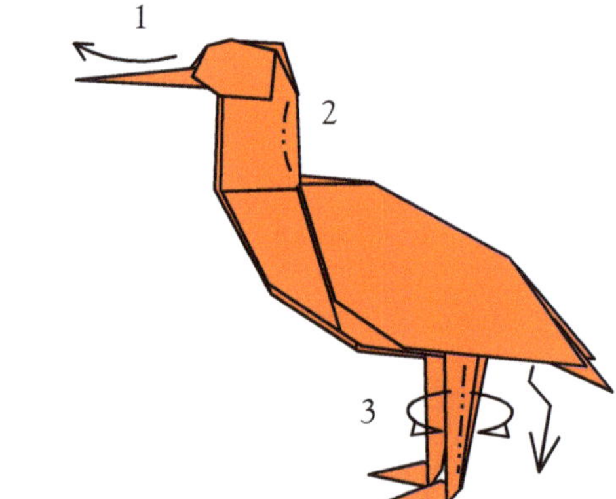

1. Curl the beak upward.
2. Shape the neck.
3. Thin and shape the legs, repeat behind.

The Avocet can stand.

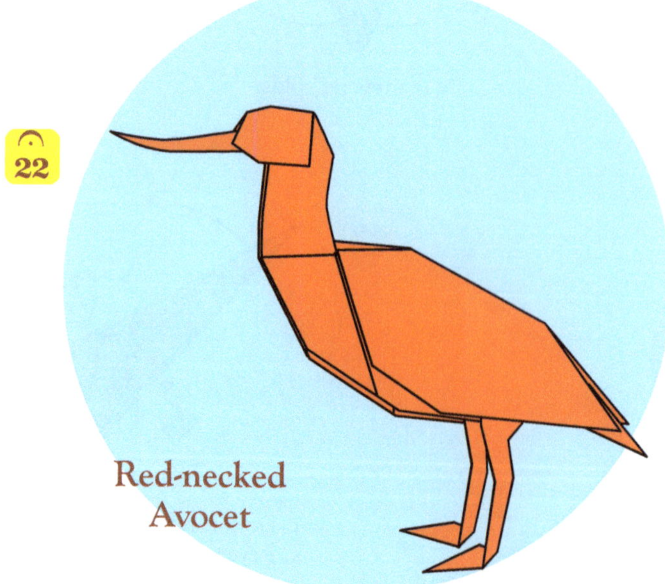

Collared Sparrowhawk

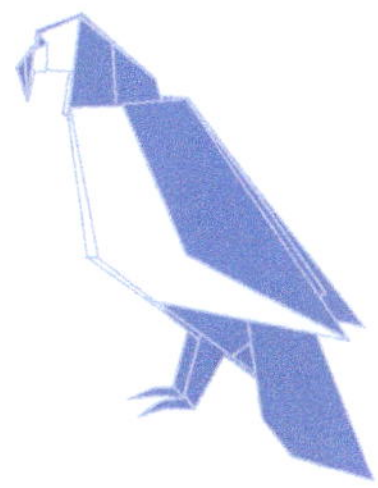

The Collared Sparrowhawk can be found throughout mainland Australia. This small bird of prey dines on insects, small mammals, and small birds. Hiding in trees, they use stealth to surprise and catch their prey in flight.

1

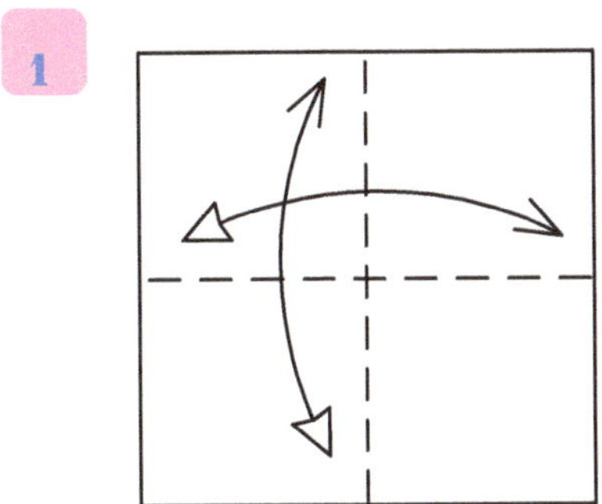

Fold and unfold.

2

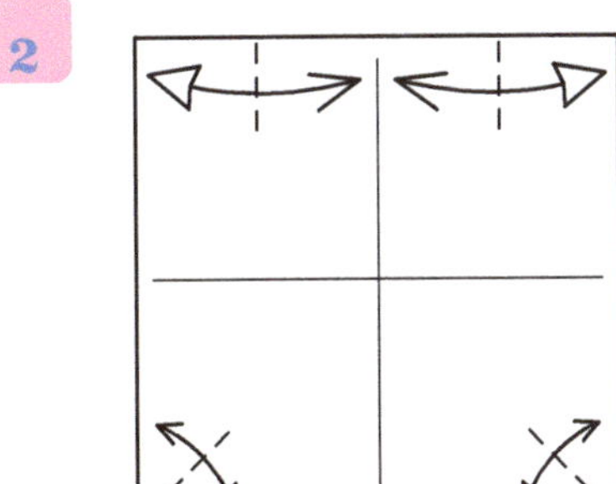

Fold and unfold.

3

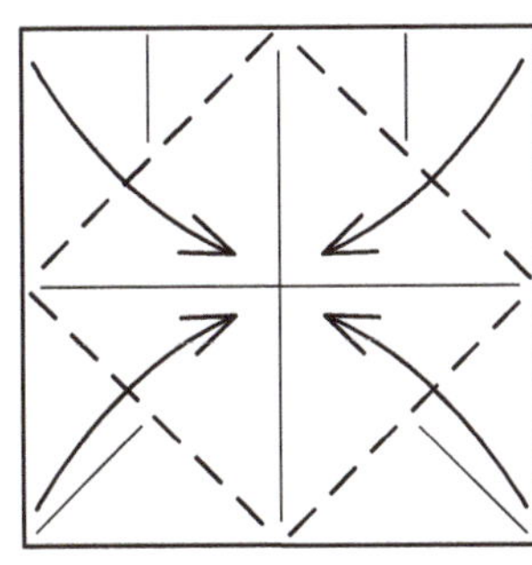

Fold to the center.

4

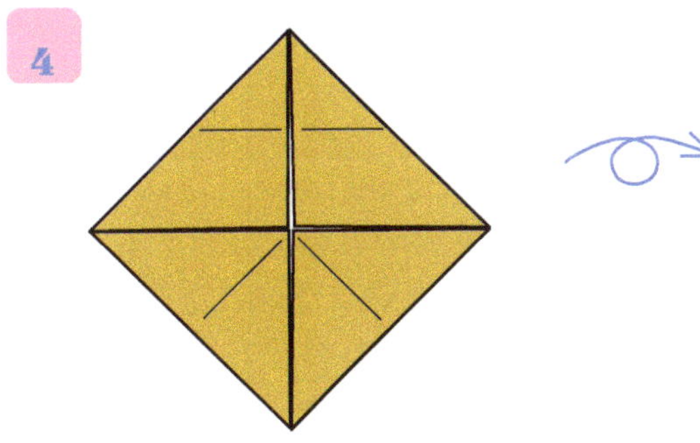

5

Fold to the center and swing out from behind. Do not crease at the top.

6

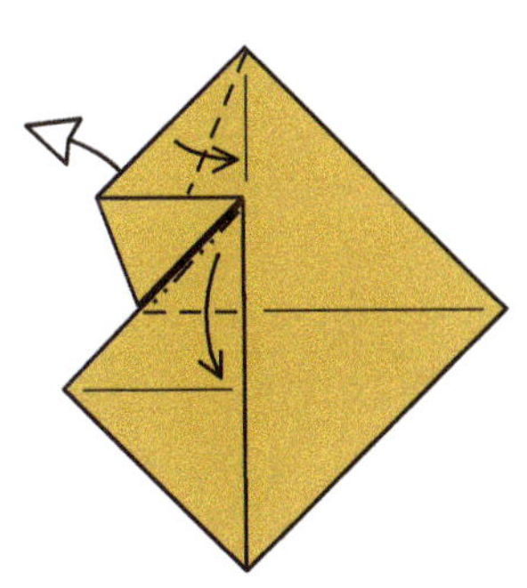

Squash-fold and swing out from behind.

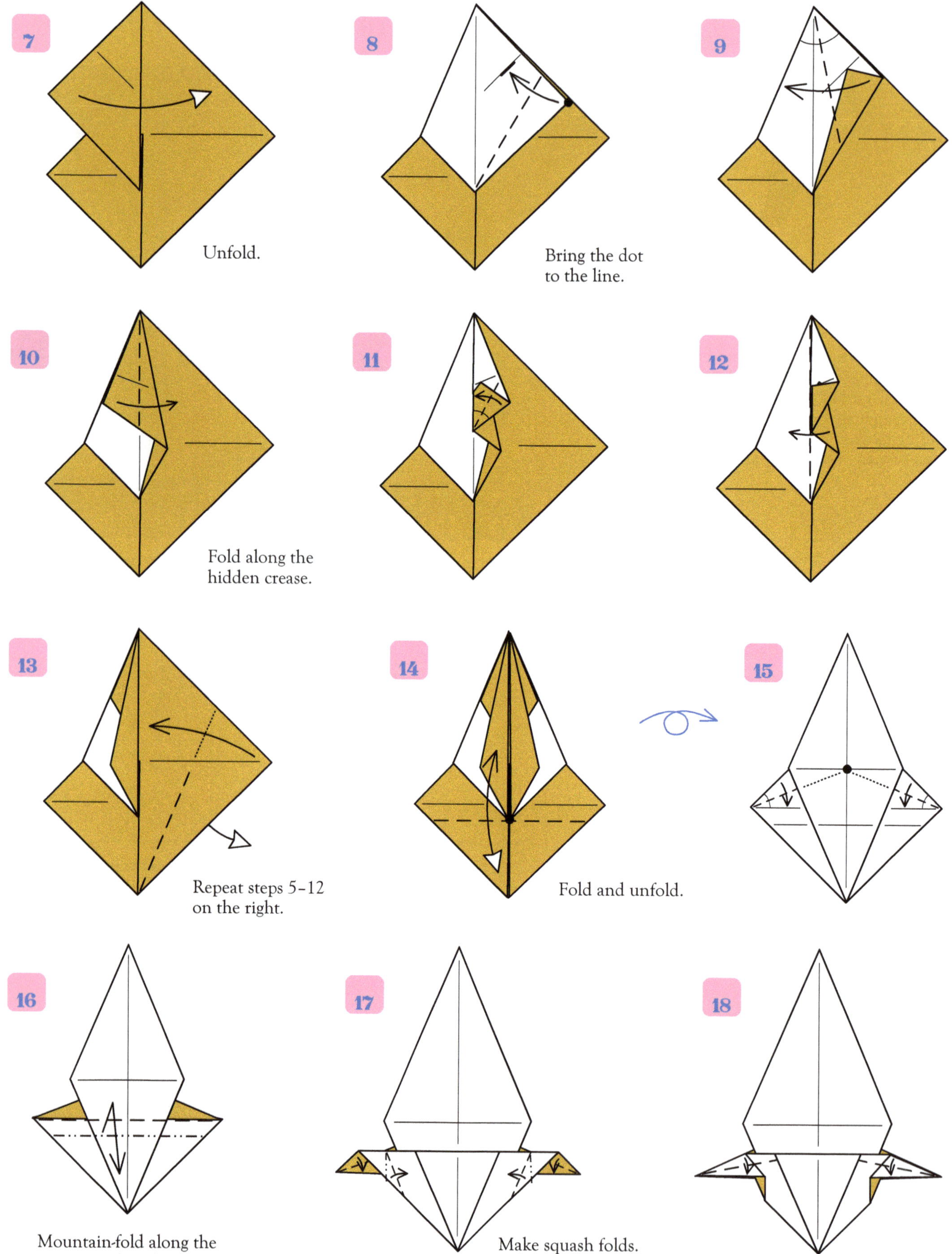
7
Unfold.
8
Bring the dot
to the line.
9
10
Fold along the
hidden crease.
11
12
13
Repeat steps 5–12
on the right.
14
Fold and unfold.
15
16
Mountain-fold along the
crease for this pleat fold.
17
Make squash folds.
18

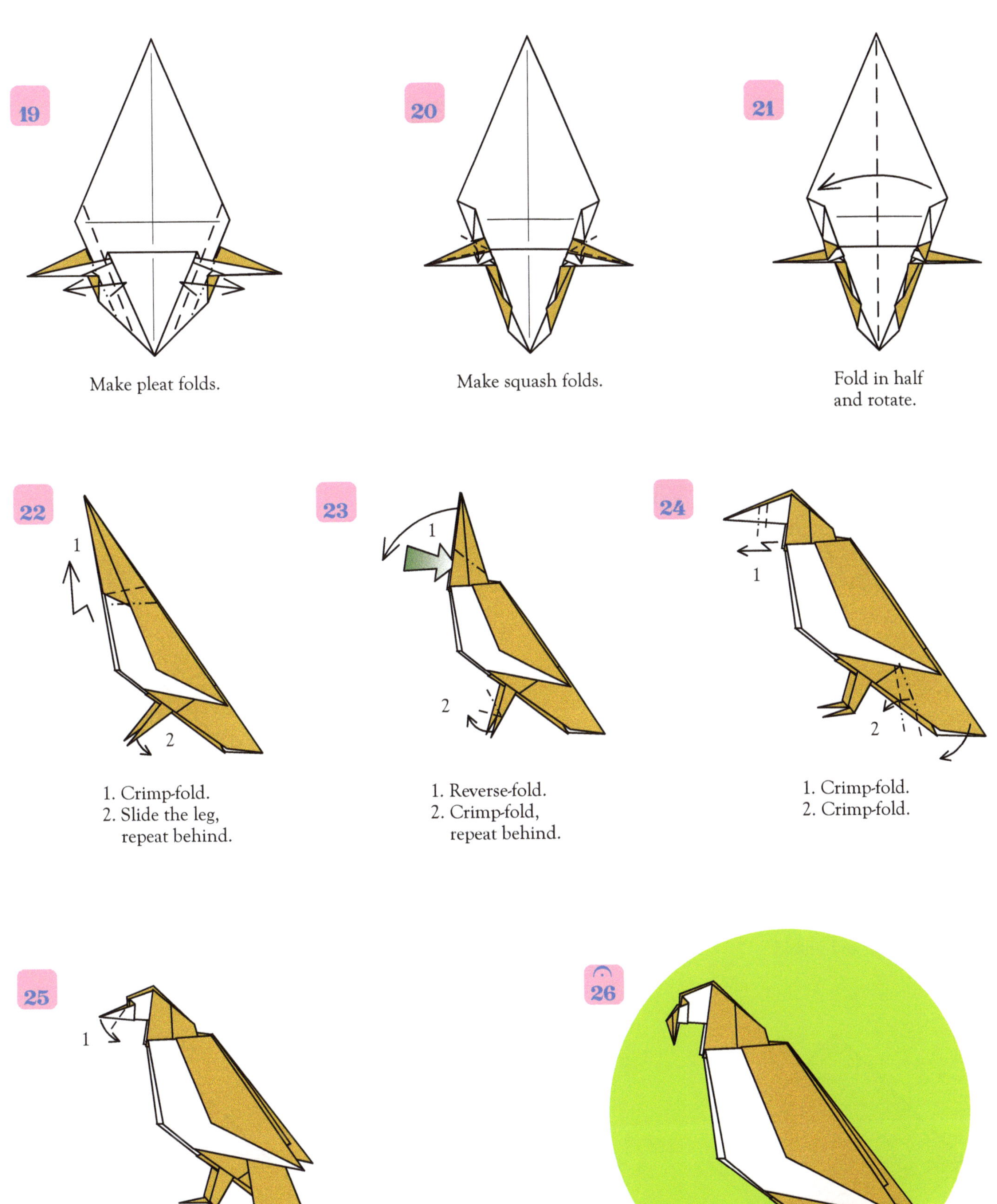

19 Make pleat folds.

20 Make squash folds.

21 Fold in half and rotate.

22
1. Crimp-fold.
2. Slide the leg, repeat behind.

23
1. Reverse-fold.
2. Crimp-fold, repeat behind.

24
1. Crimp-fold.
2. Crimp-fold.

25
1. Oustide-reverse-fold.
2. Curl the feet, repeat behind.

26

Collared Sparrowhawk

Great Cormorant

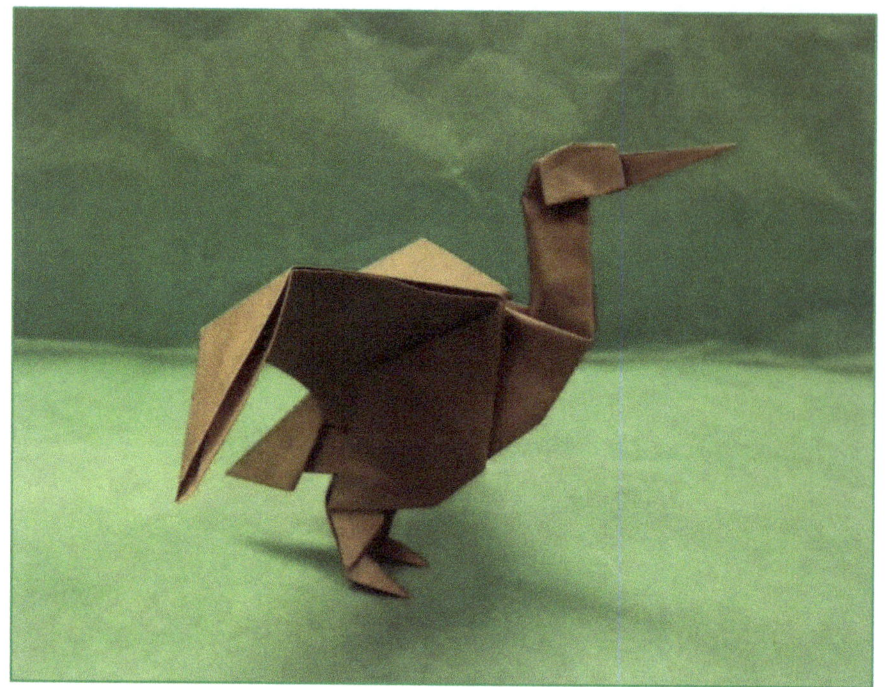

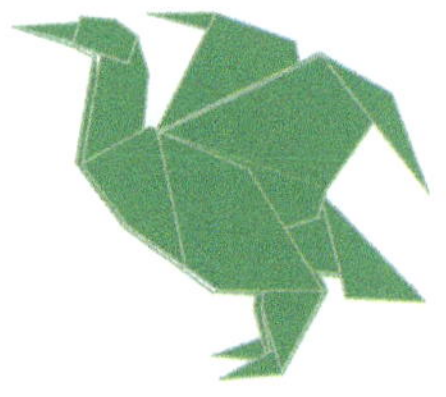

In Australia, the Great Cormorant is a large black bird that lives by the water. It dives deep into the water to catch fish with its beak. To stay warm and dry, it stands on rocks with wings outstretched. These social birds form large colonies for breeding.

1

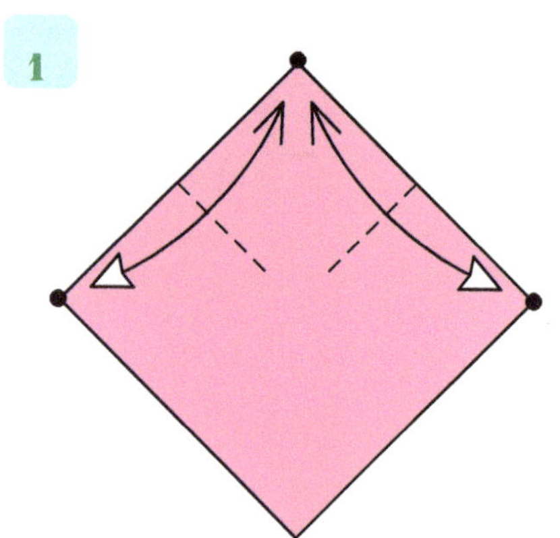

Fold and unfold.

2

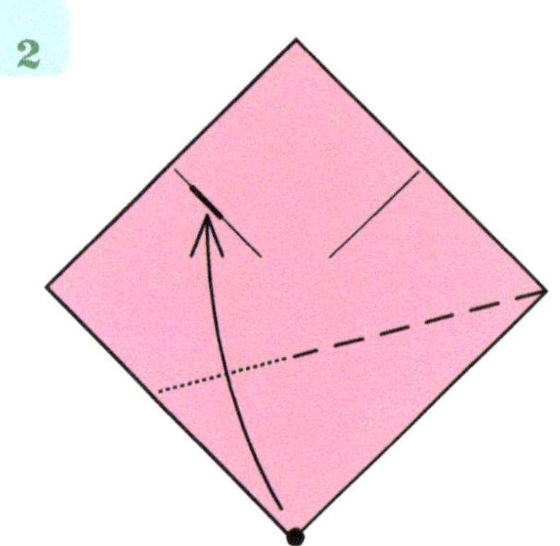

Bring the dot to the line.

3

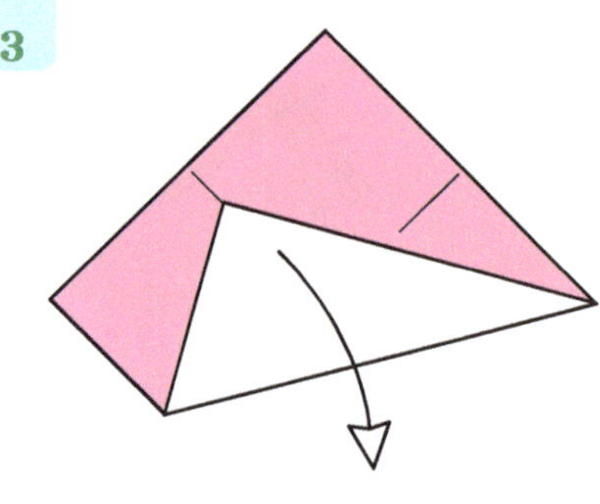

Unfold.

4

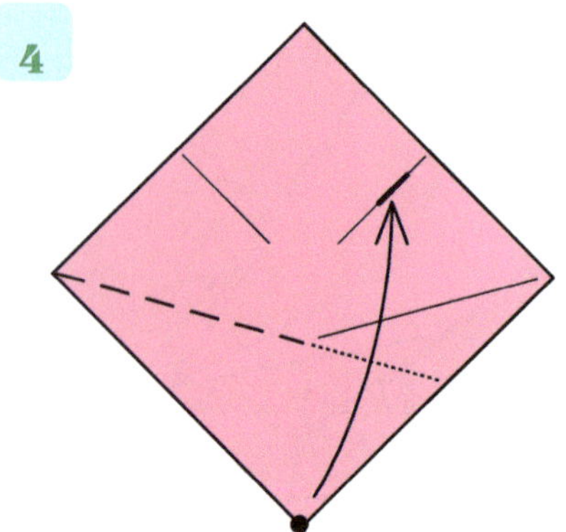

Repeat steps 2–3 in the opposite direction.

5

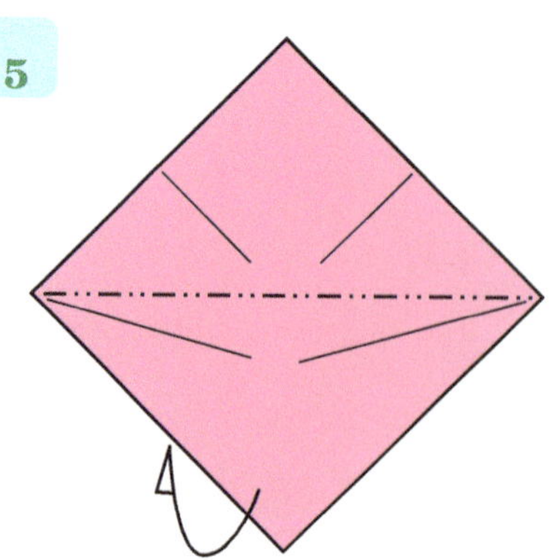

6

Fold along the creases.

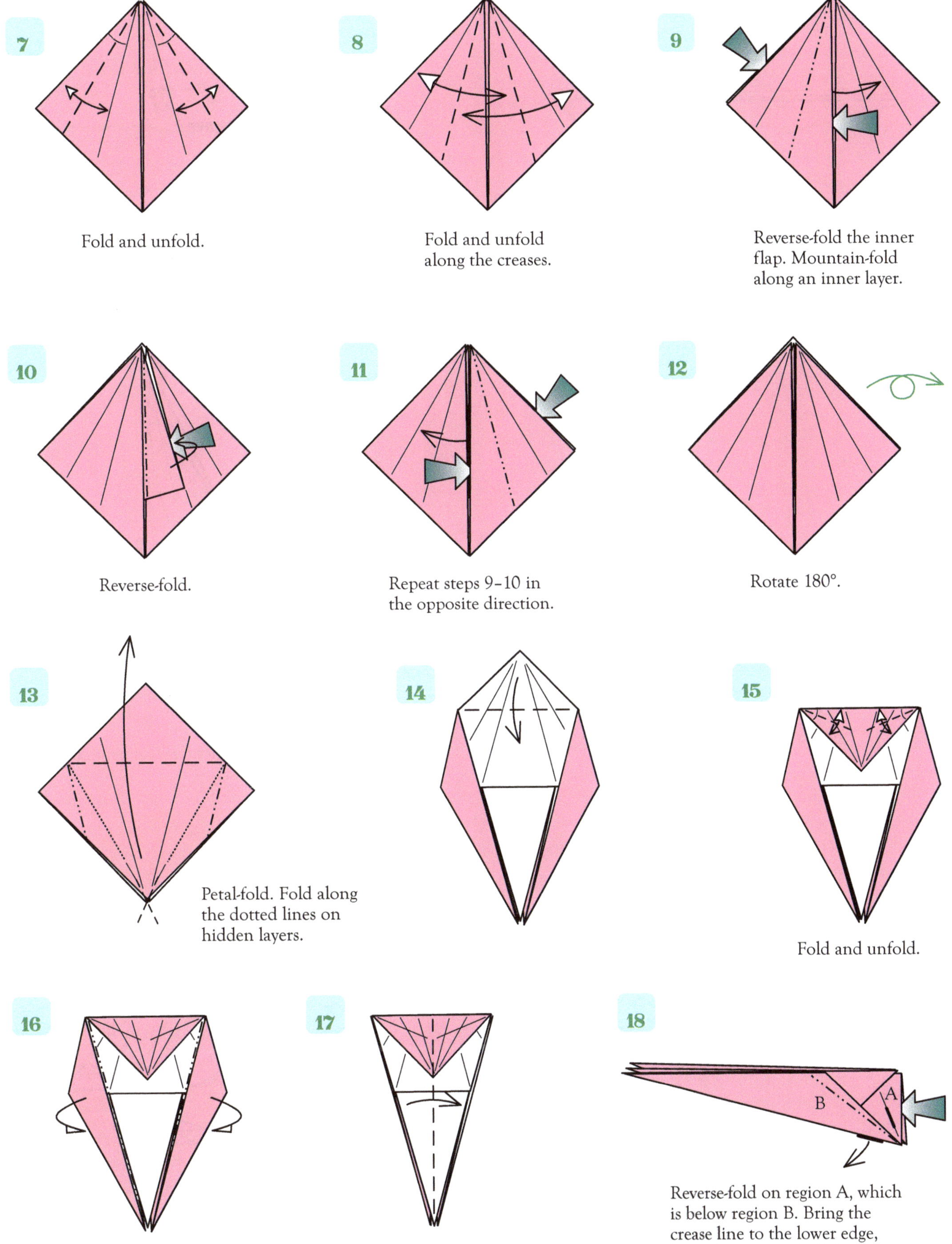
7
Fold and unfold.
8
Fold and unfold
along the creases.
9
Reverse-fold the inner
flap. Mountain-fold
along an inner layer.
10
Reverse-fold.
11
Repeat steps 9–10 in
the opposite direction.
12
Rotate 180°.
13
Petal-fold. Fold along
the dotted lines on
hidden layers.
14
15
Fold and unfold.
16
17
Fold in half and rotate.
18
B
A
Reverse-fold on region A, which
is below region B. Bring the
crease line to the lower edge,
both shown with bold lines.

19

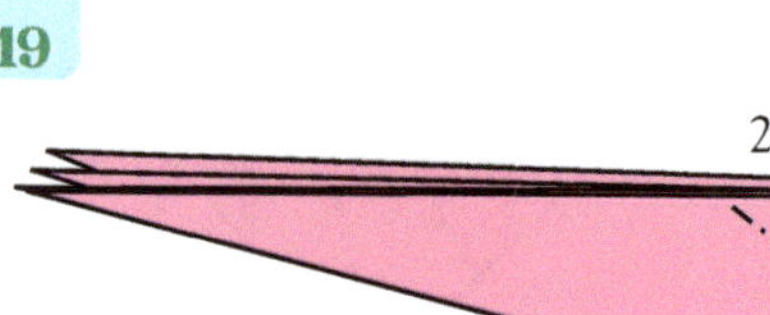

1. Reverse-fold.
2. Fold along a hidden edge, repeat behind.

20

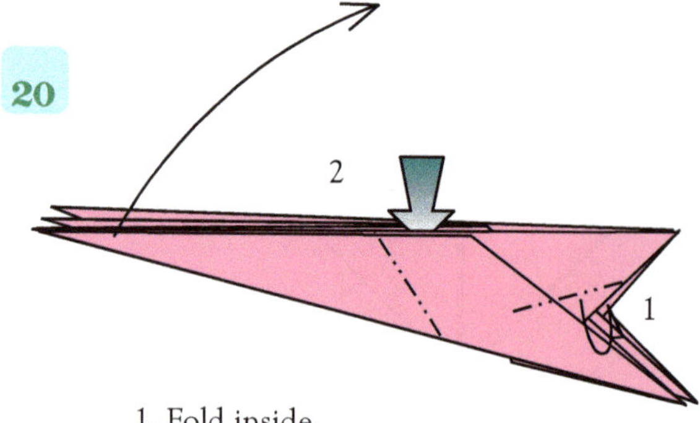

1. Fold inside.
2. Place your finger into the second pocket for this reverse fold.

Repeat behind.

21

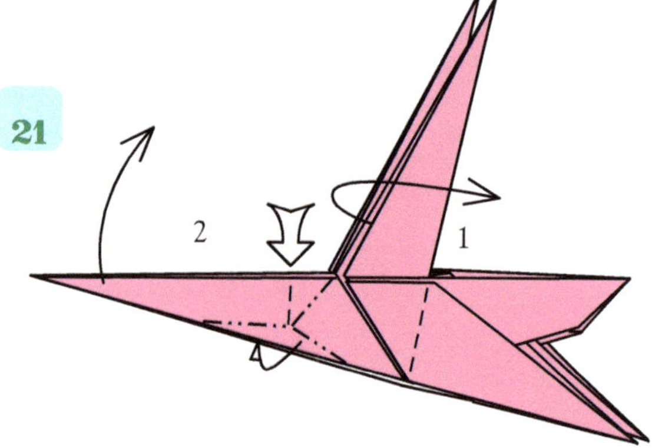

1. Fold the top layer, repeat behind.
2. Double-rabbit-ear.

22

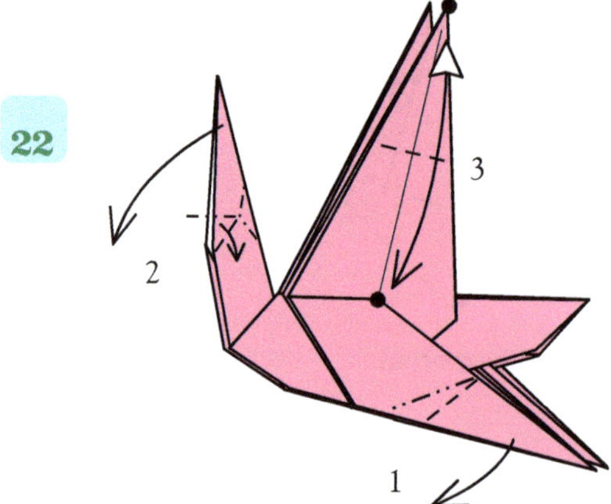

1. Crimp-fold, repeat behind.
2. Push in on the right and make a crimp fold.
3. Fold and unfold, repeat behind.

23

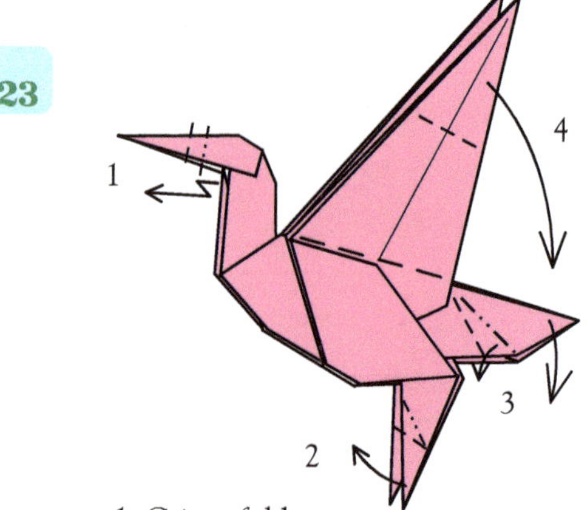

1. Crimp-fold.
2. Crimp-fold, repeat behind.
3. Crimp-fold.
4. Spread the wings, repeat behind.

The Cormorant can stand.

24

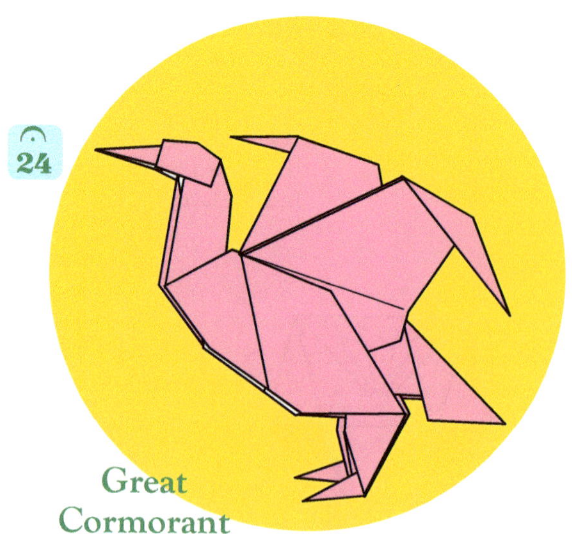

White-bellied Sea-Eagle

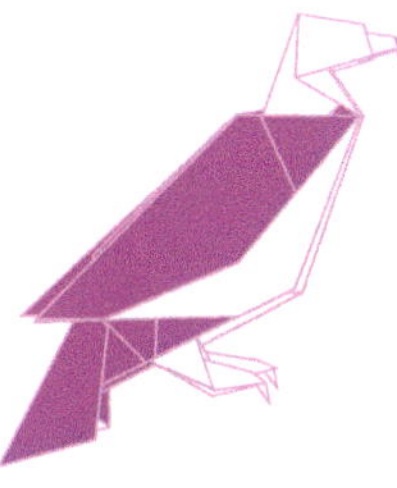

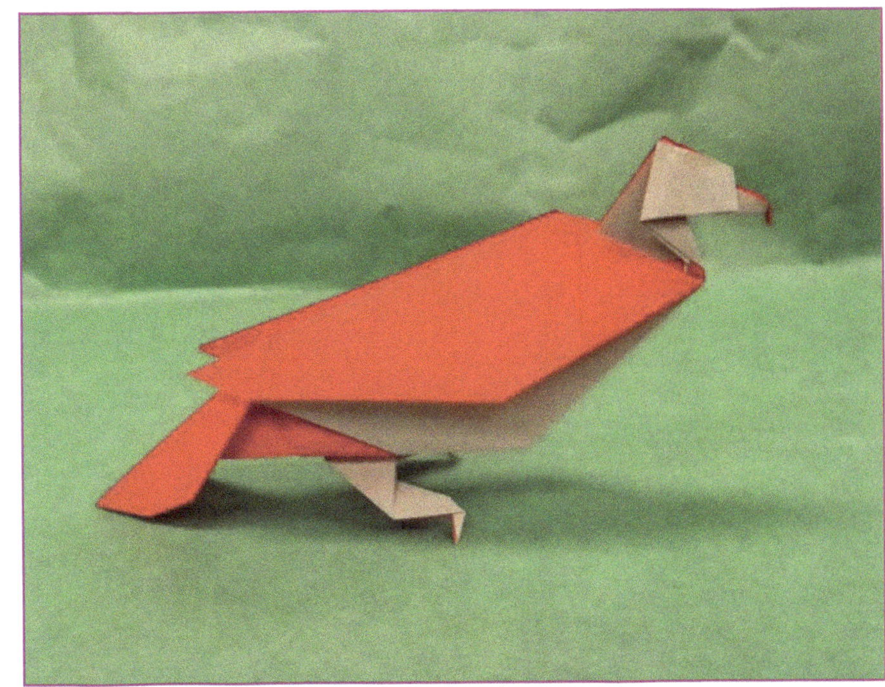

The White-bellied Sea Eagle is a large bird of prey found in coastal areas, rivers, and lakes. They feed on fish, turtles, birds, snakes and small mammals, catching them with their talons. They will force a smaller bird carrying food to drop it. They like to perch high up in tall trees and make loud honking calls.

1

Fold and unfold.

2

Fold and unfold.

3

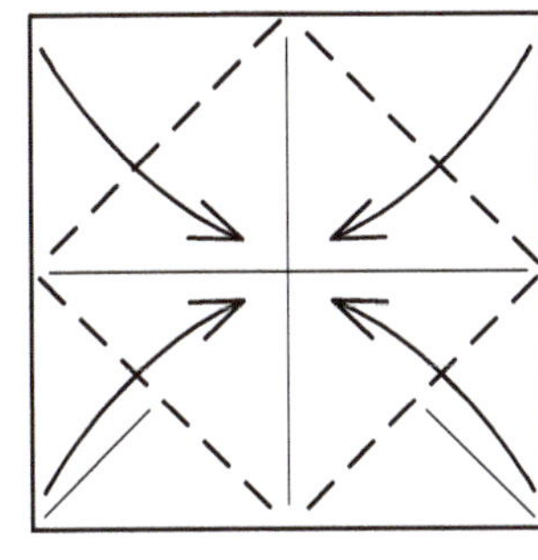

Fold to the center.

4

5

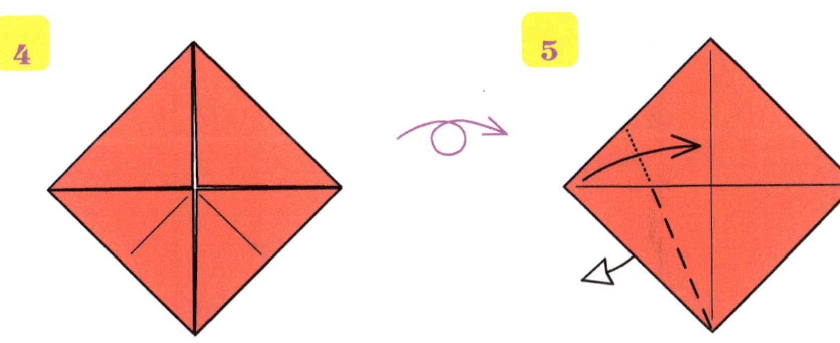

Fold to the center and swing out from behind. Do not crease at the top.

6

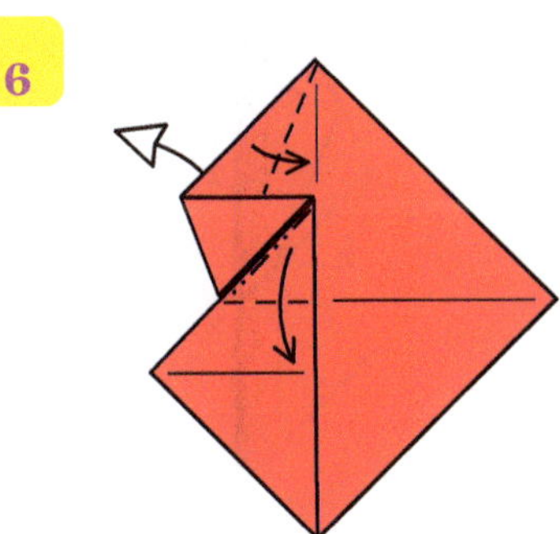

Squash-fold and swing out from behind.

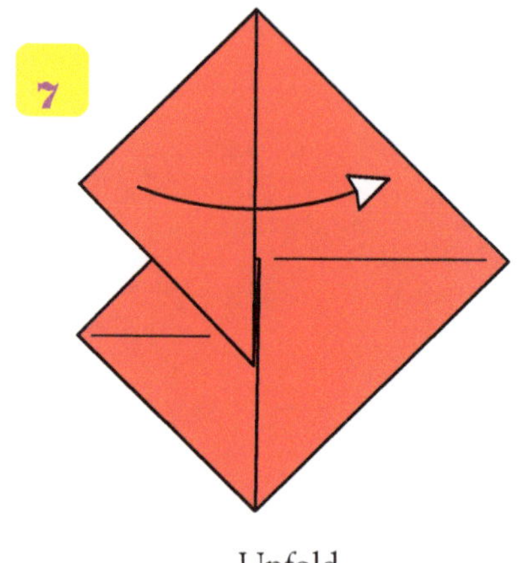

Unfold.

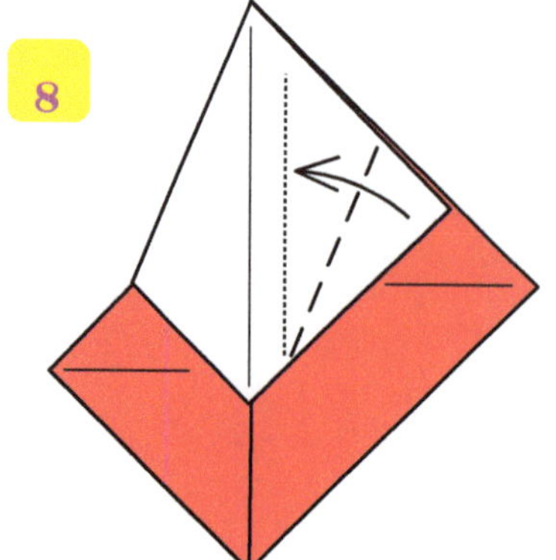

Bring the edge to
a vertical line.

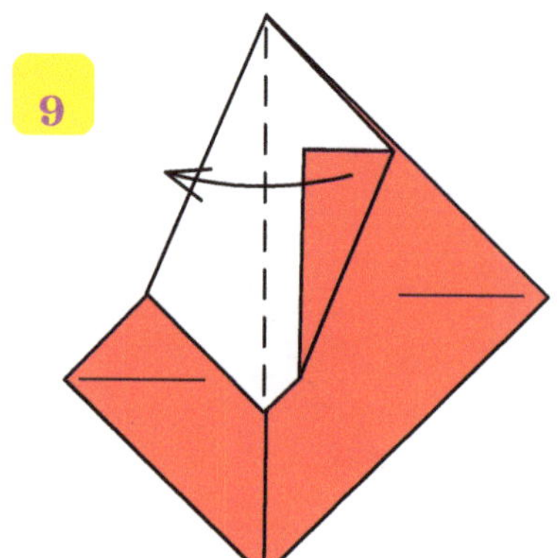

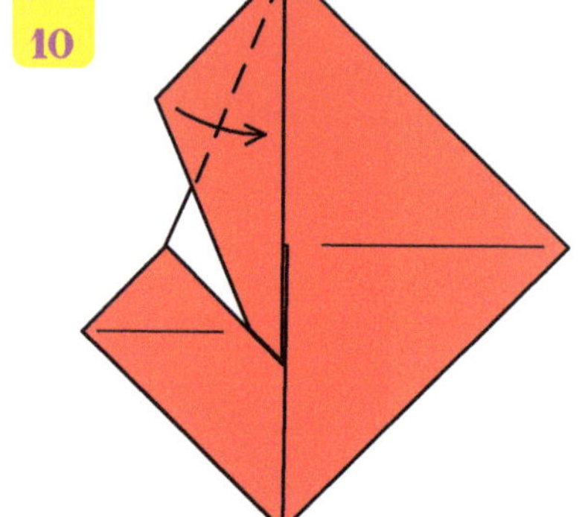

11

Repeat steps 5–10
on the right.

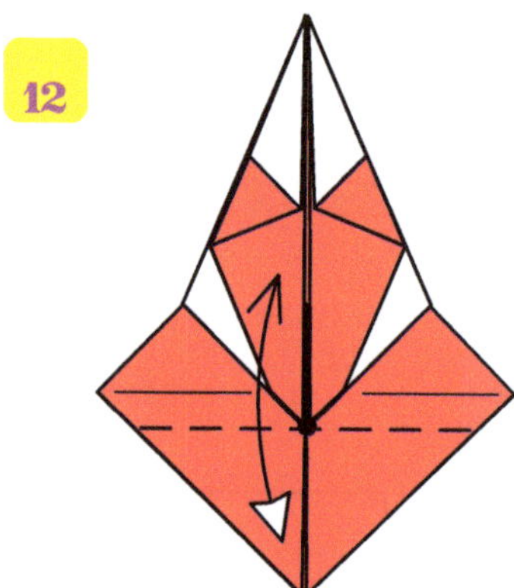

Fold and unfold.

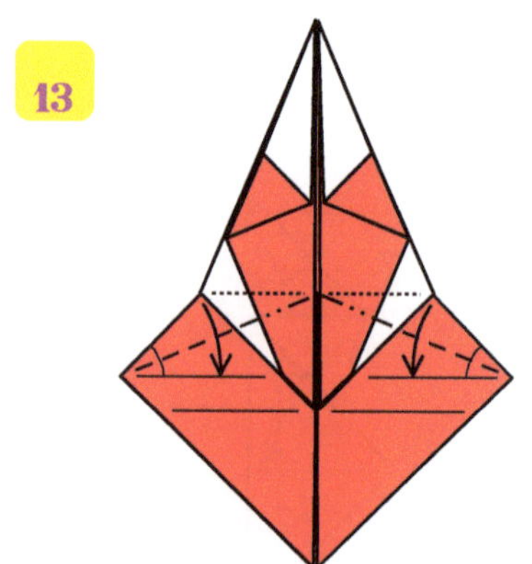

Make reverse folds.

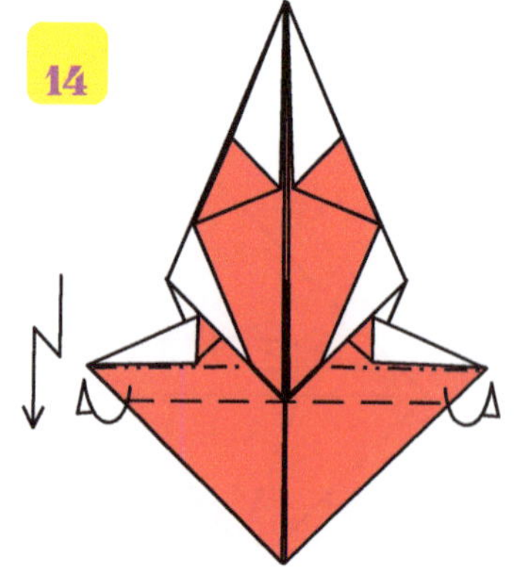

Pleat-fold.

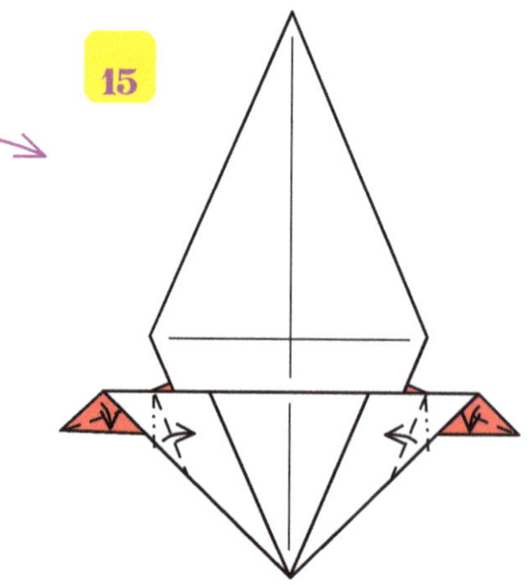

Make squash folds.

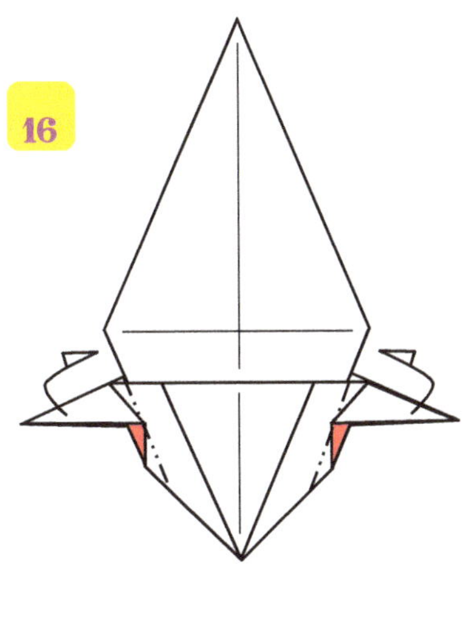

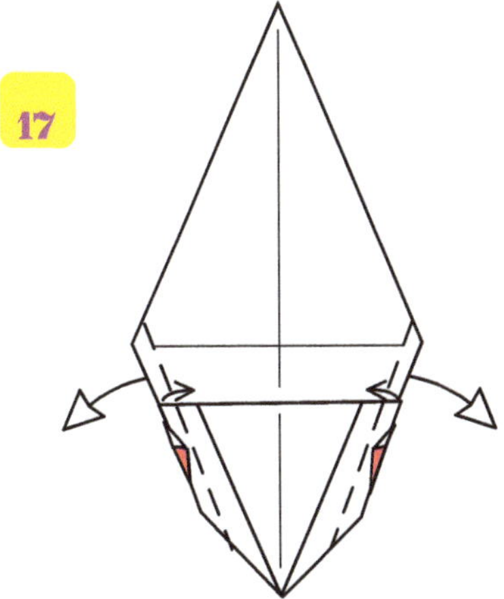

Swing out from behind.

18

Fold in half
and rotate.

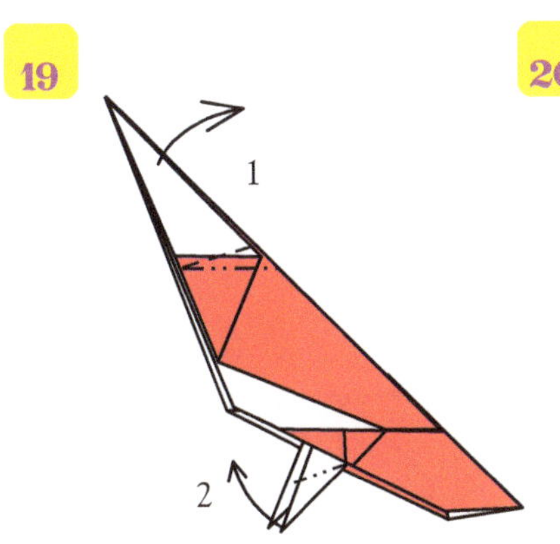

1. Crimp-fold.
2. Reverse-fold, repeat behind.

20

1. Crimp-fold.
2. Fold inside, repeat behind.
3. Reverse-fold, repeat behind.

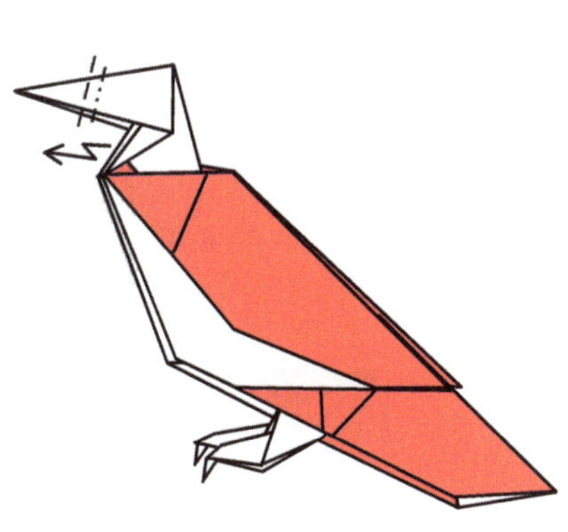

Crimp-fold.

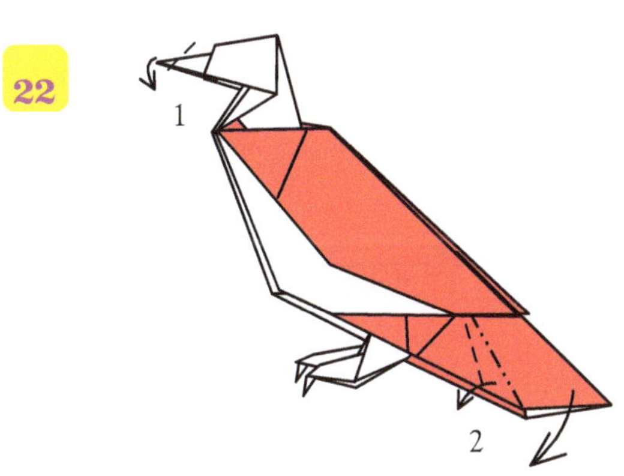

1. Outside-reverse-fold for a color change.
2. Crimp-fold.

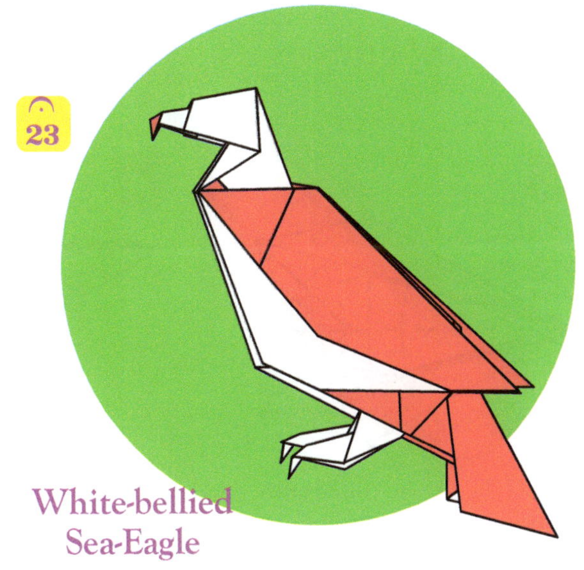

White-bellied
Sea-Eagle

Wedge-tailed Eagle

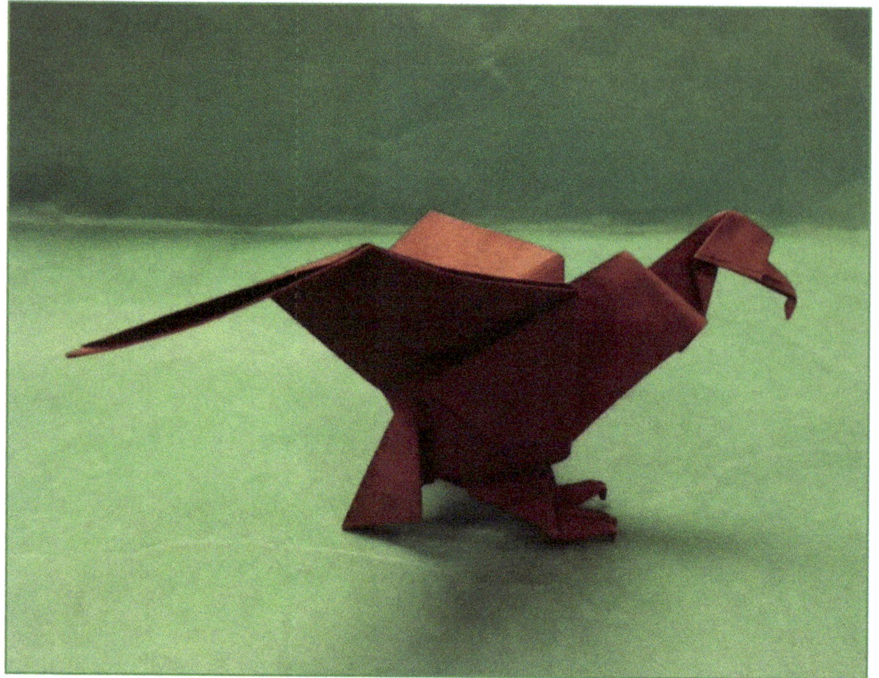

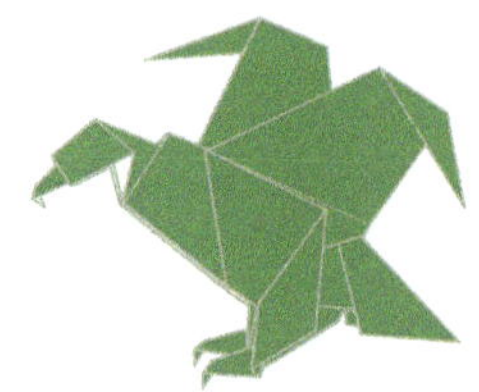

The largest bird of prey in Australia is the Wedge-tailed Eagle. Found throughout Australia, they live in forests, rainforests, savannas, in the mountains, and in the grasslands. They feed on rabbit, lizards, birds, and other mammals. Working in groups, these eagles can prey on larger mammals. They spend much time gliding or perched in high trees.

Begin with step 16 of the Great Cormorant (page 70).

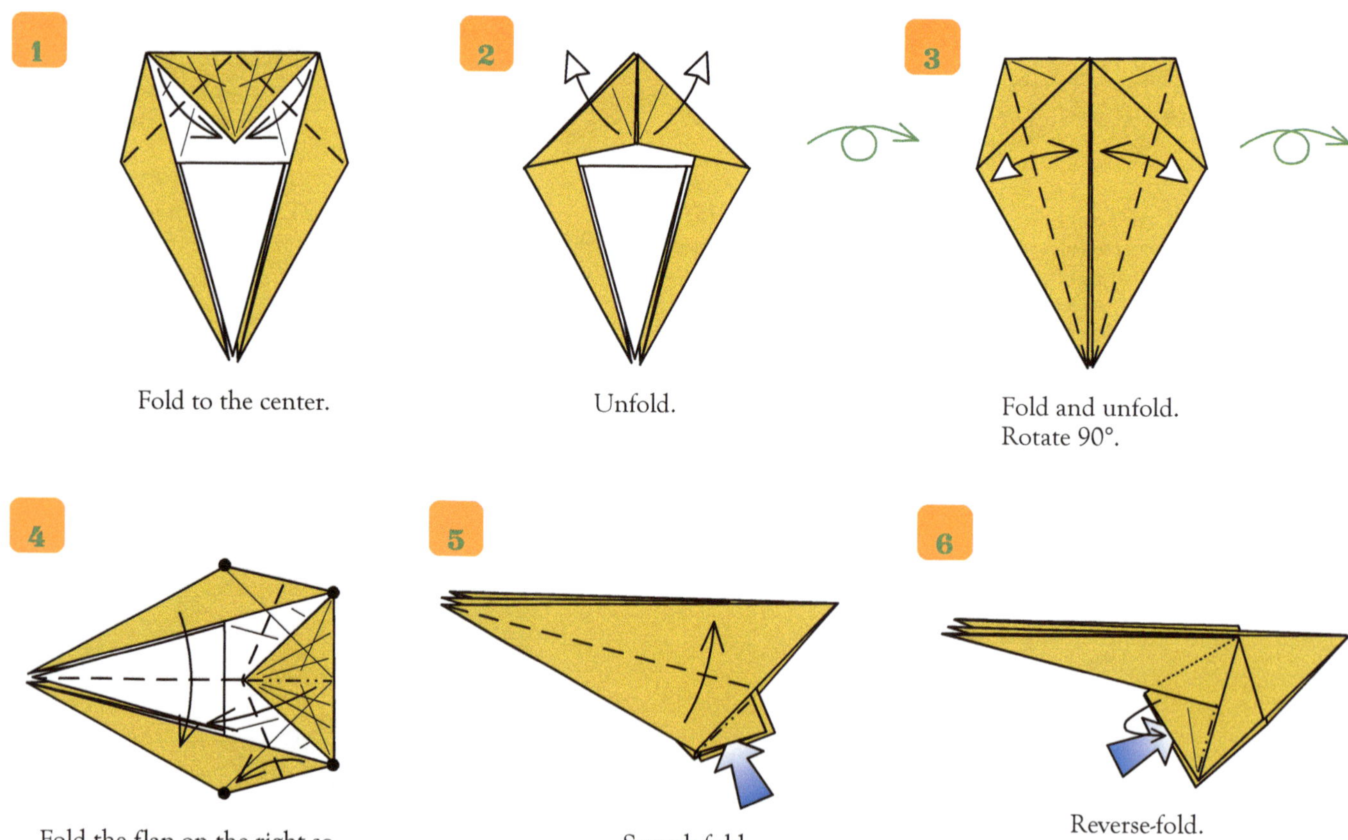

1. Fold to the center.
2. Unfold.
3. Fold and unfold. Rotate 90°.
4. Fold the flap on the right so the dots meet at the bottom, while folding in half.
5. Squash-fold, repeat behind.
6. Reverse-fold.

7

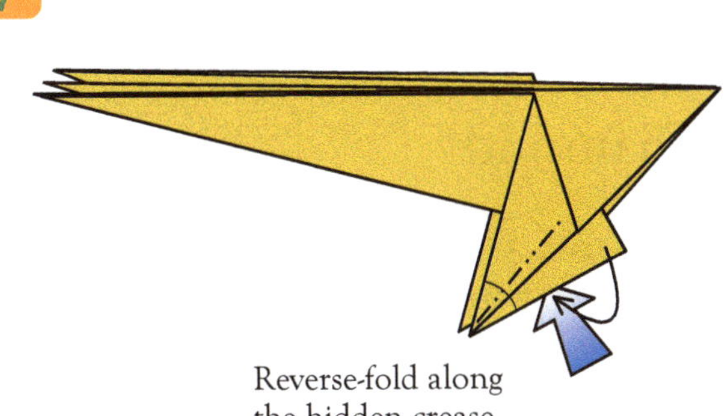

Reverse-fold along the hidden crease.

8

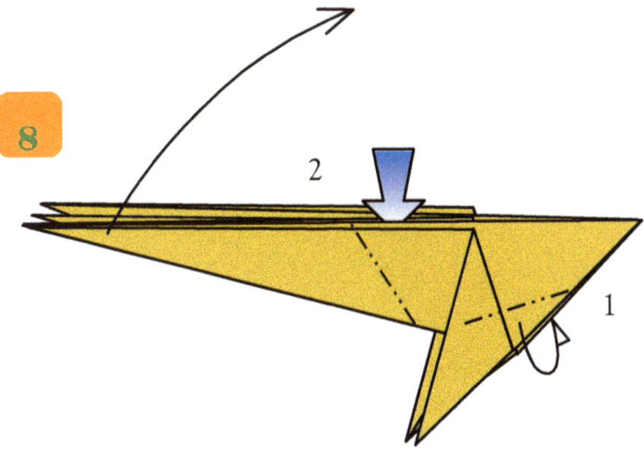

1. Fold inside.
2. Place your finger into the second pocket for this reverse fold.

Repeat behind.

9

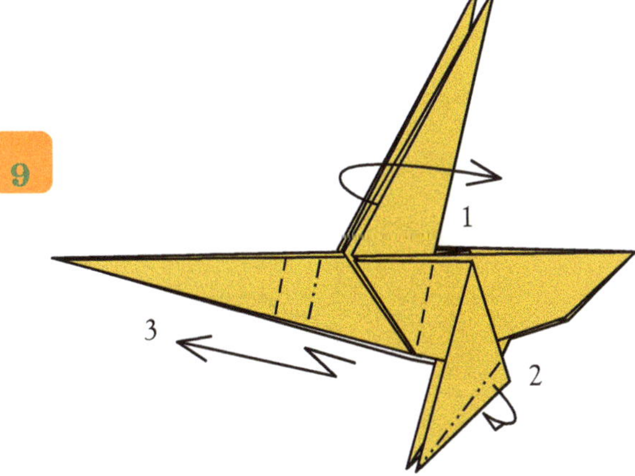

1. Fold the top layer, repeat behind.
2. Fold inside along the hidden edge, repeat behind.
3. Crimp-fold.

10

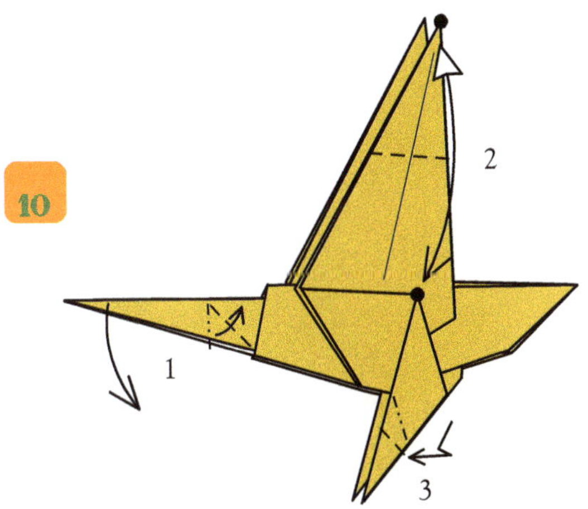

1. Crimp-fold.
2. Fold and unfold.
3. Crimp-fold, repeat behind.

11

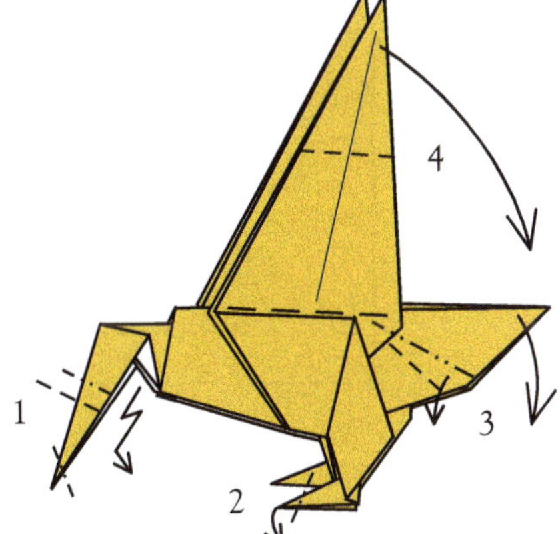

1. Crimp-fold and reverse-fold the tip.
2. Reverse-fold, repeat behind.
3. Crimp-fold.
4. Spread the wings, repeat behind.

The Eagle can stand.

12

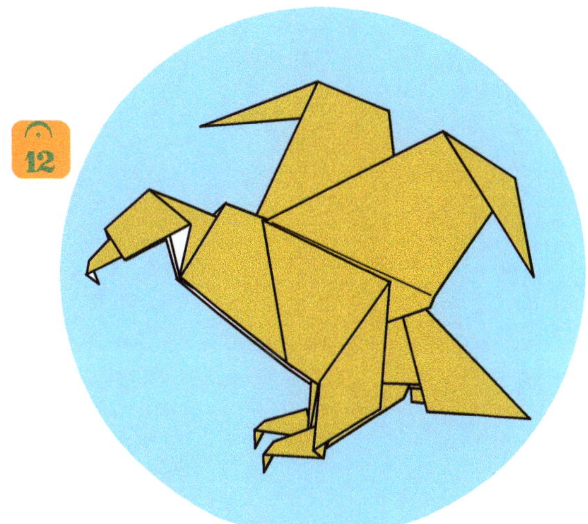

Wedge-tailed Eagle

Third Movement

Minuet of Diamonds with a Trio of Dimpled Diamonds

While these Diamonds could be the dinosaur or bird eggs, or props for the birds to perch upon, they are mainly the Dragon's jewels being protecting in their lair. At the equator of these diamonds is a polygon base. The faces are identical isosceles triangles with varying apex angles (angles at the top). For this collection, the apex angle is 180/(n + 1), where *n* is the number of sides of the polygon base. The diamonds range from a triangular to octagonal base.

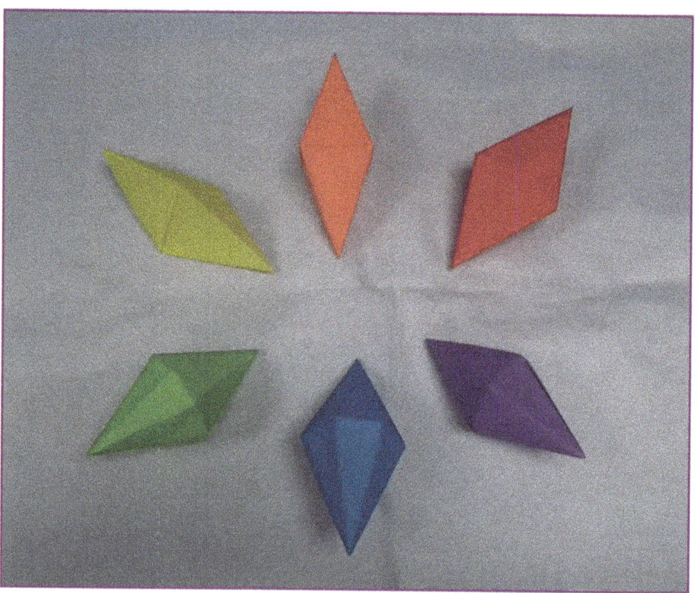

Diamond	Color	Apex Angle
Triangular	Yellow	45°
Square	Orange	36°
Pentagonal	Red	30°
Hexagonal	Purple	25.7°
Heptagonal	Blue	22.5°
Octagonal	Green	20°

Triangular Diamond

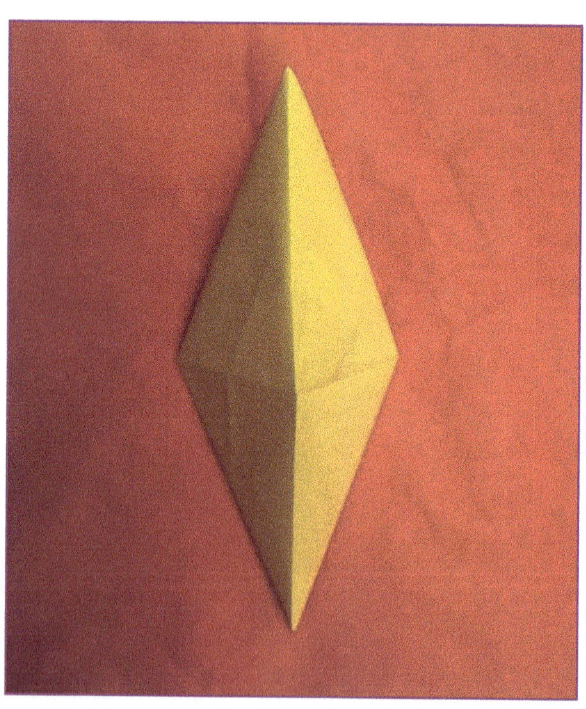

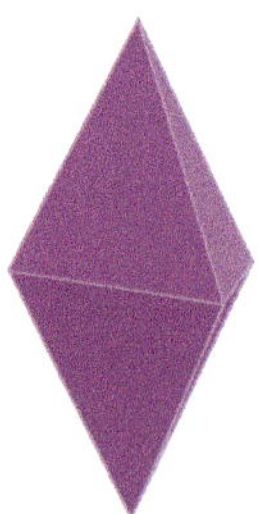

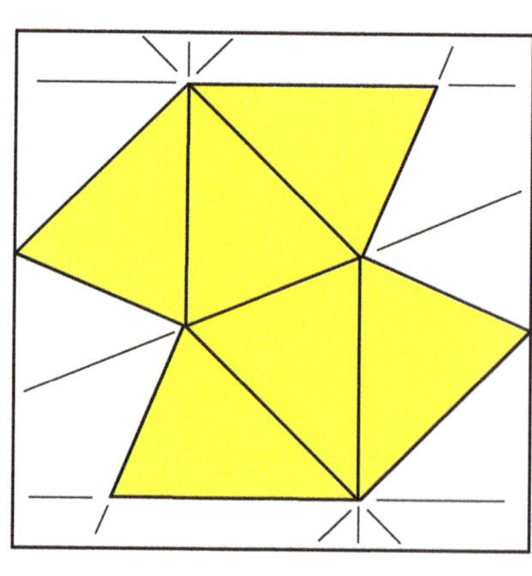

This is one of the simplest diamonds in this section but it uses several of the folding techniques as other ones. That makes it a good one to fold first. The angles of each of the six triangles are 45°,37.5°, and 37.5°. The drawing above shows the crease pattern. If the paper were rotated 180°, the crease pattern would be the same. This simplifies the folding method: whatever you do on one side, you do the same on the other.

1

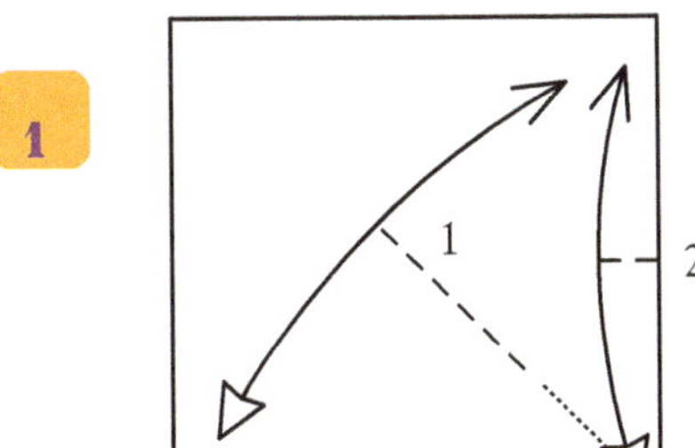

1. Fold and unfold in the center.
2. Fold and unfold on the edge.

2

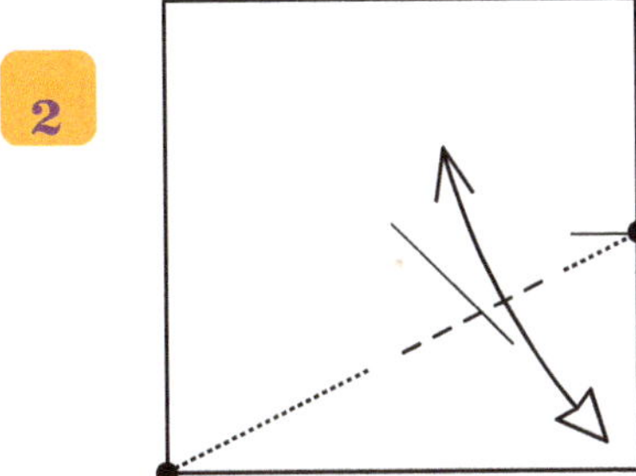

Fold and unfold through the intersection.

3

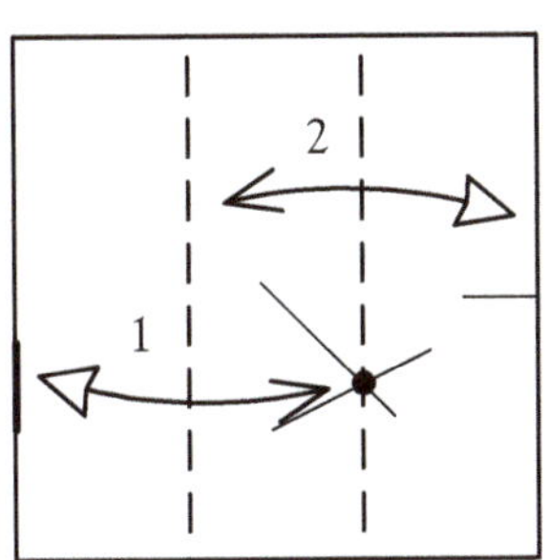

Fold and unfold.

4

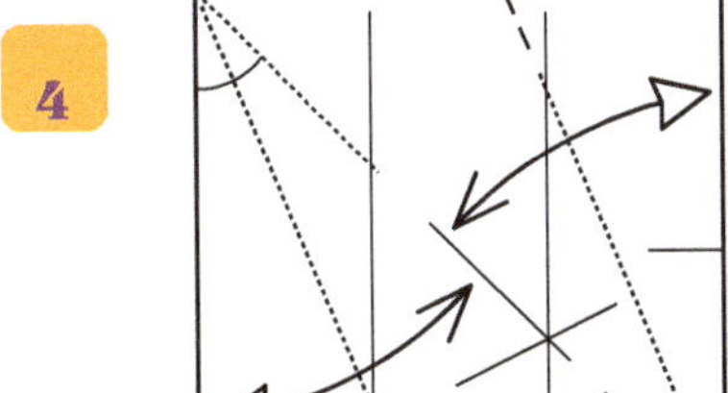

Fold to the center line and unfold.

5

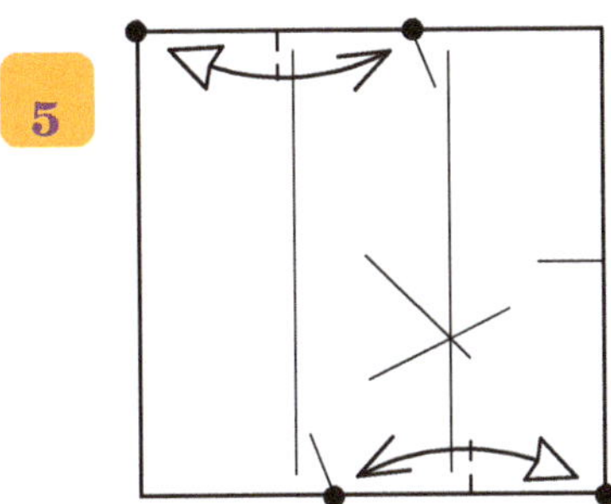

Fold and unfold on the edges.

6

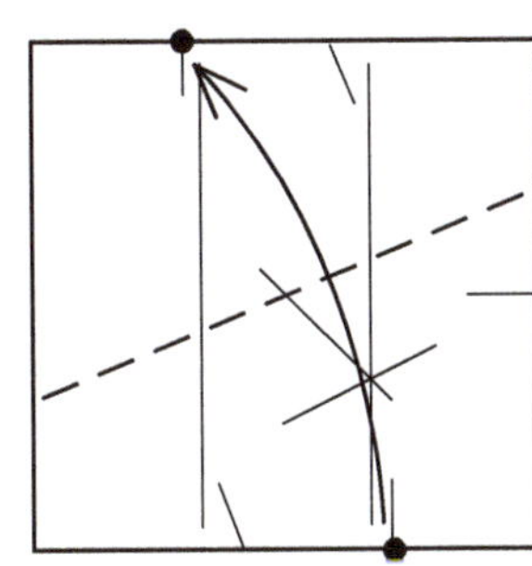

The dots will meet.

7

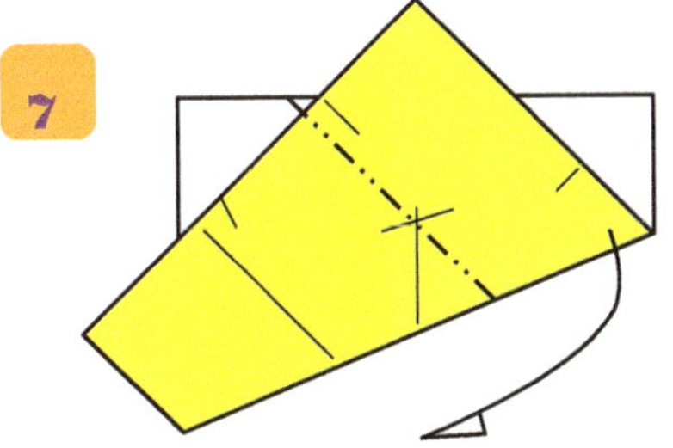

Fold behind along the crease.

8

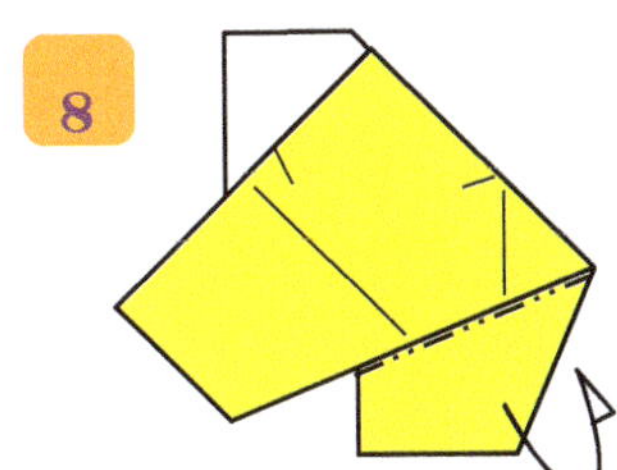

Fold behind.

9

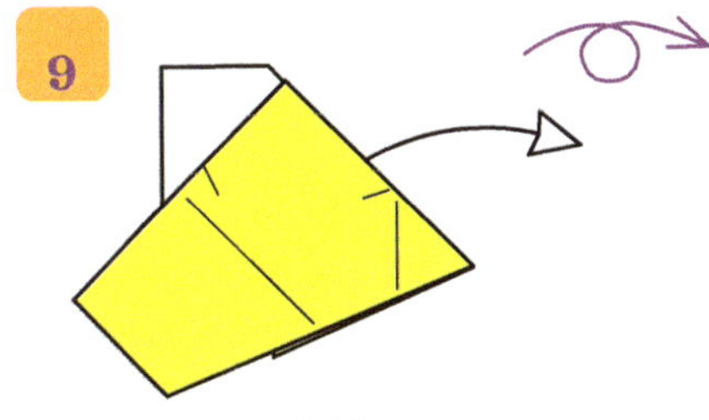

Unfold.

10

Repeat steps 7–9.

11

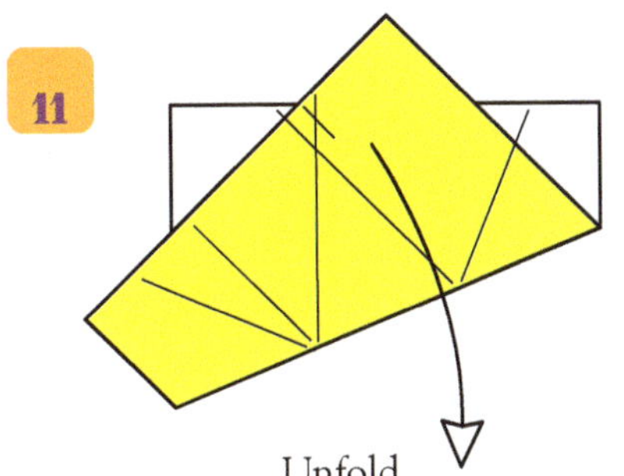

Unfold.

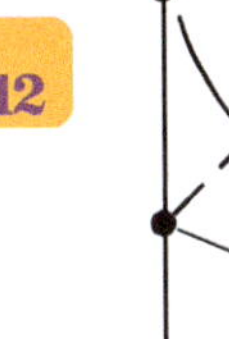

12

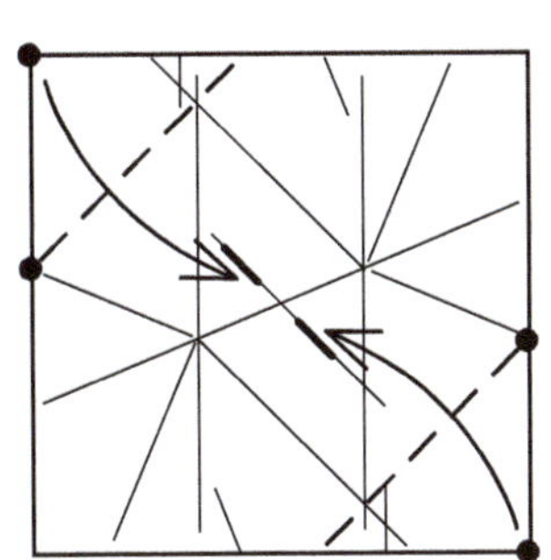

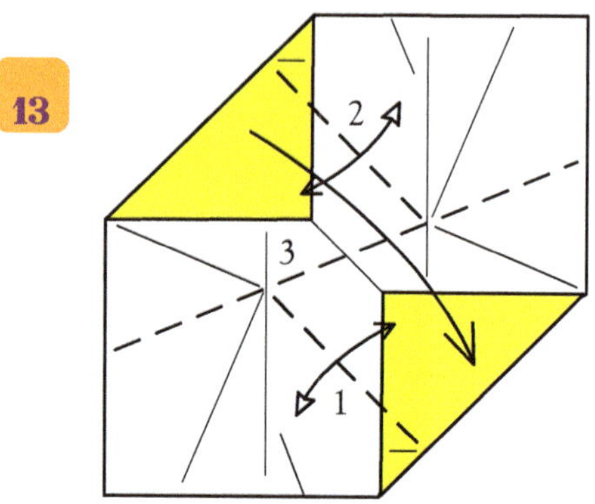

1, 2. Fold and unfold along the crease.
3. Fold along the crease.

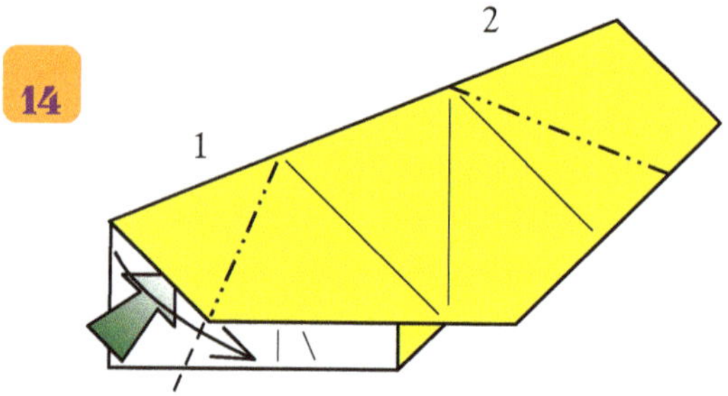

1. Reverse-fold.
2. Turn over and repeat.

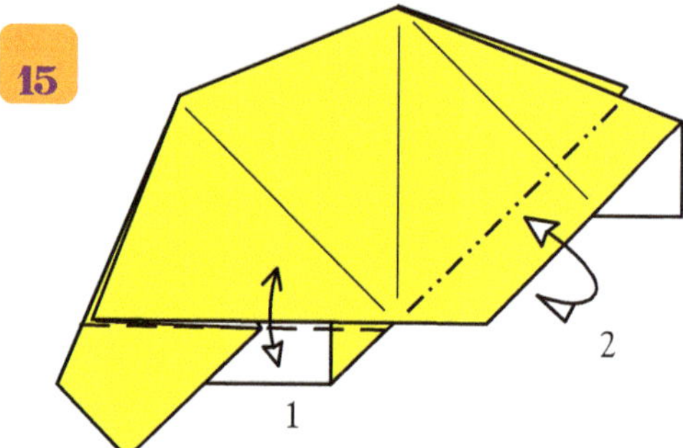

Fold and unfold.

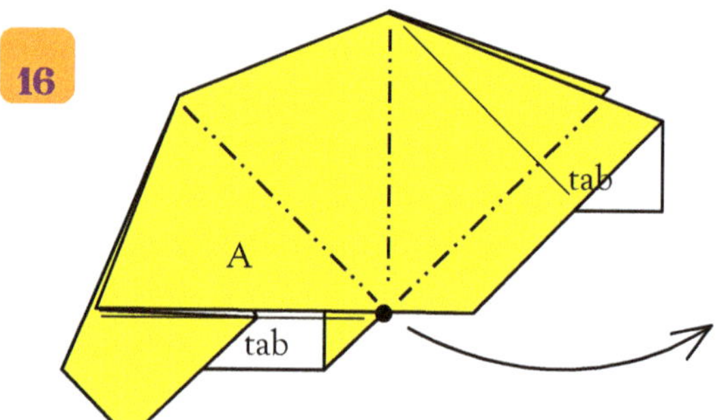

The dot will go to the right and the same below will go to the left. Follow region A.

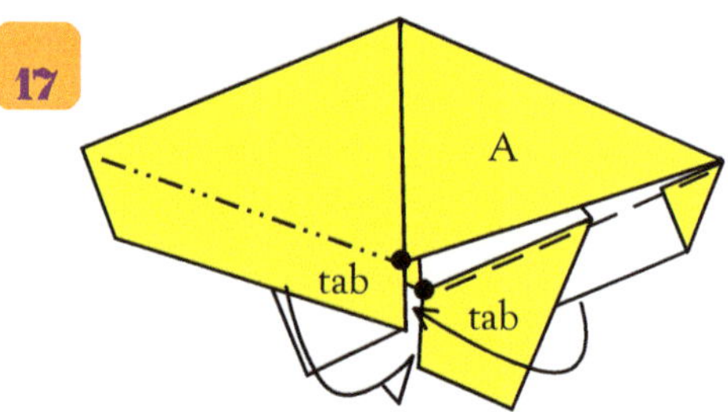

Tuck and interlock the tabs. The dots will meet.

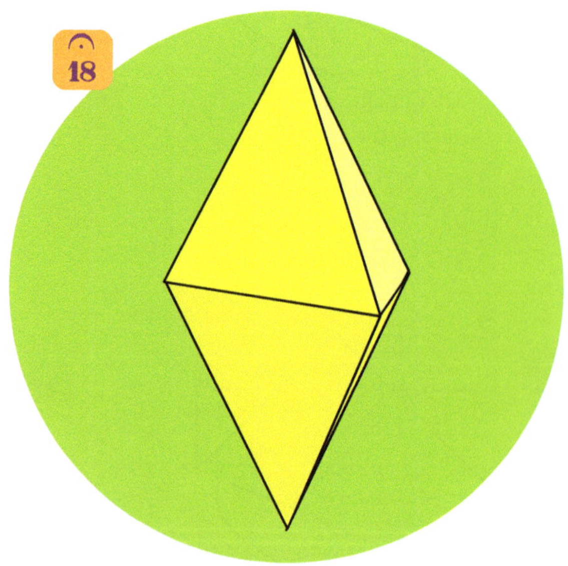

Triangular Diamond

Square Diamond

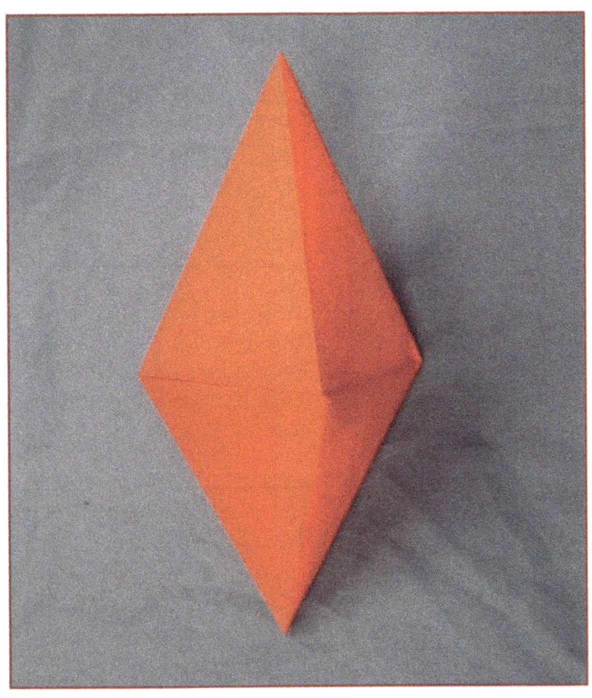

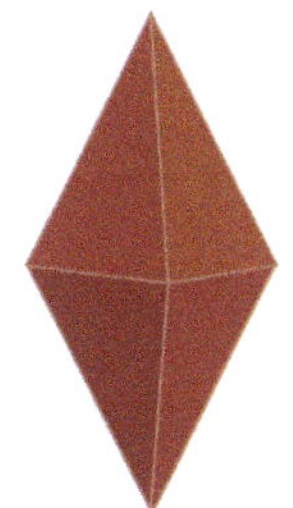

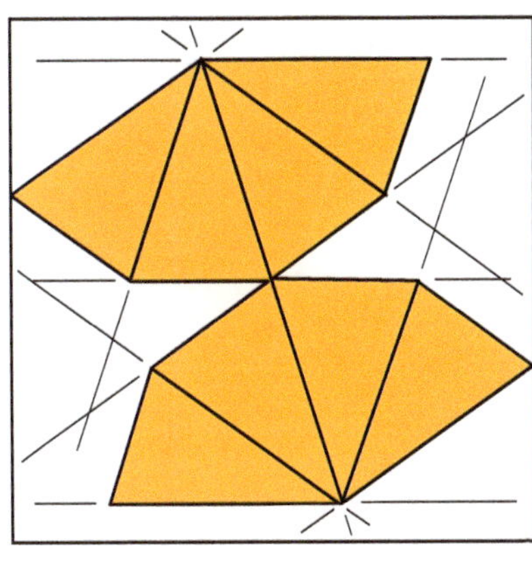

The angles of each face are 36°, 72°, and 72°. The crease patten would be the same if it was rotated 180°, so the model uses odd symmetry.

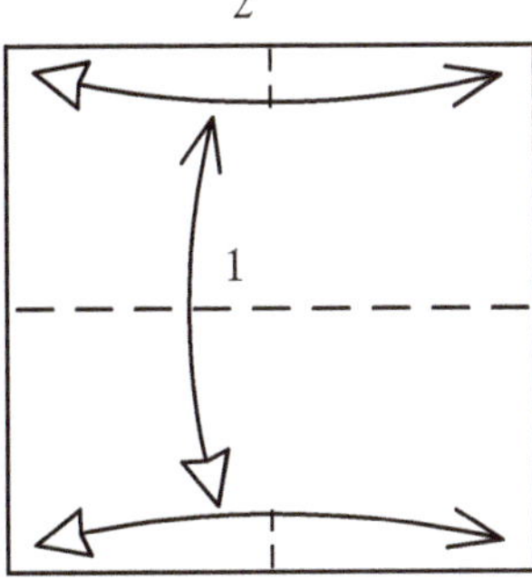

1. Fold and unfold.
2. Fold and unfold on the edges.

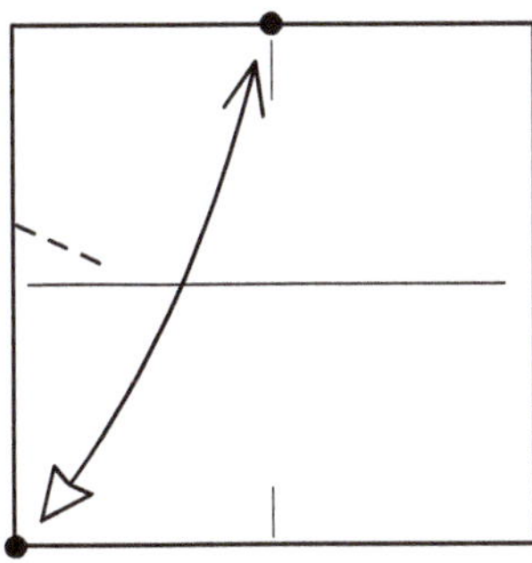

Fold and unfold on the left.

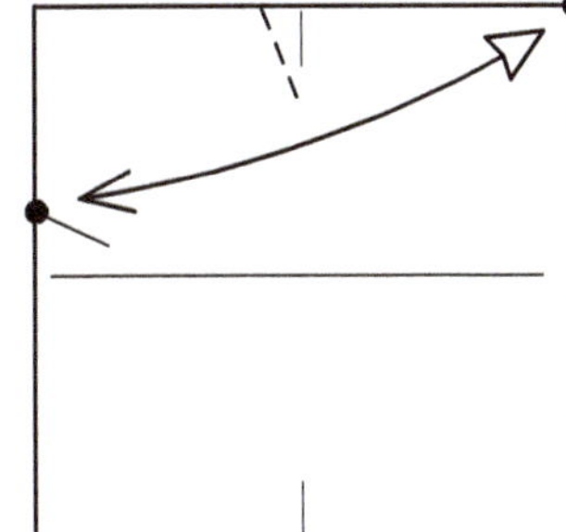

Fold and unfold on the right.

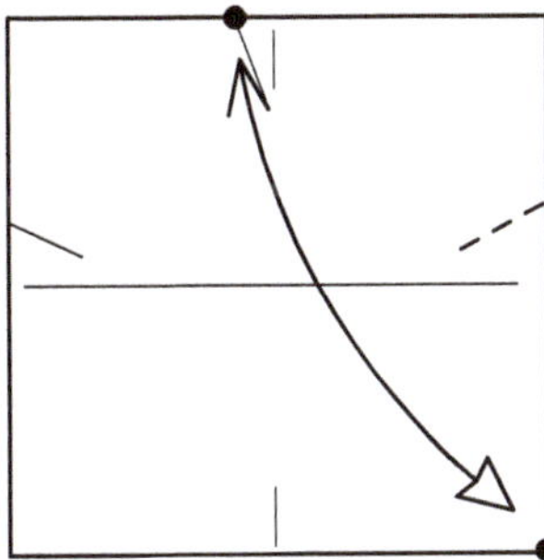

Fold and unfold on the right. Rotate 180°.

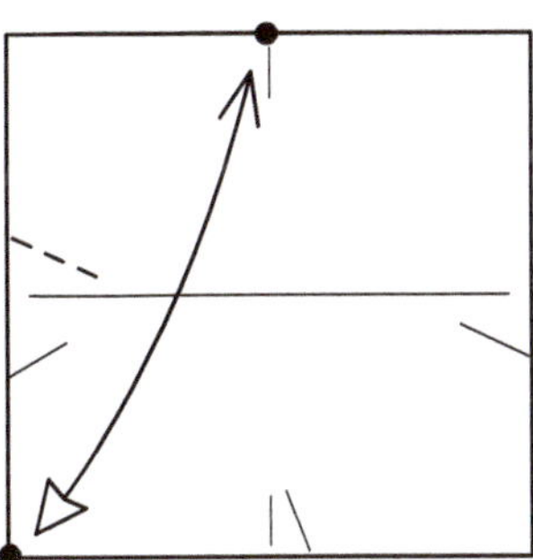

Repeat steps 2–4.

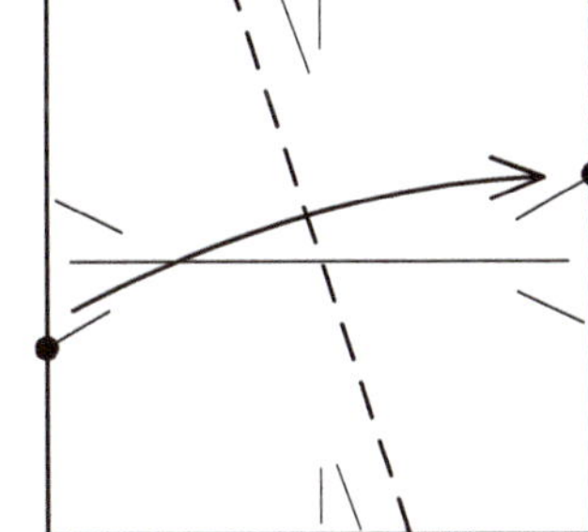

The dots will meet.

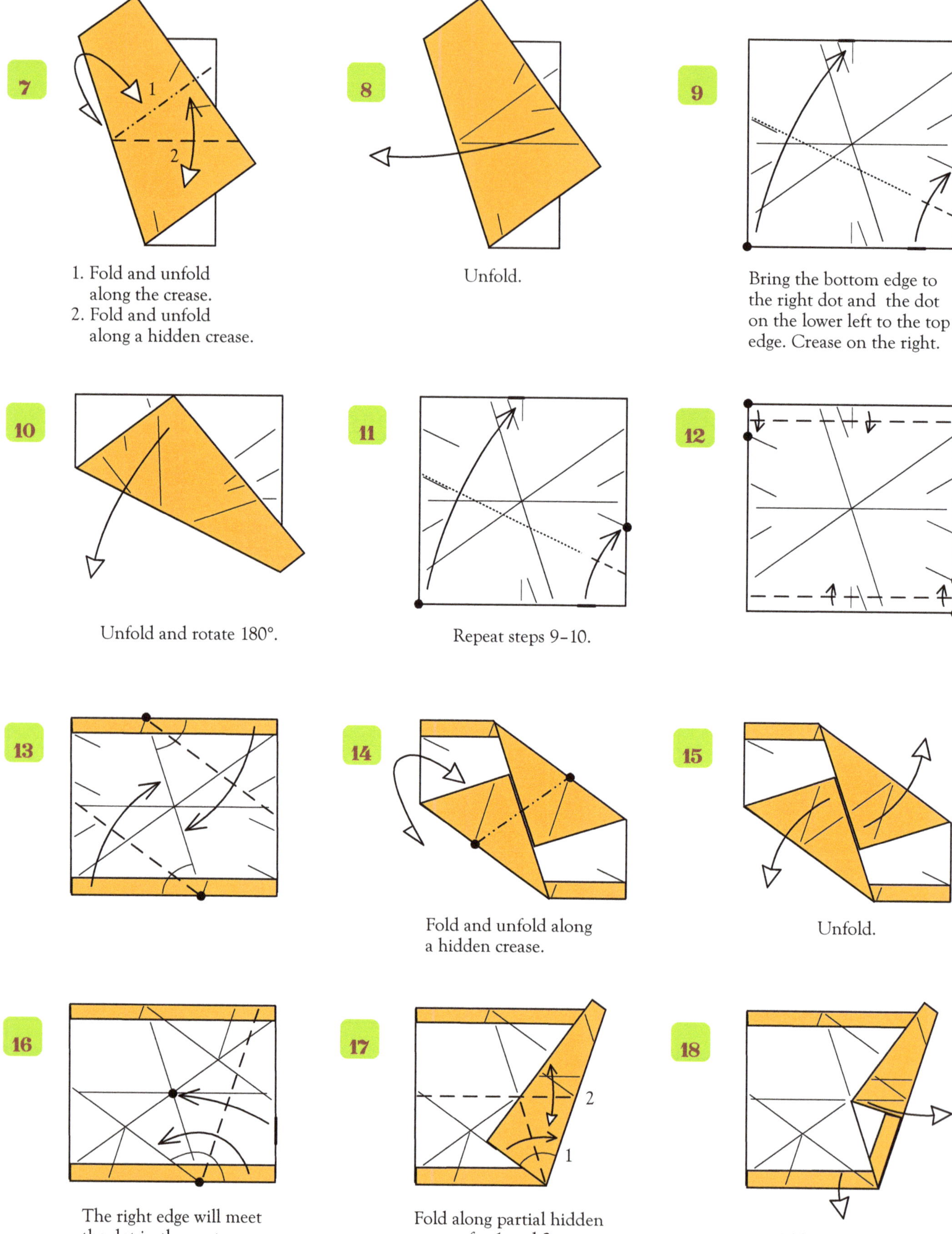

1. Fold and unfold along the crease.
2. Fold and unfold along a hidden crease.

Unfold.

Bring the bottom edge to the right dot and the dot on the lower left to the top edge. Crease on the right.

Unfold and rotate 180°.

Repeat steps 9–10.

Fold and unfold along a hidden crease.

Unfold.

The right edge will meet the dot in the center.

Fold along partial hidden creases for 1 and 2.
1. Fold to the edge.
2. Fold and unfold.

Unfold and rotate 180°.

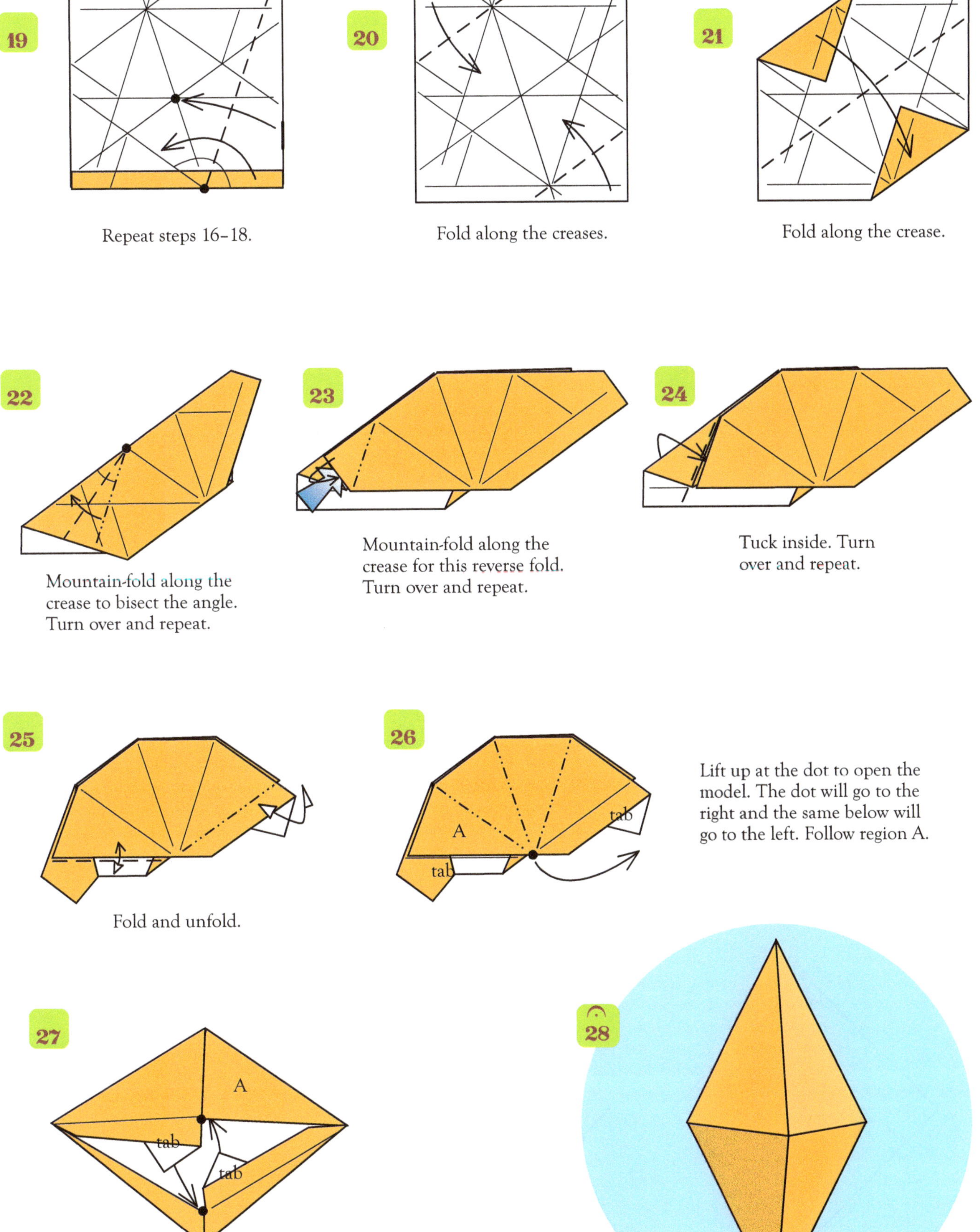
19
Repeat steps 16–18.
20
Fold along the creases.
21
Fold along the crease.
22
Mountain-fold along the crease to bisect the angle. Turn over and repeat.
23
Mountain-fold along the crease for this reverse fold. Turn over and repeat.
24
Tuck inside. Turn over and repeat.
25
Fold and unfold.
26
A
tab
tab
Lift up at the dot to open the model. The dot will go to the right and the same below will go to the left. Follow region A.
27
A
tab
tab
Tuck and interlock the tabs. The dots will meet.
28
Square Diamond

Pentagonal Diamond

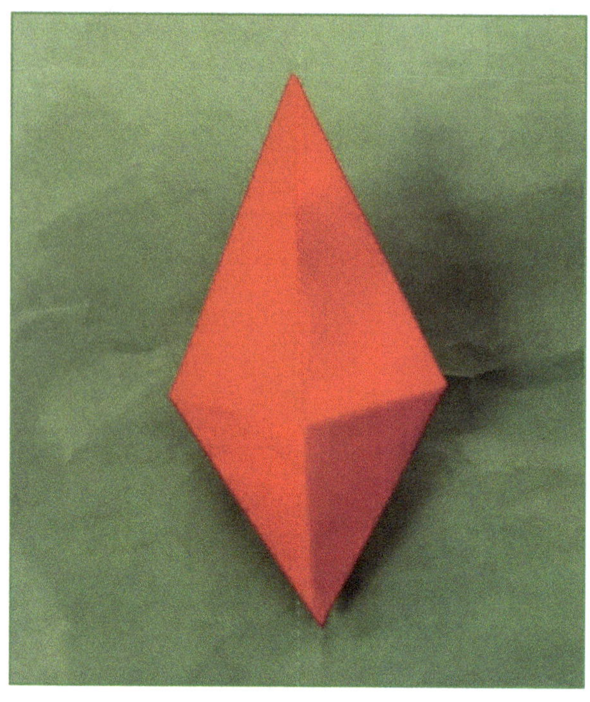

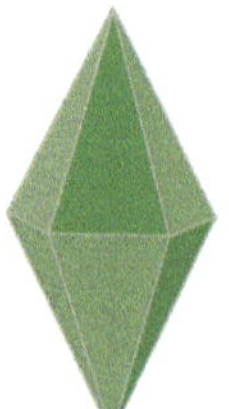

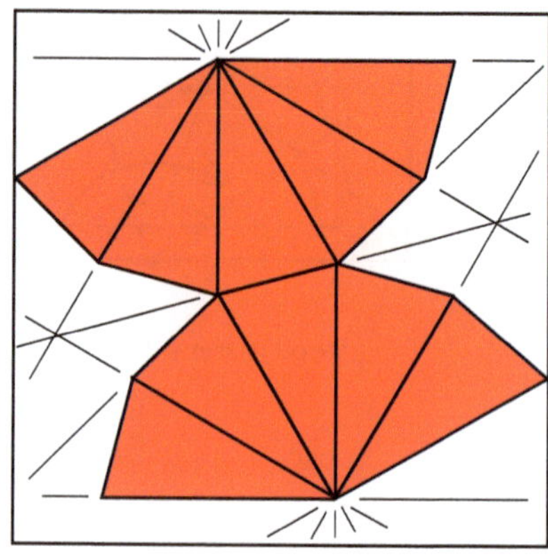

The angles of each face are 30°, 75°, and 75°. This ten-sided model uses odd symmetry.

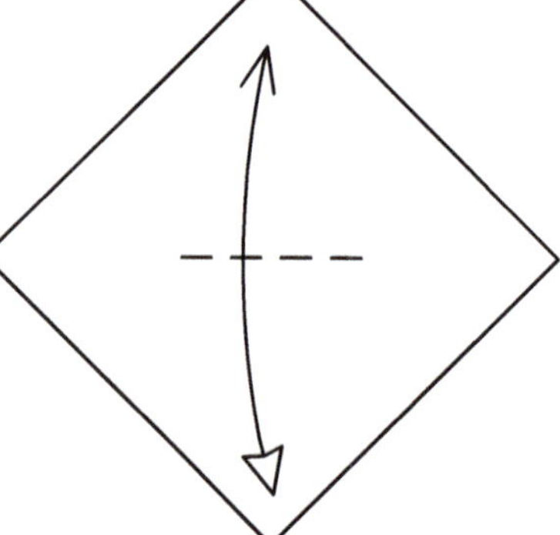

Fold and unfold.

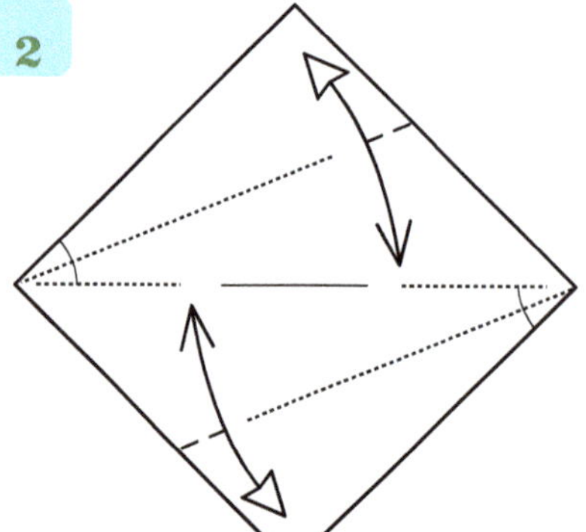

Fold and unfold along the edges.

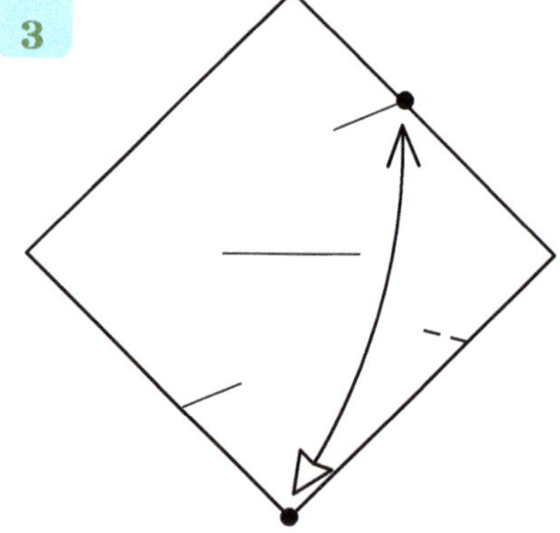

Fold and unfold on the right.

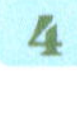

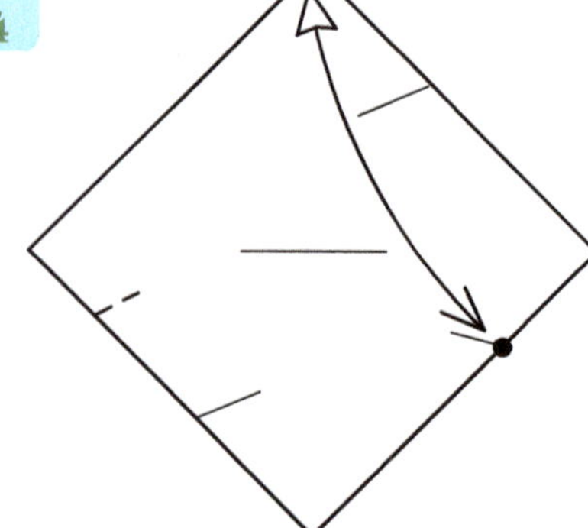

Fold and unfold on the left.

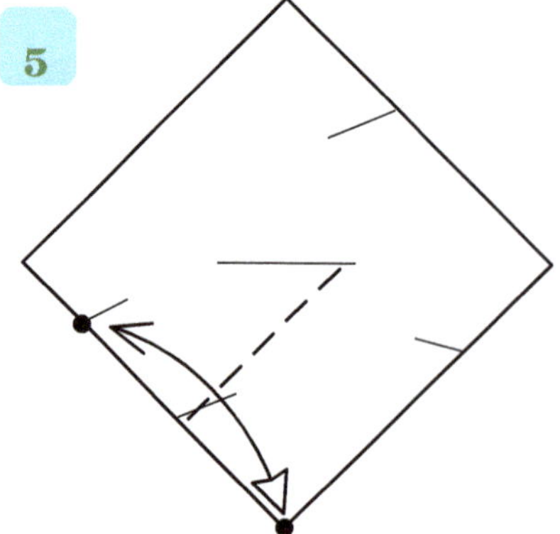

Fold and unfold on the lower half. Rotate 180°.

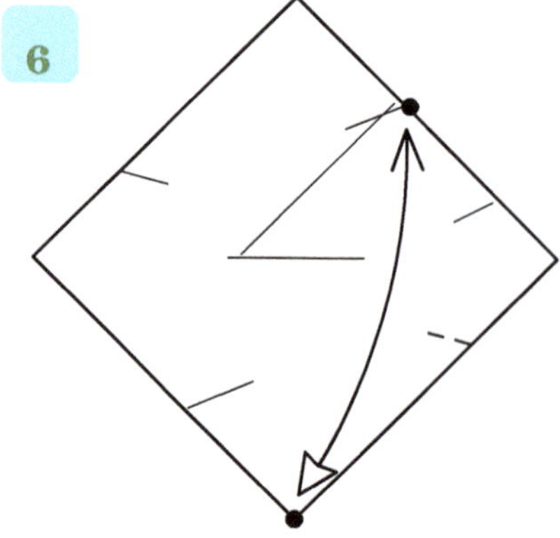

Repeat steps 3–5. Rotate 45°.

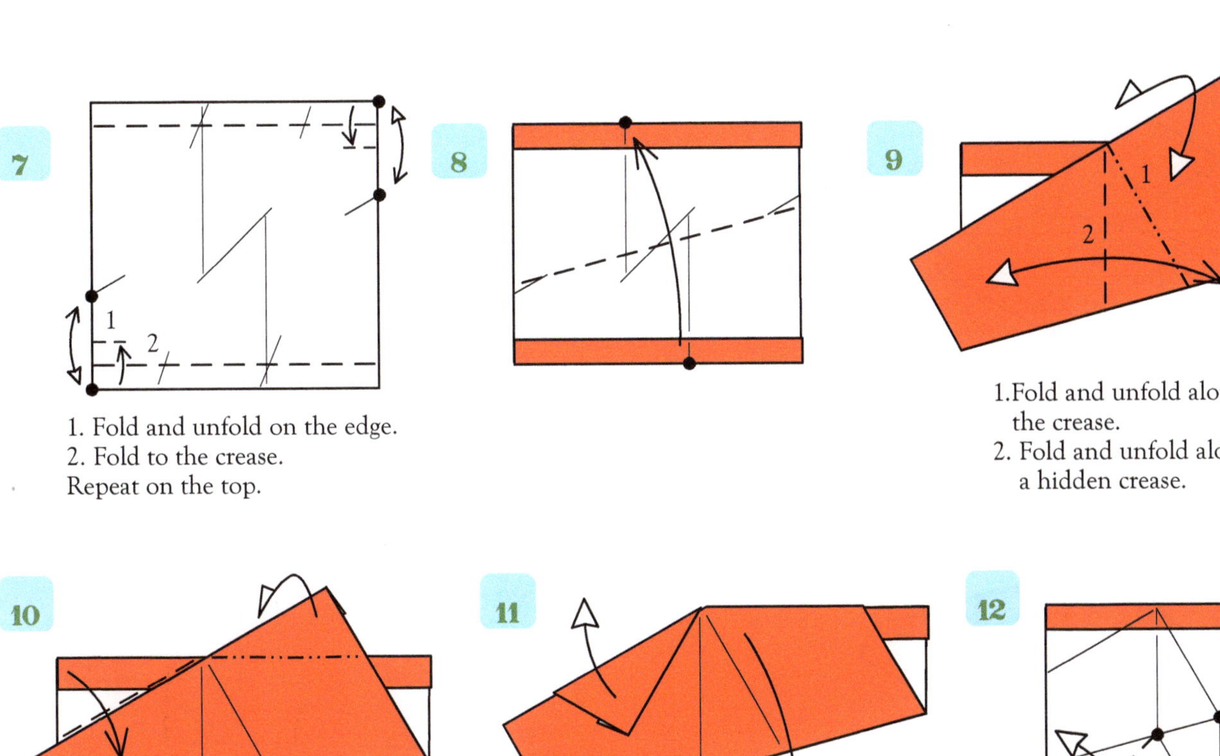

7. 1. Fold and unfold on the edge.
2. Fold to the crease.
Repeat on the top.

9. 1. Fold and unfold along the crease.
2. Fold and unfold along a hidden crease.

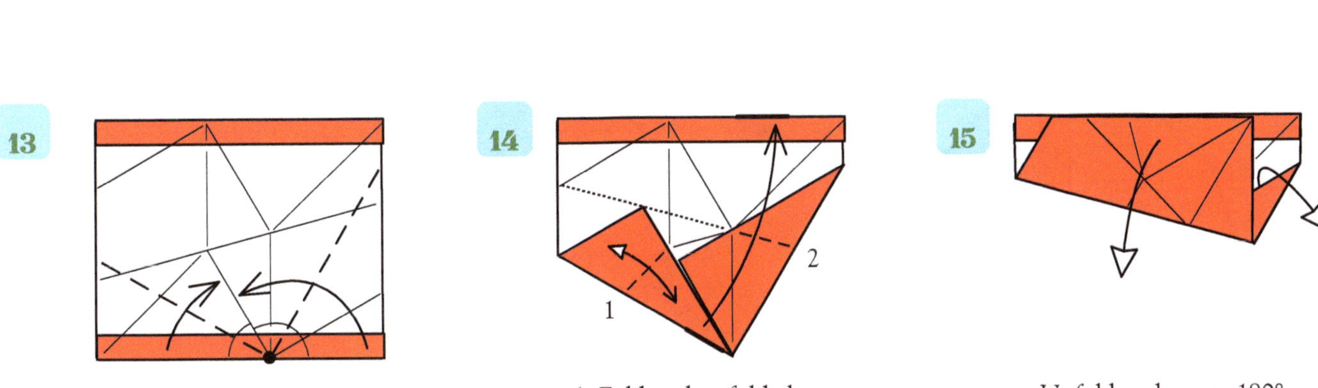

11. Unfold.

12. Fold and unfold.

13

14

15

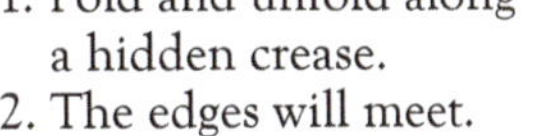

14. 1. Fold and unfold along a hidden crease.
2. The edges will meet.

15. Unfold and rotate 180°.

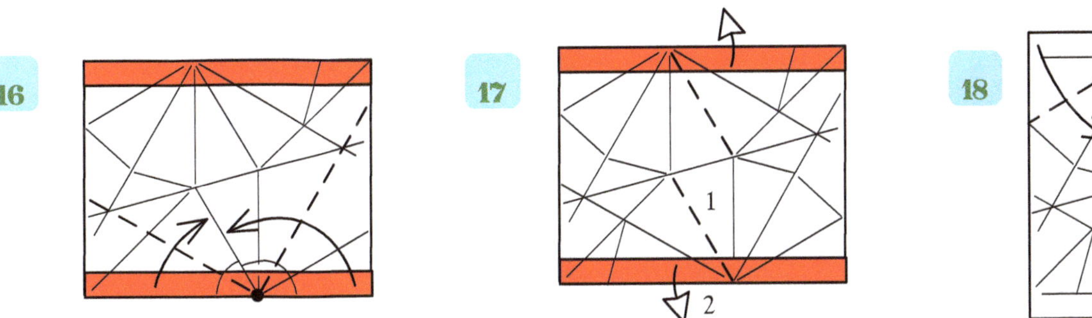

16. Repeat steps 13–15.

17. 1. Fold and unfold along the creases.
2. Unfold.

18. Fold along the creases.

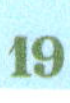

19

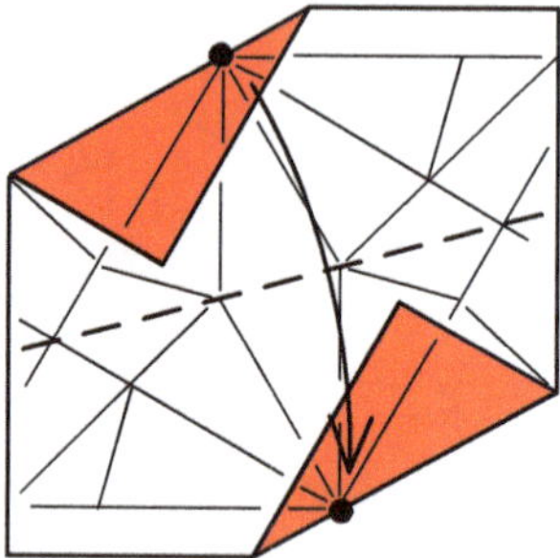

Fold along the crease.

20

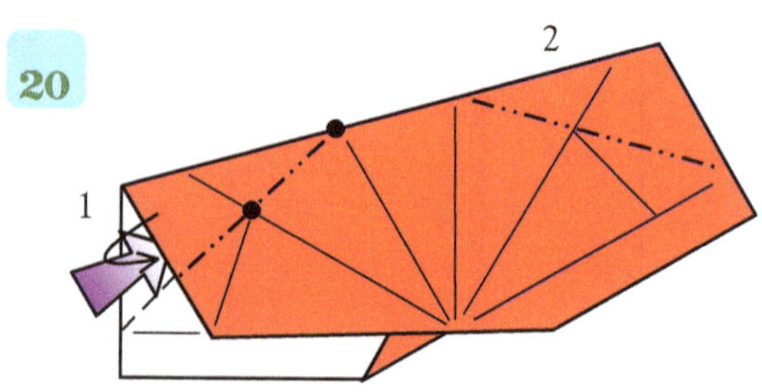

1. Reverse-fold along the crease with the dots.
2. Turn over and repeat.

21

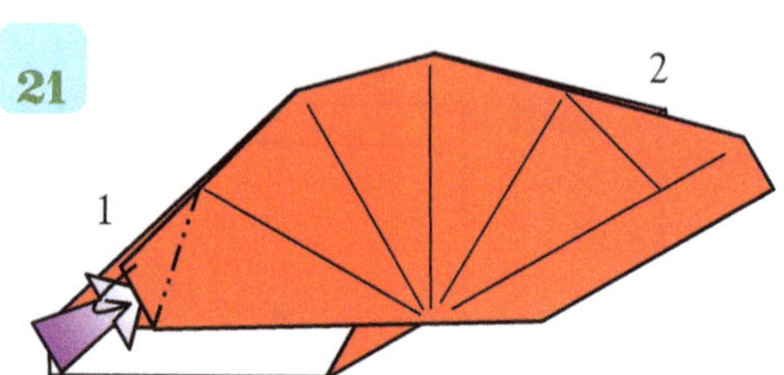

1. Reverse-fold along the crease.
2. Turn over and repeat.

22

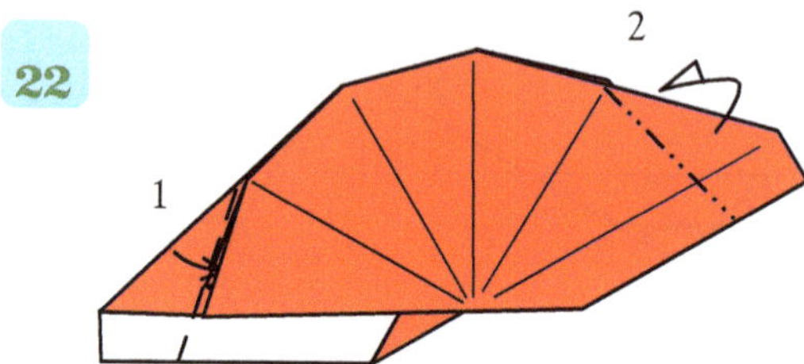

1. Tuck inside.
2. Turn over and repeat.

23

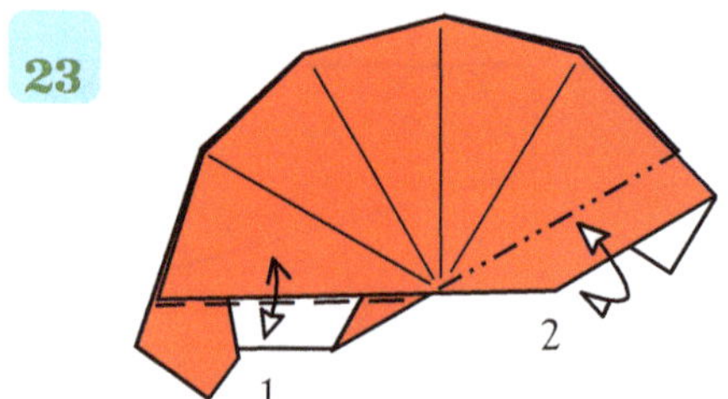

Fold and unfold.

24

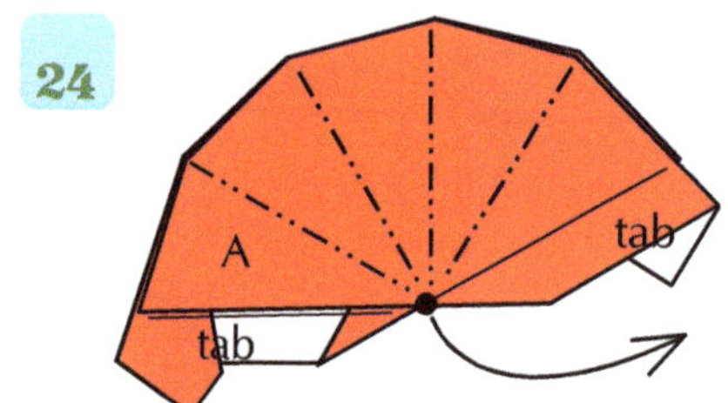

Lift up at the dot to open the model. The dot will go to the right and the same below will go to the left. Follow region A.

25

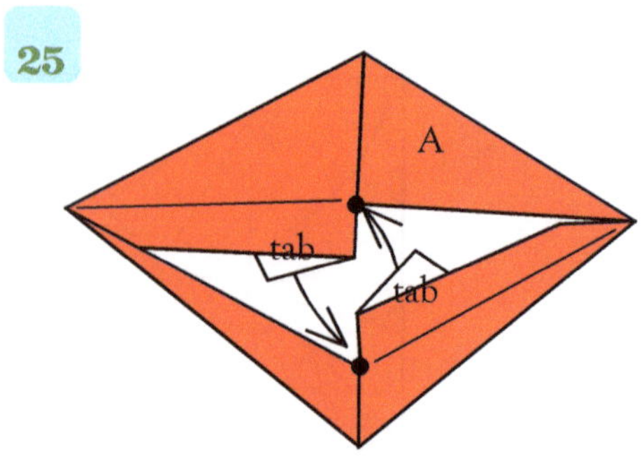

Tuck and interlock the tabs. The dots will meet.

26

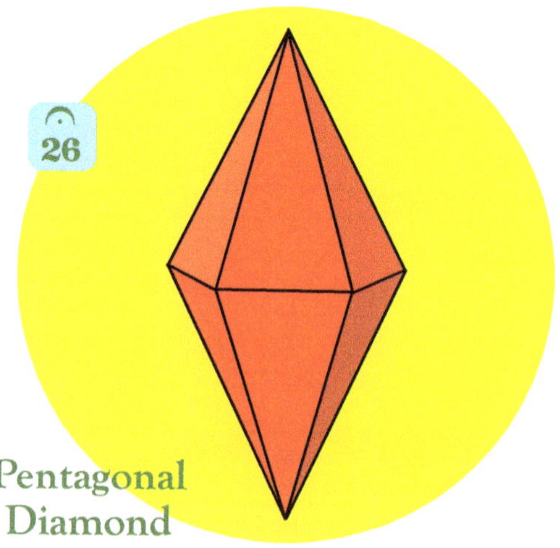

Pentagonal Diamond

Hexagonal Diamond

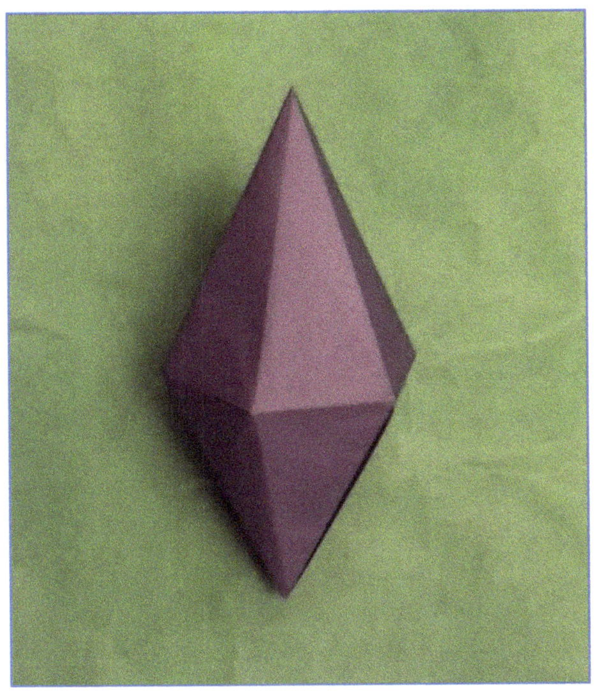

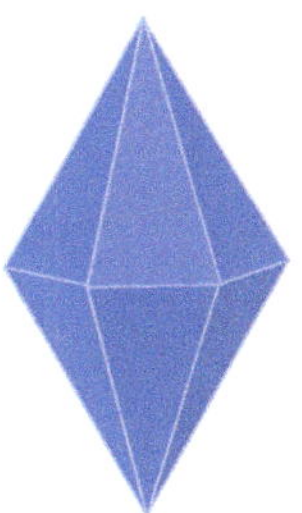

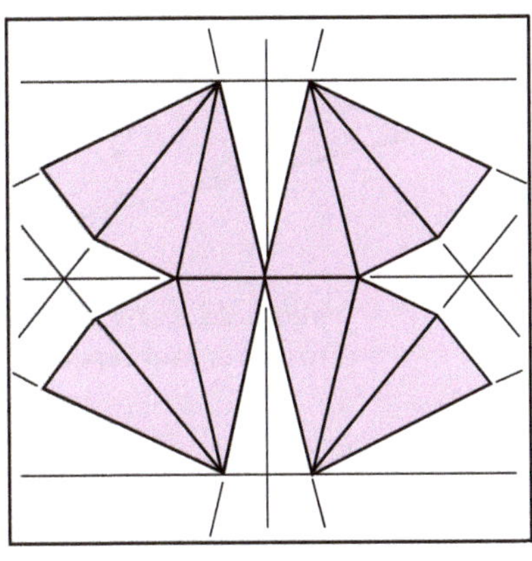

The angles of each of the twelve triangles are 26°, 77°, and 77°. The crease pattern shows a layout that is both even and odd. The even pattern is a reflection like a mirror image. The odd pattern shows that a rotation of 180° is the same.

1

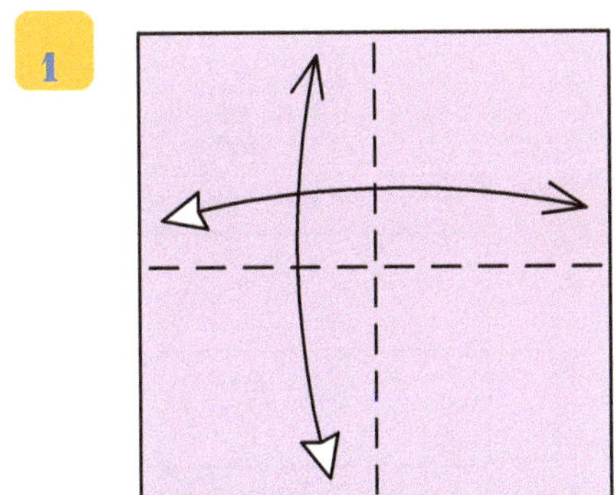

Fold and unfold.

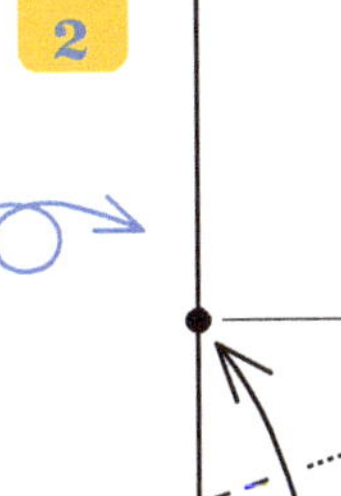

2

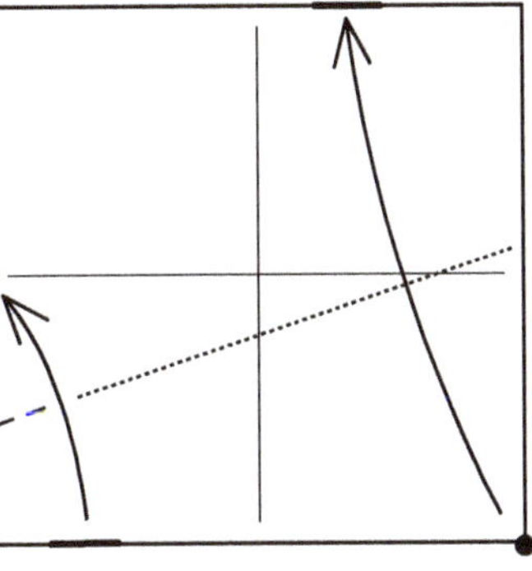

Bring the lower right corner to the top edge and the bottom edge to the left center. Crease on the left.

3

Unfold and rotate 180°.

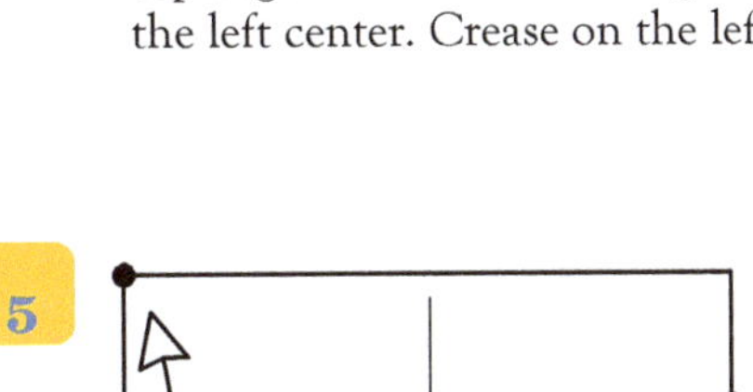

4

Repeat steps 2–3.

5

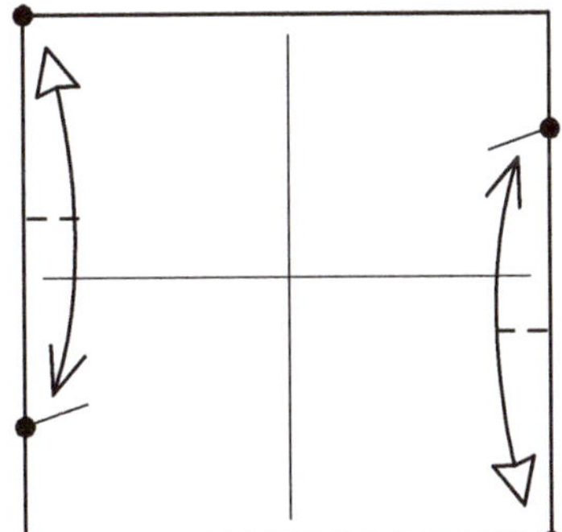

Fold and unfold on the edges. Rotate 90°.

6

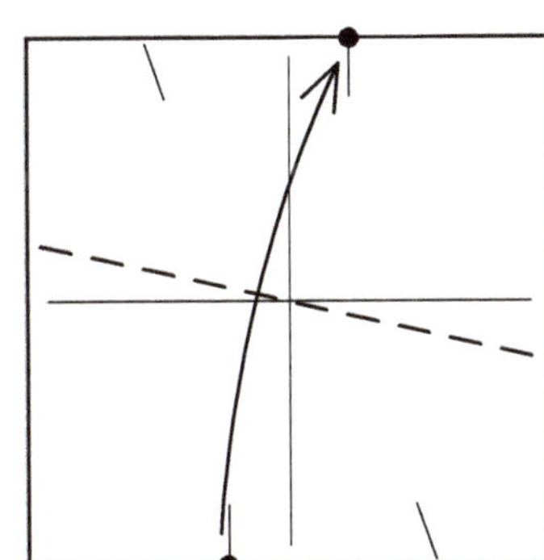

The dots will meet.

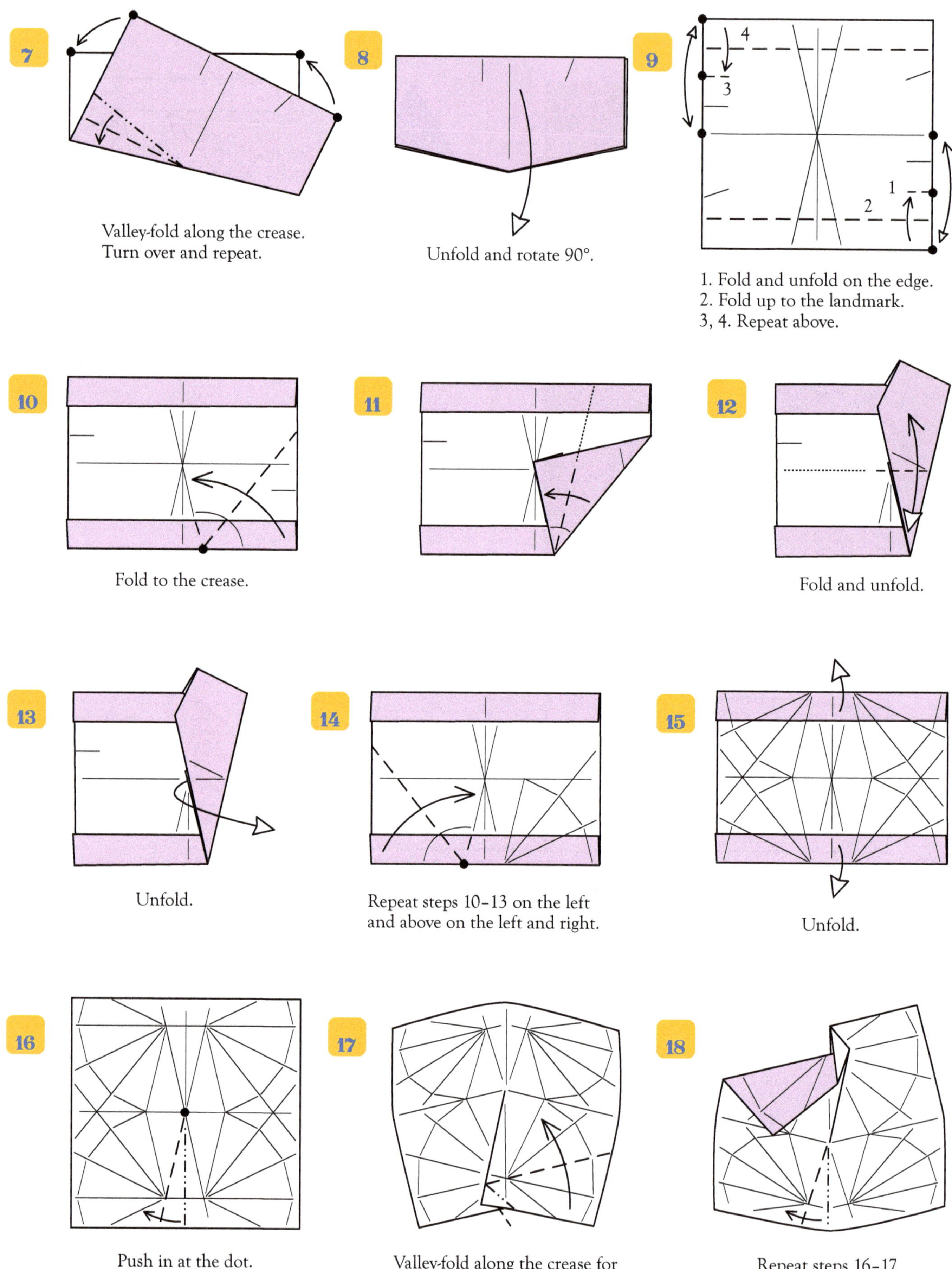

Valley-fold along the crease. Turn over and repeat.

Unfold and rotate 90°.

1. Fold and unfold on the edge.
2. Fold up to the landmark.
3, 4. Repeat above.

Fold to the crease.

Fold and unfold.

Unfold.

Repeat steps 10–13 on the left and above on the left and right.

Unfold.

Push in at the dot.

Valley-fold along the crease for this squash fold. Rotate 180°.

Repeat steps 16–17. Then flatten.

19

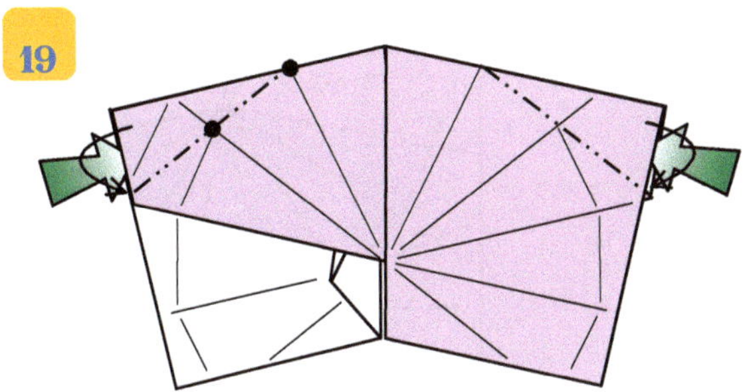

Make reverse folds along the creases with the dots.

20

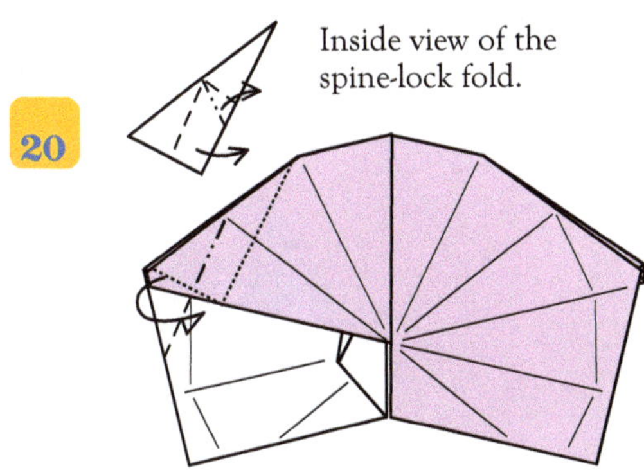

Fold the inside layers together for this spine-lock fold. Mountain-fold along the crease. Turn over and repeat.

21

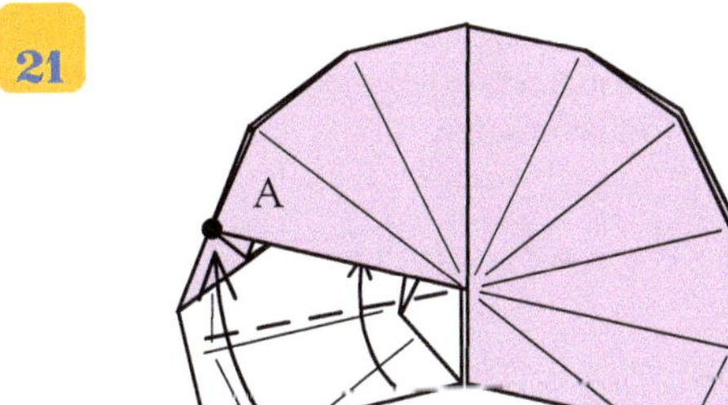

Bring the edge to the dot and tuck inside. All of the folds will be under region A. Turn over and repeat.

22

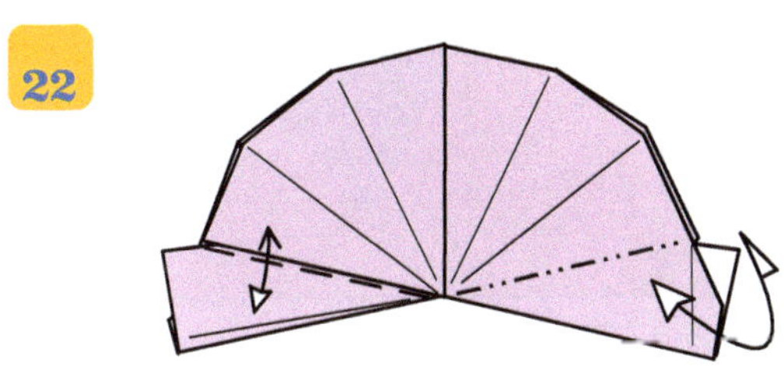

Fold and unfold.

23

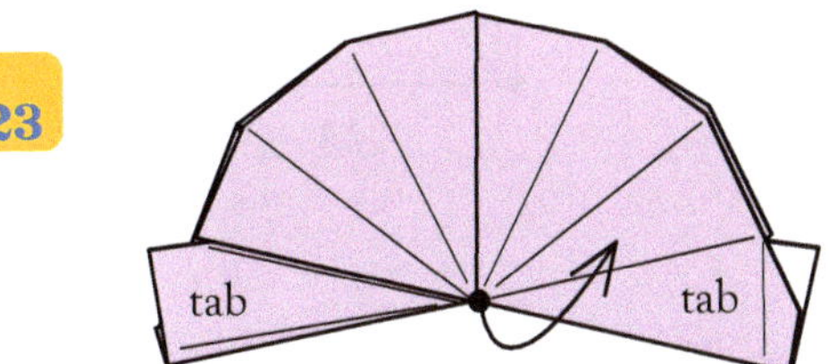

Lift up at the dot to open the model. Tuck and interlock the tabs.

24

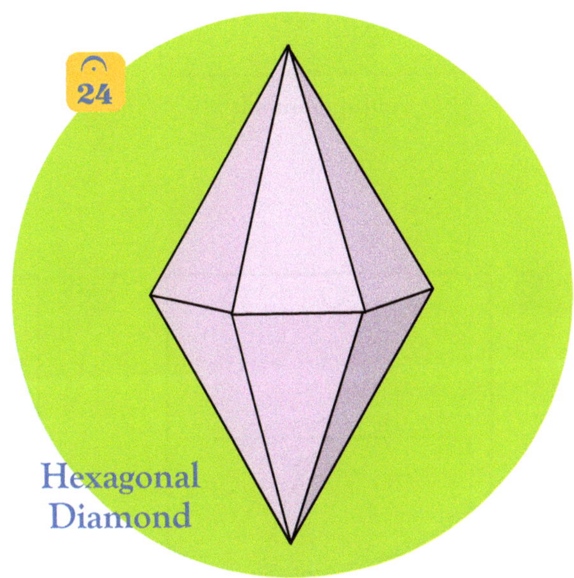

Hexagonal Diamond

Heptagonal Diamond

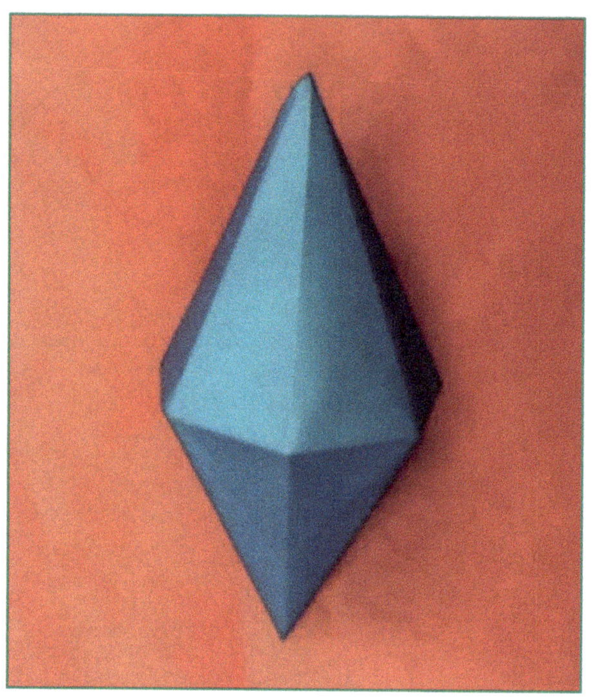

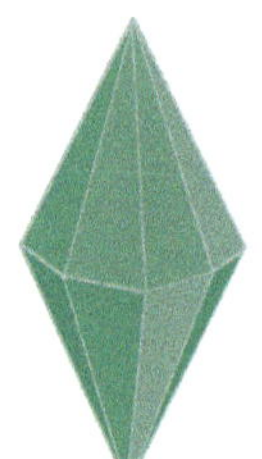

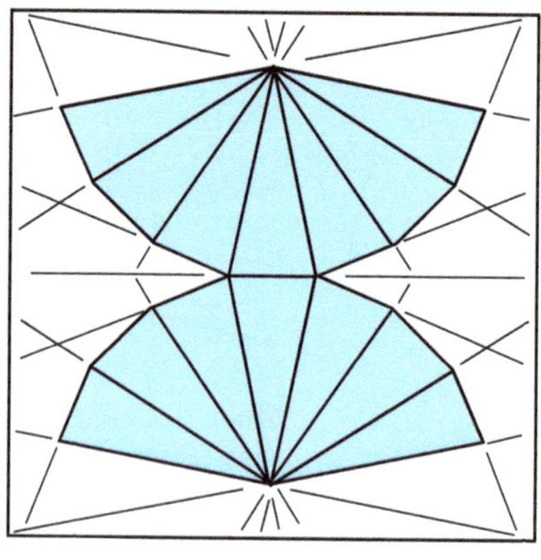

The angles of each face are 22.5°, 78.75°, and 78.75°. This fourteen-sided model uses even and odd symmetry.

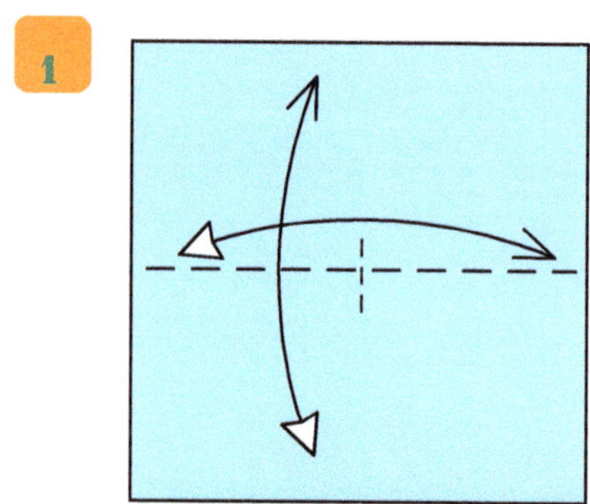

1. Fold and unfold.

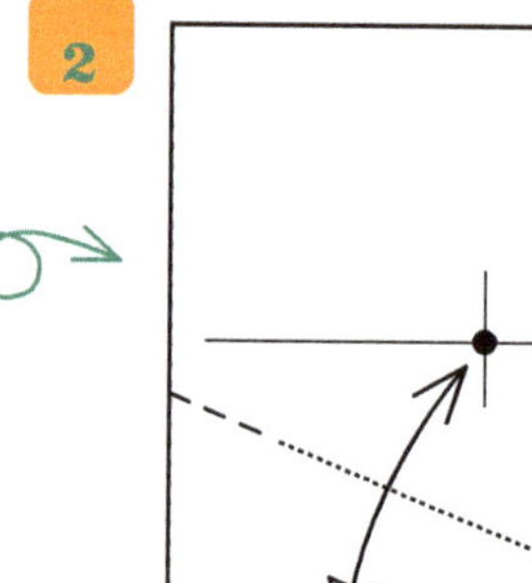

2. Fold and unfold the edge to the center. Crease on the left.

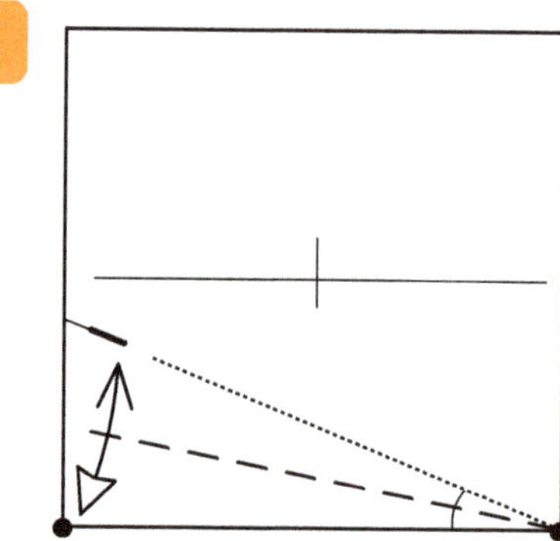

3. Fold and unfold to bisect the angle.

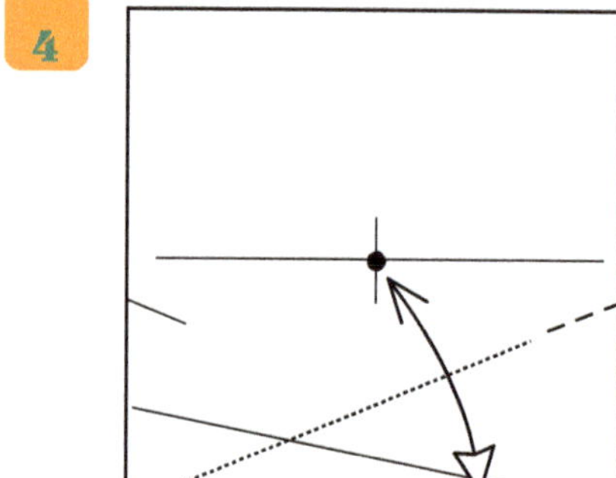

4. Repeat steps 2–3 in the other direction. Rotate 180°.

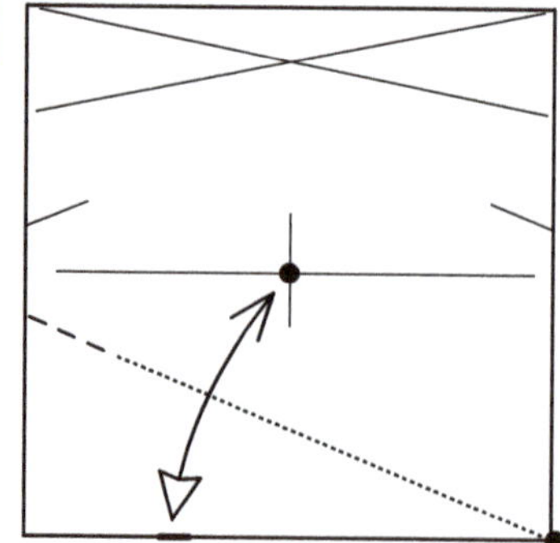

5. Repeat steps 2–4.

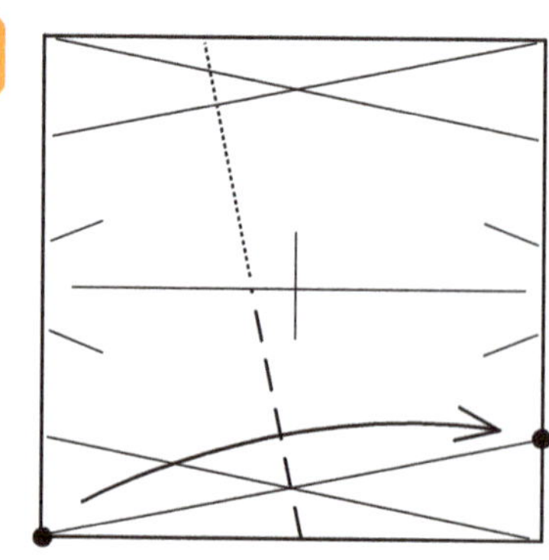

6. Crease on the lower half.

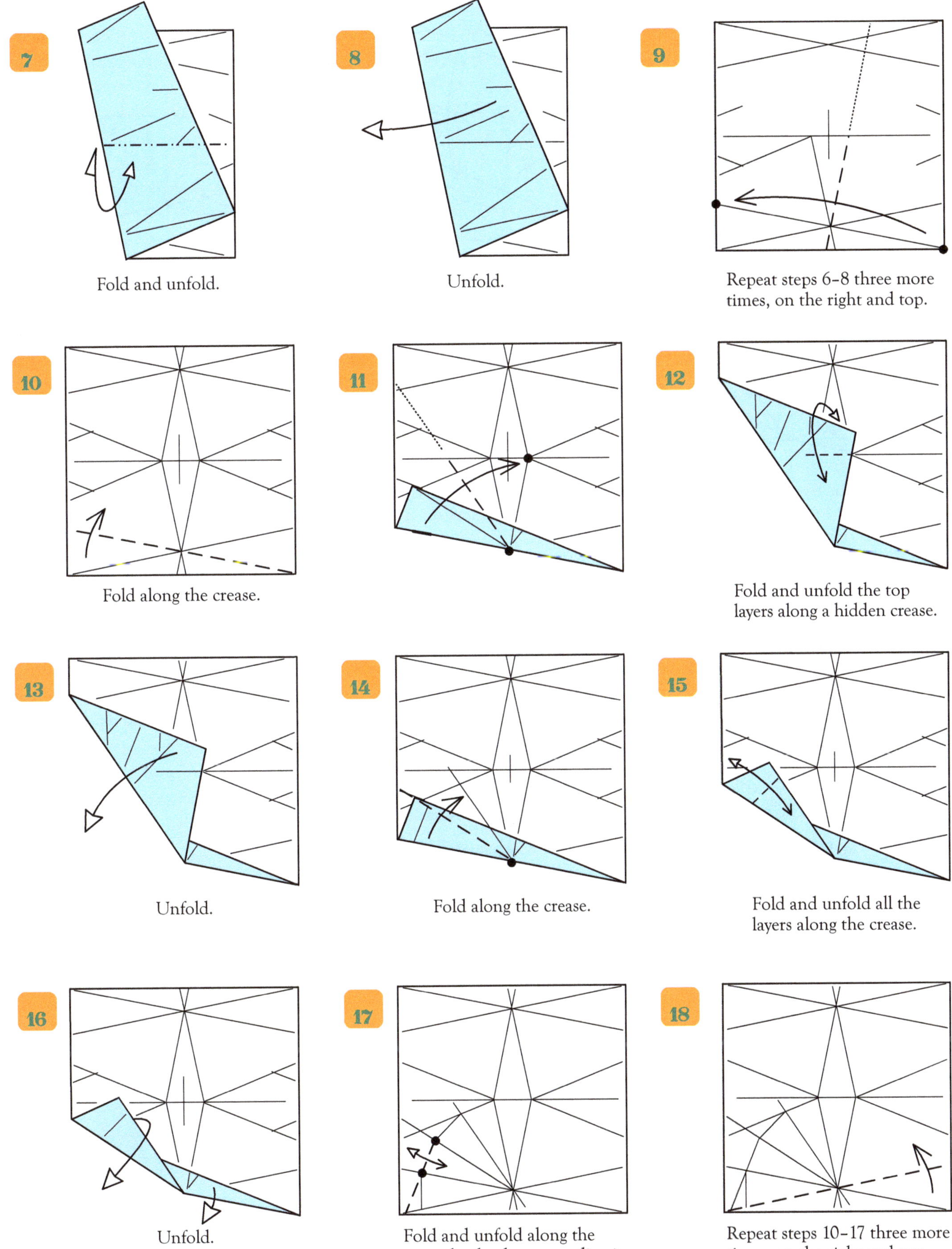

Fold and unfold.

Unfold.

Repeat steps 6–8 three more times, on the right and top.

Fold along the crease.

Fold and unfold the top layers along a hidden crease.

Unfold.

Fold along the crease.

Fold and unfold all the layers along the crease.

Unfold.

Fold and unfold along the crease by the dots, extending it.

Repeat steps 10–17 three more times, on the right and top.

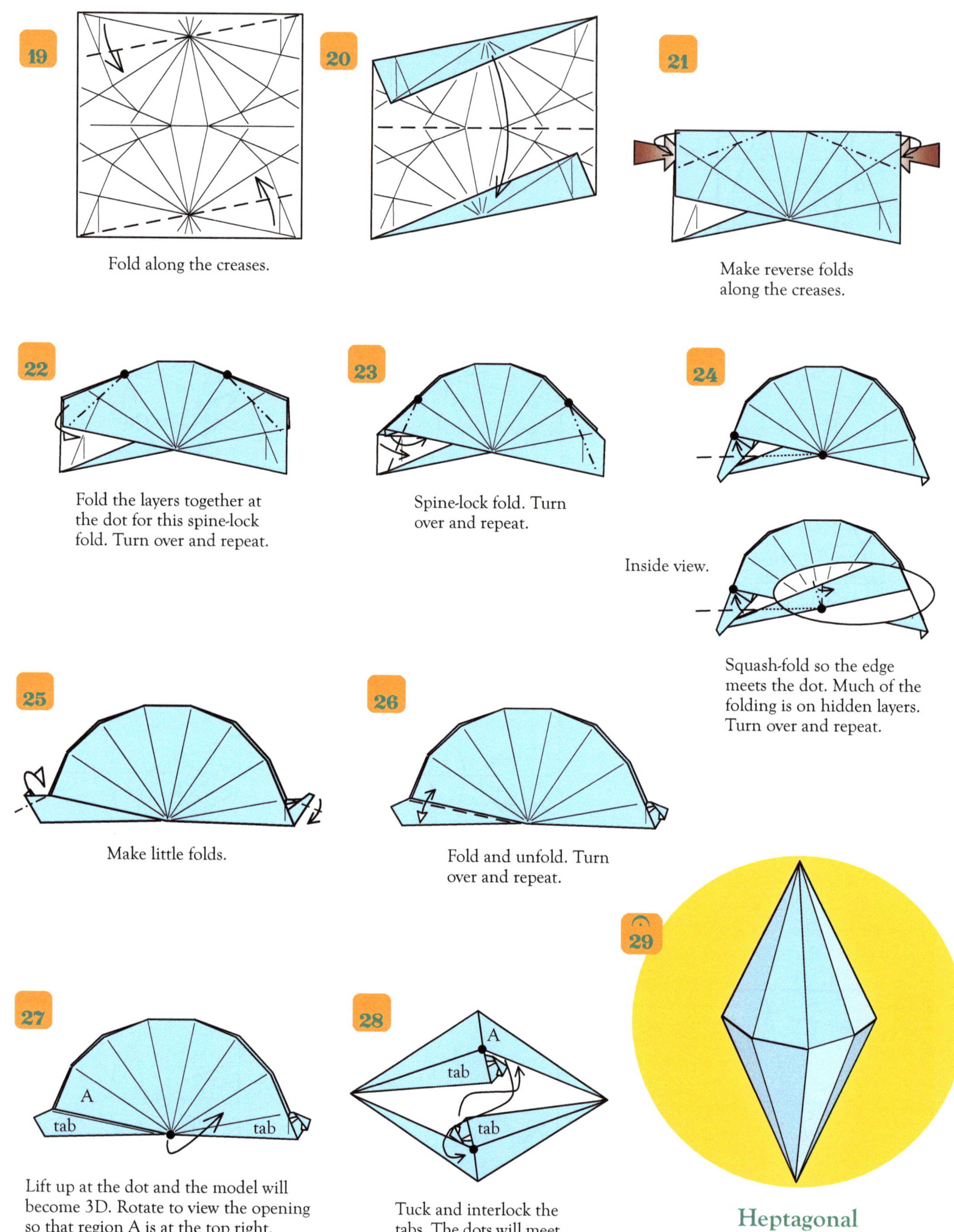

Fold along the creases.

Make reverse folds along the creases.

Fold the layers together at the dot for this spine-lock fold. Turn over and repeat.

Spine-lock fold. Turn over and repeat.

Inside view.

Squash-fold so the edge meets the dot. Much of the folding is on hidden layers. Turn over and repeat.

Make little folds.

Fold and unfold. Turn over and repeat.

Lift up at the dot and the model will become 3D. Rotate to view the opening so that region A is at the top right.

Tuck and interlock the tabs. The dots will meet.

Heptagonal Diamond

Octagonal Diamond

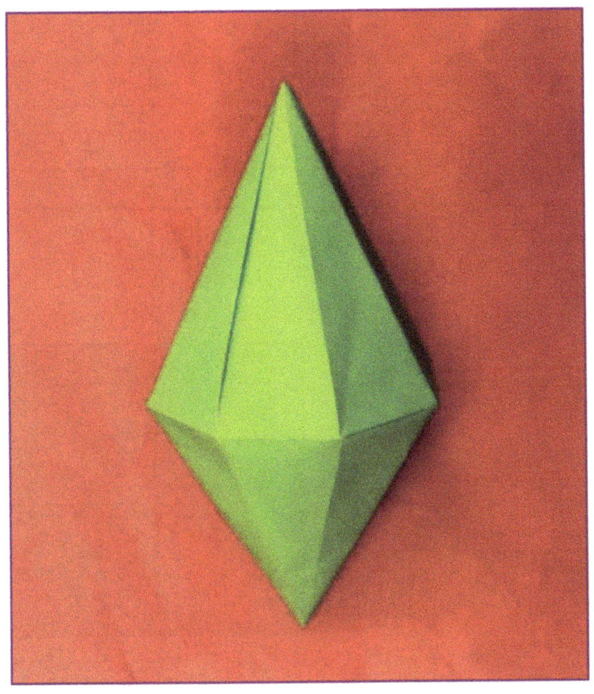

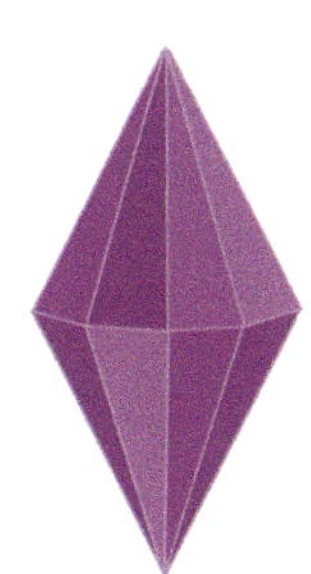

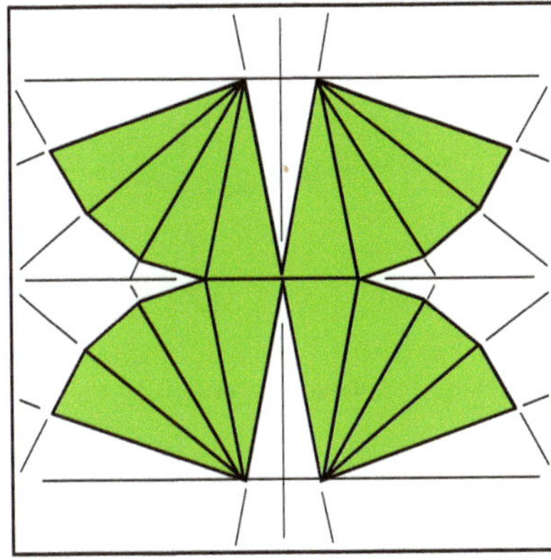

The angles in each of the triangles of this sixteen-sided diamond are 20°, 80°, and 80°.

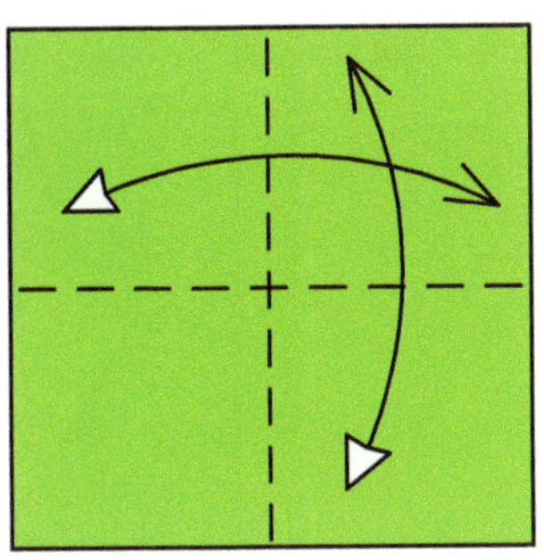

1 Fold and unfold.

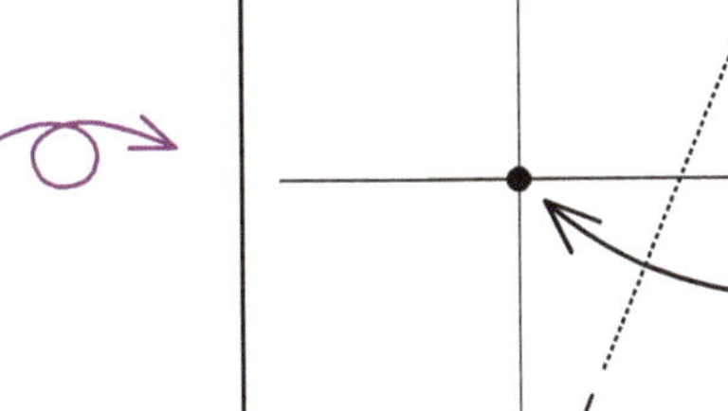

2 Bring the edge to the center and crease at the bottom.

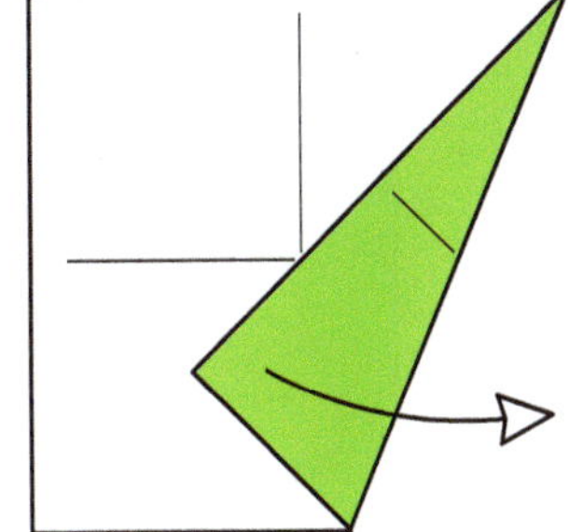

3 Unfold and rotate 180°.

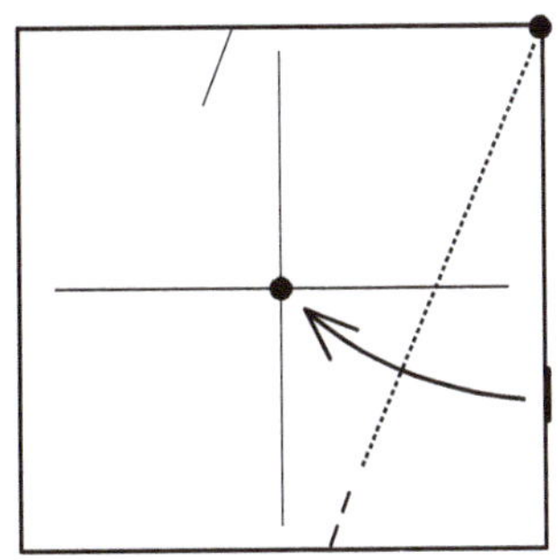

4 Repeat steps 2–3.

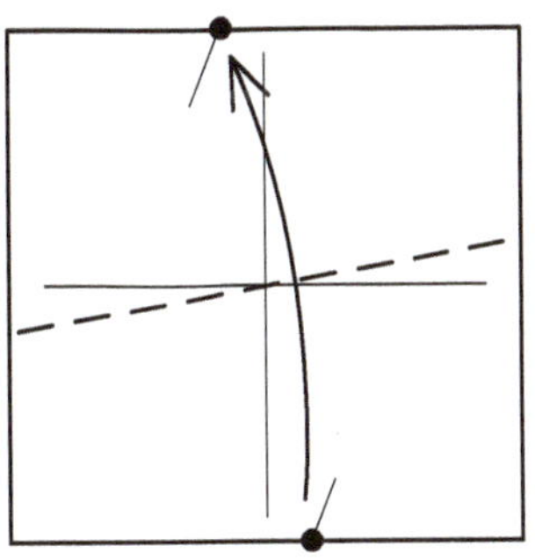

5 The dots will meet.

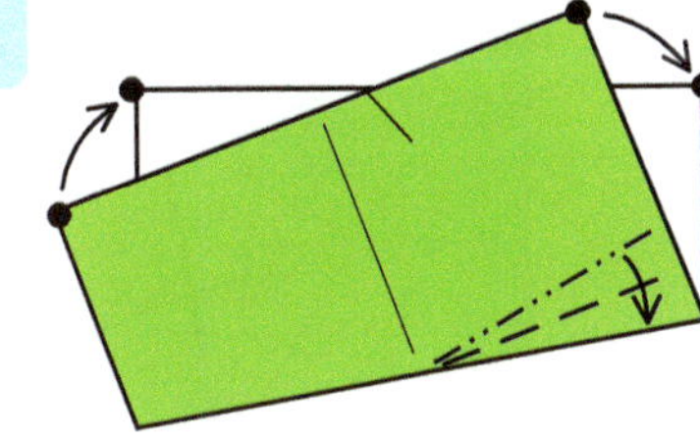

6 Valley-fold along the crease. Turn over and repeat.

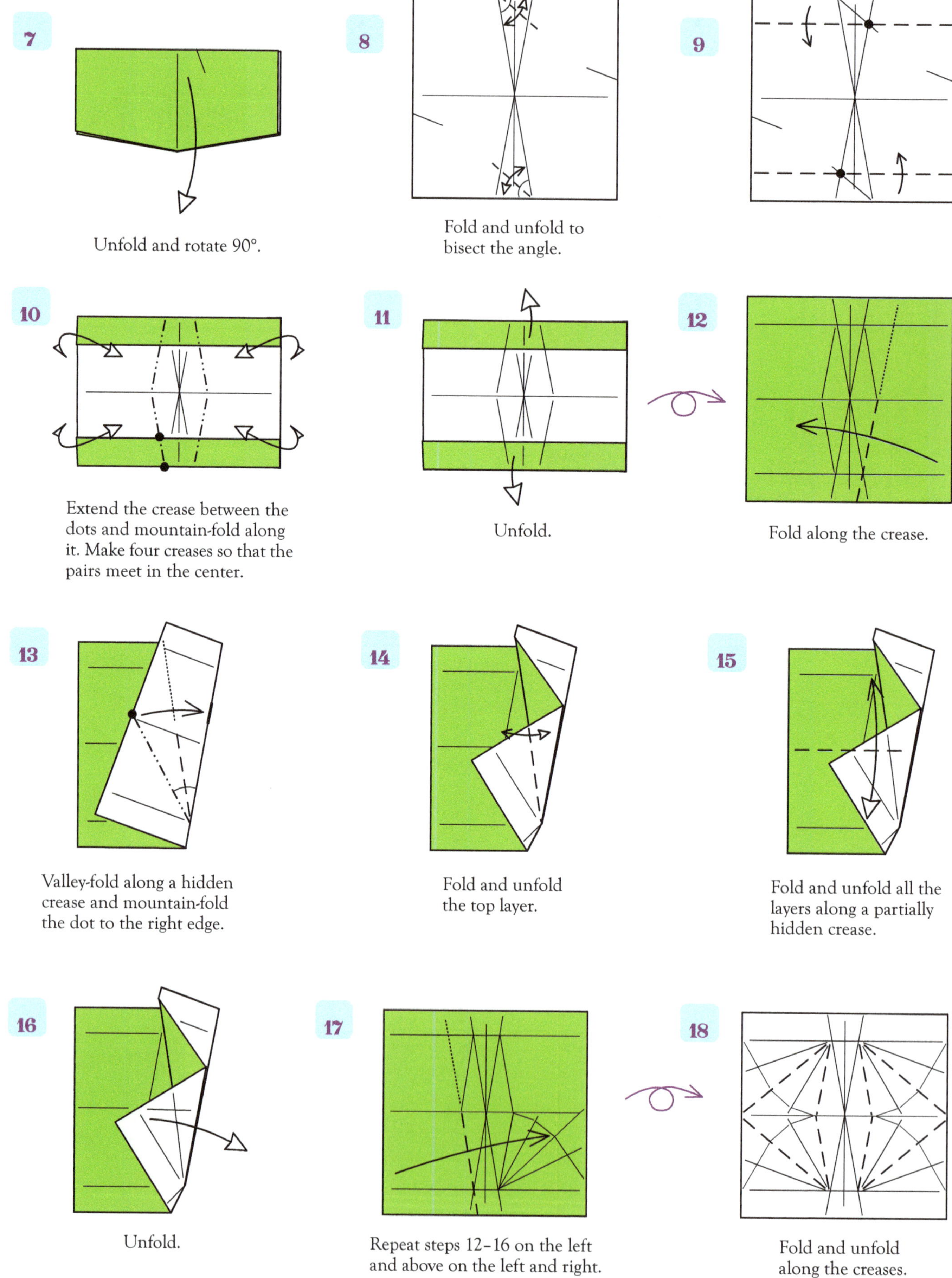

Unfold and rotate 90°.

Fold and unfold to bisect the angle.

Extend the crease between the dots and mountain-fold along it. Make four creases so that the pairs meet in the center.

Unfold.

Fold along the crease.

Valley-fold along a hidden crease and mountain-fold the dot to the right edge.

Fold and unfold the top layer.

Fold and unfold all the layers along a partially hidden crease.

Unfold.

Repeat steps 12–16 on the left and above on the left and right.

Fold and unfold along the creases.

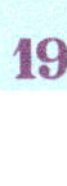

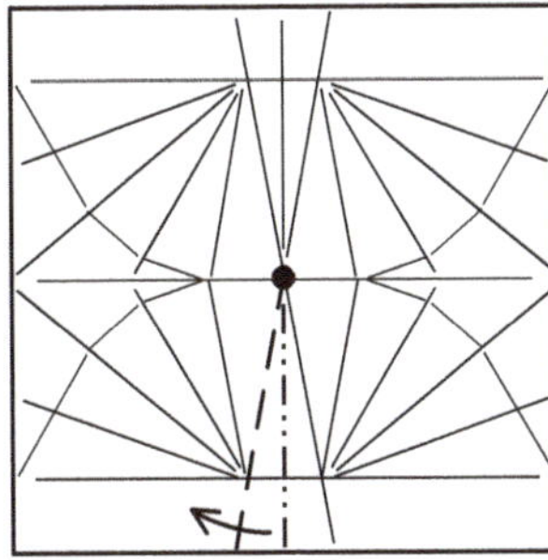

Push in at the dot.

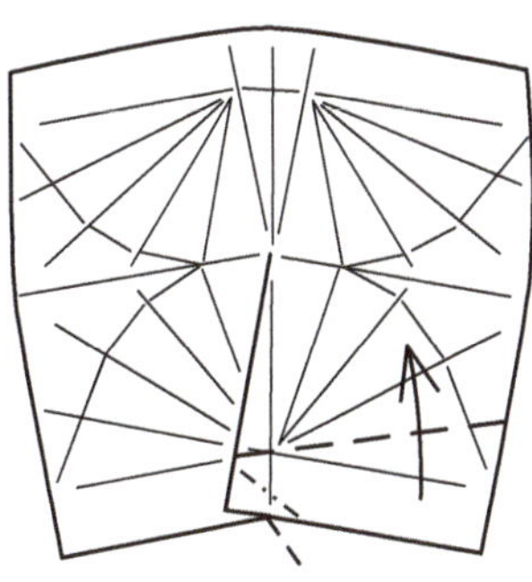

Valley-fold along the crease for this squash fold. Rotate 180°.

21

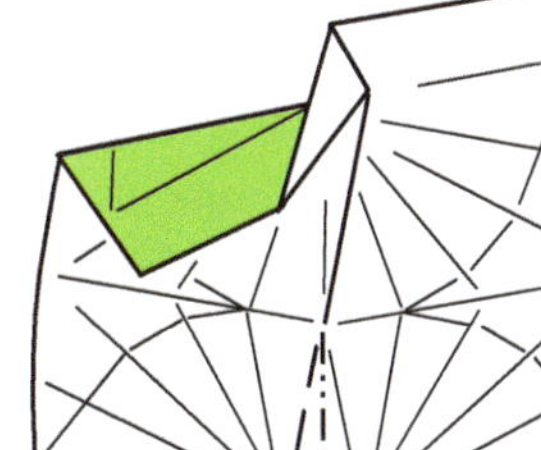

Repeat steps 19–20. Then flatten.

22

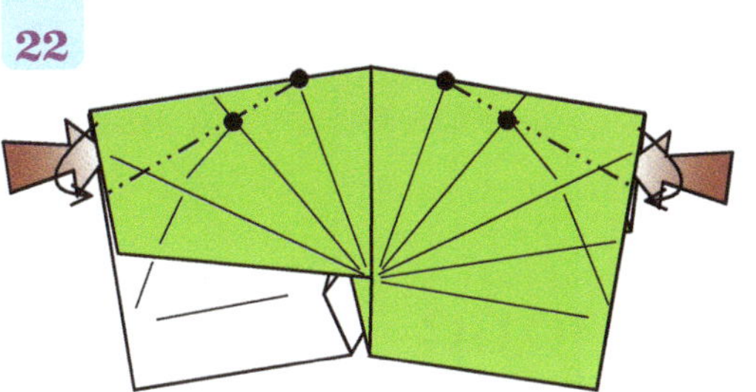

Make reverse folds along the creases with the dots.

23

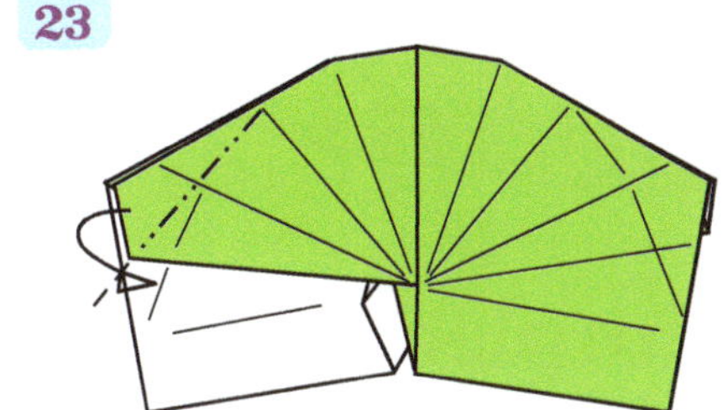

Fold the inside layers together for this spine-lock fold. Turn over and repeat.

24

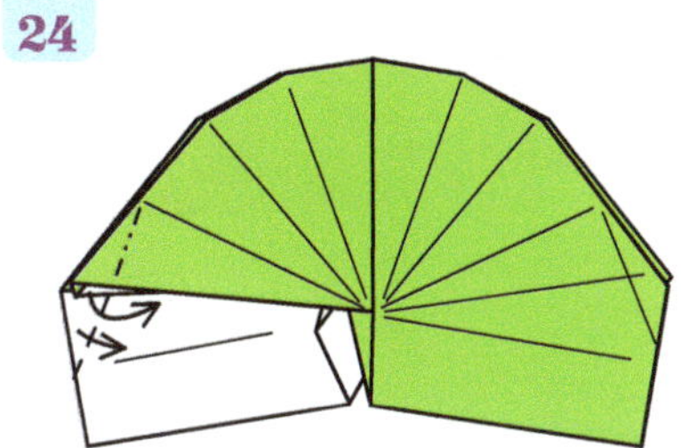

Fold the inside layers together for this spine-lock fold. Turn over and repeat.

25

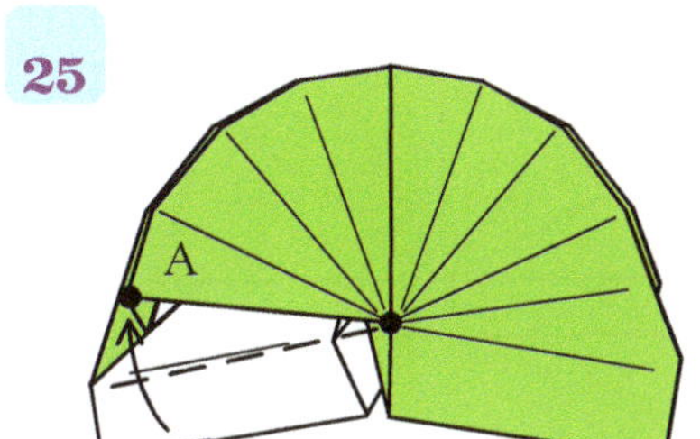

Bring the edge to the dot and tuck inside. All of the folds will be under region A. Turn over and repeat.

26

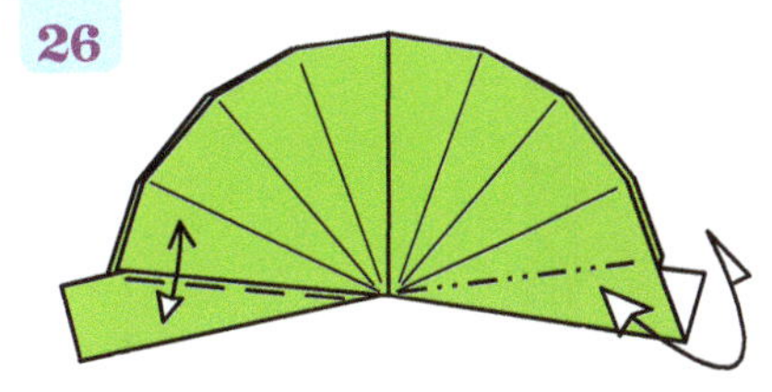

Fold and unfold.

27

tab tab

Lift up at the dot to open the model. Tuck and interlock the tabs.

28

Octagonal Diamond

Trio of Dimpled Diamonds

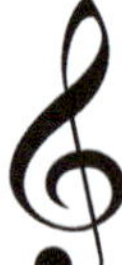

This minuet of Diamonds has a trio of Dimpled Diamonds. Alternate sides of the Diamonds are sunken. These jewels are the prized possessions of the Dragons. Should you capture these treasures, keep them safe before the Dragons find them.

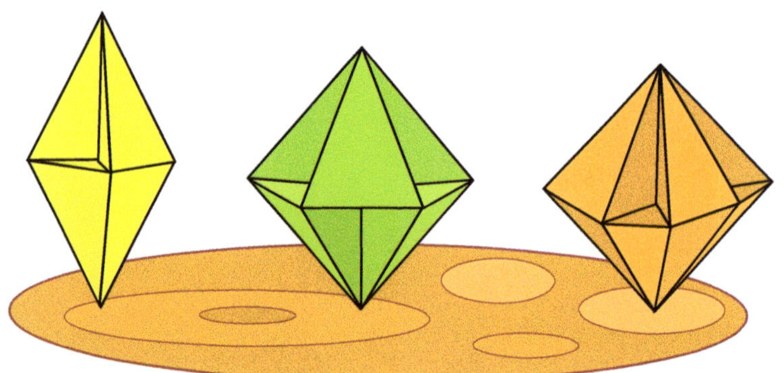

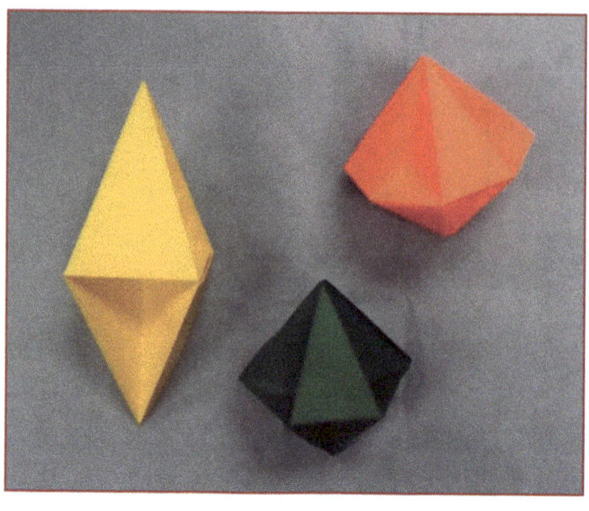

Dimpled Square Diamond

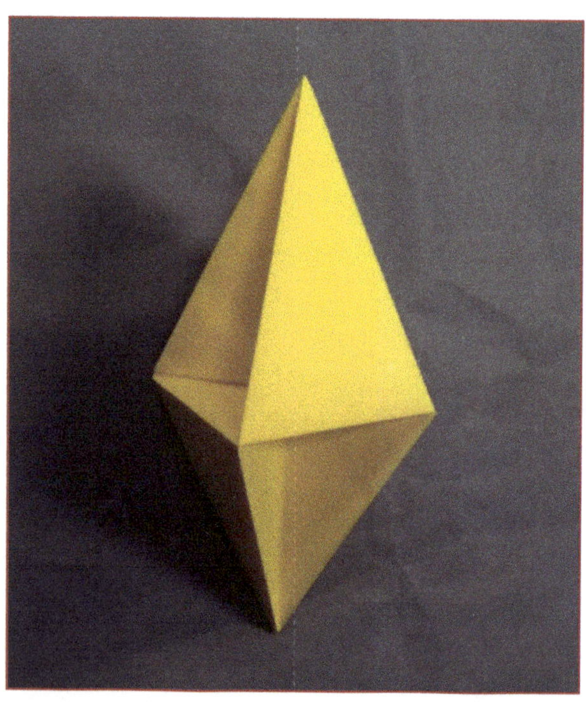

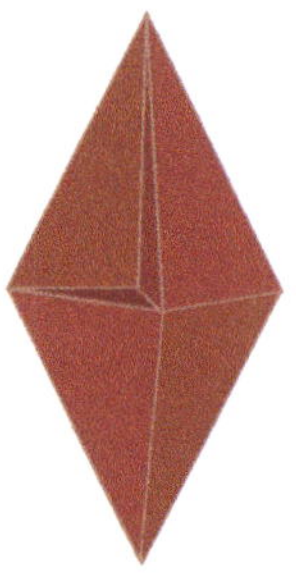

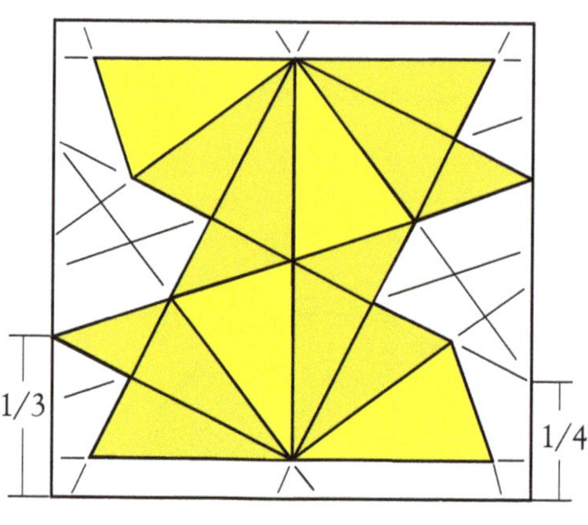

For this dimpled square diamond, four alternating sides are sunken. The darker regions show the sunken sides. Odd symmetry is used.

1

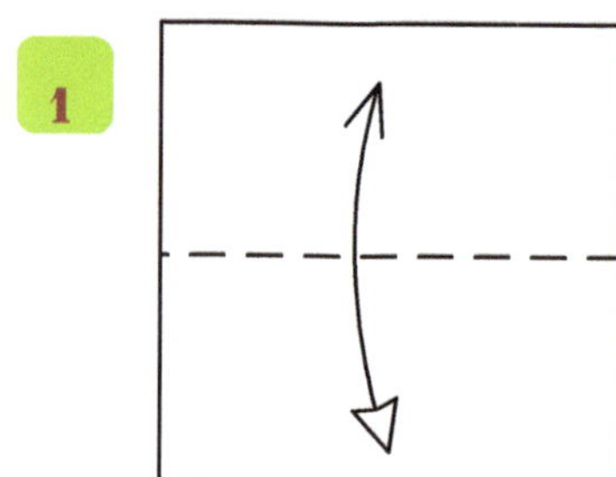

Fold and unfold.

2

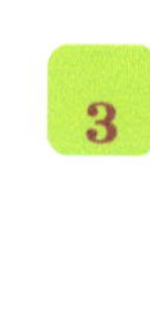

Fold and unfold on the left and right by the edges. Rotate 90°.

3

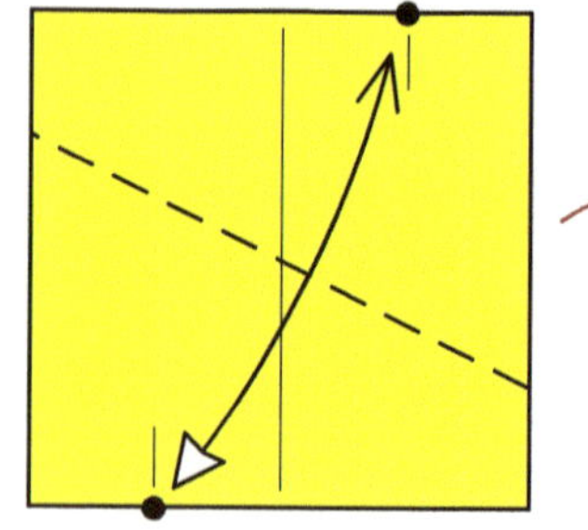

Fold and unfold.

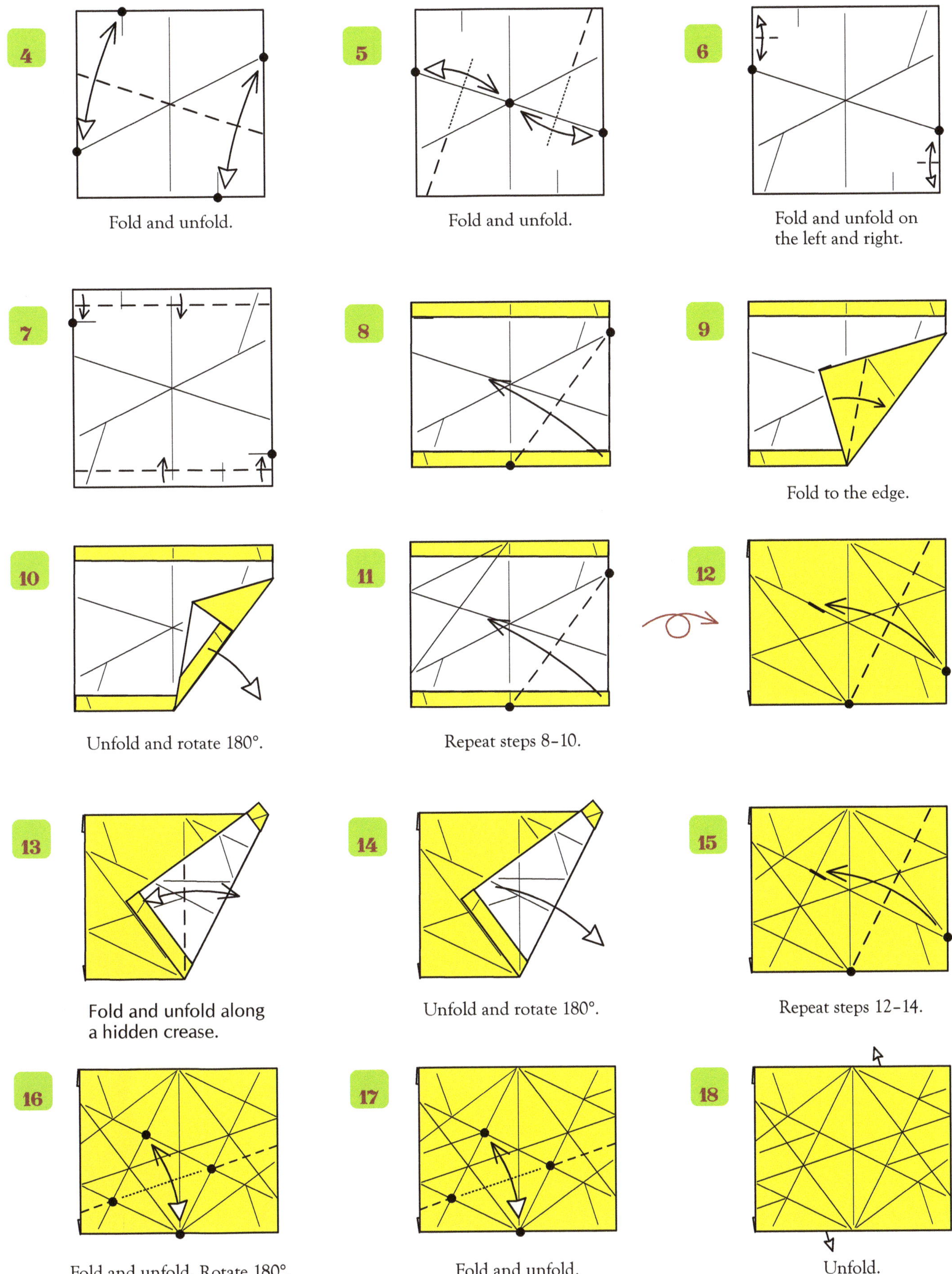
4
Fold and unfold.
5
Fold and unfold.
6
Fold and unfold on the left and right.
7
8
9
Fold to the edge.
10
Unfold and rotate 180°.
11
Repeat steps 8–10.
12
13
Fold and unfold along a hidden crease.
14
Unfold and rotate 180°.
15
Repeat steps 12–14.
16
Fold and unfold. Rotate 180°.
17
Fold and unfold.
18
Unfold.

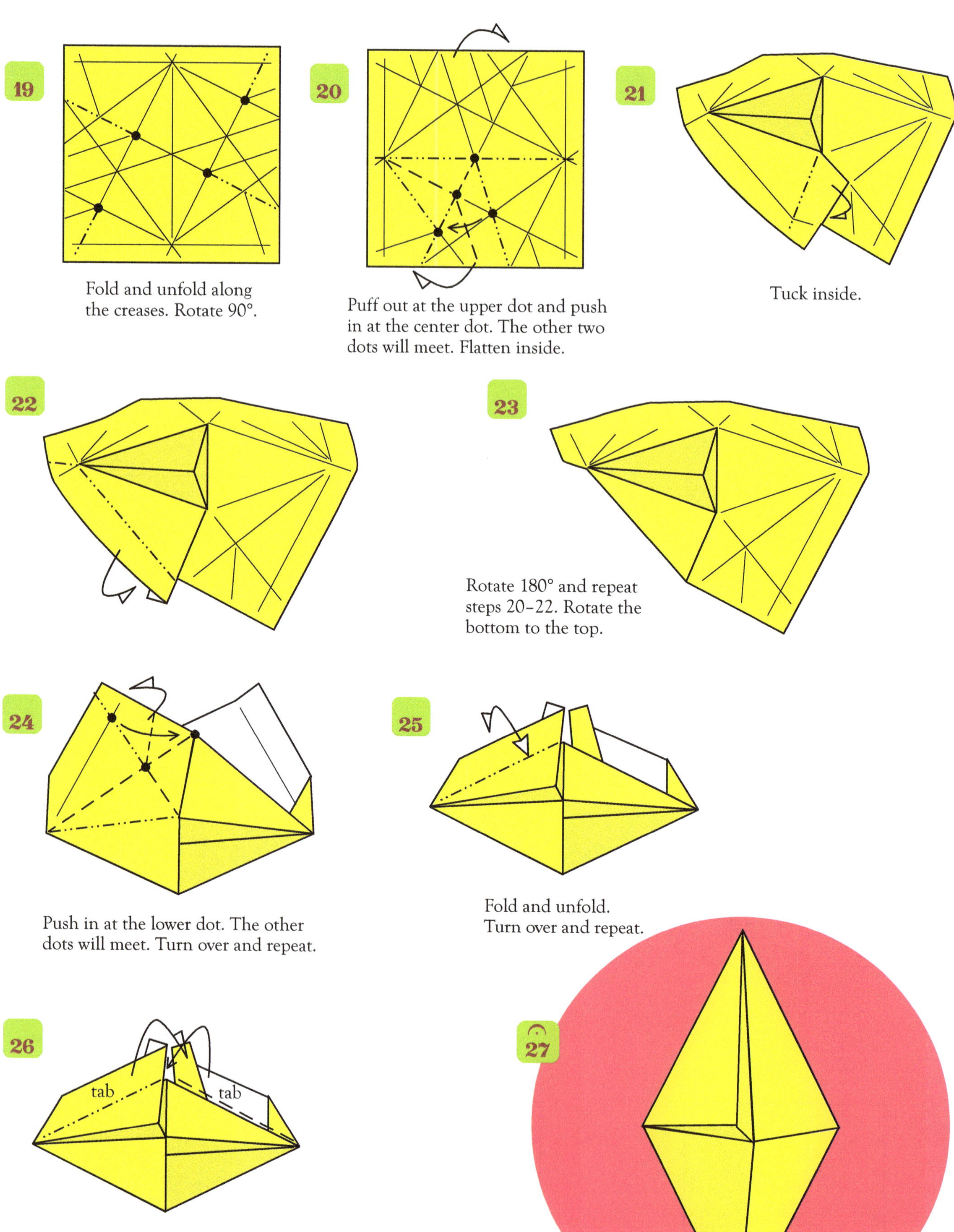

Fold and unfold along the creases. Rotate 90°.

Puff out at the upper dot and push in at the center dot. The other two dots will meet. Flatten inside.

Tuck inside.

Rotate 180° and repeat steps 20–22. Rotate the bottom to the top.

Push in at the lower dot. The other dots will meet. Turn over and repeat.

Fold and unfold. Turn over and repeat.

Interlock the tabs to close the model.

Dimpled Hexagonal Diamond

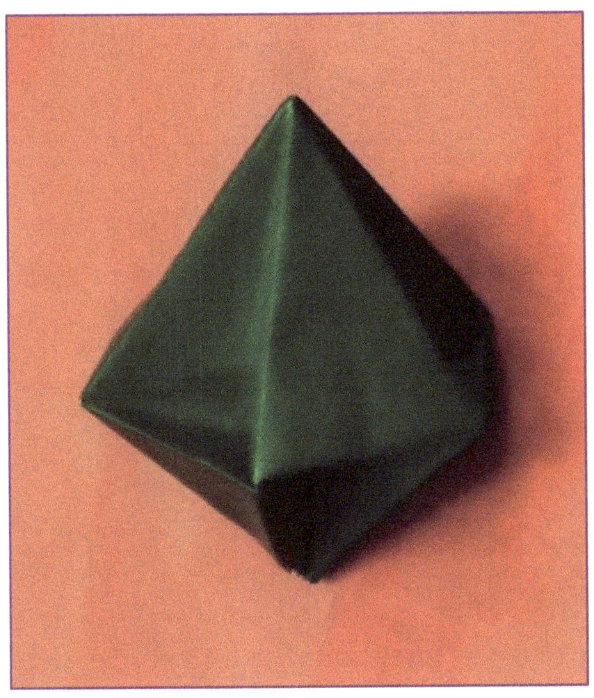

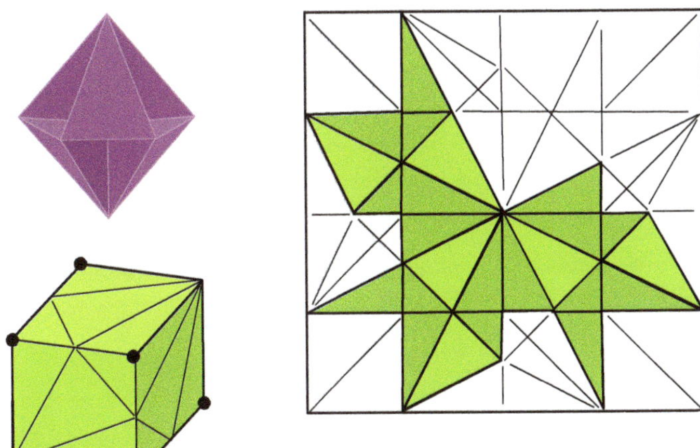

This model comes from a cube where six of the eight corners are sunken, as shown in the middle picture. The layout shows 3/4 square symmetry. The darker regions represent the sunken sides.

1

Fold and unfold.

2

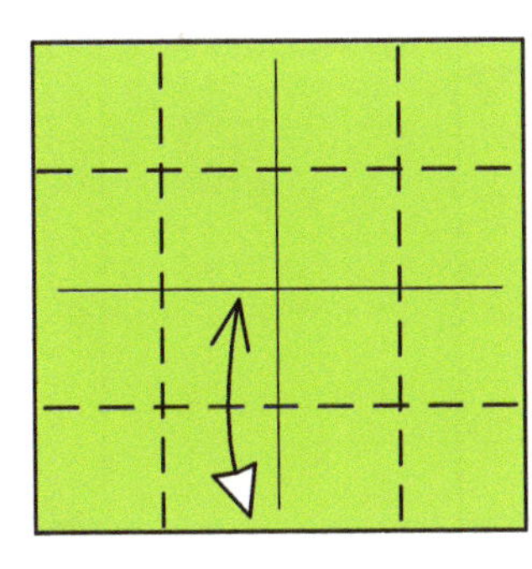

Fold and unfold four times.

3

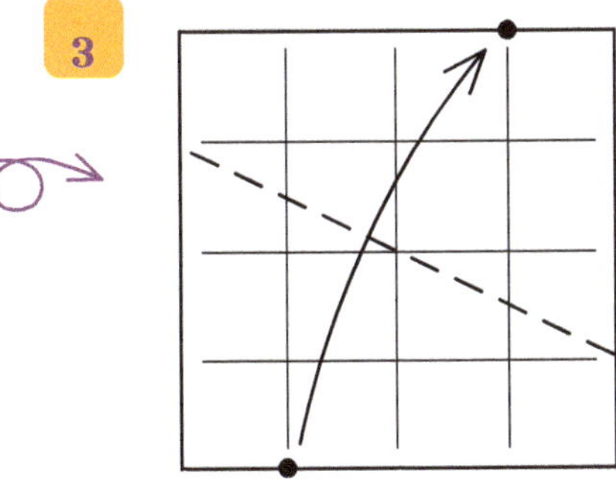

4

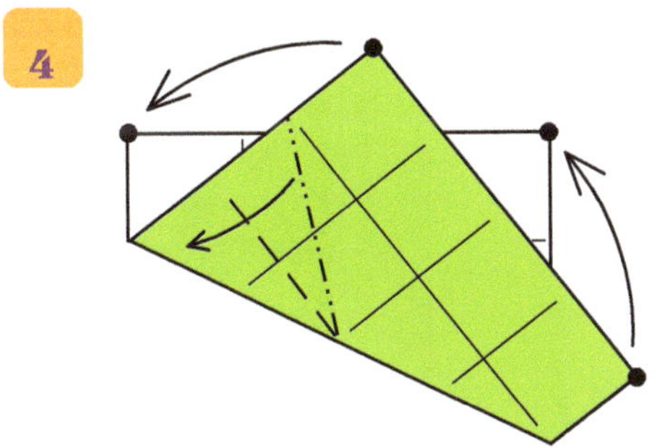

Valley-fold along the crease. Turn over and repeat.

5

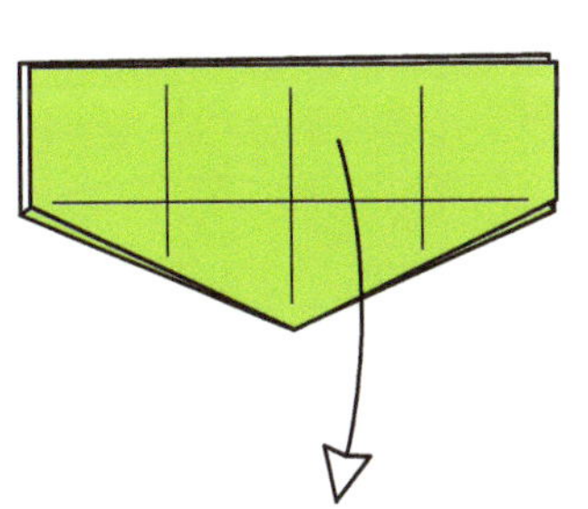

Unfold and rotate 90°.

6

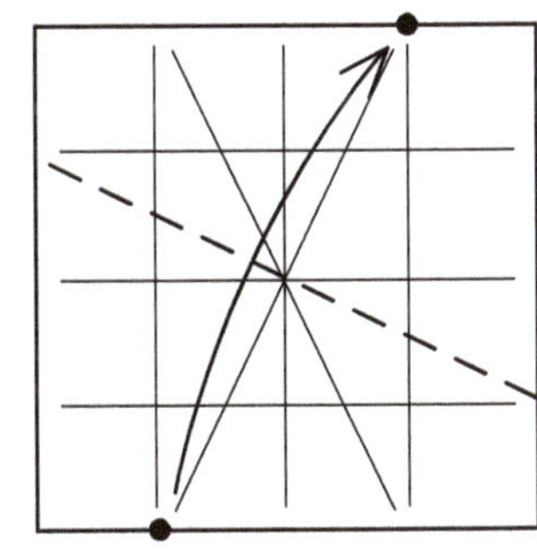

Repeat steps 3–5.

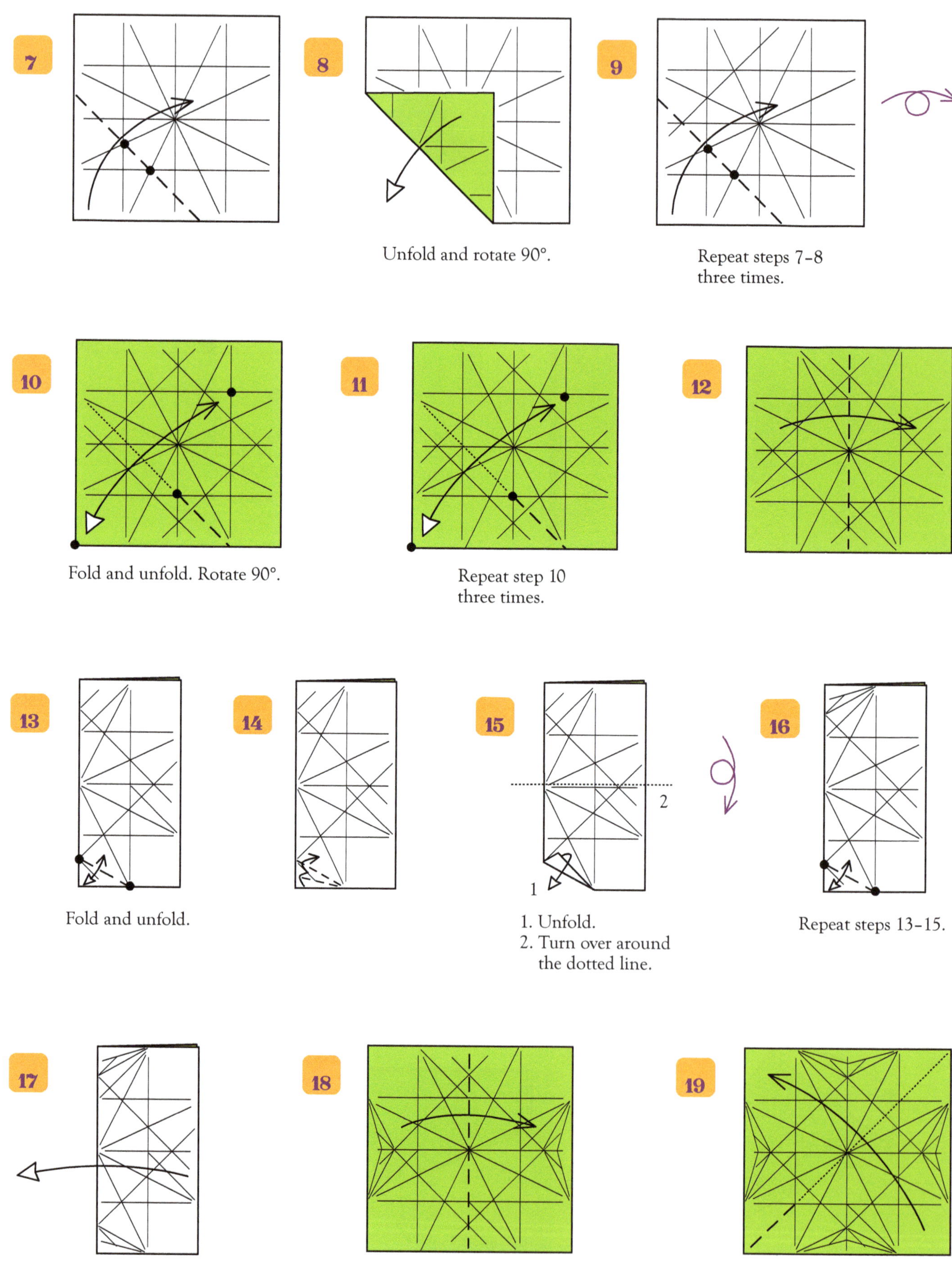

Unfold and rotate 90°.

Repeat steps 7–8
three times.

Fold and unfold. Rotate 90°.

Repeat step 10
three times.

Fold and unfold.

1. Unfold.
2. Turn over around the dotted line.

Repeat steps 13–15.

Unfold and rotate 90°.

Repeat steps 12–17.

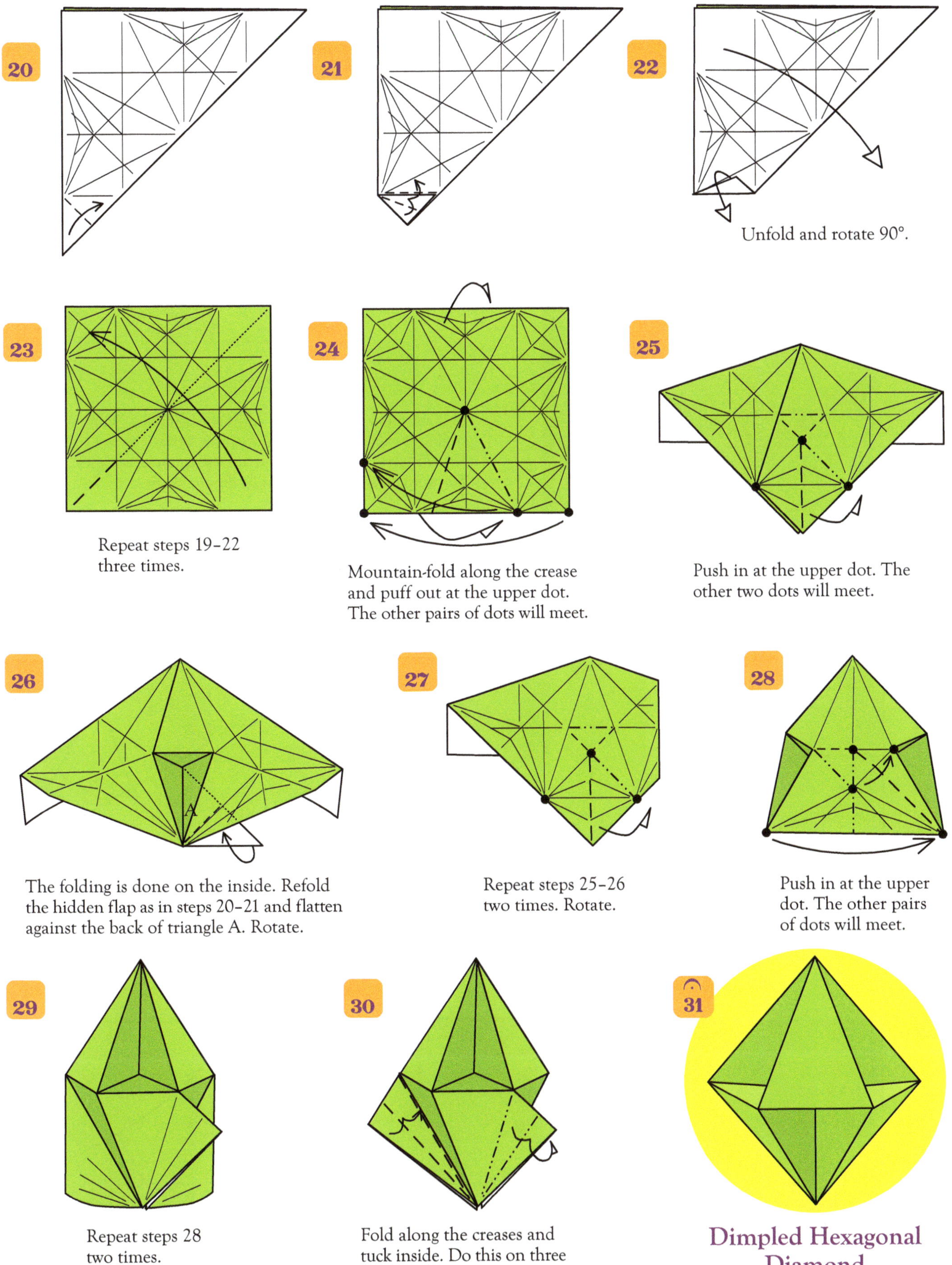

Dimpled Hexagonal Diamond

Dimpled Octagonal Diamond

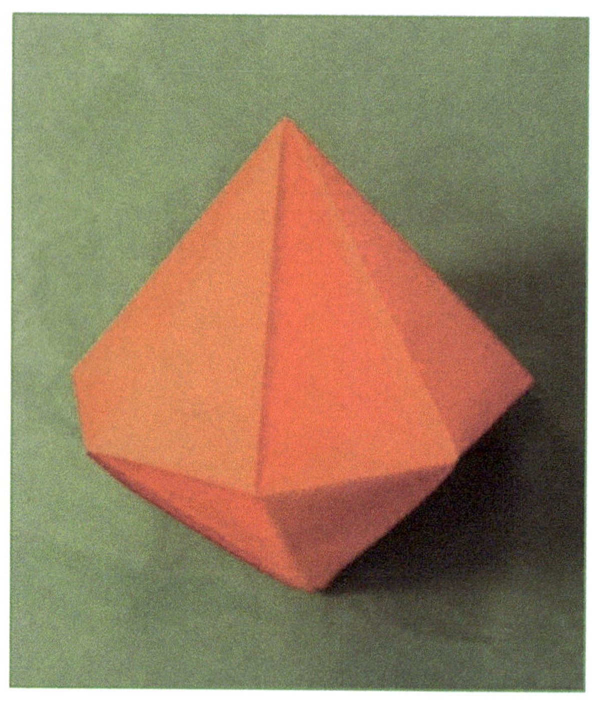

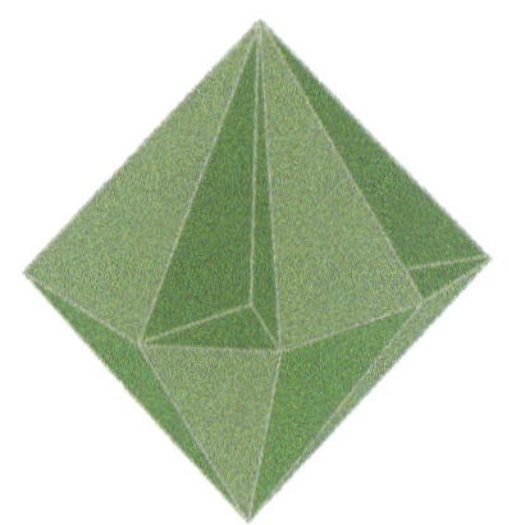

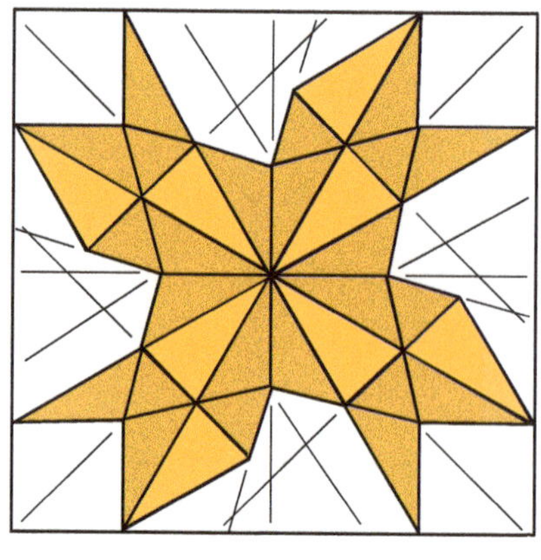

This dimpled diamond has eight sunken sides. The angles of each of the eight nonsunken triangles are 30°, 75°, and 75°. The layout shows square symmetry. The sunken sides are shown in darker shades.

1

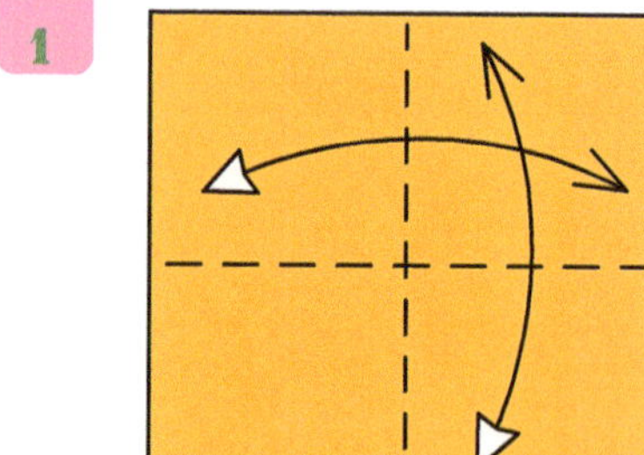

Fold and unfold.

2

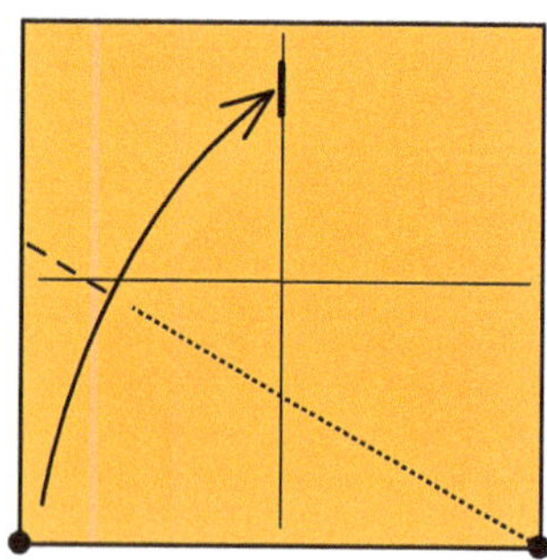

Bring the corner to the line. Fold on the left.

3

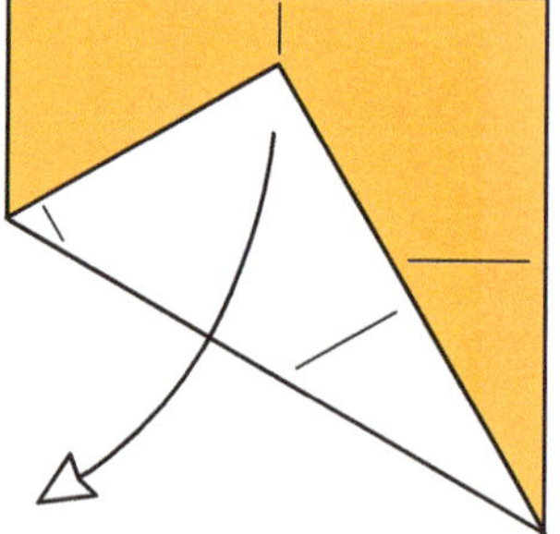

Unfold.

4

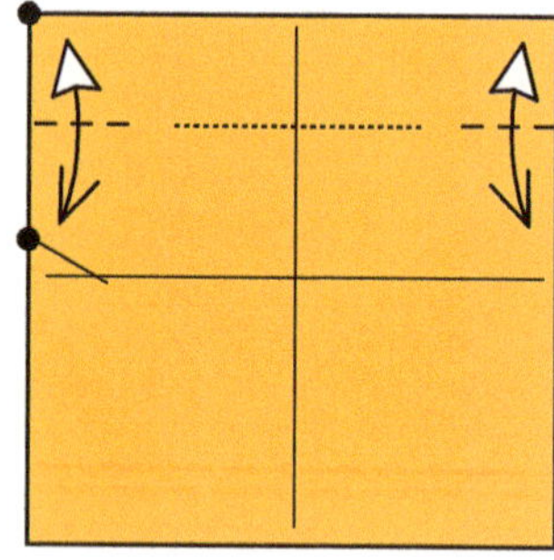

Fold and unfold on the left and right. Rotate 180°.

5

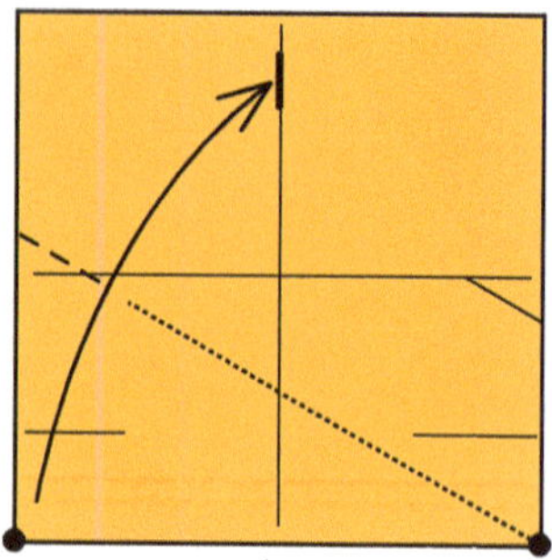

Repeat steps 2–4.

6

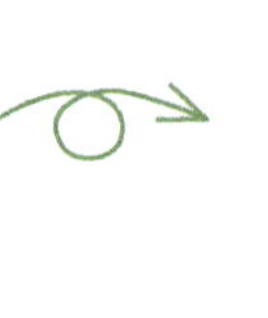

Fold and unfold.

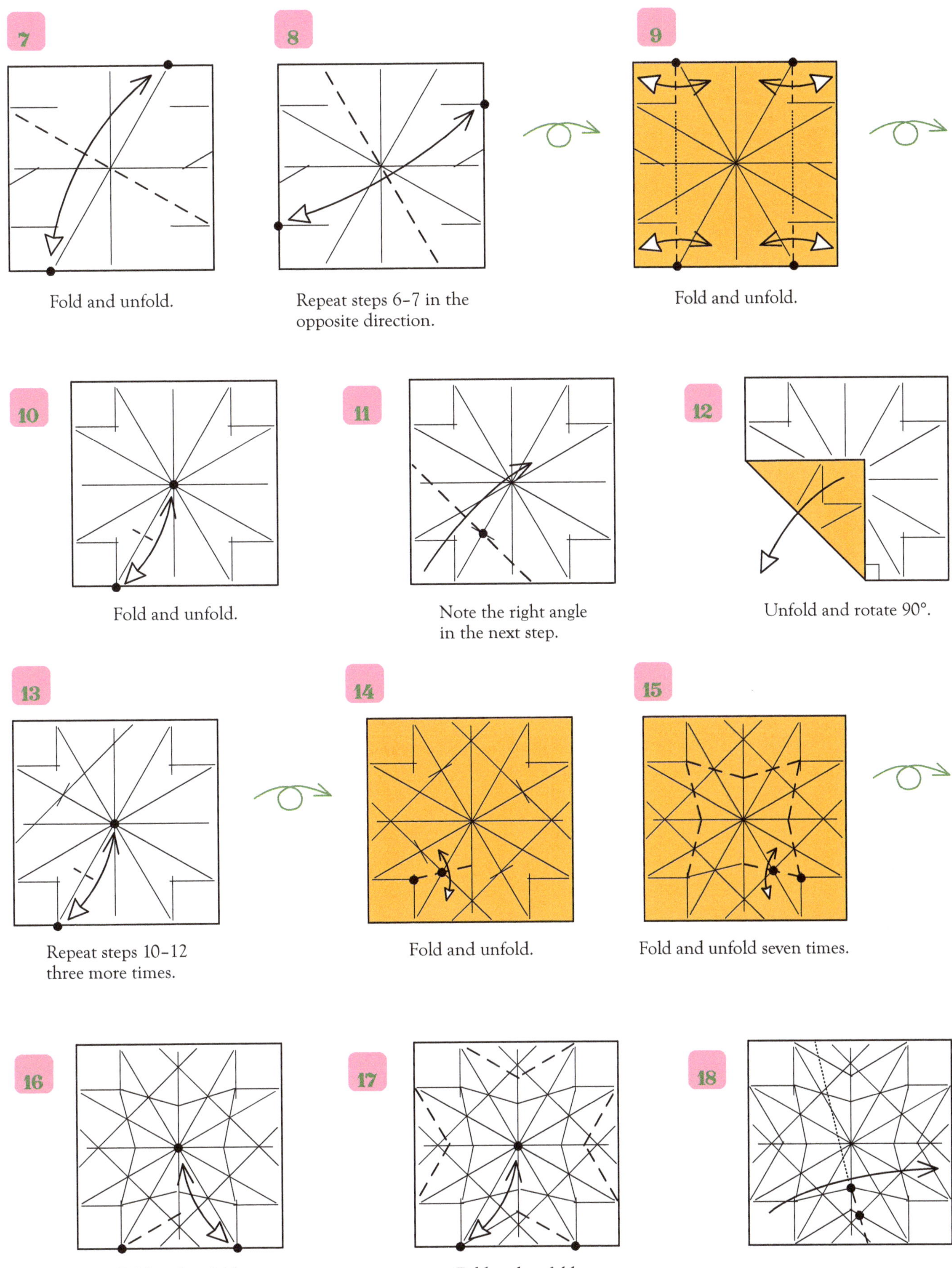
7
Fold and unfold.
8
Repeat steps 6–7 in the opposite direction.
9
Fold and unfold.
10
Fold and unfold.
11
Note the right angle in the next step.
12
Unfold and rotate 90°.
13
Repeat steps 10–12 three more times.
14
Fold and unfold.
15
Fold and unfold seven times.
16
Fold and unfold.
17
Fold and unfold.
18

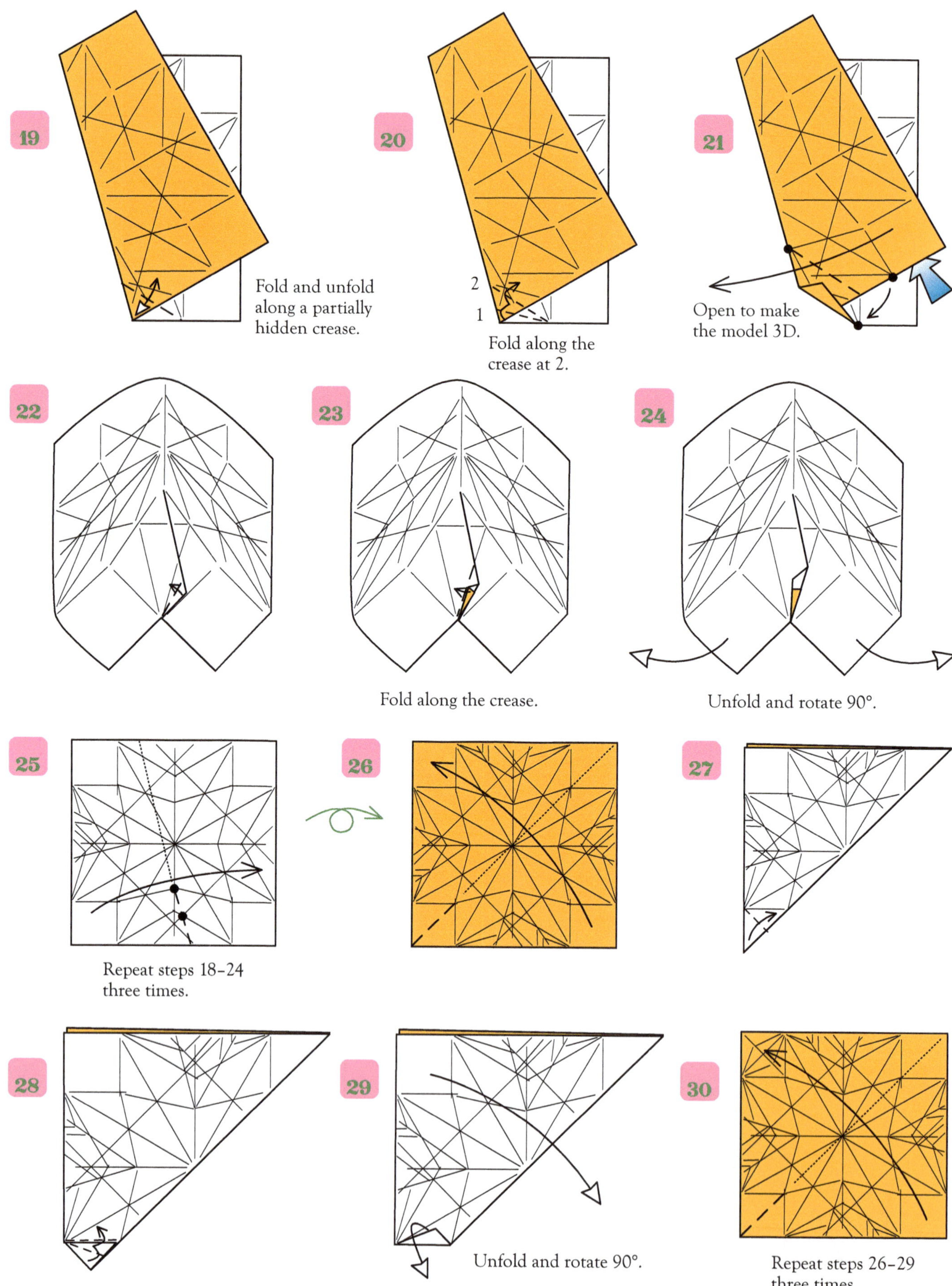

Fold and unfold along a partially hidden crease.

Fold along the crease at 2.

Open to make the model 3D.

Fold along the crease.

Unfold and rotate 90°.

Repeat steps 18–24 three times.

Unfold and rotate 90°.

Repeat steps 26–29 three times.

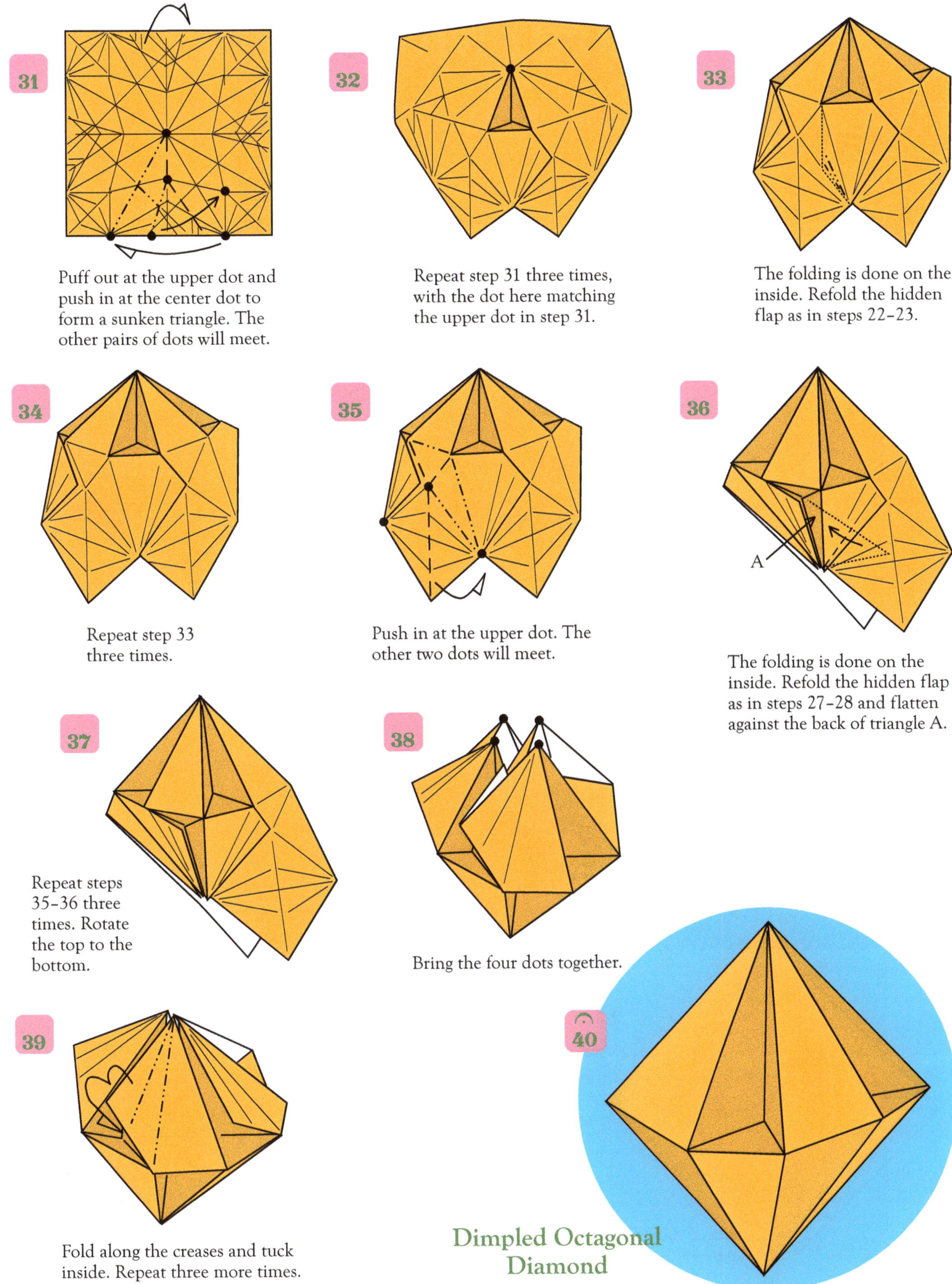
31
Puff out at the upper dot and push in at the center dot to form a sunken triangle. The other pairs of dots will meet.
32
Repeat step 31 three times, with the dot here matching the upper dot in step 31.
33
The folding is done on the inside. Refold the hidden flap as in steps 22–23.
34
Repeat step 33 three times.
35
Push in at the upper dot. The other two dots will meet.
36
A
The folding is done on the inside. Refold the hidden flap as in steps 27–28 and flatten against the back of triangle A.
37
Repeat steps 35–36 three times. Rotate the top to the bottom.
38
Bring the four dots together.
39
Fold along the creases and tuck inside. Repeat three more times.
40
Dimpled Octagonal Diamond

Fourth Movement

Presto: Flight of the Dragons

𝄢 While Dragons are imaginary, it is possible that dinosaur bones, found a long time ago, along with unusual sea sightings, suggested such creatures. It is also possible that small animals, during the age of dinosaurs, knew to fear large scaled creatures with claws and possible wings. As this instinct continued to evolve, humans were able to communicate this thought. Fold these Dragons well and you will gain super powers.

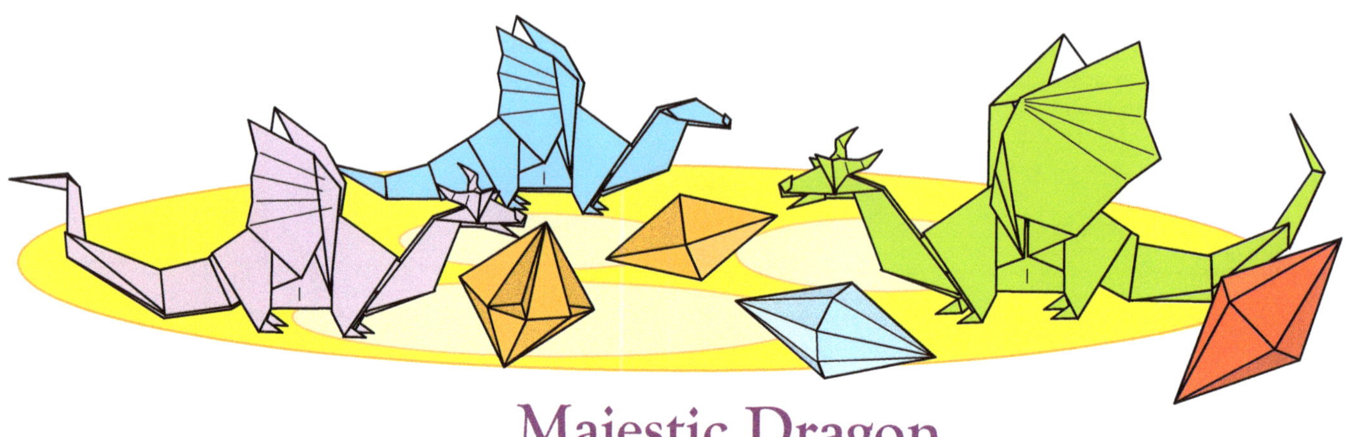

Majestic Dragon

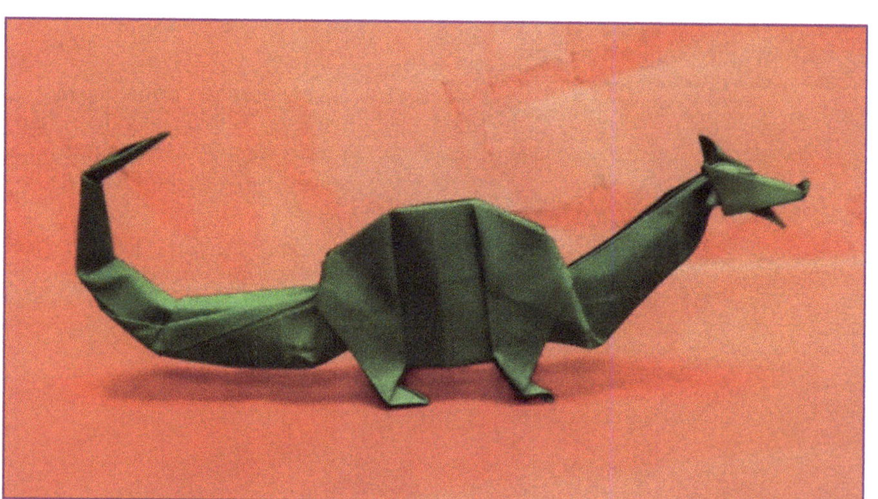

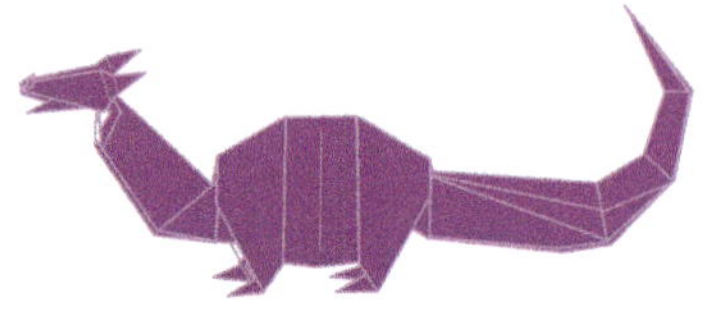

Unlike other dragons, the Majestic Dragon will protect you. It resides in deep caverns with its treasures. Fold it carefully and it will present you with a treasure. This dragon can change into anything, from an earthworm, to the entire universe. All you have to do is unfold it and refold it into anything! However, the Majestic Dragon is happier to stay put and hide in its cave.

1

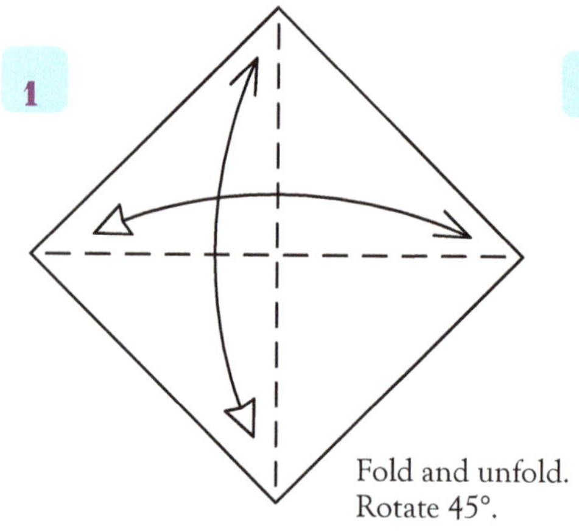

Fold and unfold. Rotate 45°.

2

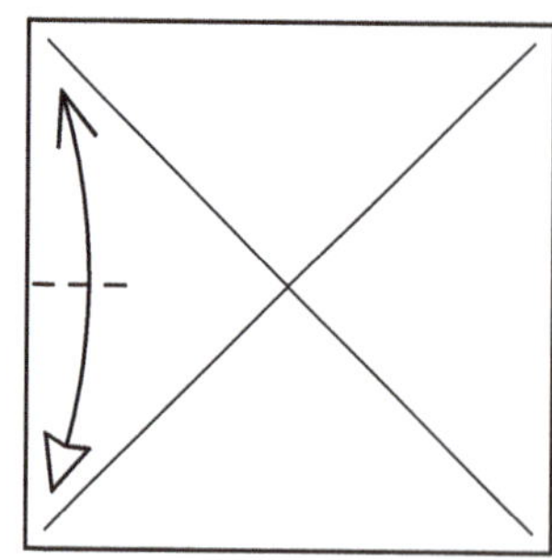

Fold and unfold on the left.

3

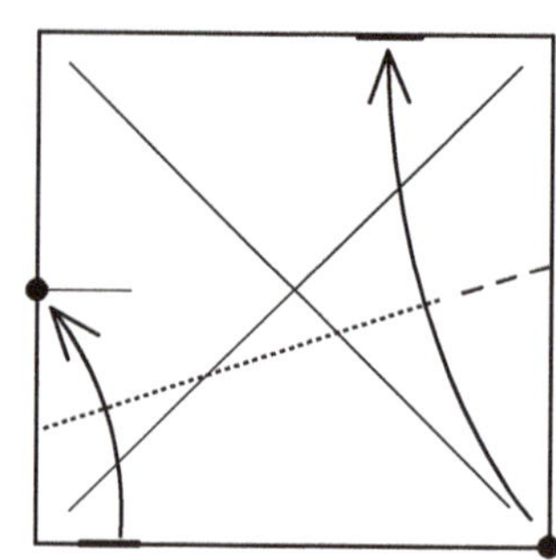

Bring the lower right corner to the top edge and the bottom edge to the left center. Crease on the right.

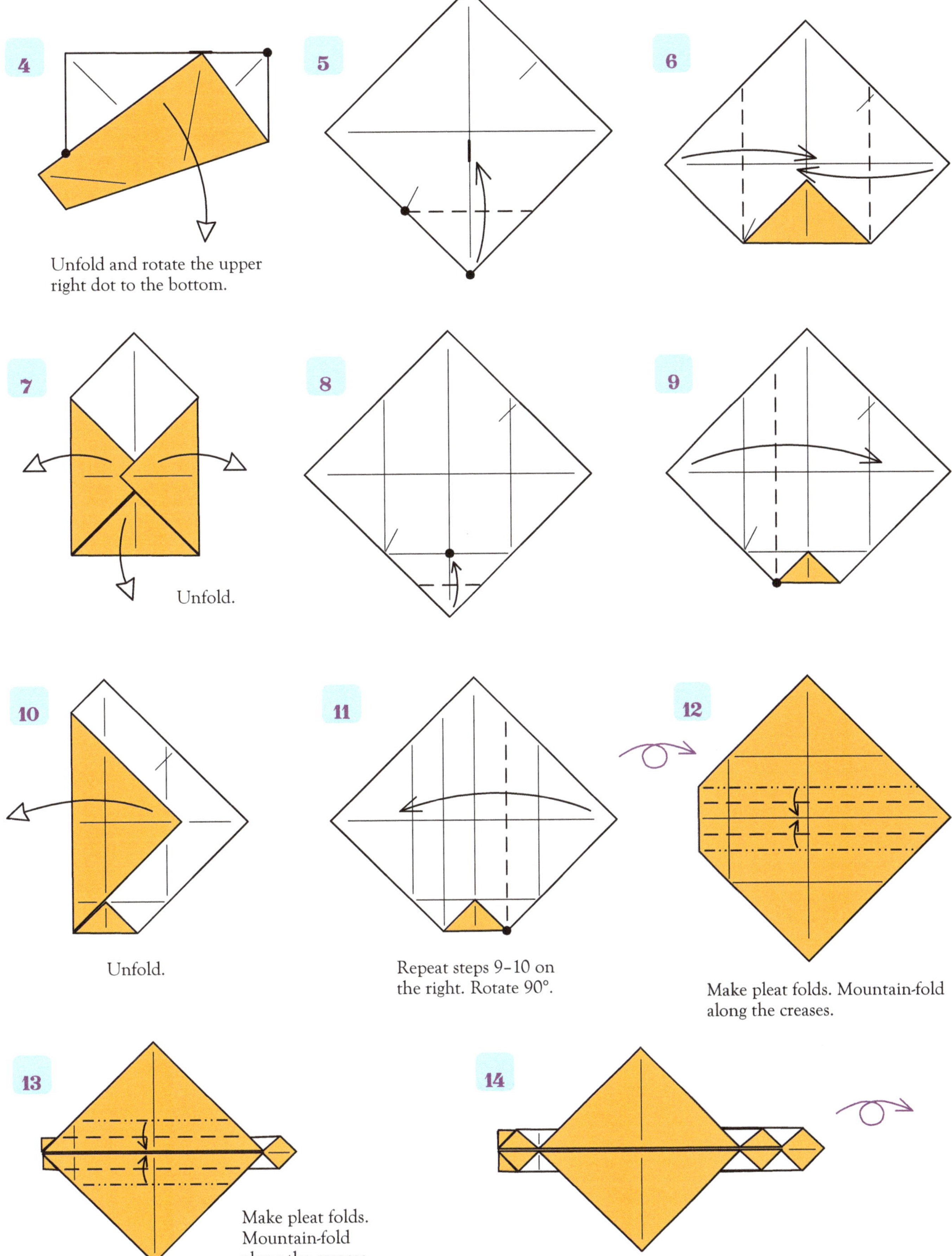
4
Unfold and rotate the upper right dot to the bottom.
5
6
7
Unfold.
8
9
10
Unfold.
11
Repeat steps 9–10 on the right. Rotate 90°.
12
Make pleat folds. Mountain-fold along the creases.
13
Make pleat folds. Mountain-fold along the creases.
14

15

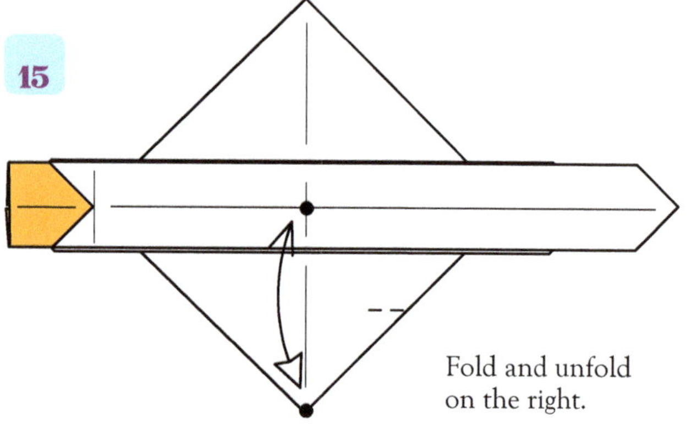

Fold and unfold on the right.

16

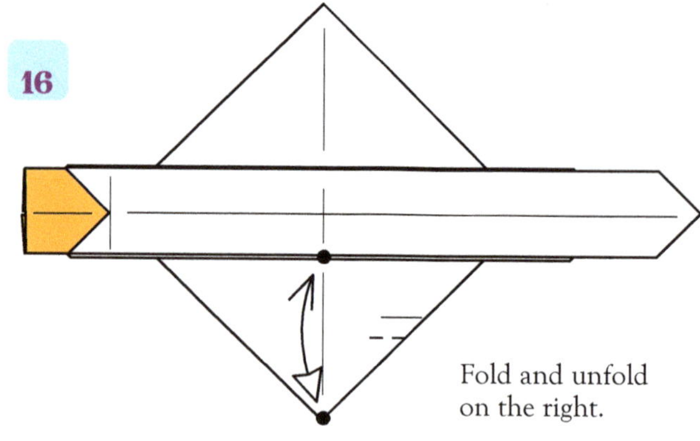

Fold and unfold on the right.

17

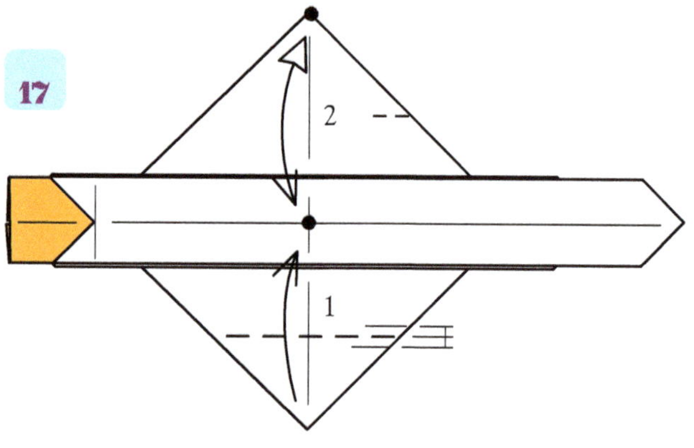

1. Fold up half way between the creases.
2. Repeat steps 15–16 on the top.

18

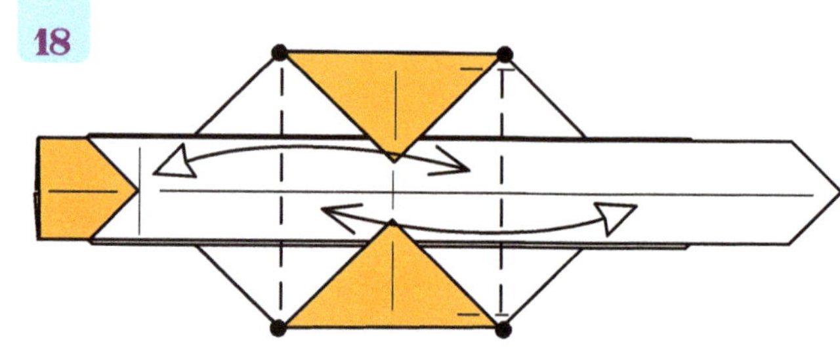

Fold and unfold.

19

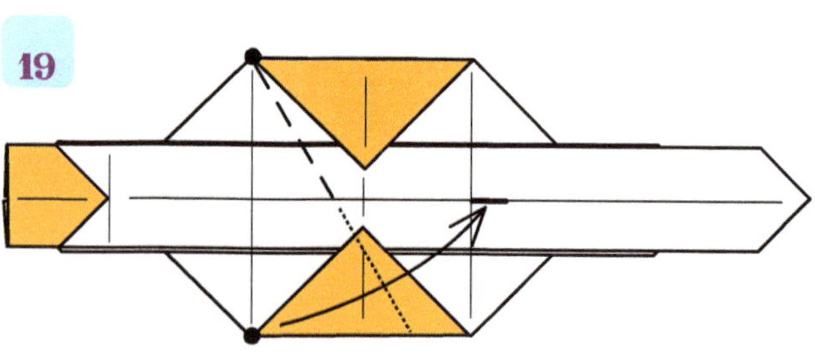

Bring the lower dot to the line. Crease on the top.

20

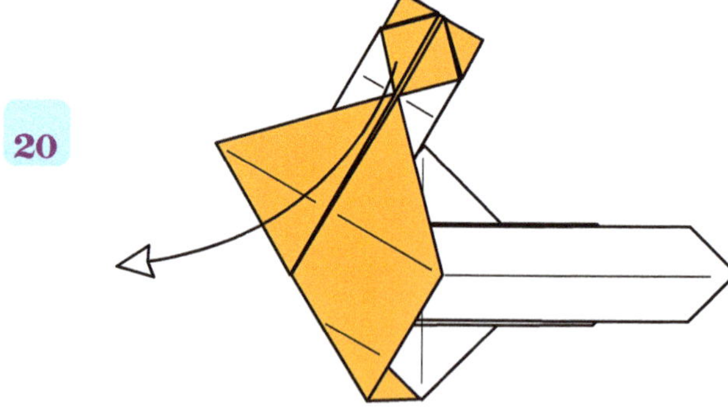

Unfold.

21

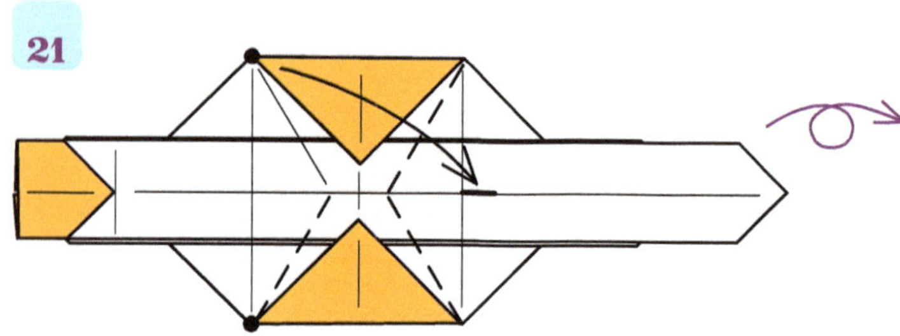

Repeat steps 19–20 three times.

22

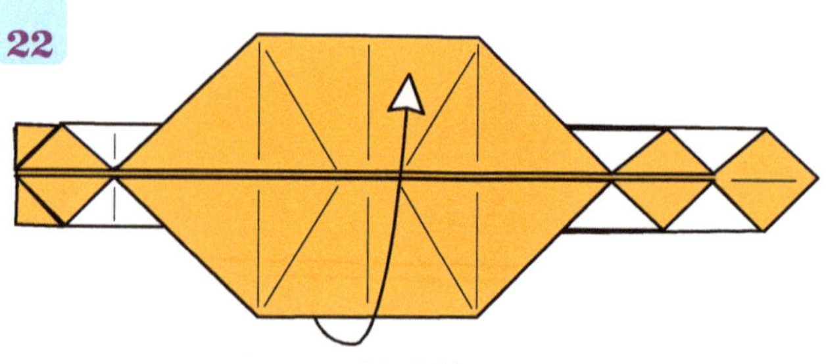

Unfold.

23

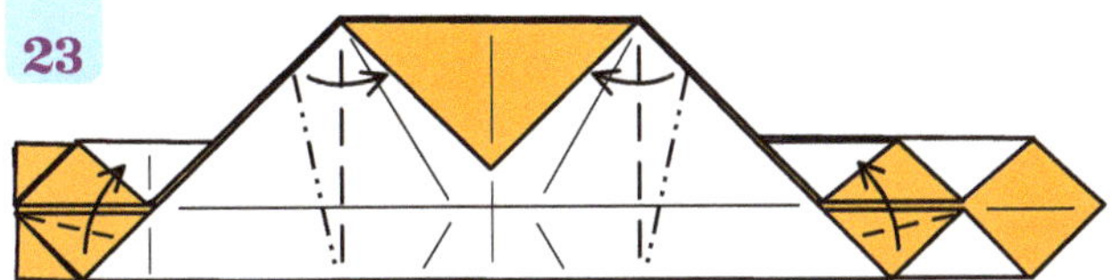

Make squash folds. Valley-fold along the creases.

24

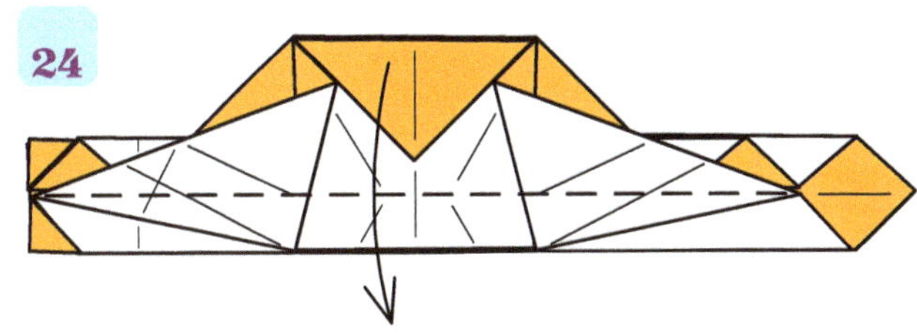

25

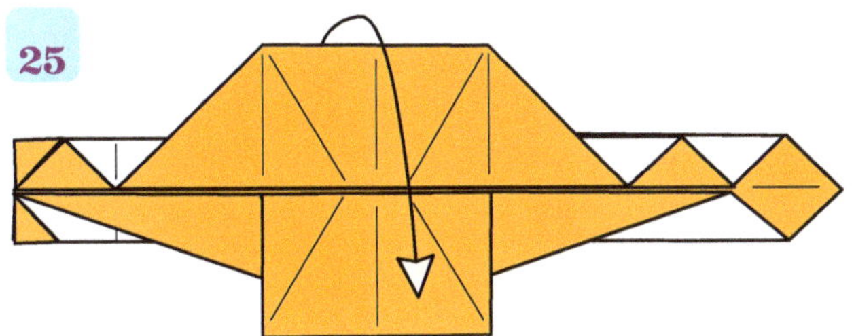

Repeat steps 22–24 on the top.

26

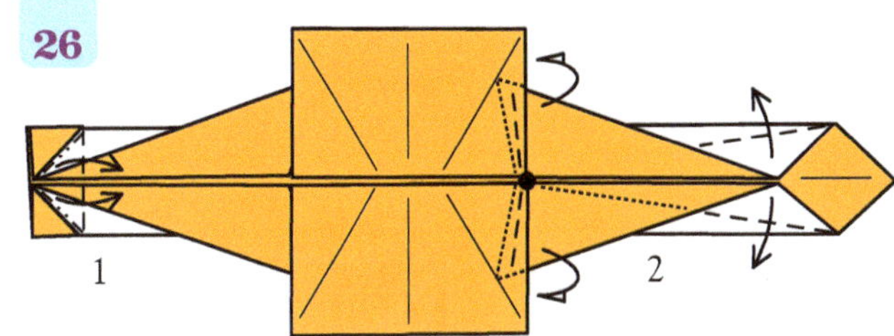

1. Make squash folds.
2. Pivot at the dot for these squash folds. Some of the folds are hidden under the center flaps.

27

28

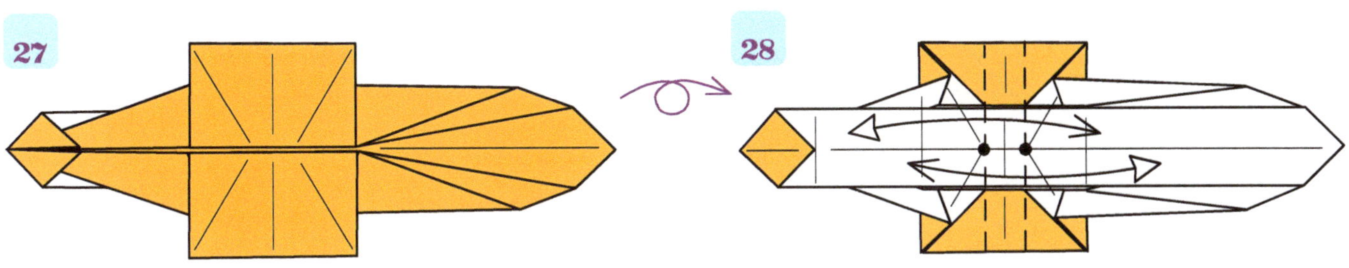

Fold and unfold.

29

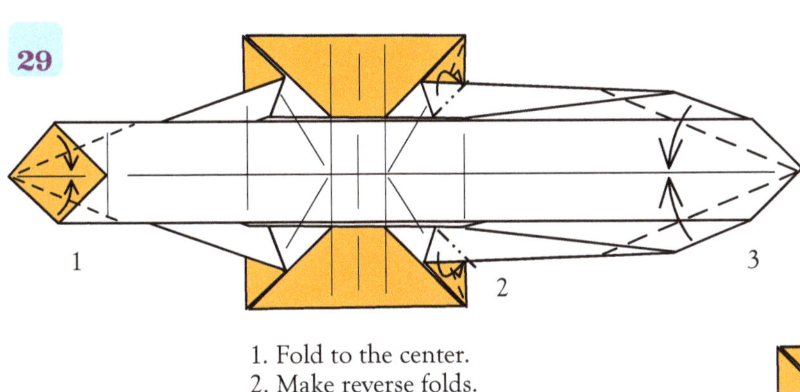

1. Fold to the center.
2. Make reverse folds.
3. Fold to the center.

30

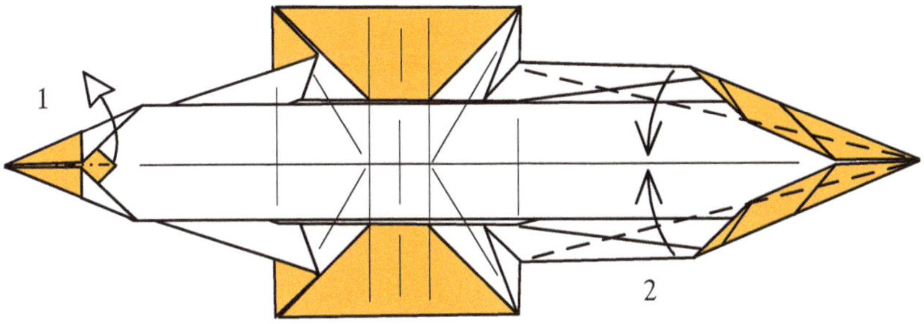

1

2

1. Pull out.
2. Fold to the center.

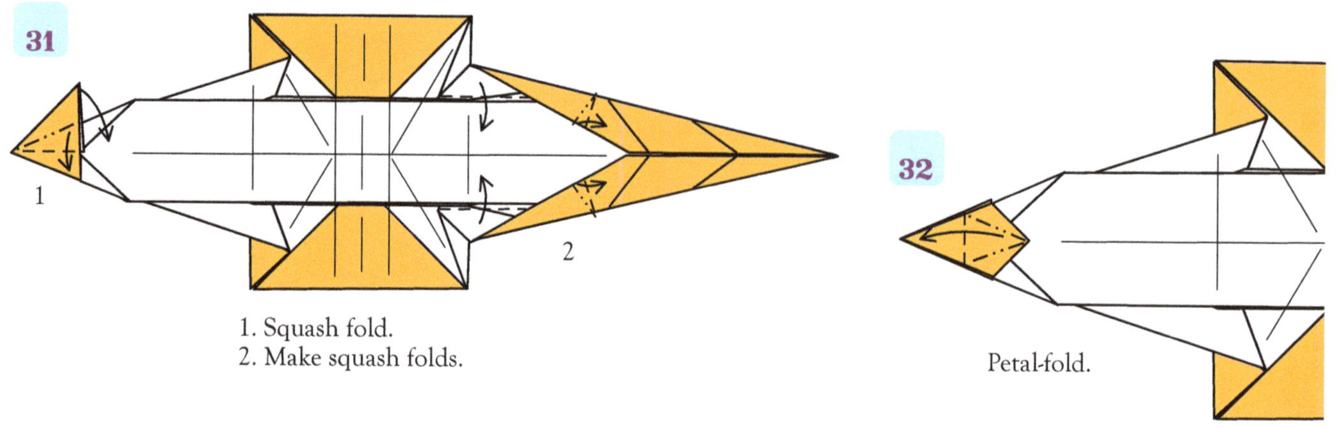

31: 1. Squash fold.
2. Make squash folds.

32: Petal-fold.

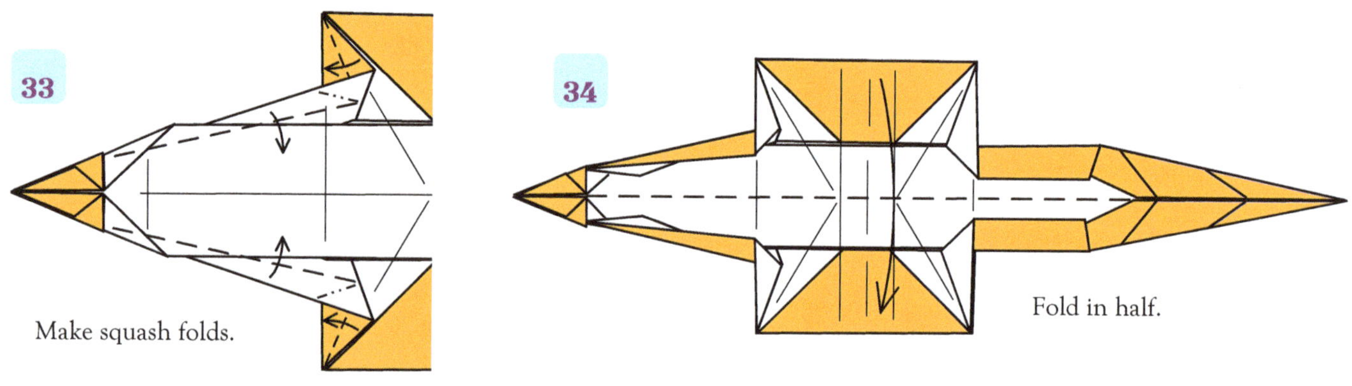

33: Make squash folds.

34: Fold in half.

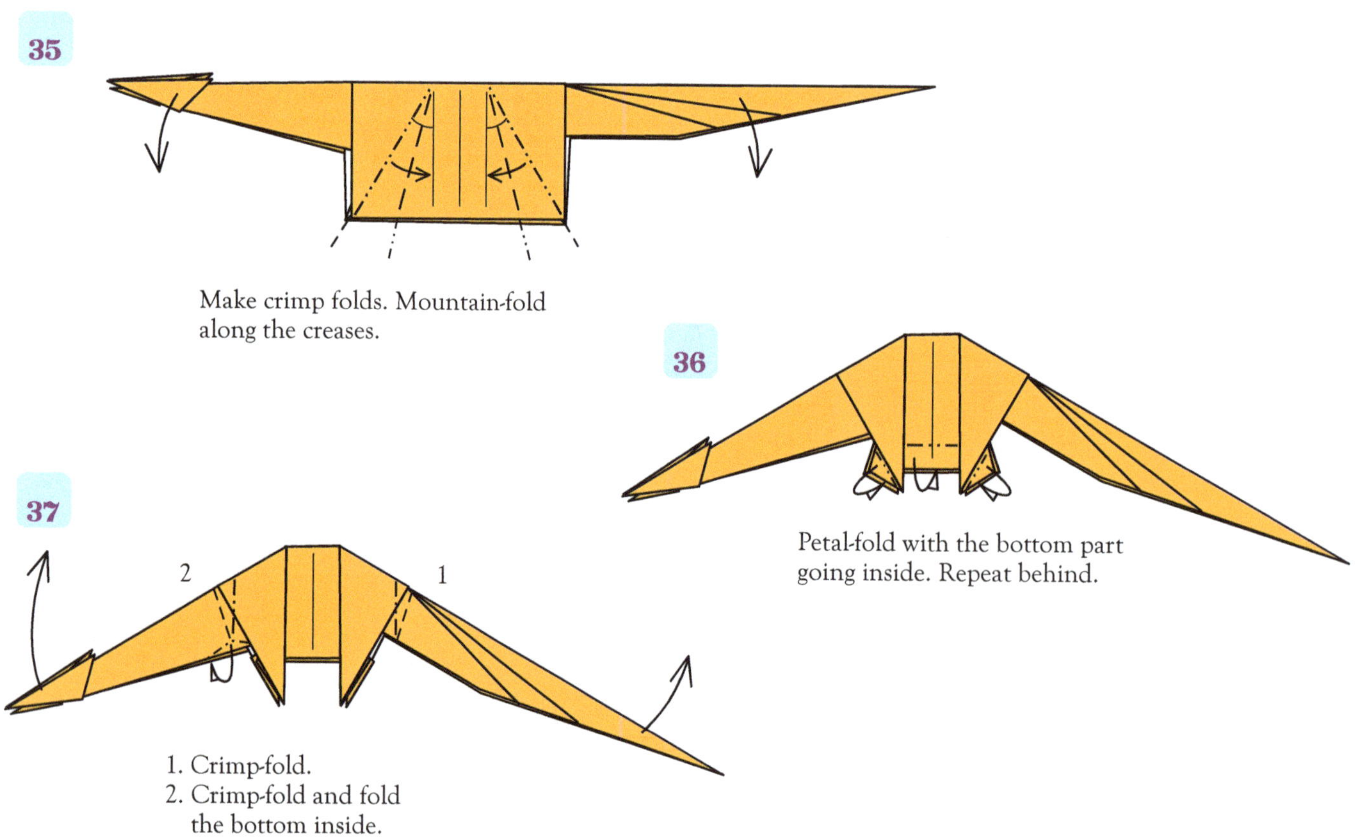

35: Make crimp folds. Mountain-fold along the creases.

36: Petal-fold with the bottom part going inside. Repeat behind.

37: 1. Crimp-fold.
2. Crimp-fold and fold the bottom inside.

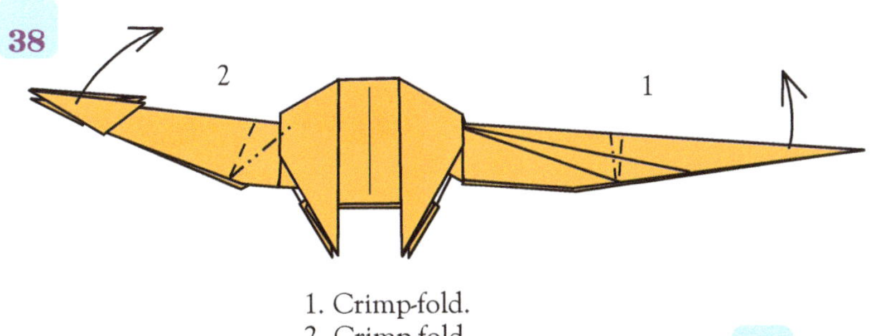

1. Crimp-fold.
2. Crimp-fold.

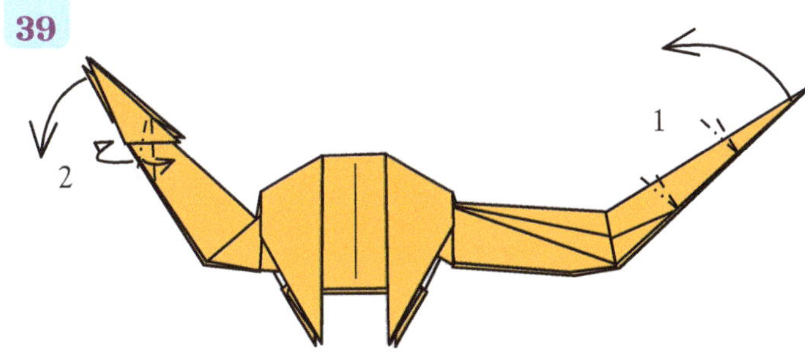

1. Make crimp folds.
2. Crimp-fold.

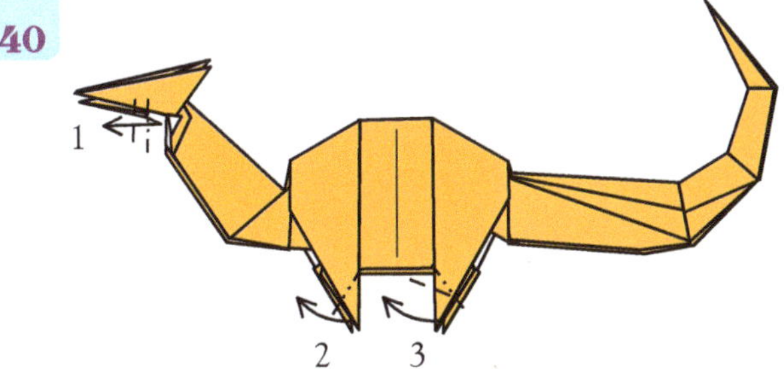

1. Crimp-fold.
2. Reverse-fold, repeat behind.
3. Crimp-fold, repeat behind.

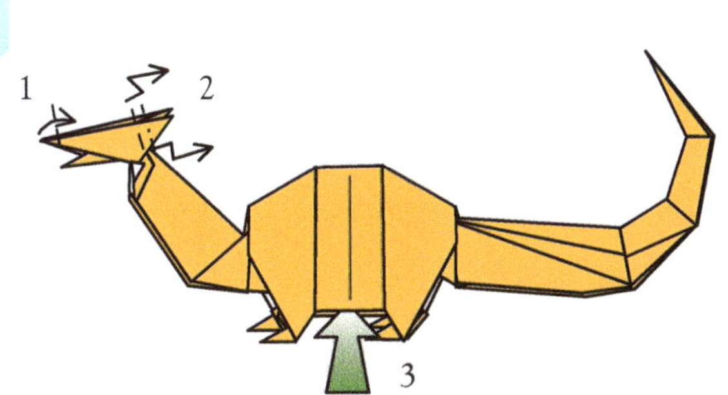

1. Outside-reverse-fold and spread the tip.
2. Pleat-fold the horn, repeat behind.
3. Round out the body.

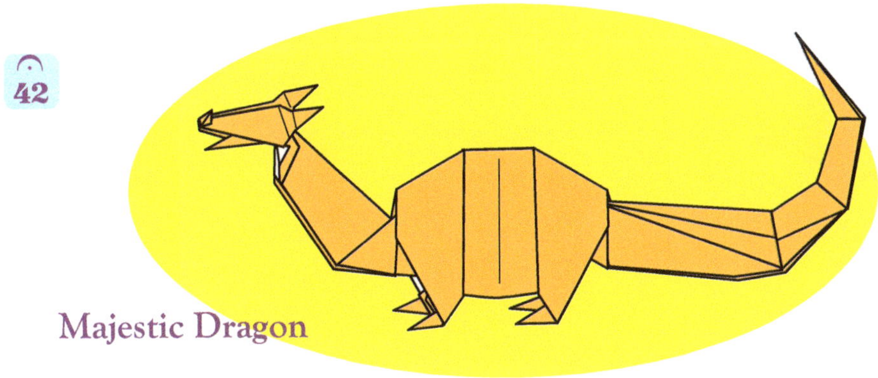

Majestic Dragon

Chinese Dragon

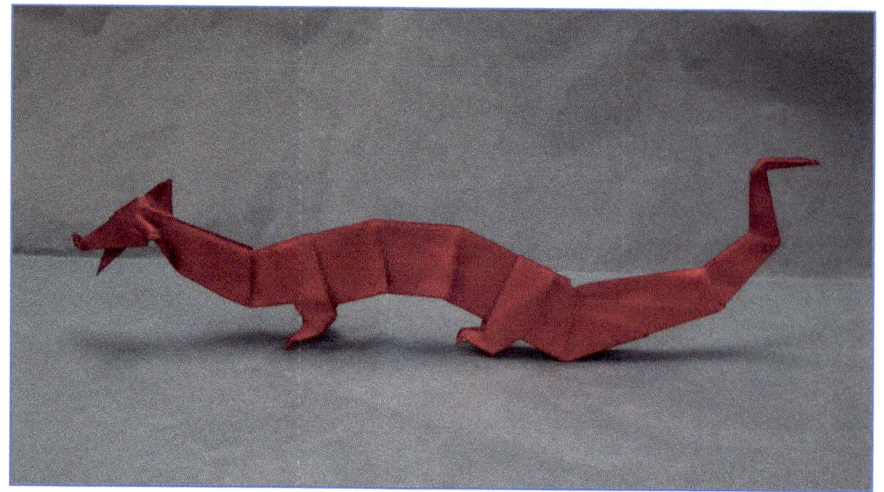

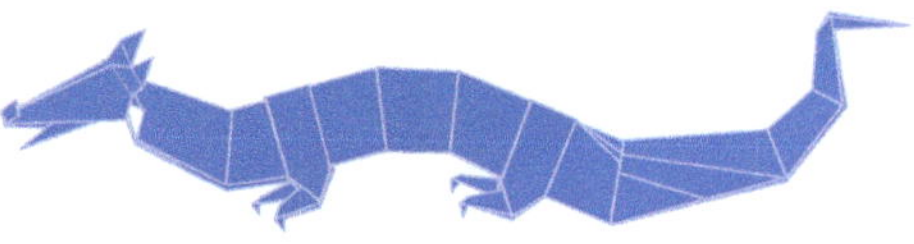

The Chinese Dragon is a symbol of strength, power, and good luck. This Dragon also controls rain and weather. While it has no wings, it can still fly because of its mystical powers. The Chinese use this dragon in several expressions, such as "A dragon among men" to describe someone exceptionally skilled. You, too, will have the power of the Chinese Dragon when you fold it.

1

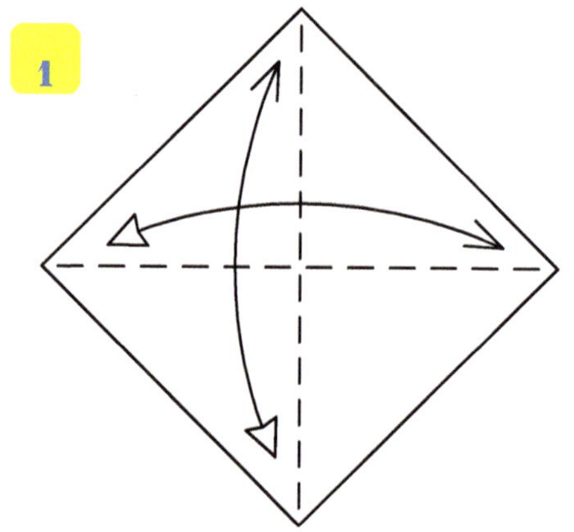

Fold and unfold.
Rotate 45°.

2

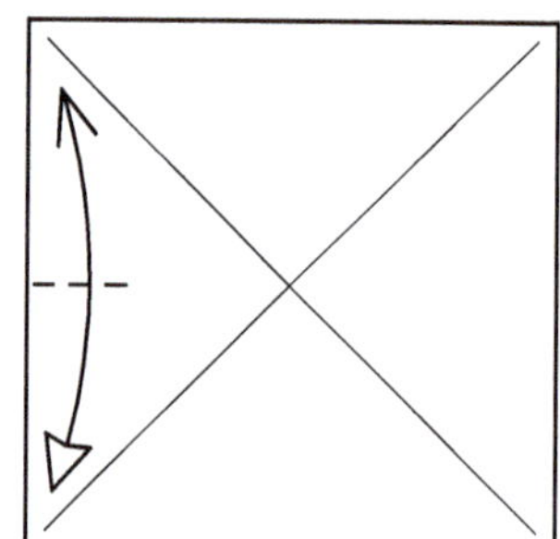

Fold and unfold on the left.

3

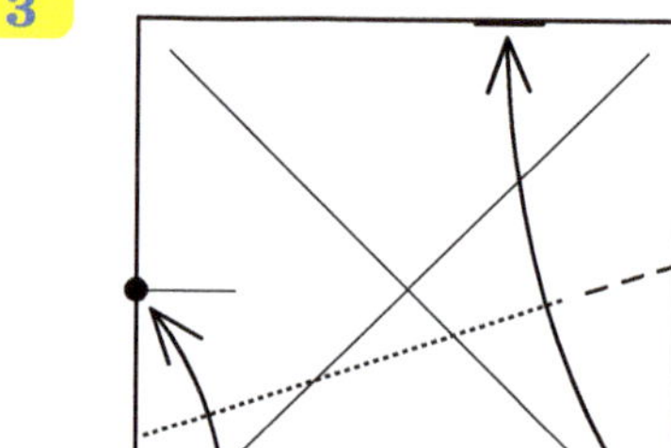

Bring the lower right corner to the top edge and the bottom edge to the left center. Crease on the right.

4

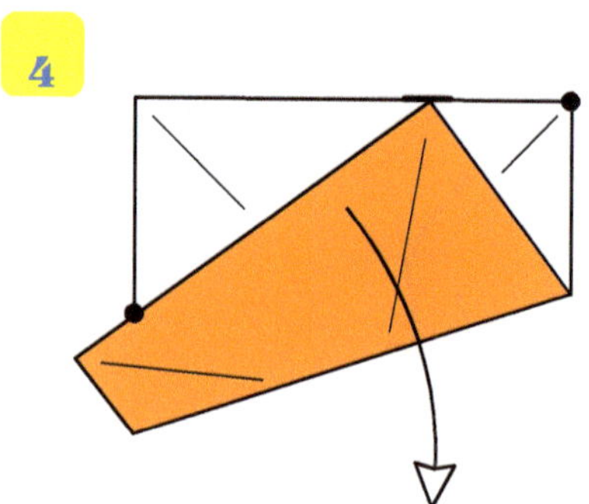

Unfold and rotate the upper right dot to the bottom.

5

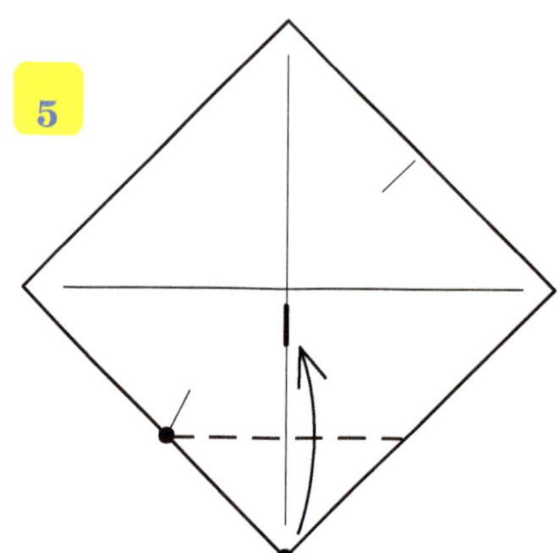

6

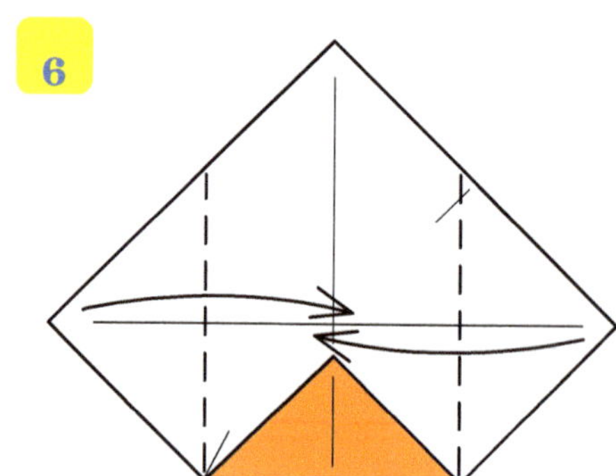

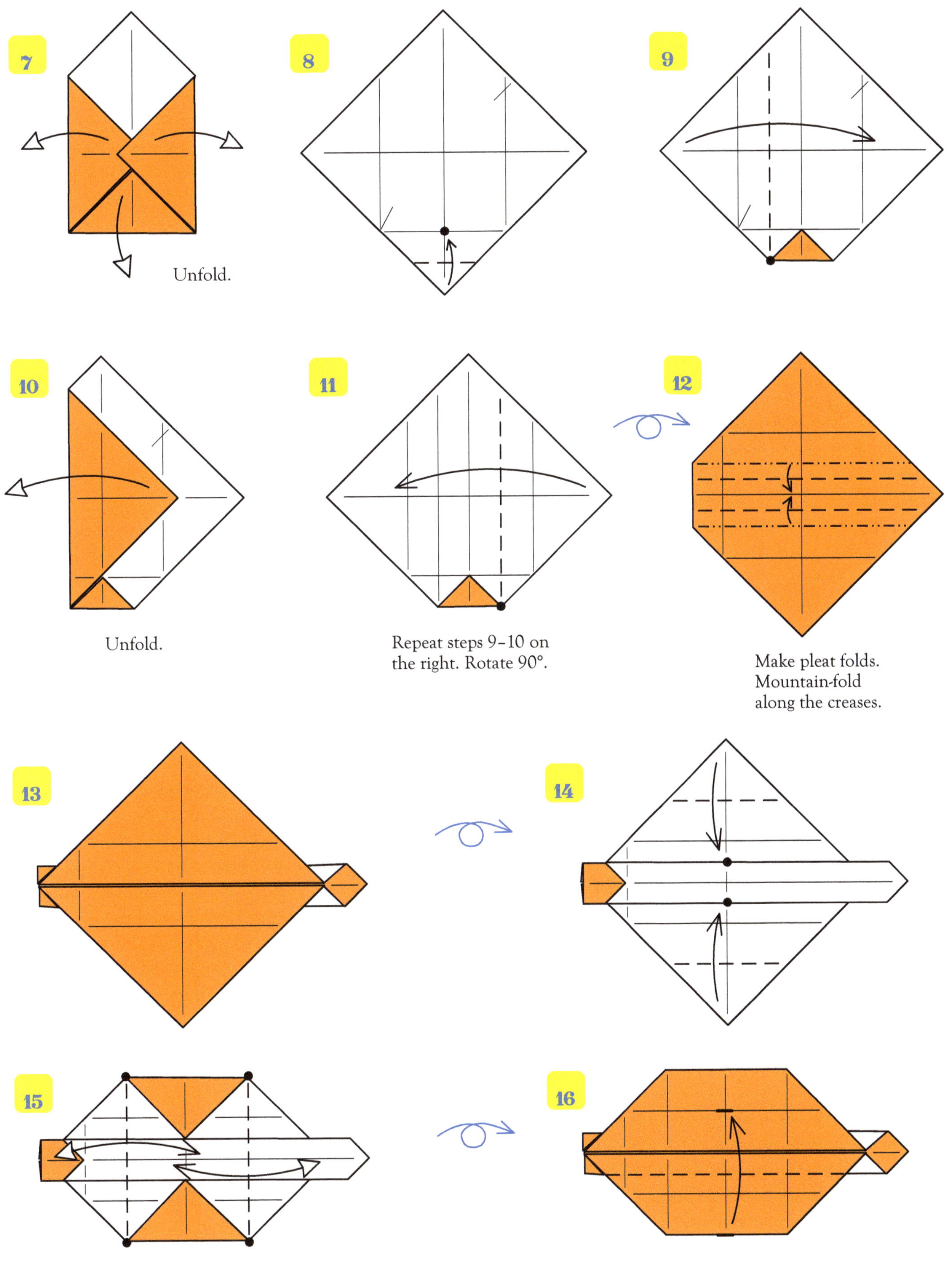

7
Unfold.
8
9
10
Unfold.
11
Repeat steps 9–10 on the right. Rotate 90°.
12
Make pleat folds. Mountain-fold along the creases.
13
14
15
Fold and unfold.
16

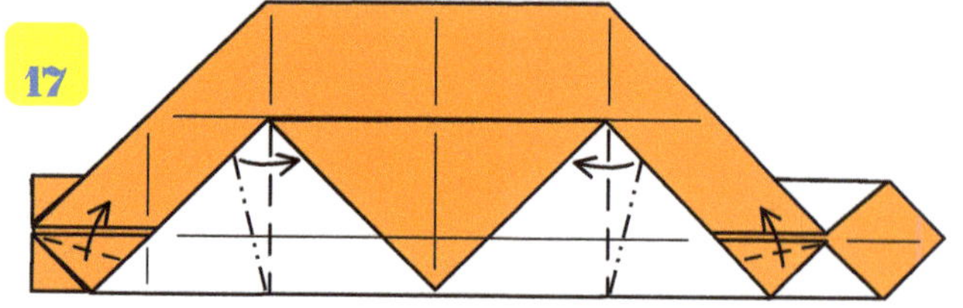

Make squash folds. Valley-fold along the creases.

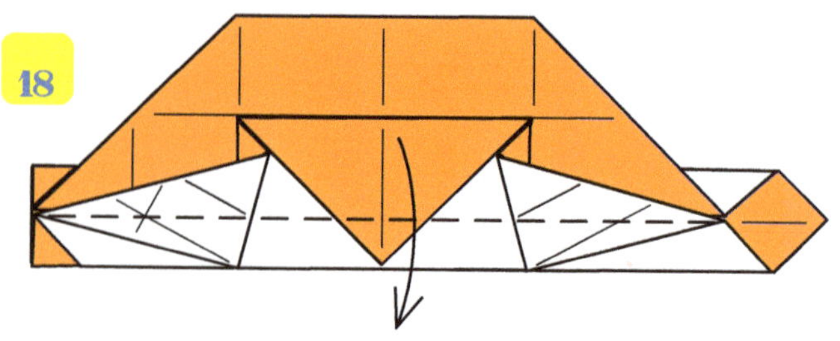

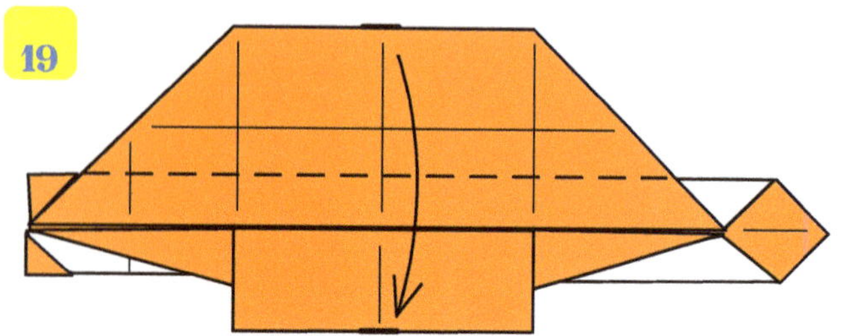

Repeat steps 16–18 on the top.

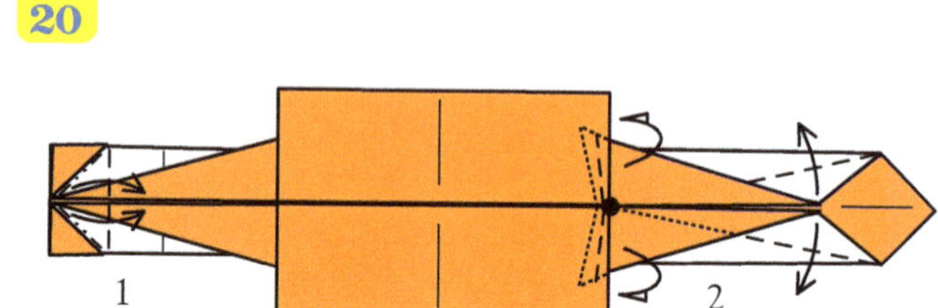

1. Make squash folds.
2. Pivot at the dot for these squash folds. Some of the folds are hidden under the center flaps.

21

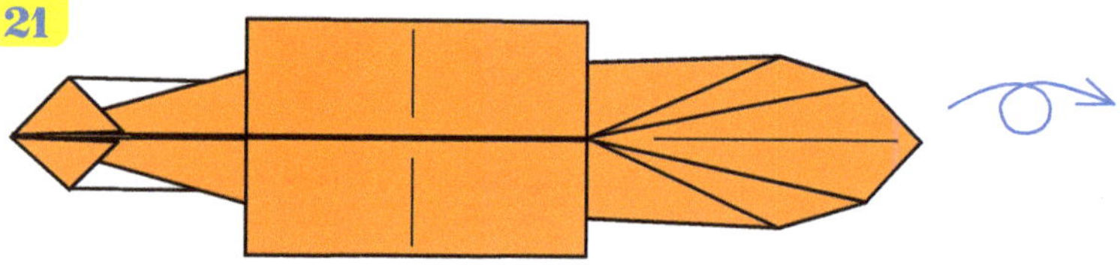

22

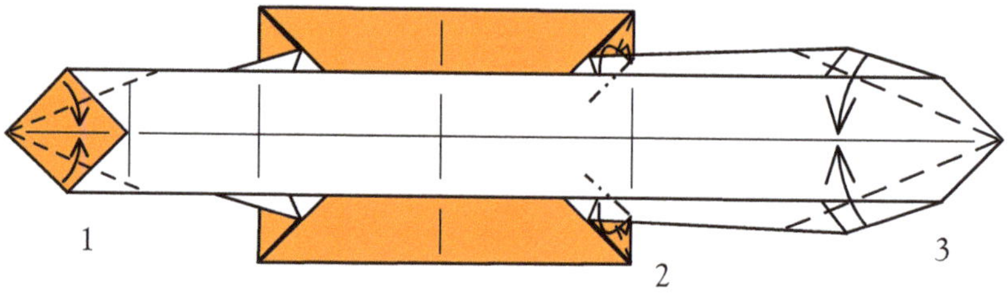

1. Fold to the center.
2. Make reverse folds.
3. Fold to the center.

23

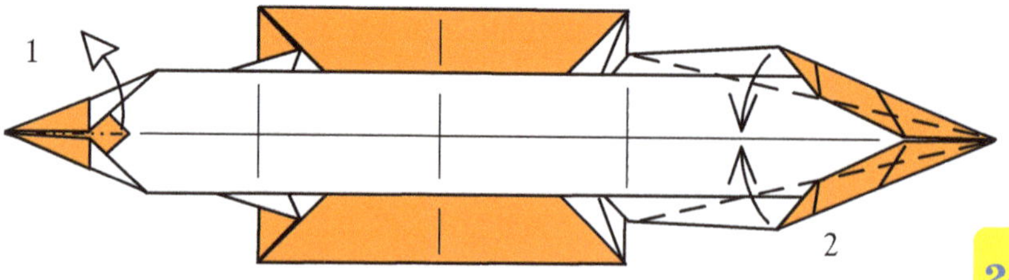

1. Pull out.
2. Fold to the center.

24

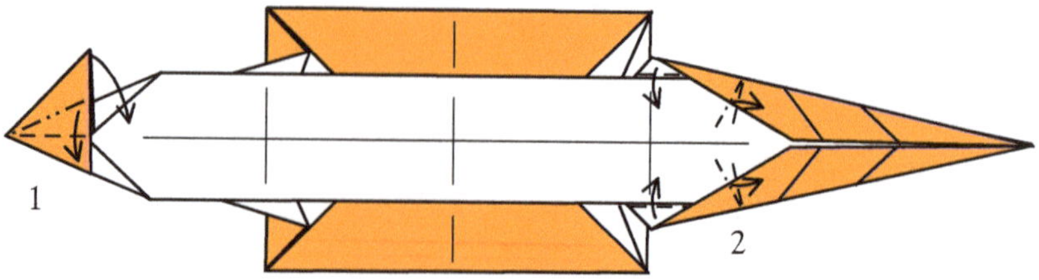

1. Squash fold.
2. Make squash folds.

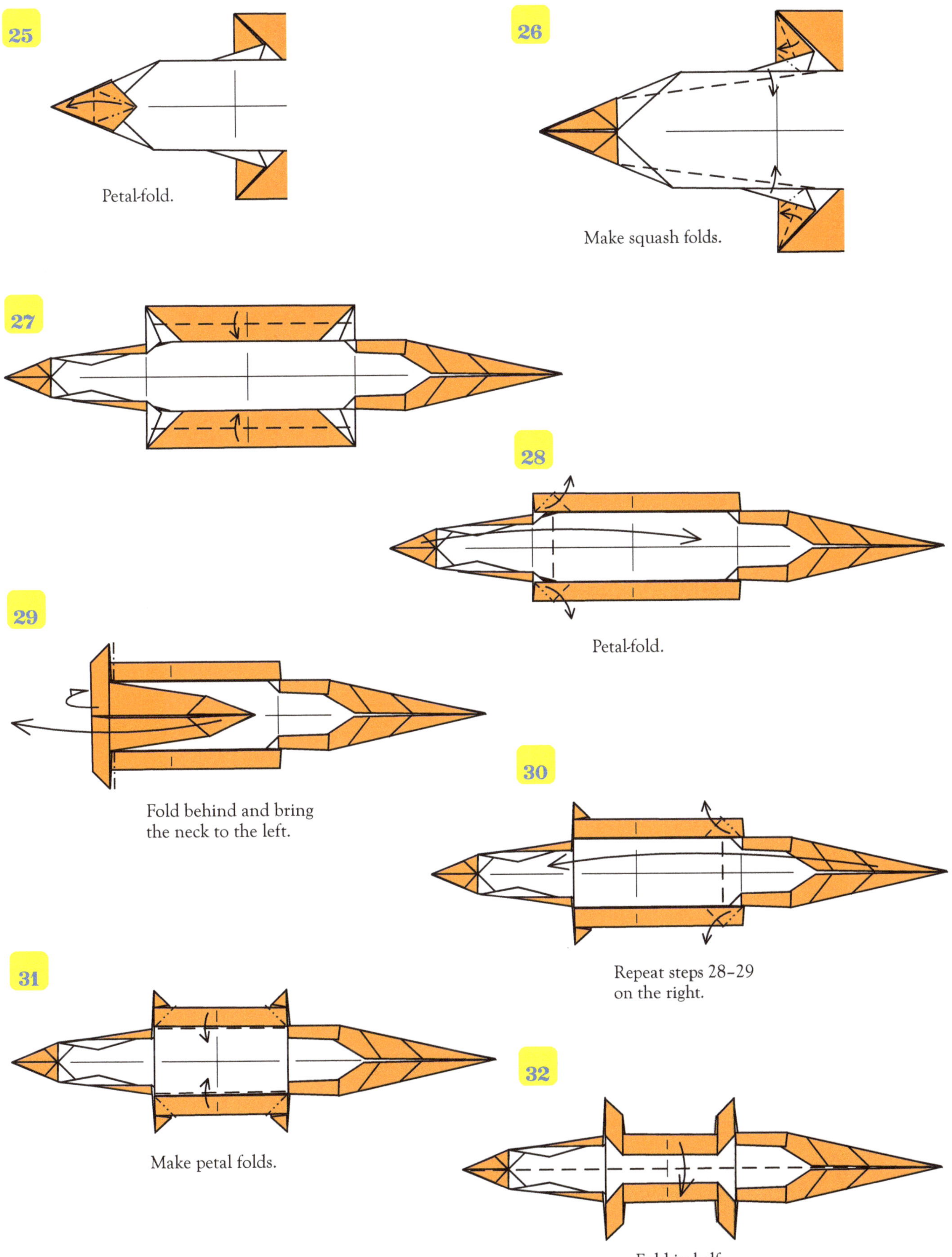
25
Petal-fold.
26
Make squash folds.
27
28
Petal-fold.
29
Fold behind and bring the neck to the left.
30
Repeat steps 28–29 on the right.
31
Make petal folds.
32
Fold in half.

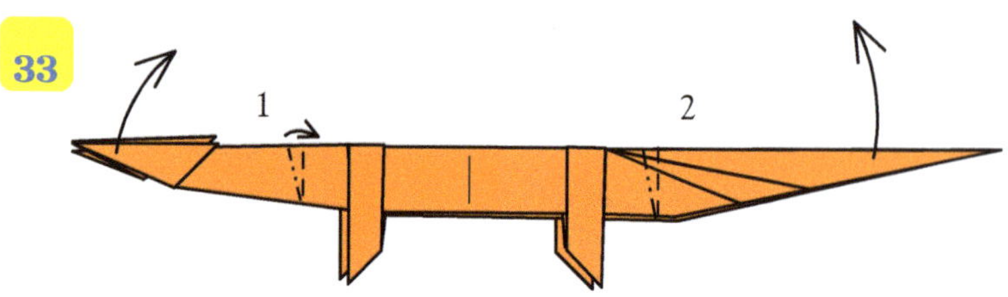

Make crimp folds at 1 and 2.

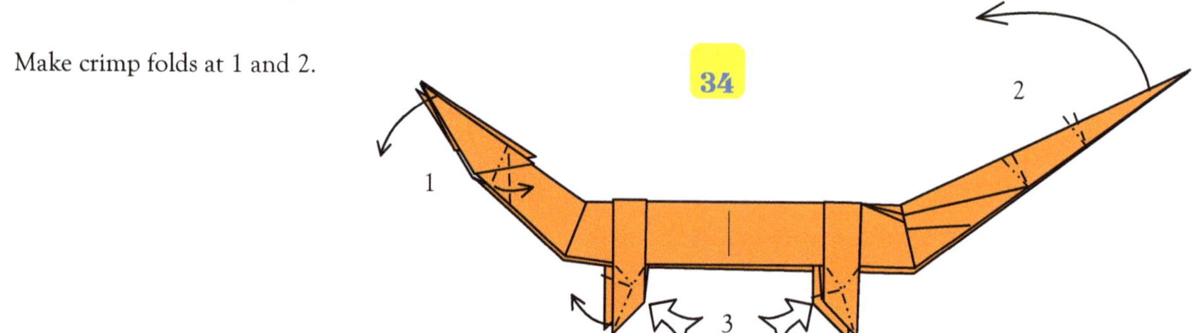

1. Crimp-fold.
2. Make crimp folds.
3. Form the feet. This is similar to a double-rabbit ear. Repeat behind.

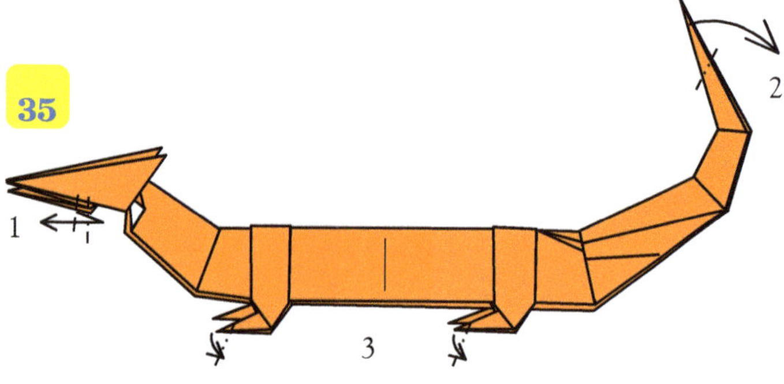

1. Crimp-fold.
2. Reverse-fold.
3. Make small reverse folds, repeat behind.

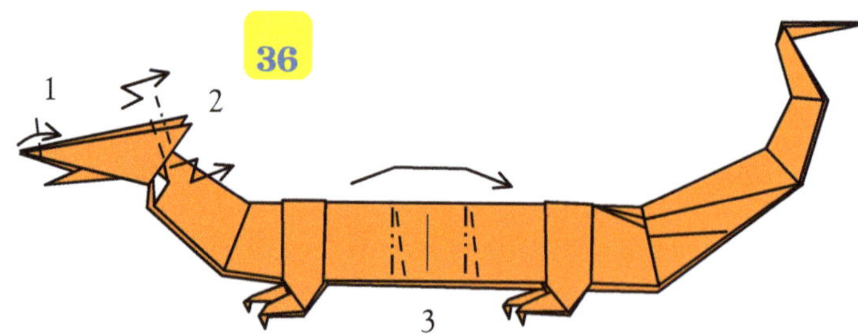

1. Outside-reverse-fold and spread the tip.
2. Pleat-fold the horn, repeat behind.
3. Make crimp folds.

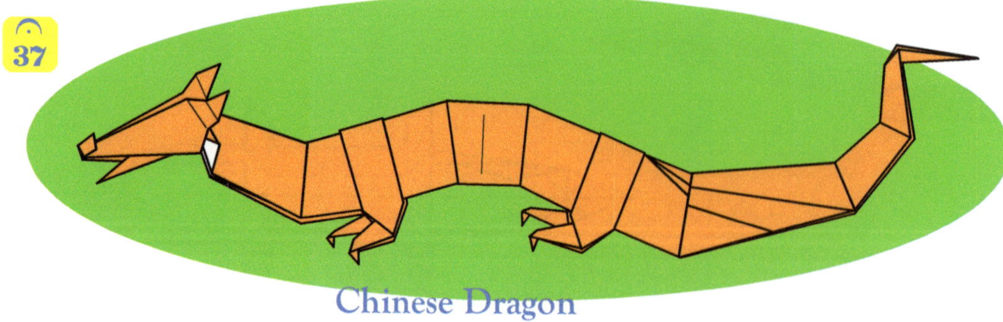

Chinese Dragon

Baby Dragon

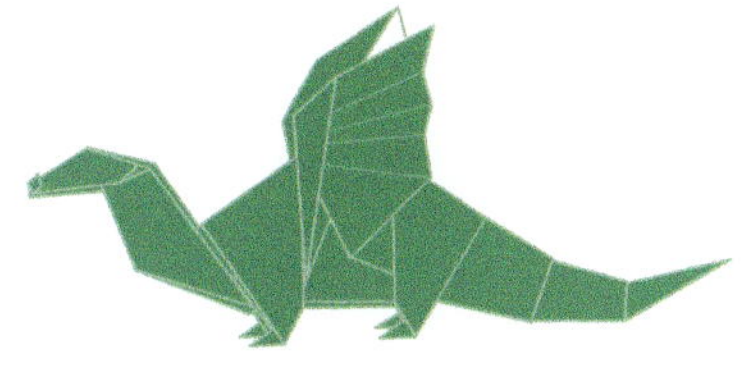

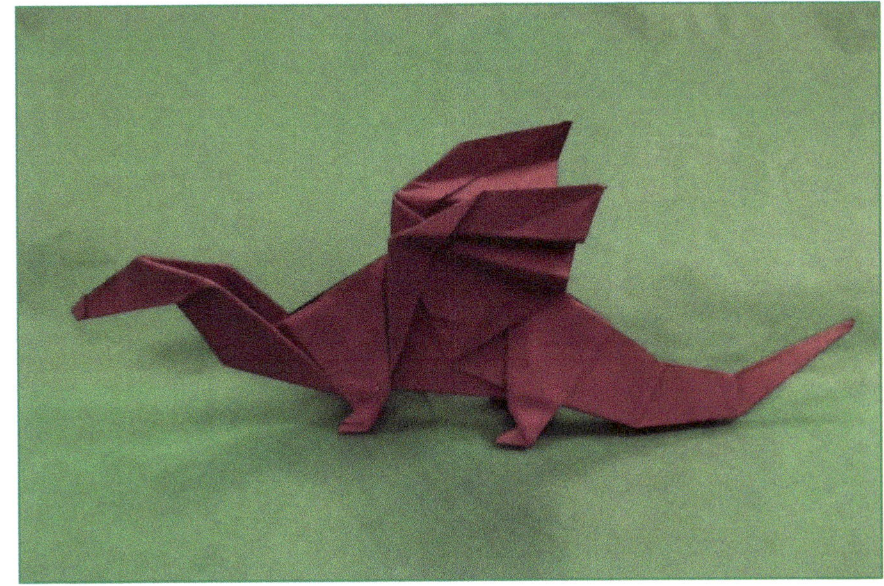

The Baby Dragon is the youngest in the family of Western Dragons. The wings are too small for it to fly and it has not yet found its powers. About all it can do is breathe fire. If it is hungry, or wants to move, it will let you know by breathing fire. Keep it content and it will be happy and grow to a benevolent, powerful creature. But be careful, if it is not happy, it will only develop better skills at breathing fire. Fold carefully.

1

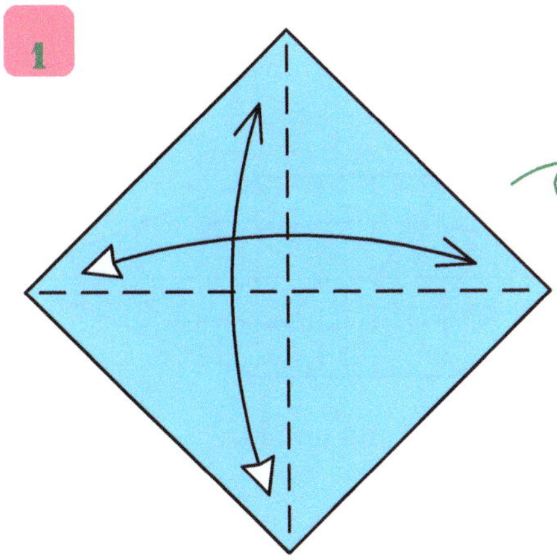

Fold and unfold.

2

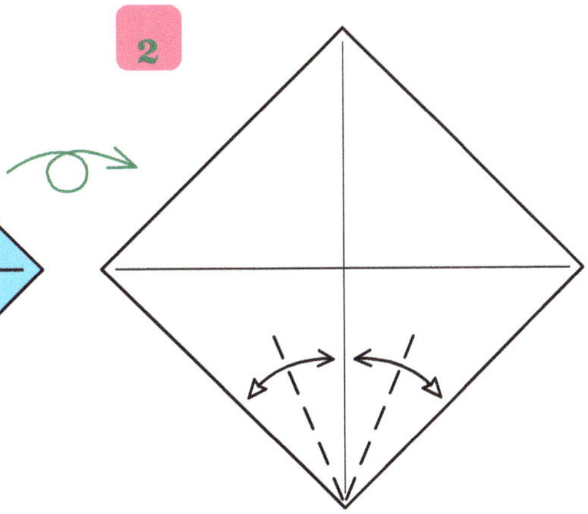

Fold and unfold.
Rotate 90°.

3

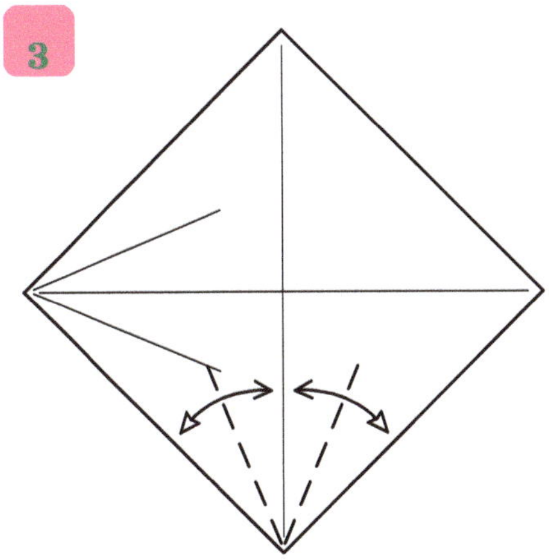

Repeat step 2 three times.

4

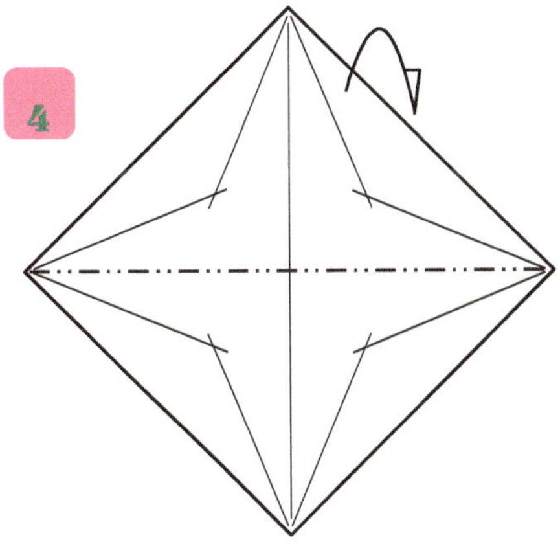

5

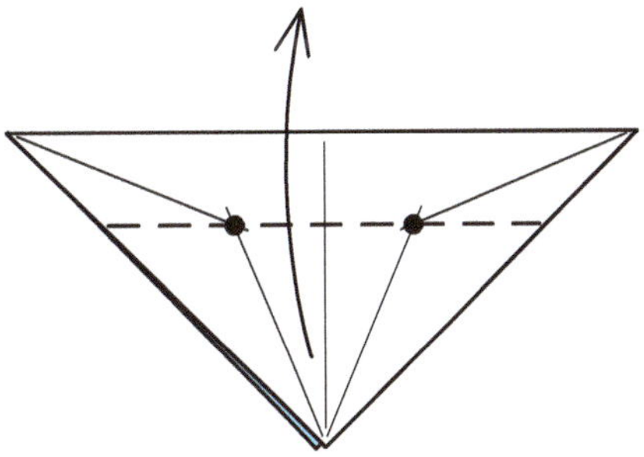

Repeat behind.

6

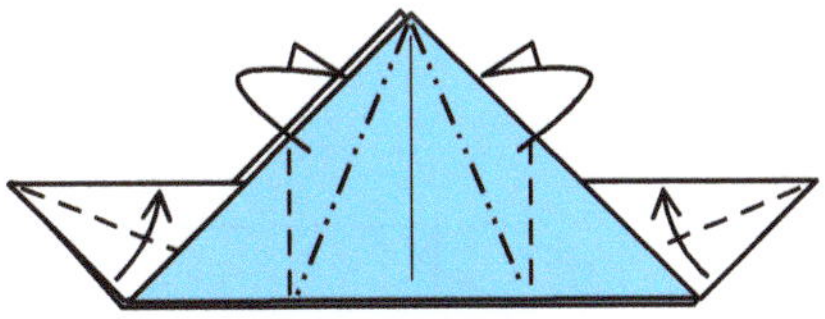

Fold along several of the creases. Repeat behind.

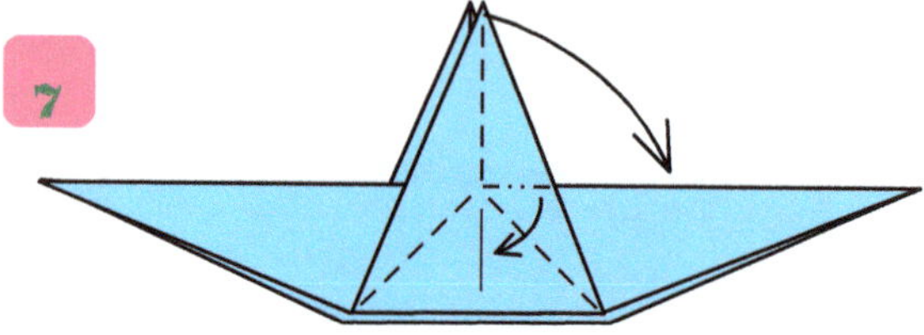

Rabbit-ear, repeat behind.

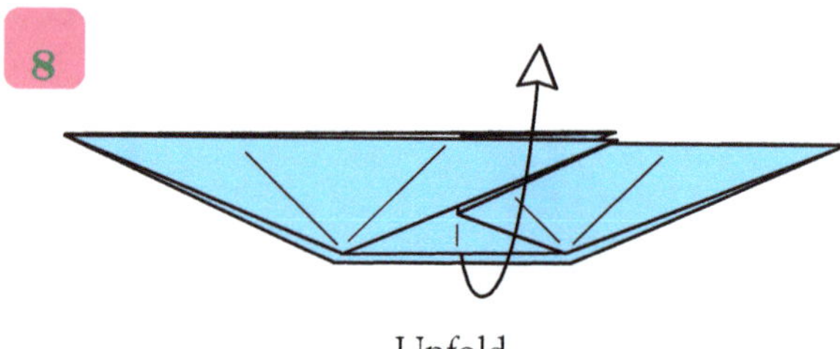

Unfold.

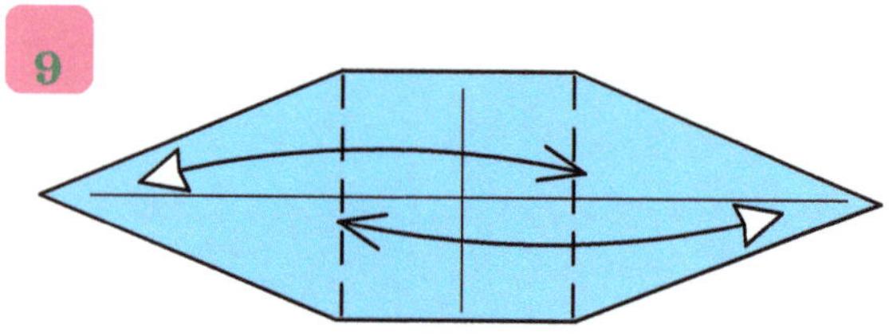

Fold and unfold.

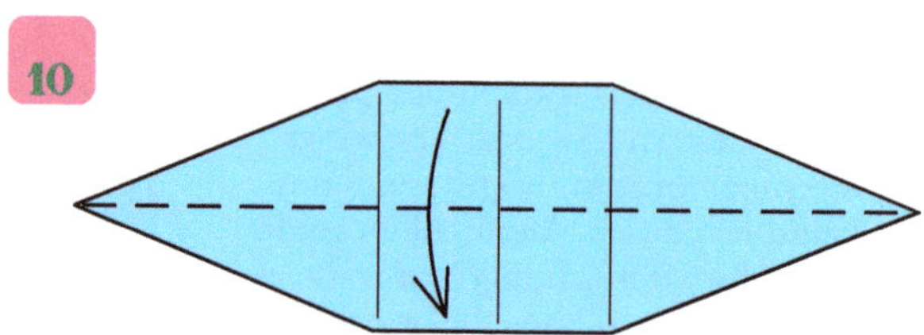

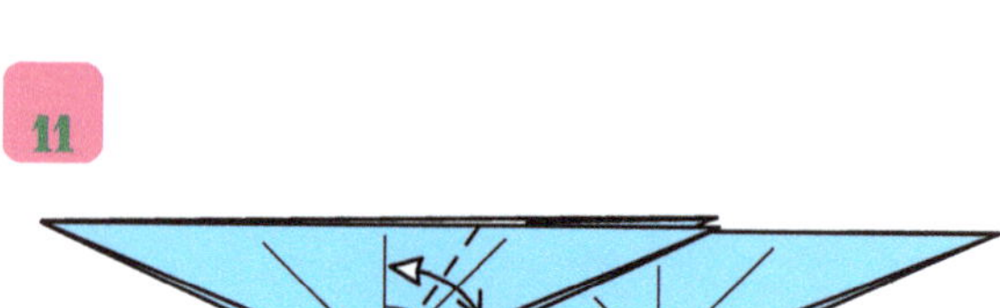

Fold and unfold.

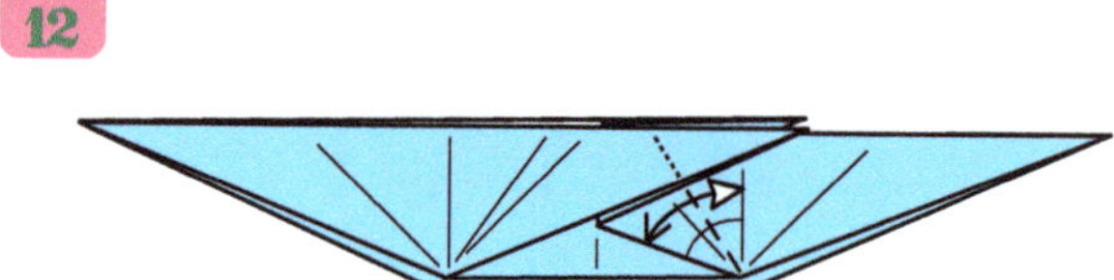

Fold and unfold.

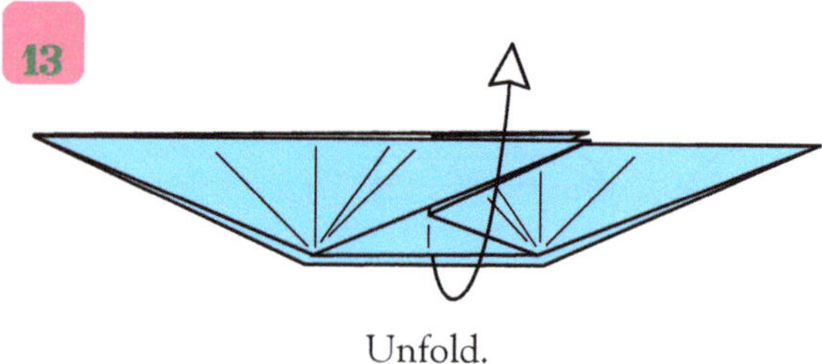

Unfold.

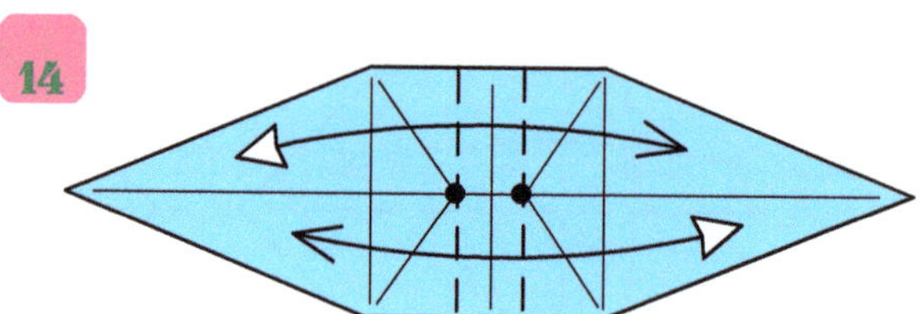

Fold and unfold.

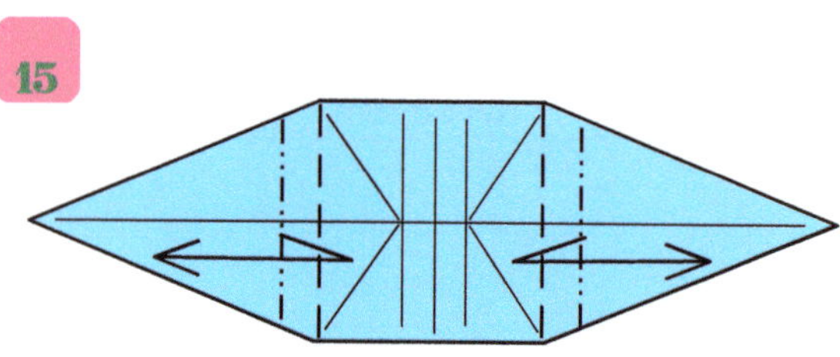

Make pleat-folds.

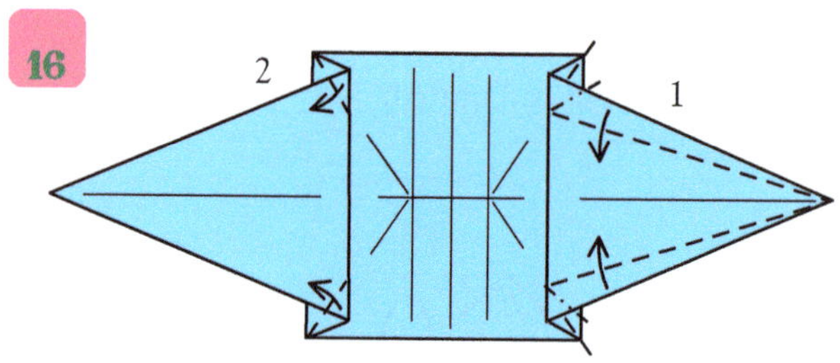

1. Make squash folds.
2. Make valley folds.

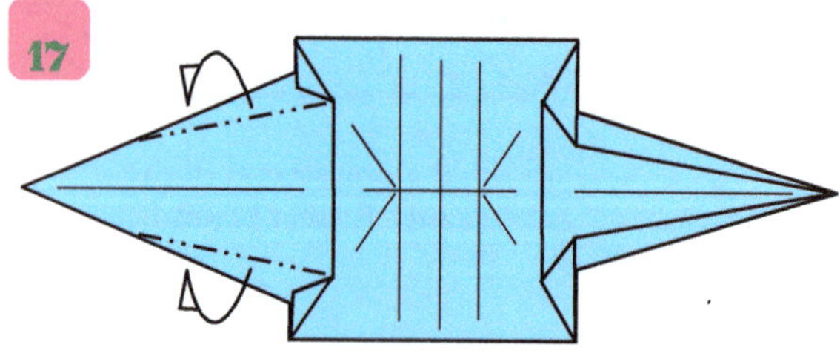

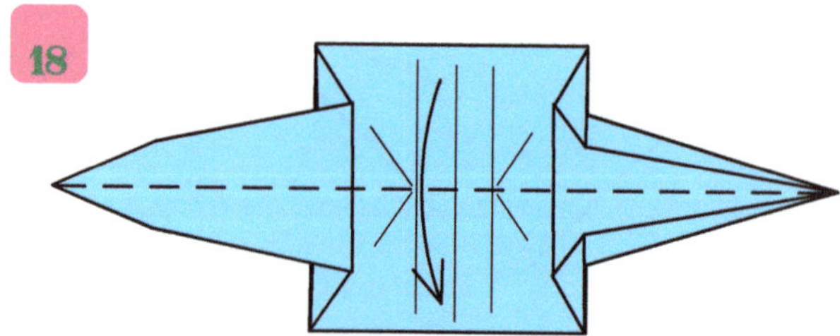

19

20

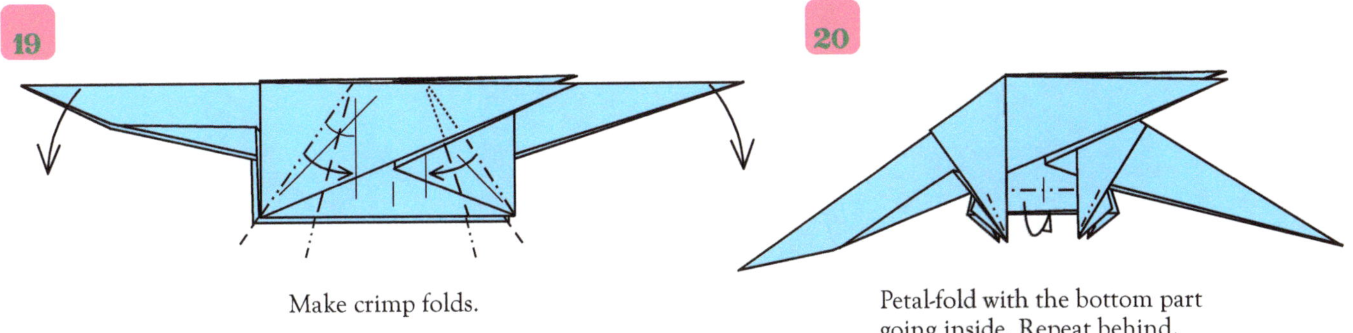

Make crimp folds.

Petal-fold with the bottom part going inside. Repeat behind.

21

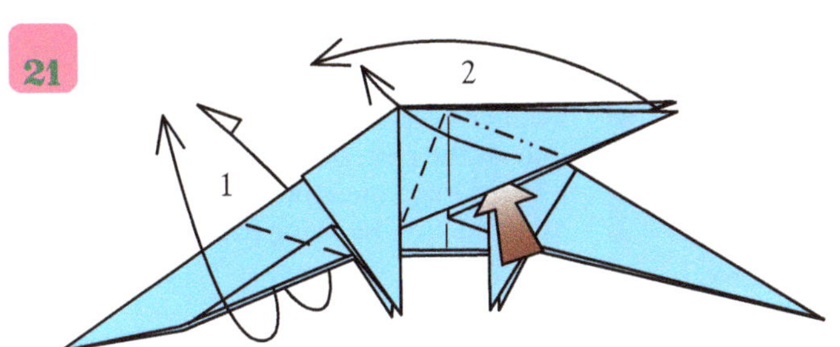

1. Outside-reverse-fold.
2. Squash-fold, repeat behind.

22

1. Squash-fold, repeat behind.
2. Make crimp-folds.

23

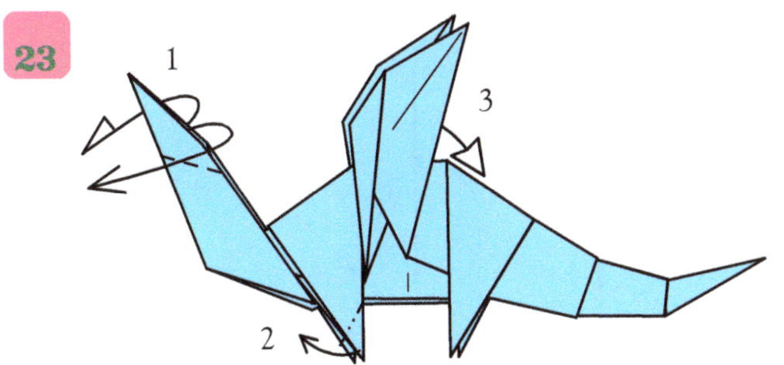

1. Outside-reverse-fold.
2. Reverse-fold, repeat behind.
3. Pull out some paper, repeat behind.

24

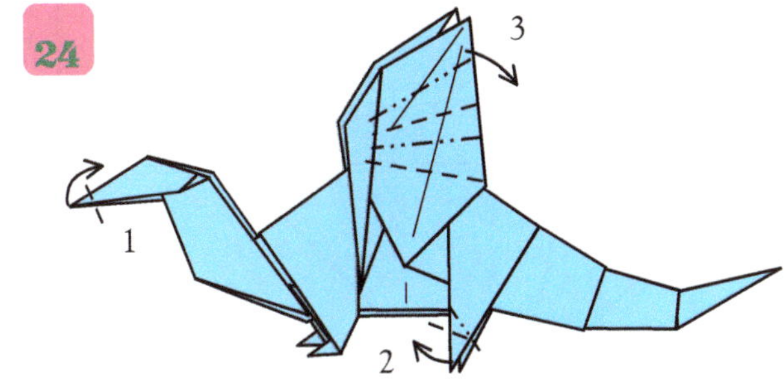

1. Outside-reverse-fold and spread.
2. Crimp-fold, repeat behind.
3. Pleat-fold, repeat behind.

25

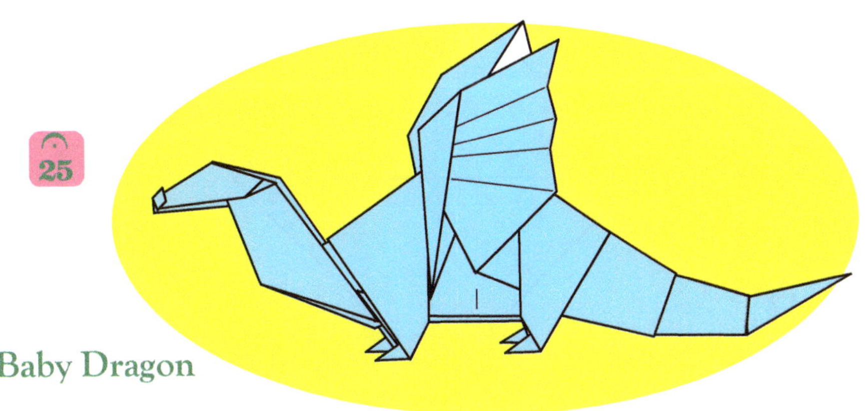

Baby Dragon

Juvenile Dragon

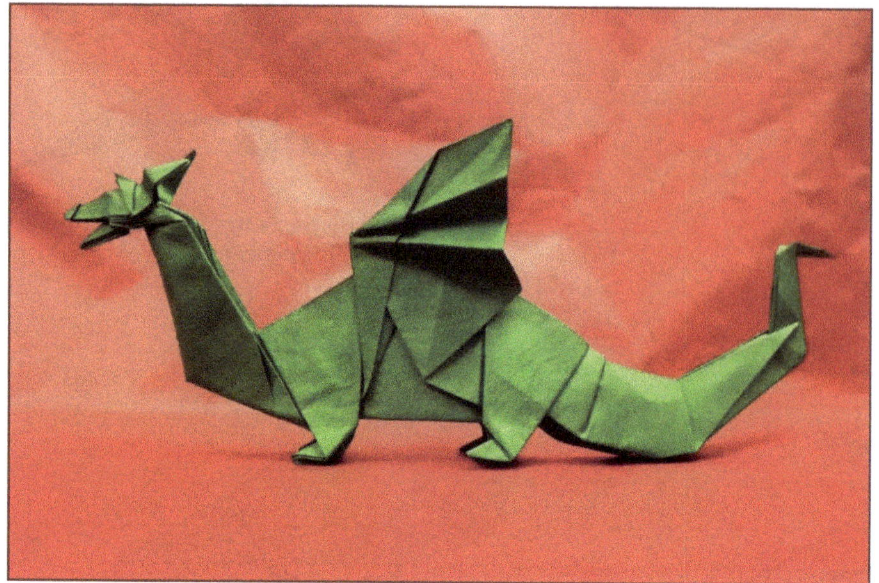

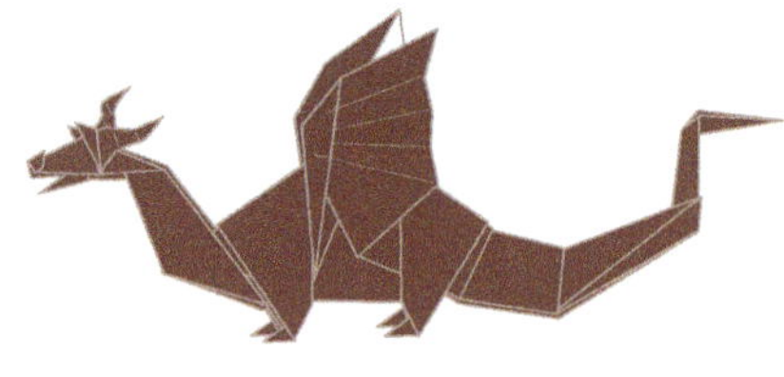

The Juvenile Dragon can fly, breathe fire, and protect its owner. Still, it is always challenging other dragons, as it finds its own strength. The better you fold it, and from the right colors, the more power it will possess, and you will help guide it down the path of prosperity. If it sees a Baby Dragon nearby, it will not bother to breathe fire, knowing that the baby will.

1

Fold and unfold. Rotate 45°.

2

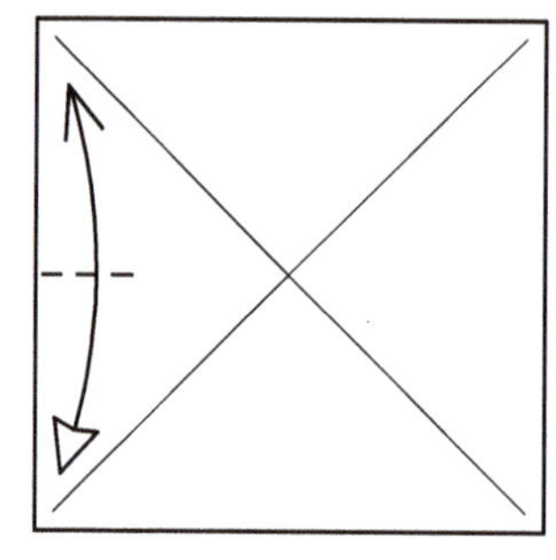

Fold and unfold on the left.

3

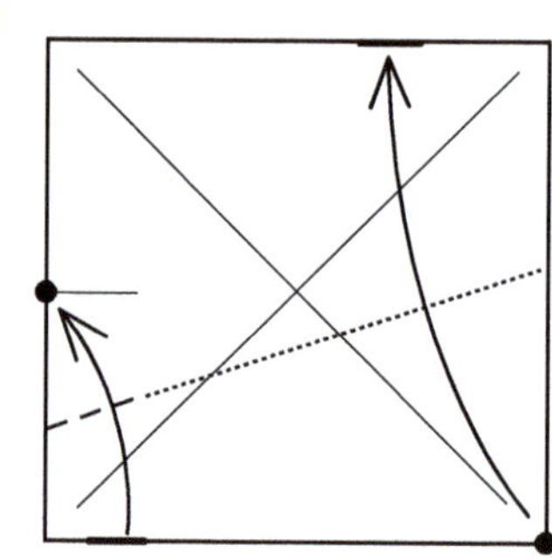

Bring the lower right corner to the top edge and the bottom edge to the left center. Crease on the left.

4

5

6

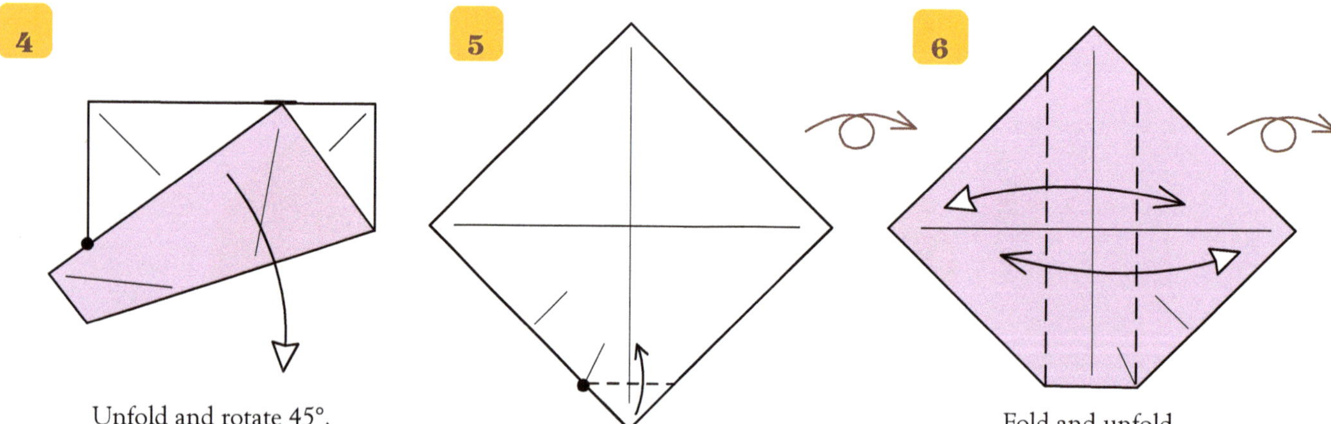

Unfold and rotate 45°.

Fold and unfold.

7

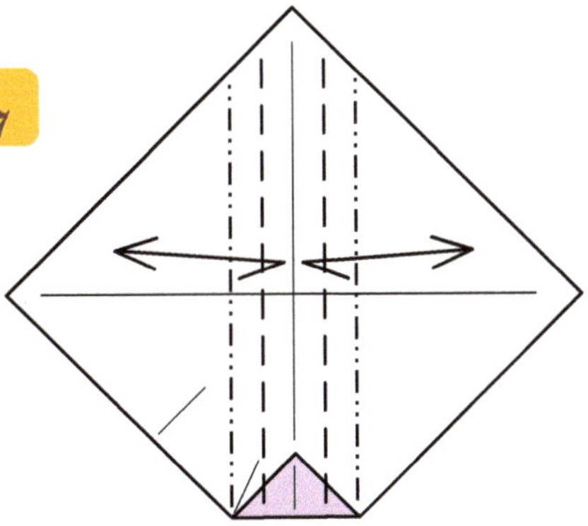

Make pleat folds. Mountain-fold along the creases. Rotate 90°.

8

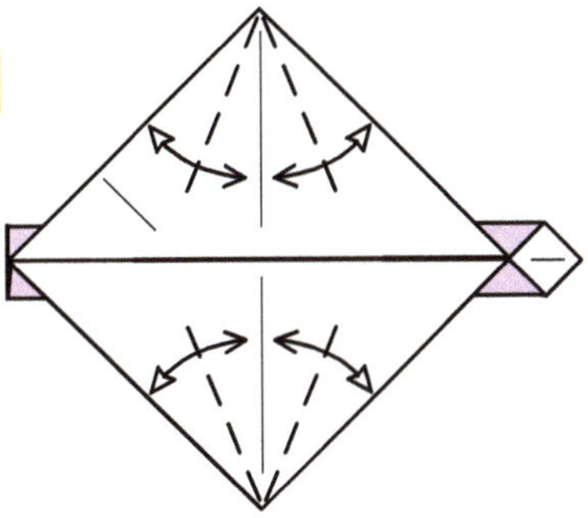

Fold and unfold.

9

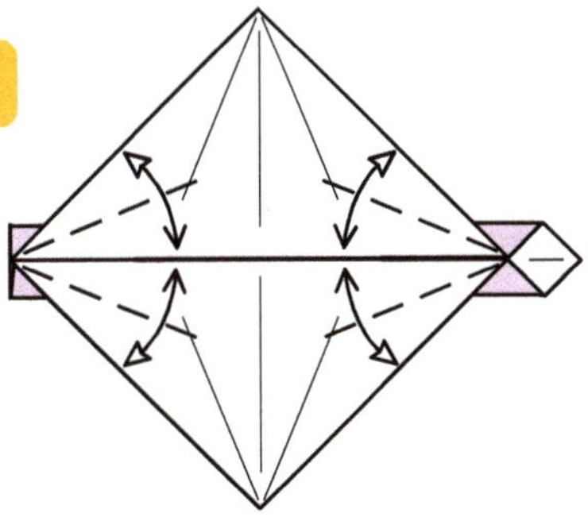

Fold and unfold.

10

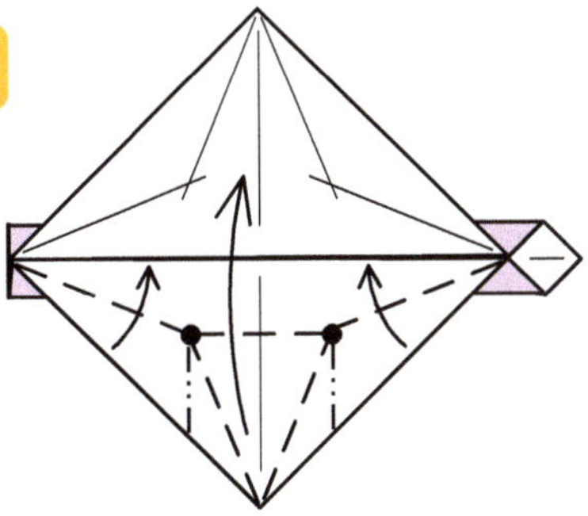

Fold along the creases.

11

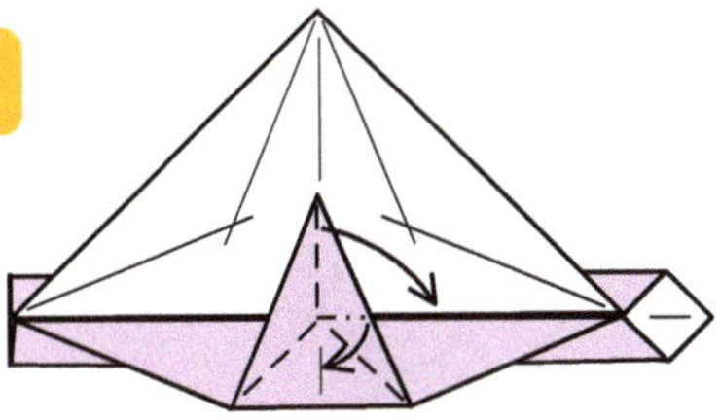

Rabbit-ear.

12

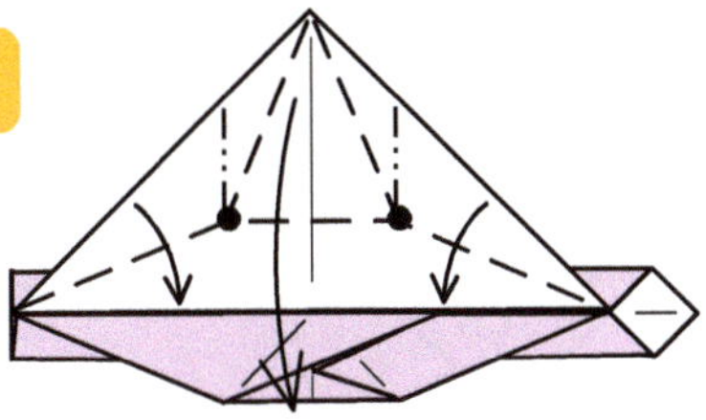

Repeat steps 10–11 on the top.

13

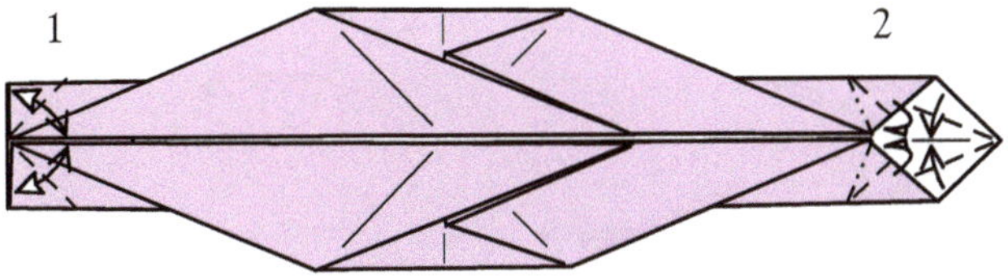

1

2

1. Fold and unfold.
2. Make reverse folds.

14

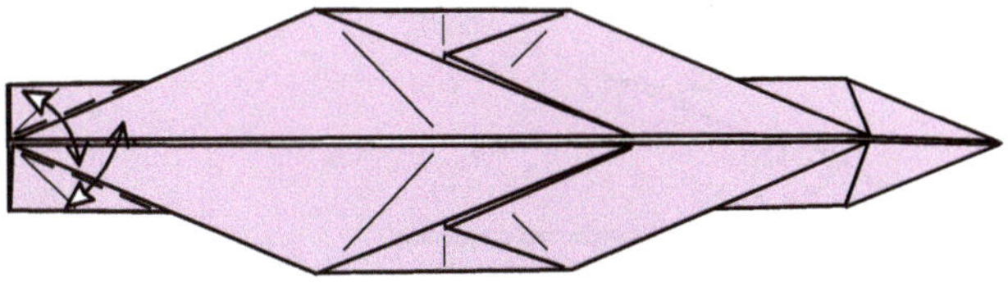

Fold and unfold.

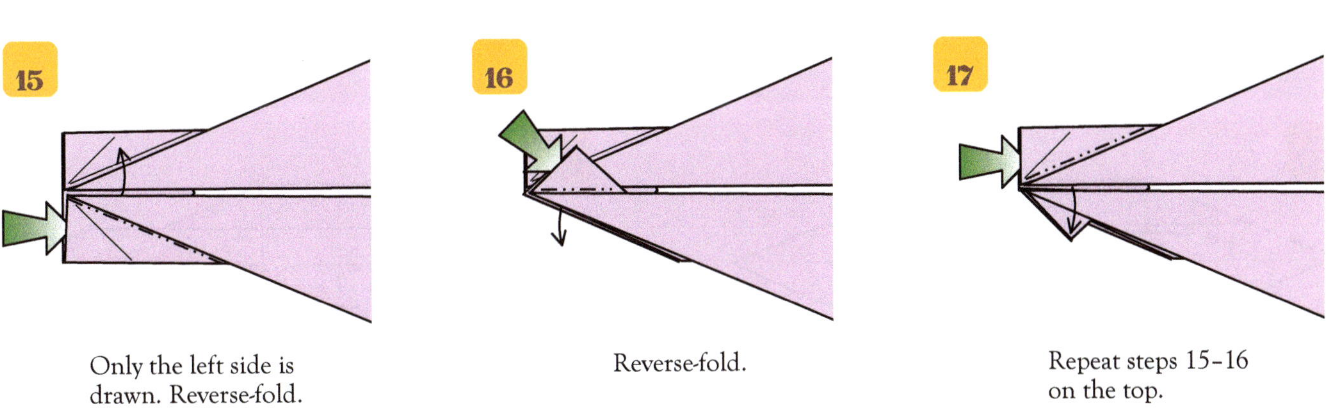

Only the left side is drawn. Reverse-fold.

Reverse-fold.

Repeat steps 15–16 on the top.

18

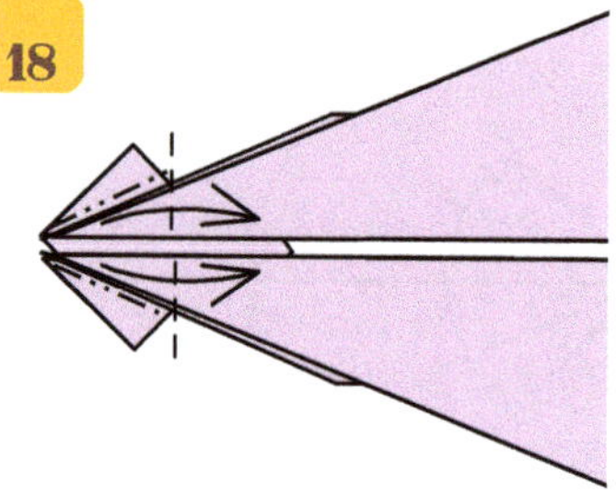

Make squash folds.

19

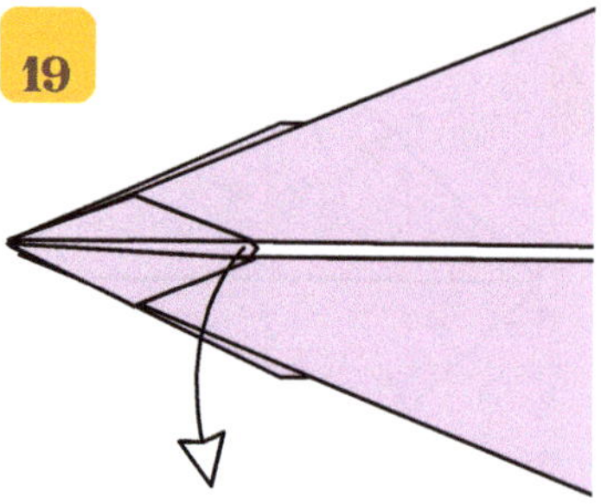

Pull out the hidden corner.

20

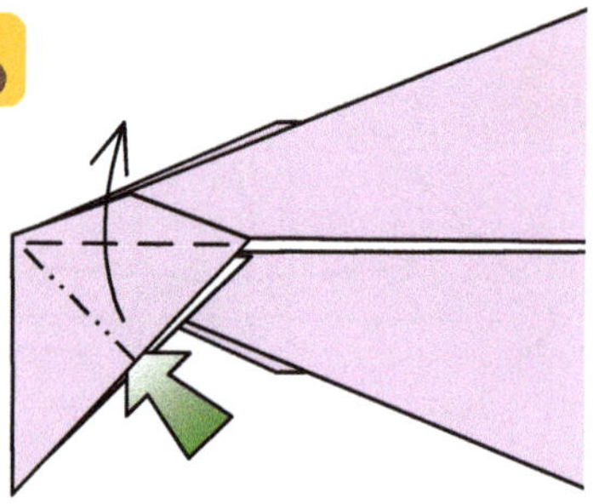

Squash-fold.

21

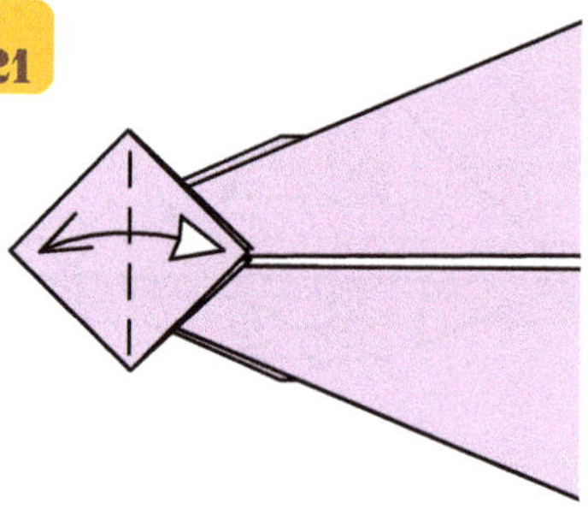

Fold and unfold.

22

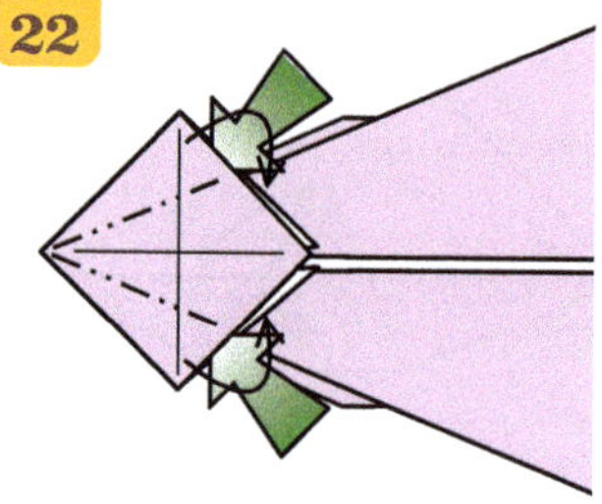

Make reverse folds.

23

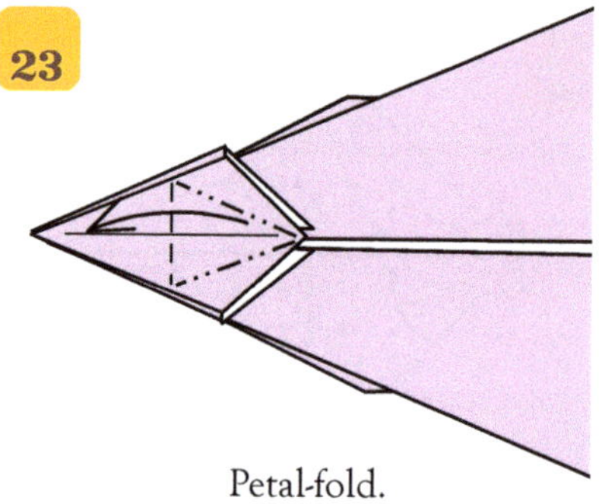

Petal-fold.

24

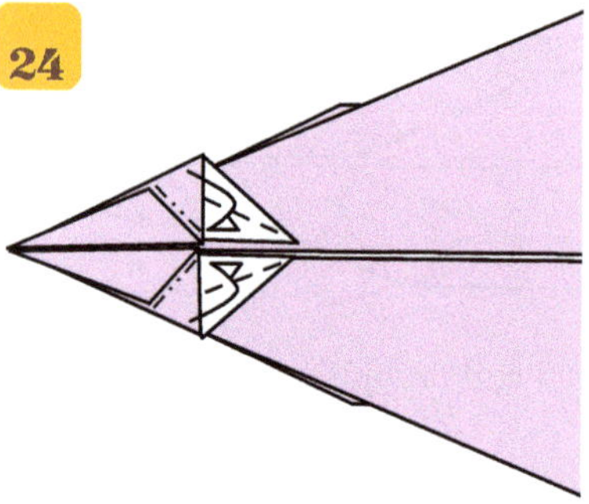

Reverse folds.

25

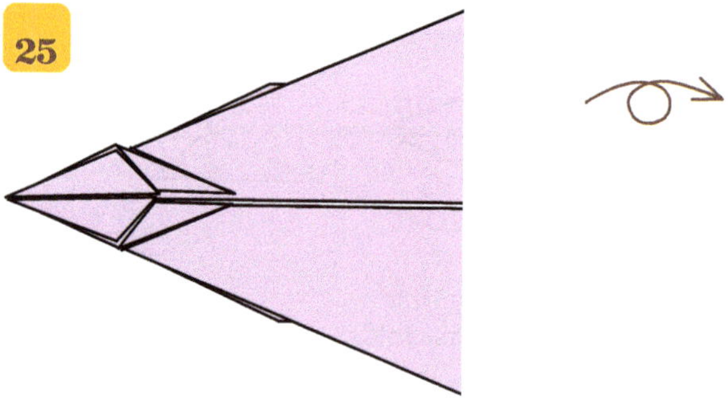

26

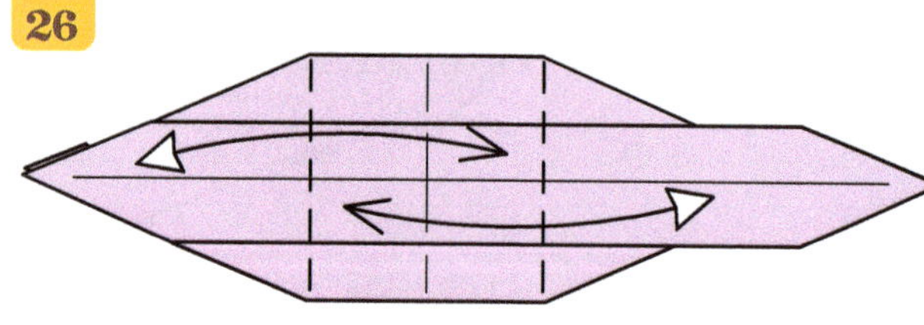

Fold and unfold.

27

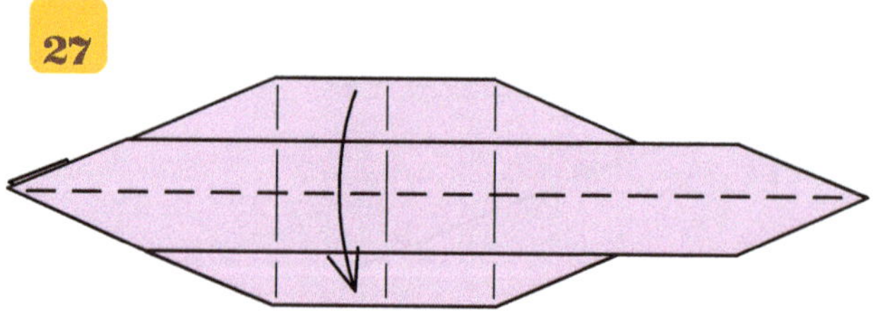

Fold in half.

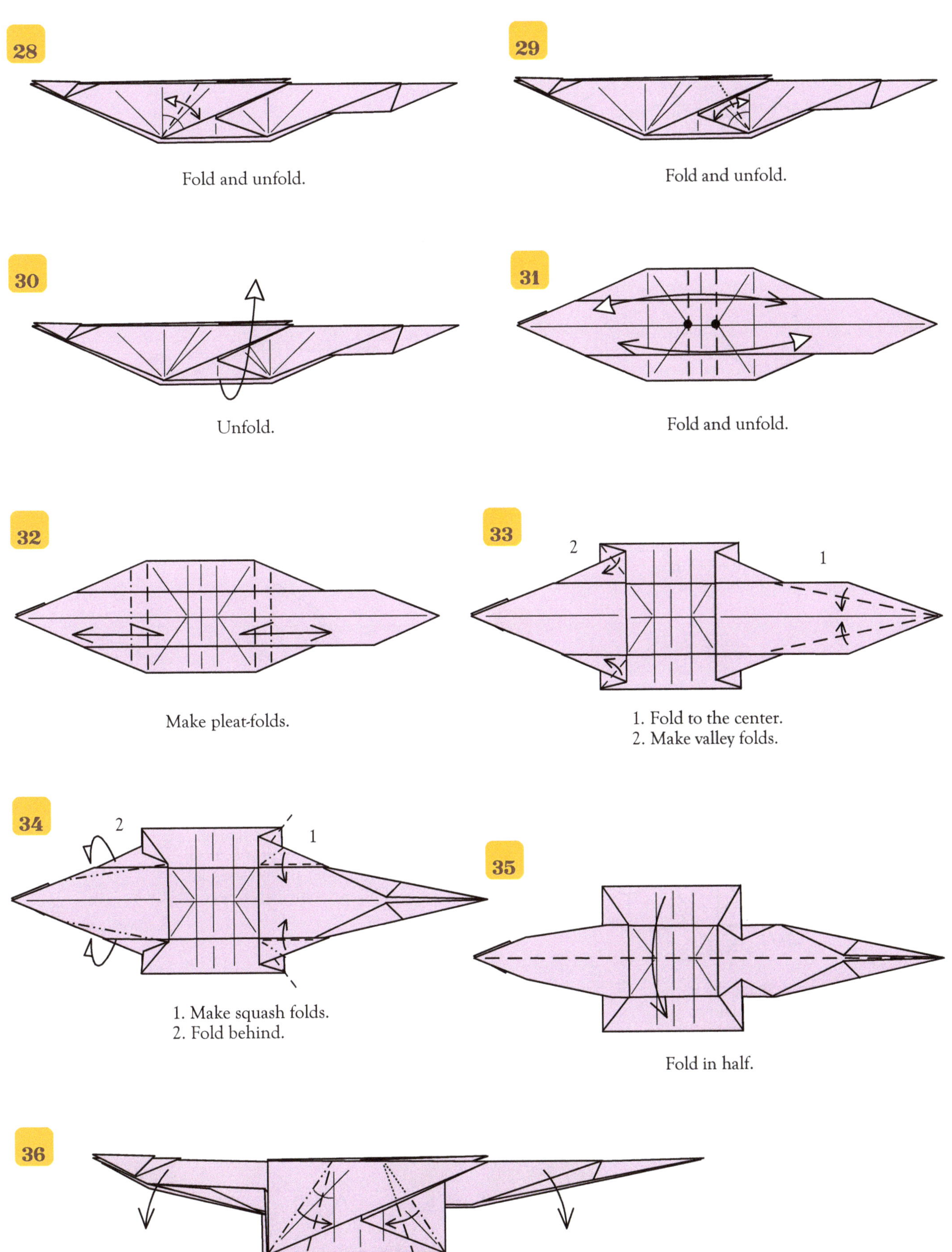
28
Fold and unfold.
29
Fold and unfold.
30
Unfold.
31
Fold and unfold.
32
Make pleat-folds.
33
2
1
1. Fold to the center.
2. Make valley folds.
34
2
1
1. Make squash folds.
2. Fold behind.
35
Fold in half.
36
Make crimp folds.

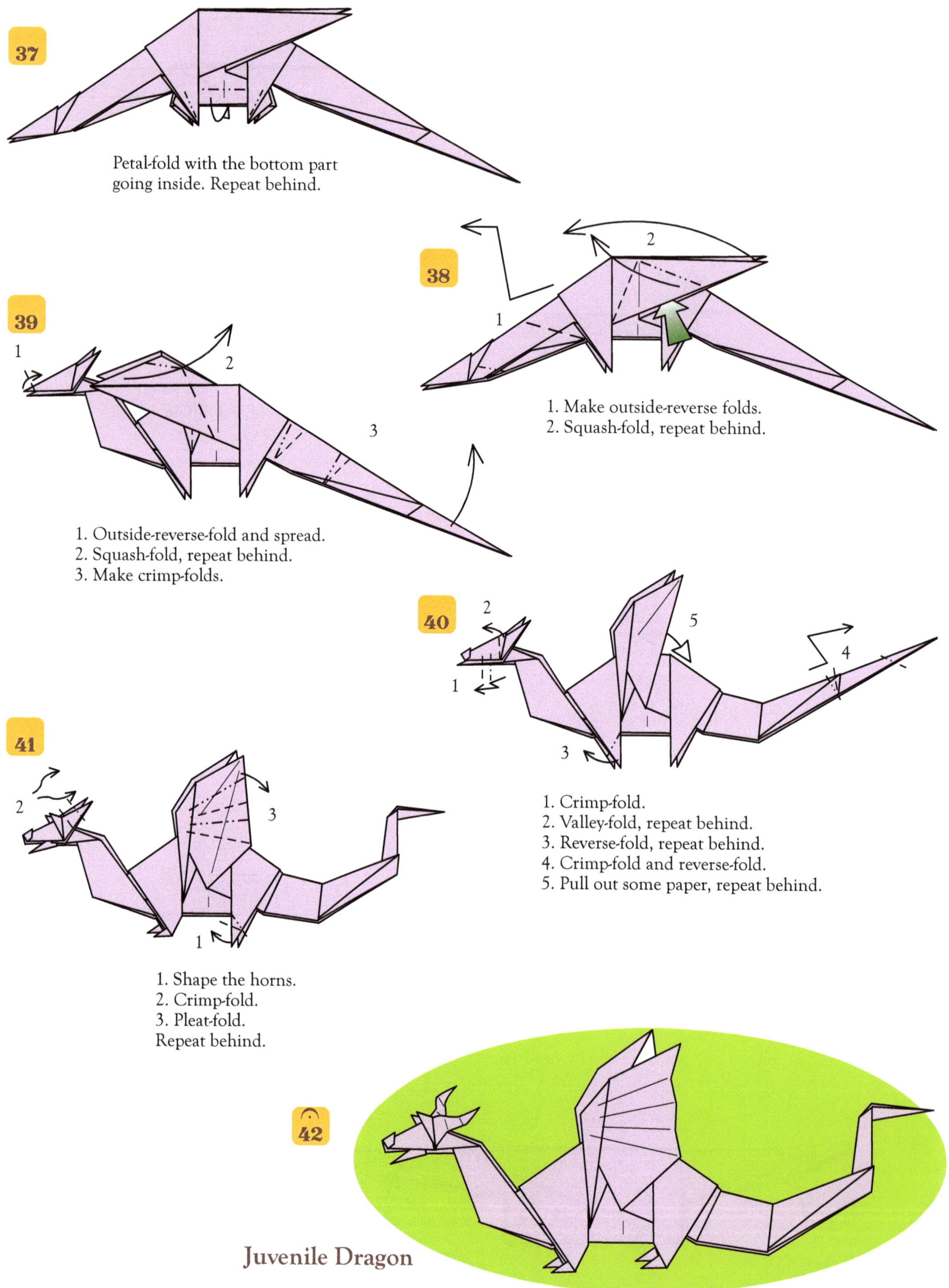
37
Petal-fold with the bottom part going inside. Repeat behind.
38
1
2
1. Make outside-reverse folds.
2. Squash-fold, repeat behind.
39
1
2
3
1. Outside-reverse-fold and spread.
2. Squash-fold, repeat behind.
3. Make crimp-folds.
40
1
2
3
4
5
1. Crimp-fold.
2. Valley-fold, repeat behind.
3. Reverse-fold, repeat behind.
4. Crimp-fold and reverse-fold.
5. Pull out some paper, repeat behind.
41
1
2
3
1. Shape the horns.
2. Crimp-fold.
3. Pleat-fold.
Repeat behind.
42
Juvenile Dragon

Full-Grown Dragon

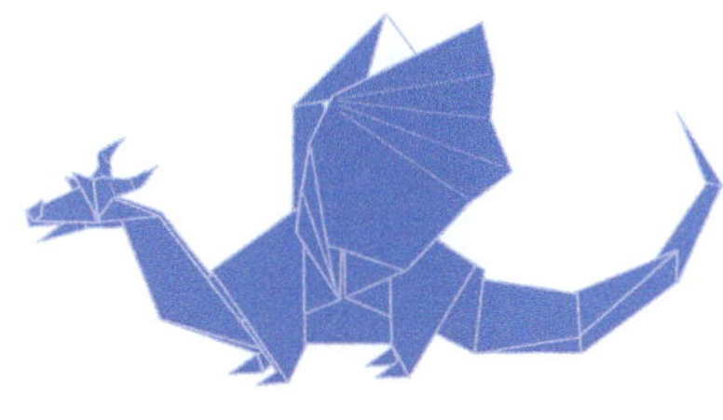

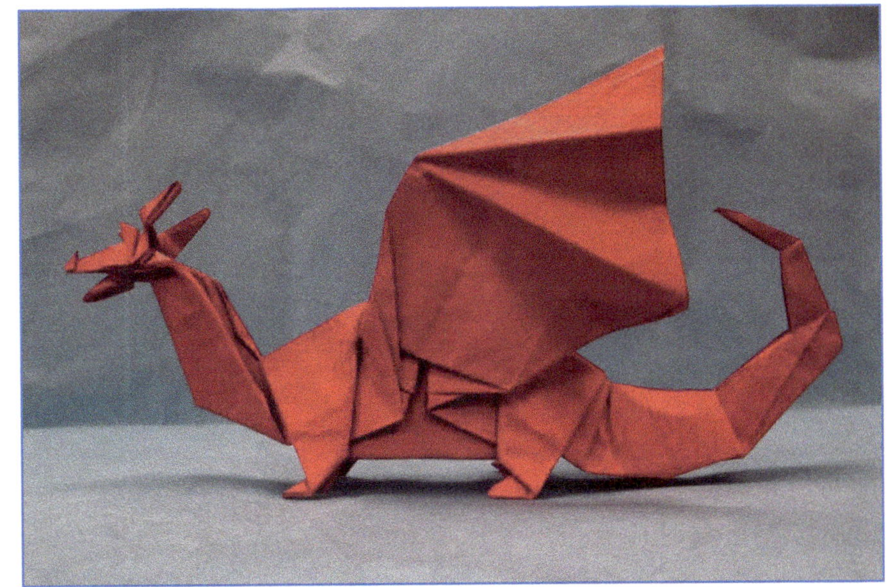

With fully developed wings, the Full-Grown Dragon can fly anywhere, and take you along for the ride. But be careful, this dragon could be evil. If you have already folded the Baby and Juvenile Dragons, then this dragon will be happy and bring good luck. Folding multiple Full-Grown Dragons will grant you more power and exceptional skills.

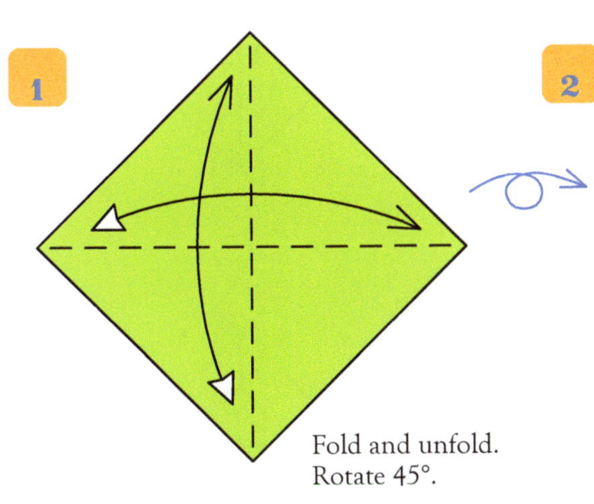

Fold and unfold. Rotate 45°.

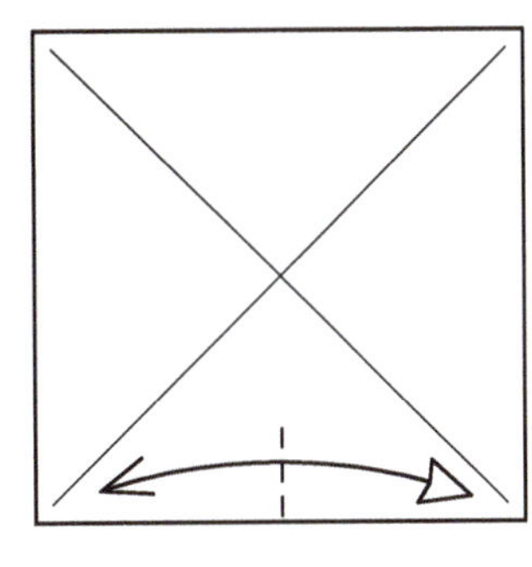

Fold and unfold on the bottom.

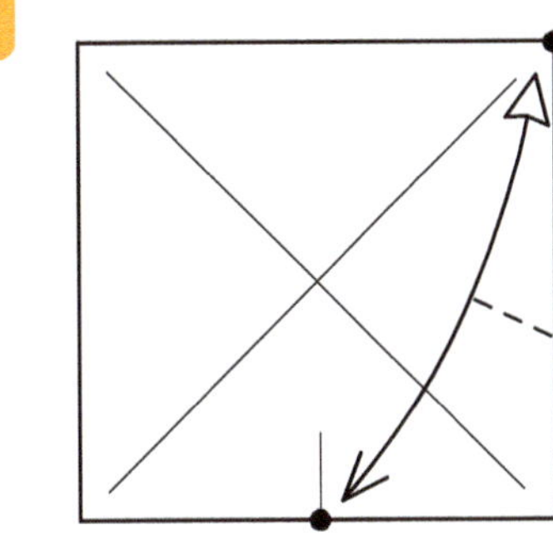

Fold and unfold on the right.

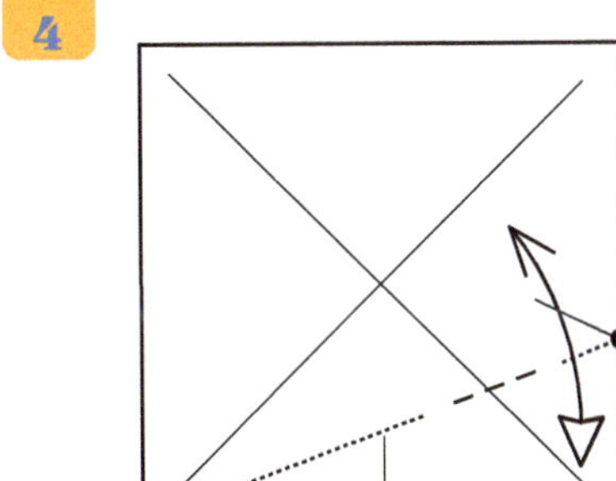

Fold and unfold on the diagonal. Rotate so the dot on the left goes to the right.

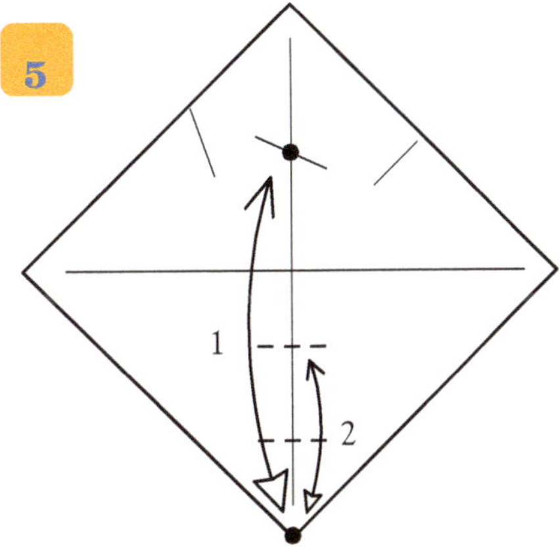

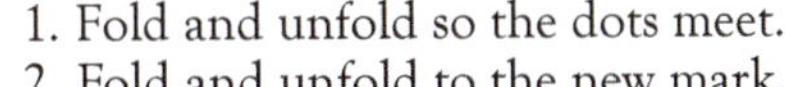

1. Fold and unfold so the dots meet.
2. Fold and unfold to the new mark.
Only fold on the diagonal.

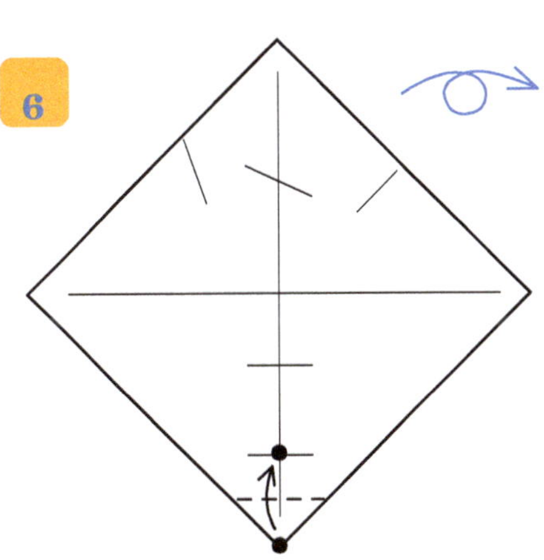

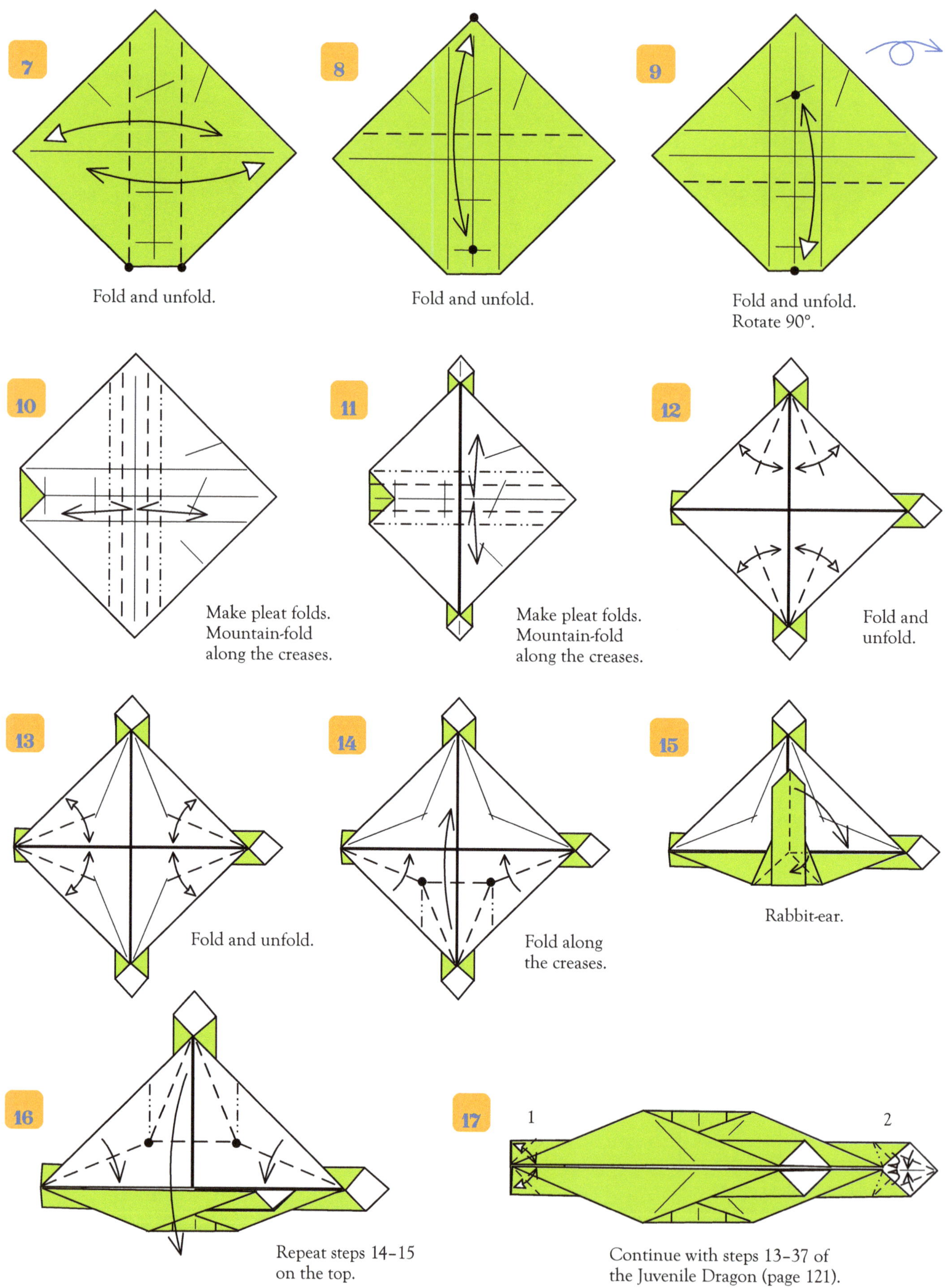
7
Fold and unfold.
8
Fold and unfold.
9
Fold and unfold.
Rotate 90°.
10
Make pleat folds.
Mountain-fold
along the creases.
11
Make pleat folds.
Mountain-fold
along the creases.
12
Fold and
unfold.
13
Fold and unfold.
14
Fold along
the creases.
15
Rabbit-ear.
16
Repeat steps 14–15
on the top.
17
1
2
Continue with steps 13–37 of
the Juvenile Dragon (page 121).

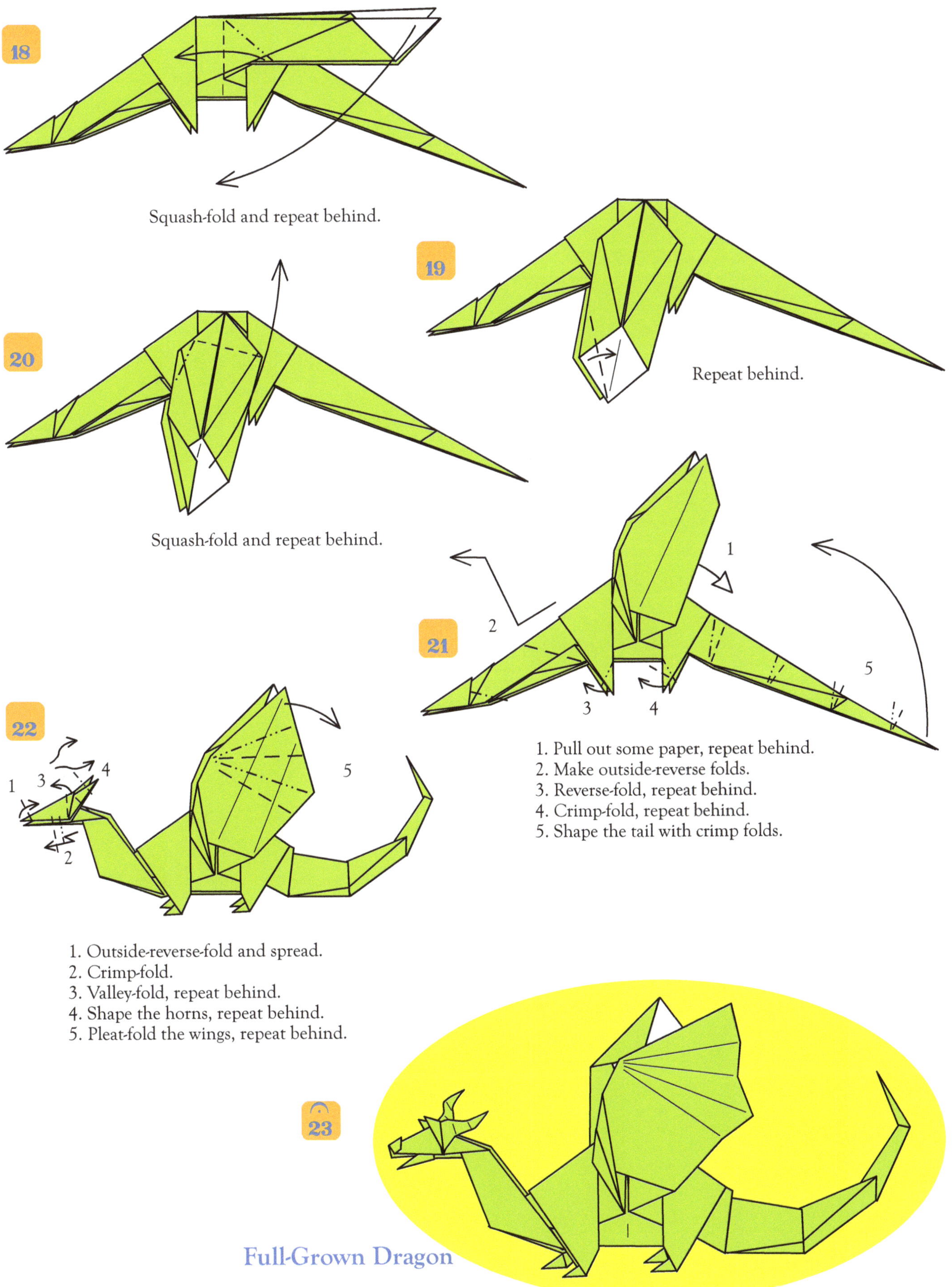
18
Squash-fold and repeat behind.
19
Repeat behind.
20
Squash-fold and repeat behind.
21
1
2
3
4
5
1. Pull out some paper, repeat behind.
2. Make outside-reverse folds.
3. Reverse-fold, repeat behind.
4. Crimp-fold, repeat behind.
5. Shape the tail with crimp folds.
22
1
2
3
4
5
1. Outside-reverse-fold and spread.
2. Crimp-fold.
3. Valley-fold, repeat behind.
4. Shape the horns, repeat behind.
5. Pleat-fold the wings, repeat behind.
23
Full-Grown Dragon

www.ingramcontent.com/pod-product-compliance
Ingram Content Group UK Ltd.
Pitfield, Milton Keynes, MK11 3LW, UK
UKHW050144280726
14058UKWH00006B/813

9 781877 656507